SHADOW SYNDROMES

SHADOW SYNDROMES

JOHN J. RATEY, M.D.

AND

CATHERINE JOHNSON, Ph.D.

BANTAM BOOKS
NEW YORK TORONTO LONDON SYDNEY AUCKLAND

This edition contains the complete text of the original hardcover edition.
NOT ONE WORD HAS BEEN OMITTED

SHADOW SYNDROMES
A Bantam Book / published by arrangement with Pantheon Books, a division of
Random House, Inc.

PUBLISHING HISTORY

Pantheon hardcover edition / 1997
Bantam trade paperback edition / June 1998

To Jimmy
and
To John's patients

CONTENTS

SHADOW SYNDROMES

INTRODUCTION

The Biology of Everyday Life

IT WAS SIGMUND FREUD who, nearly a hundred years ago, first told us that there is no such thing as normal. "Every person," he wrote, ". . . is only normal on the average. His ego approximates to that of the psychotic in some part or other and to a greater or lesser extent."

Needless to say, Freud would not have put much stock in the paragons of mental health our American culture has produced: Ozzie and Harriet, the Brady Bunch, Ronald Reagan—all, in Freud's view, would be seen as simple fantasies of robust good cheer and rational living. There is always, in the world of Freud, a dark side of the moon. Nothing is as it seems; no one is truly normal.

Today the advancing neuroscience of the twentieth century is proving Freud right: probably none of us is "normal"—normal in the sense of possessing a brain in which every part and system works as well as every other part and system—and all functions lie well within an optimal range. Such a brain may in fact be a logical impossibility; it is possible that genius (or simply talent) in one realm develops as a result of deficits (or weaknesses) in another—that in order to be a genius in, say, physics, you must be a relative "nongenius" in linguistic skills, or in social ability. The autistic savant may be the prototype here; often an autistic child with an extraordinary talent (most often in computation or drawing) will lose that talent as he or she develops more normal capabilities in social interaction and language. As language "comes in," drawing and mental computation "go out." A mute child with an extraordinary capacity to draw objects from memory—a capacity exceeding that of Picasso at the same age—will, as she finally begins to acquire her first words in late childhood, see her drawing abilities ebb away until they are gone. A similar principle may be at work in the normal brain; we may "pay" for our talents, both cognitive and emotional, with relative deficits elsewhere. Thus the idea of possessing a brain that functions optimally in all respects may simply not be a possibility in the real world. All brains possess their relative weaknesses.

Beyond this, the brain is an evolving organ: we human beings have existed for only 100,000 years (dinosaurs lived for 160 million), and our brains are still in their evolutionary infancy. The brain is a work in progress, with some positive adaptations no doubt still to come. Thus all of us have our mental glitches, some more serious and some less so.

That is the topic of this book: shadow syndromes, the subtle differences in our brains that can shape our lives. What they are (or what we are beginning to suspect they are), and when and how we can address them.

■□ BIOPSYCHIATRY THEN AND NOW

While it is not necessary to know a great deal about the brain to read this book, a brief look at how we have gotten where we are today may help. To start, neuropsychiatry has undergone a major conceptual shift since the 1960s. In those days everyone was speculating about neurotransmitter levels in mental illness. (Neurotransmitters are the chemicals, like dopamine and serotonin, that carry messages between the brain's nerve cells.) Researchers focused upon neurotransmitters—or, rather, the breakdown products of neurotransmitters that can be found in blood and urine—because, given the technology of the day, that was what they *could* study. Blood, urine, spinal fluid: these were the substances researchers could actually collect and measure. We could not look inside the skull.

It was an incredibly exciting period which, inevitably, produced the one-neurotransmitter–one-disorder theory of mental illness: this was the idea that mental illness was caused by simple "chemical imbalances" in the brain. In 1965 the dopamine theory of schizophrenia, which held that this severe mental illness was caused by too much dopamine in the brain, was developed. Later, researchers advanced equivalent theories concerning other disorders.

The problem with this approach was that it turned out to be too simple. The one-neurotransmitter–one-disease model was highly appealing, but it did not bear up under close scrutiny. When neurologists measured people's dopamine—and lab technicians went through whole swimming pools of urine trying to make the case—all too often they found that the dopamine levels of normal people and schizophrenics turned out to be the same.

Psychiatry underwent a similar sequence of initial enthusiasm followed by dashed hopes in the late 1960s when scientists discovered that low levels of norepinephrine were roughly correlated with low mood—and that imipramine, one of our first antidepressants, raises levels of norepinephrine in the brain. Too little norepinephrine equals depression; that was the wonderfully simple formula researchers embraced.

At the time, this was very exciting research, and there followed at fifteen-year period during which researchers believed they would soon be able actually to quantify levels of depression simply by measuring a patient's level of MHPG in the blood. (MHPG is a major metabolite, or by-product, of norepinephrine when the body breaks it down.) For a time, the development of a simple blood test for depression and a clear-cut treatment seemed at hand. But ultimately this proved to be a blind alley.

The advent of the brain scan changed everything. Brain scans allow neurologists to move inside the skull—to look at the brain's structure and watch the brain in action as it processes thoughts and emotions. We now have available a new echo-planar magnetic resonance imaging technique that can capture an image of the brain changing every 25 *milliseconds*. In the words of Dr. Joel Yager of UCLA's Neuropsychiatric Institute, soon we will actually be able to watch the "mind boggle."

Thus far, this approach has been enormously fruitful. Alan Zametkin of the National Institute of Mental Health has discovered certain areas of the brain involved in attention deficit disorder, areas that appear to be metabolizing glucose too slowly compared to normal brains; others have found the areas affected in obsessive-compulsive disorder—areas which, in this case, appear to be metabolizing glucose too quickly.

Now that we can actually look at the brain in action, we have begun, inevitably, to think in terms of brain geography as well as chemistry. In the future we will speak of certain areas of the brain, areas we call microenvironments, and we will think of medication in terms of its ability to target those locations. We will also be adding the elements of time and recursivity to the mix: the way in which a change in one location of the brain, over time, filters out to cause changes in other locations. These downstream changes feed back, in turn, into the original site of alteration, affecting it once again. This does not mean that all talk of chemical imbalances will fade away, but instead that the notion of a chemical imbalance will become more precise as neuroscience advances. Presently, of course, our knowledge of the brain's geography remains sketchy, and readers will notice that throughout this book we often refer to high and low levels of neurotransmitters like serotonin and dopamine. Whenever such observations occur, the reader should assume that the full story has yet to be uncovered.

In terms of treatment, a focus on the brain's geography, timing, and recursivity tells us that often we do not really know why a medication works as well as it does. Take Prozac, for instance. Prozac is known to raise serotonin levels in the brain, so naturally psychiatrists concluded that it is the rise in serotonin that relieves the depression. But in fact this rise takes place the first day a patient takes the pill, yet the depression does not lift until three to six weeks later. Obviously, something else is going on—something that has to do with the brain's geography and timing, with the particular areas of the brain in which Prozac does or does not find docking sites, and with feedback loops between and among these areas.

Thus, in the future we will see the language of "brain chemicals," "imbalances," and "levels" joined, and sometimes replaced, by the language of microenvironments, timing, and recursivity. Already, psychiatrists talk about "frontal-lope types": these are the sticky people we can't get off the telephone. Such people often have problems involving differences in the frontal lobe, hence the nickname. It is a population that has become known by the *place* in their brain that is not working properly—not by the neurotransmitter that is "out of balance."

■ NORMAL PEOPLE AND THEIR PROBLEMS

When we think about life in terms of the brain's geography and timing, we quickly develop a real appreciation for Freud's dictum that normal people are not all that normal. The brain is infinitely complex, and a difference in just one tiny area can produce major differences in behavior and emotion—either for good or for ill. Because everyone's brain is different, it is easy to see why all of us may end up with our own particular brain-based emotional difficulties, as well as with our own unique talents and strengths.

The biology of the brain's development in early life also points to the possibility that all of us may end up with our own unique mental issues. At the moment of conception tiny differences in genetic endowment from one child to the next will result in major differences in their fully developed brains. Then, as the fetal brain grows, small differences in the biology of the mother's womb (due to hormones, nutrition, viruses, drugs, cigarettes, etc.) will also produce significant differences in the finished brain.

Before birth the brain proceeds through a complex process of neuron migration. During migration, nerve cells must move from the "neural tube," where they begin life, to their final location in the brain—a process that, when it goes awry, can produce a tangled set of neurons. (Schizophrenia is thought to result from just such a scrambled migration process.) After birth the brain begins a process of cell-pruning in which it kills nerve cells it does not use. Once again, subtle flaws, or just subtle differences, in this process can produce dramatic differences in the person we see. (A 1995 study of adult autistic men found that their brains were larger-than-average in size, an anomaly that could be due to insufficient pruning, among other things.) In short, the very complexity of the brain's development makes it likely that all of us end up with parts of our brain that "grew well" and parts that did not grow as well. Every brain is unique, and every brain is going to have its problems. From the outside those problems are going to look like emotional issues, or cognitive deficits, or both.

Even if we are lucky enough to come into this world with a brain that processes information and deflects stress with the best of them, some of us will not make it to middle age with those capacities intact. One of the important truths in life—a truth that is sometimes lost in the rush to the new biology—is that the biology of our brains is not fixed at birth. The brain develops in response to its environment, which means that painful life experiences leave their mark. We now possess a fair amount of evidence indicating that psychological trauma actually alters the *physical* makeup of the brain, that a single episode of major depression in response to a devastating life event scars not only our souls but our gray matter as well. Moreover, some psychiatrists now speculate that, like the long-distance runner's knees, the brain's capacity to handle stress may decline with age. In short, even the golden baby who begins life with a happy face and bright eyes is likely to acquire a few dents and scrapes along the way.

Thus, whether for reasons of inborn genetics or reasons of the inevitable wear and tear of life, we may all have our mental "weaknesses." And until recently, these weaknesses were seen simply as personality flaws that we, typically, blamed on our parents. The man who can't talk about his feelings, the mother who screams at her children one moment and smothers them in kisses the next, the wallflower, the loner, the needy neighbor you can't get off the telephone, the absent-minded professor, the confirmed bachelor, the overprotective mom who won't take her children to the park for fear they might catch a bug, the husband who tantrums like a four-year-old while his children cower before him, the gifted person who cannot seem to live up to his or her potential—all of these "types" have always seemed to be just that: types. The thought that such ordinary, everyday phenomena as a bad temper or an "inferiority complex" (a popular problem back in the 1950s) might have a biological basis has, until recently, not crossed our minds.

But neuropsychiatry is now discovering that a great deal of what we thought was due to (poor) upbringing in fact is heavily influenced by the genetics, structure, and neurochemistry of the brain. Every one of the troublesome personalities made famous by our popular press likely has its roots in an unsuspected brain difference: the Peter Pan syndrome, the Cinderella complex, the women who love too much, the men who can't love, the codependent—the list goes on. All of these people are doubtless going to turn out to have brain differences that contribute to their Peter Pan–ness or their Cinderella-ness or their codependentness. Of course, differences in the brain cut both ways: as studies of artists with manic-depressive illness have shown, a brain difference that handicaps us in one realm may also endow us with greater capacities in another. Our purpose in writing this book is not to pathologize every nook and cranny of everyday life, but to offer help for those areas in which our brain differences do hurt more than help. Until now there has been no biologically based help for the difficult personalities among us because no one has suspected that their problems might have biological facets.

That is the purpose of this book: to look again at the biology of everyday life one hundred years later—this time from the vantage point of twentieth-century neuropsychiatry. Our question in this book is: when we—or someone we love—are behaving at our worst, or simply behaving irrationally, what role does biology play? And: how do genuine problems in life, problems like a difficult childhood or a parent who drinks, interact with our biology to create the character traits and flaws that are not just written into our characters but into our neurons as well?

■□ SHADOW SYNDROMES: PEOPLE WITH MILD FORMS OF SERIOUS DISORDERS

In order to take a second look at normal "craziness," we can learn from the kinds of craziness that are not so normal. When we speak of schizophrenia or severe manic-depression, there is no question in anyone's mind that the person is ill. And it is easy enough for us to believe that these illnesses are biological in origin (though it was not so long ago that these illnesses, too, were blamed upon bad parents).

The confusion begins when one sees patients who do not fit the classic categories, but who nevertheless have very real difficulties in life. Are these difficulties due entirely to upbringing and environment, or do they, too, have some basis in the brain's biology? Modern psychiatry has been struggling to make sense of these people for fifty years. Doctors diagnose their patients according to the syndromes described in DSM-IV, the *Diagnostic and Statistical Manual,* Fourth Edition. A syndrome is a set of behaviors that consistently appear together: a set of behaviors the patient, the doctor, or the patient's friends and family can observe and describe. A syndrome is *not,* at this point, a physical marker like the positive result on a test for HIV antibodies that establishes a diagnosis of HIV-positive. When a psychiatrist diagnoses the syndrome of panic disorder, for example, he cannot—yet—perform an MRI (magnetic resonance imaging) that tells him whether the patient does or does not qualify for the diagnosis (although we may be closest to such a test for this particular disorder). Instead, he looks for symptoms: a pounding chest, rapid heartbeat, shortness of breath or hyperventilation, sweating or coldness and changes in temperature regulation, the fear that one is having a heart attack, sometimes a feeling that the person is going to pass out, sometimes a feeling that he or she is going to go crazy. This is the set of symptoms that make up the syndrome.

The problem is, every patient is different—including every patient with the same diagnosis. As a result, the number of syndromes recognized by practicing psychiatrists has leapt in the forty years since the first edition of the DSM appeared in 1952. That volume described 60 categories of abnormal behavior. DSM-II, published in 1968, more than doubled this number to 145 syndromes, and DSM-III raised the total to 230. The DSM-IV, which appeared in 1994, lists 382 distinct diagnoses, plus an additional 28 floating, or unassigned, diagnoses—which brings us today to a total of 410 different possible diagnostic labels. What the ever-increasing number of possible diagnoses means is that a person who comes into a psychiatrist's office complaining of being depressed, for example, could be categorized as belonging to one of four major categories—bipolar disorder, major depression, "other specific affective disorders," or "atypical affective disorder"—with several subcategories included within each of these main categories. (A patient diagnosed as bipolar could then be further characterized as "mixed," "manic," or "depressed," for instance.) It is a complex business.

As time goes by, we find that the art of diagnosis grows ever more fragmented; seemingly sound diagnostic categories keep breaking down. Emotional problems do not fit the "concrete blocks" of the DSM-I, -II, -III, or -IV; real people come into the office with bits of this and pieces of that. A patient might show signs of panic disorder, signs of major depressive disorder, and signs of a narcissistic personality disorder all in the same package. He or she may have parts of a whole array of syndromes, and yet not suffer from all of the symptoms of any one syndrome. Or he may fit every aspect of a syndrome down to the smallest detail and yet be so mildly affected compared to other people suffering from that problem that even a good therapist might miss the diagnosis. Finally, a patient may exhibit only one or two symptoms from a particular syndrome, a condition long known as a *forme fruste* in conventional medicine. A patient with a *forme fruste* of Graves disease, for instance, might have the bulging eyes without the sweaty hands, rapid heartbeat, irritability, and weight loss that accompany a full-blown case of the illness. A *forme fruste* is an incomplete expression of an illness, though the term is little used today. We have chosen to replace it here with the phrase shadow syndrome because the meanings of the word shadow, both literal and metaphorical, capture the nature of a mild mental disorder. In the literal sense, a shadow is an indistinct form of something all too vivid and real, just as a shadow syndrome is an indistinct and seldom obvious form of a severe disorder. And metaphorical shadows cast a pall across a day that might otherwise be sunny and clear. This is what shadow syndromes do in the realms of work and love: they cast a shadow.

Not only are there a number of very troubled people who do not fully fit the DSM categories; there are also many, many not-so-troubled people who do fit these categories, to some degree. When we look at everyday people wending their way through everyday life, we notice that most people seem to have minor bits of this syndrome, small pieces of that.

A close friend, for instance, may fit one or two of the criteria for an "atypical" depression. She is pessimistic, worried, anxious about the future. Maybe she eats too much in response to stress, and her love life is a mess. And yet she has never experienced a true, flat-out, stay-in-bed-with-the-covers-over-your-head crash. She is not *depressed*.

How do we think about this person? Traditionally, we would see her in psychological terms as the victim of parents who did not offer praise, or were too demanding, or drank too much, or did not talk about feelings, or generally inflicted upon her the particular constellation of bad habits and character flaws they themselves possessed. As her friend, we may log hours on the telephone offering reassurance that she is a good person who will find happiness in life, countless other hours sifting through her childhood looking for clues. We pour precious time and energy into our friend's difficulties, and yet, for all the effort, neither we nor our suffering friend suspects that there might be something biological going on. Neither of us thinks, Depression.

Or take the case of a woman married to a man who cannot control his temper. Living with him is like living on a fault line; his loved ones never know when the ground beneath their feet will explode. The children fear him; his wife's blood pressure shoots up the moment she hears his key in the lock. But she loves him because when he is not shouting he is wonderful. Energetic, full of life, funny, up for adventures of all sorts. A natural with the kids.

Here again, what are we to think of this person? How do we explain his behavior? Perhaps we see him in moral terms, as simply a bad person, at least when he tantrums. Perhaps we see him in psychological terms as the victim of a bad childhood; perhaps we see him in political terms as a man who, living in a male-dominated society, feels free to vent his angriest feelings while women learn to suppress theirs. Perhaps we think all of these things and more. And certainly we could be right.

But what we don't think, again, is biology. We don't think: manic-depression. We don't think this because, while this person does have unpredictable mood swings, he is nothing like the florid cases of manic-depression that land their sufferers in psychiatric wards. His mood swings may be difficult to live with, but they seem like the kind of thing many people have. Many normal people.

And in fact, significant numbers of people do live with wildly veering moods. Many, many families struggle along with a parent (or a child) who can turn an entire household upside down faster than a tornado can flip a car across a field of corn. It is not an easy life, but it is certainly a common one. It lies within the bounds of normalcy.

Therapists of all stripes have always paid a great deal of attention to the struggles of the normal, but troubled, people whom sociologists have called the "worried well." There is a name for them: YAVIS, an acronym that stands for the "young, attractive, verbal, intelligent, and successful" patients all therapists want to see. These are the patients who thrive in therapy, who can take what they learn there and use it to turn their lives around.

Until now neurologists and experimental biopsychiatrists have not paid the YAVIS much heed. After all, YAVIS are doing so well in life, relatively speaking, that their problems seem to be entirely of their environment's making, nothing to do with a flaw in the brain. But today this is changing. Neurologists and experimental biopsychiatrists are taking a second look at the normal problems of normal people. And what we are finding is the existence of what one prominent psychiatrist, Dr. Michael Liebowitz of Columbia University, calls subsyndromal behavior—behavior that fits only part of a syndrome but not all. A shadow syndrome. A person with a shadow syndrome is a person who does not fit the DSM's concrete blocks, a person who may have only some parts of a mental illness that, if he suffered from the full-blown syndrome, would be unmistakable.

In a way, the very mildness of his illness adds to his problems because it is likely to go undiagnosed. An educated, middle-class person who experiences a complete version of a DSM syndrome has a good chance of getting the help he or she needs. Such a person in the midst of a full-blown clinical depression will either seek out the services of a psychiatrist, or will have family members who seek them out for him or her.

But the "subsyndromal" person, the person who is only a "little bit" manic-depressive, or a "little bit" clinically depressed, is likely to struggle on alone, wondering what is the matter with him—or, all too often, what is the matter with *everyone else*. As he continues to act out the partial illness his biology harbors, he incurs the wrath of family and friends, all of whom hold him responsible for his behavior—and all of whom, more than anything else, want him just to *stop*.

But stopping a biologically driven behavior is not a simple matter. We can't just stop doing something our brain compels us to do. We understand this when it comes to severe mental illnesses; we understand that a schizophrenic cannot just stop hallucinating because his friends and family want him to. But we are far from understanding this truth when it comes to mild and hidden forms of mental illness. We have not yet learned that a mildly depressed young woman suffering from too-low levels of serotonin cannot simply decide to feel like a person whose brain is flooded with bountiful levels of this crucial neurotransmitter in the critical microenvironments, wherever those ultimately prove to be. Her biology is as compelling to her as the schizophrenic's is to him. It is the same story with the tantrum-throwing husband. If the man with the bad temper has an incompletely expressed rage disorder, he is not "choosing" to rage at his family; the chemistry of his brain is suffusing him with feelings of rage that he is not going to be able to turn off simply by willing it. To a very significant degree, he is at the mercy of his own flawed biology.

■ PERSONAL RESPONSIBILITY IN THE AGE OF BIOLOGY

Life changes when we begin to realize that people can have subtle, hidden, or partial mental disorders. For one thing, the impulse to blame loses it power. Think how much time we spend blaming people, or blaming their parents, for their problems. We blame the parent who shouts for being mean and uncaring, and we blame his mother for teaching him to shout by having shouted herself.

The act of self-blame can be most painful of all. The profound and corrosive sense of shame we feel over ways of being that have been "given" to us by our biology is akin to the deep shame felt by the child who wets his bed—a behavior now known to be a soft sign of a neurological difference in the brain. Shame begins to lift when we understand that subtle differences in the brain can create important differences in behavior.

The notion of the shadow syndrome also helps us to see that talk therapy needs to address our biological selves as well as our psychological selves. Before his awareness of shadow syndromes and subsyndromal behaviors began to grow, John worked with patients in primarily psychodynamic terms. Now he, like many of his colleagues, is changing. Recently, a new patient came to his office seeking a consultation concerning her son. She was a fearful woman, a full-time mother who was highly protective of her only child, a little boy of six who had begun kindergarten at a small, very expensive private school—a school that offered an environment nearly as sheltered and intimate as his home.

But the school year had not gone well. The boy, who had never been allowed to attend a preschool, cried every morning at the thought of leaving his mother. Nothing the mother or the boy's teachers had done could help him to overcome his terror at the separation. They had tried having the mother stay in the classroom for the first week; they had tried having her drop the boy off decisively with a cheerful kiss and wave goodbye; they had tried having him bring a favorite toy from home that he could keep with him throughout the day. Still, he sobbed for an hour every time his mother left, and gave every indication of being in fragile condition for the rest of the day once his tears had dried.

Just a few years ago John would have approached the mother's problem in purely psychodynamic terms. He might have explored the possibility that this patient was a lonely and frightened woman, perhaps a sexually repressed wife who had displaced her adult need for a man's love onto her son, a little boy who was responding to his mother's problems by faithfully enacting his own role in her drama. The boy's fear of school would make sense as an unconscious form of cooperation with his mother's unspoken need for his loyalty. John and the mother might have devoted months to a psychotherapy intended to help her come to these insights for herself.

But today John sees this patient's situation very differently. Today he would see her little boy as suffering not from an overprotective mother (or not solely from this, at any rate), but from a shadow syndrome of panic episode with a school phobia attached. The mother, too, suffers from her own biologically based anxiety disorder. It is a mild and partial disorder; like so many people, she does not neatly fit the relevant DSM categories. But when we look, we can see that it is there. She has always been an anxious sort; she was anxious as a small child. Since becoming a mother her anxieties have crystallized around her son, but if she had not had a child, she clearly would be just as anxious about something else.

As for the little boy, very likely he is his mother's son—in the biological sense as much as the psychological. He has inherited her partial anxiety disorder, and a child with an anxiety disorder can be expected to manifest unusually intense separation anxiety at his age. He is not necessarily acting out his mother's unconscious drama, though he could be; even if he *is* acting out her drama, he is acting out his own biology as well. A happy and robust mother who feared nothing in this world might have trouble getting this child off to school, too. It is in his nature to be more fearful than other children.

This understanding of mother and son represents a radical shift from the days before we understood how pervasive the reach of the brain's biology is. And it points therapist and patient in new directions when it comes to treatment. John's first goal with this woman today is not to explore her psychosexual relation to her son, though he might well get to that, but to educate her in the signs, symptoms, and causes of mild anxiety disorder. John would tell her what we know, and what we theorize, about how the brain produces excessive levels of fear. He might suggest she try a medication such as BuSpar, which helps normalize the brain of a biologically anxious person, and he might suggest that her son try a small dose of Prozac, which has been shown to be highly effective for children who suffer acute separation anxiety.

He might also work with a behavioral approach, using the "desensitization" techniques that have proven so effective with phobic patients. Recent research has shown that behavior therapy can actually affect the physical functioning of the brain in patients with obsessive-compulsive disorder; it is important to understand that biology and environment are always linked. Just as the biology of the brain can affect thoughts and actions, thoughts and actions can influence biology. A course of behavior therapy for an anxious patient may alter that part of the brain involved in creating the anxiety.

Finally, John and his patient might also pursue a course of traditional psychotherapy. To say that a problem is biologically based is not to say that it has no unconscious significance. This woman, with her biologically given vulnerability to anxiety, could certainly also be a sexually repressed mother who has made her son into her stand-in husband. This is a woman who has lived all her life with a brain that is overreactive to frightening stimuli, a biological fact that has shaped her character in countless ways. It is not just our parents who "warp" our personalities; our biology can shape and distort our character as well. It is hard to grow up with a fearful (or excessively angry or excessively aroused) biology, and the child forms his personality around the biological givens of his brain.

Eventually, a mood disorder, even a very mild or partial one, can become a person's character: in time character wraps around biology. One long-term study of depressed women found that the social problems created by their sadness and withdrawal persisted even after their depressions had lifted. These were women whose illness had permeated their characters; they had developed "depressive" ways of thinking and acting that went beyond the mood disorder itself. We all know people who have become depressive in character as well as mood. These are the "eyeores" of life, A. A. Milne's sad-sack donkey friend to Pooh; they are the people who see the glass as half empty—and who are put off by people who observe that it is equally half full. Committed depressives often dislike cheerful people, seeing them as vapid, superficial, and dull. They can be critical and deflating; they puncture people's balloons. If they have an intellectual bent they may be prone to everyday Freudianisms, always probing beneath the surface to discover the dark realities below. They believe that the depths of character are inevitably dark and dire; they dismiss all surface shine as illusion. They are the people who never say yes. Instead, they say maybe.

The depressive personality does not spring full-blown from the womb. It takes years of living, day in and day out, in a state of mild melancholy and woe to make the sad songs of depressive biology one's own. But once character has shaped itself around even a very mild disorder, more than an antidepressant is required to turn back time. Complicating matters is the fact that the depressive personality (or hypomanic personality or ADD personality or whatever the case may be) very often does not wish to change in any fundamental way. At most such a person simply hopes to feel a bit better in the day to day. But she most adamantly does *not* wish to become Donna Reed (and it will always be Donna Reed—or a Donna Reed clone—who is her model of what happy people are like; more often than not, the depressive personality simply does not appreciate the naturally upbeat). All people act to preserve their essential identities, and once depression has become identity a person will act to protect her mild depression by rejecting the lives and examples of people who are content.

Thus, in the case of John's patient, quite apart from beginning a course of antianxiety medication she will no doubt need psychotherapy to undo the damage her hidden disorder has caused, to relearn who she is and who she can be apart from her anxieties. She may need psychotherapy simply to convince her that, for her own sake, a fundamental change in character would be a good thing.

Such a therapy would also look at the ways in which her family and life experiences may have interacted with her inborn biology to create the problems she has today. Here again, to see personality as growing out of biology is not to dismiss our environments as a major source of who and what we are. Biology and environment always come together, each affecting the other. A child with an innately anxious temperament who is born to a parent with an innately anxious temperament may grow up to be a different person from the child with the anxious temperament whose mother does not share his difficulty. The point of the "new" biology is not to dismiss environment; it is to understand how environment and biology work together to create the person.

Nor does the new biology release us from personal responsibility. While it is true that we have only so much capacity to resist our biology, our responsibility in this new era is to acknowledge our biology, understand our biology, and take whatever steps we need to take in order to prevent that biology from harming our lives or the lives of those we love. It is not acceptable to plead "bad" brain chemicals as an excuse for bad behavior. The husband with the severe rage episodes is *not* within his rights to say to his family: "This is just me. I was born this way, this is the way my brain works. I can't help it." His responsibility is to do something about the way his brain works.

How does he go about this? First, he listens. He must try to see himself as his loved ones see him rather than charging full steam ahead with whatever angry impulses he is feeling in the moment. He needs to see himself as the frighteningly unpredictable bully that, from a small child's perspective, he is.

He also needs to consult a doctor, and to listen to what that doctor tells him. As a responsible adult, he should educate himself fully in the ways of his brain chemistry. Then, working with his doctor and his family, he needs to create tools he can use to short-circuit his biologically based rage response to daily life. Perhaps he and his wife can develop a "time-out" strategy; perhaps when he feels rage coming on, they can agree that he will spend some time alone until it passes.

And finally, if behavioral and supportive psychotherapy are not sufficient to help him make the changes he needs to make, his responsibility may extend to taking whatever medication will restore his brain to smoother functioning. There is a strong Puritan ethic in our country concerning drugs; countless articles have been published decrying the concept of taking a pill to be happy. But the authors of such essays forget that all mental illnesses, including the mild, everyday ones, have more than one victim. Al-Anon estimates that every alcoholic's addiction intimately affects at least four other people, and the same can be said of the shadow syndromes as well. Emotional problems affect the whole family—often the workplace as well—not just the person with the problem. A husband who takes lithium, BuSpar, a beta-blocker, or an antidepressant such as Prozac or Norpramin to help modulate his temper is not just taking a pill to be happy, he is taking a pill to make his *children* happy. He is taking a pill not as an "escape" or a "quick fix" or an "easy way out," but as a gesture of responsibility toward his family.

As for the personal responsibility of those whose mild disorders are less obviously distressing to others—people with subtle depressions, phobias, or anxiety disorders that hurt mainly themselves—it is a matter of personal choice whether one wishes to become "better than well," in the words of Peter Kramer, whose book *Listening to Prozac* introduced the concept of the *forme fruste* (or shadow syndrome, as we call it) to the public. However, whether or not "well" is truly well is another question. A twelve-year study of nearly three thousand adults found that those with *mild* depression—a persistent state of discouragement falling short of true depression—suffered a significantly greater rate of heart disease than did those who were not mildly depressed. Controlling the sample for sex, age, smoking, drinking, and blood pressure, the Centers for Disease Control found that the mildly depressed suffered a rate of death from heart attack four times greater than the nondepressed, as well as a higher rate of nonfatal heart disease.

It is important to add that the issue of negative emotions and physical health remains unsettled. Many studies have found a link between such feelings as cynicism and hostility, for instance, and heart disease. But others have not. The same will no doubt hold true for any connection between mild depression and physical illness. Nevertheless, the evidence is suggestive. The negative emotions that accompany subtle differences in the brain may not be so harmless as we have long assumed.

■□ COMING TO KNOW THE BRAIN

The new neurology can affect our sense of who we are. Where once we thought of ourselves as the victims of dysfunctional families, some of us are beginning to see ourselves, instead, as the "victims" of dysfunctional brain chemistry—and our parents as, perhaps, victims of the same chemistry themselves. We are beginning to understand ourselves in new ways, not just as a collection of personality traits, but as a collection of biological traits as well.

Borrowing from science fiction, John predicts that within the next decade computer programs will come into being that will allow people to sit down and map out their biological profiles. People will play a series of games and perform a series of tasks that measure a multitude of variables: how good our attention is and how well we can stay focused (this test has already been used to study the relatives of schizophrenics, who often show subtle signs of cognitive differences even though they are not themselves schizophrenic), what level of interest in a task you need in order to sustain focus, what your level of irritability is compared to other people, your level of impulsiveness (the tendency to speak or act before you think), reactivity (the brain's over- or under-reaction to stimuli in the environment), arousal levels, mood variability, shyness, novelty-seeking, and so on. These tests will even be subtle enough, eventually, to be able to give you a reading on your level of defensiveness, or how likely you are to refuse to believe anything the test tells you about yourself!

The value of this futuristic exercise will lie in its ability to tell you what biologically based traits make you tick. Knowledge is power: if you know that you characteristically move through life with very high arousal levels, you can create ways to temper this trait. You can discuss it with family, friends, therapists, or others who share this trait; you can read about it; you can educate yourself as to what it means that, say, your levels of the stress hormone cortisol are elevated even when you sleep (something that has been found to be true of some depressed patients). You can learn to recognize those times when this trait is getting in your way, as well as those occasions when it helps. Rather than being driven by your biology, the goal will be to use knowledge of your biology to drive the chariot yourself.

For this is ultimately everyone's hope: to sit in the driver's seat of our own lives. Choice and a new sense of freedom: these are the benefits to come from the dawning age of neuropsychiatry. The point is not to create a cheery citizenry of model beings; no researcher seeks to erase each and every trace of the shadow syndromes from our collective lives. All of the shadow syndromes bestow blessings as well as troubles, and the blessings can be reason enough to learn to live with the troubles. Mental perfection for all is not a goal of neuroscience; it is not even a theoretical possibility, as we will see.

The hope, instead, is to give people a new understanding of themselves and others; an understanding they can use to make the changes they wish and hope to make. There are those who will protest that if the problems we talk about in this book are perfectly normal, then why worry? If everyone possesses some mental something that trips him up from time to time, aren't we all playing on an even field? Shouldn't we simply soldier on?

The answer is that in truth, for many of us, normalcy is not good enough. This should come as no surprise. The fact that a dark temper or a pessimistic character may be normal does not mean that either is easy to live with. A number of social commentators have criticized the universalism of the recovery movement, the claim by so many authors and therapists and talk-show denizens that *all* families are codependent, *all* families dysfunctional. But however we might feel about such sweeping declarations, it is important to confront the emotional reality from which they arise. Many, many people live daily with emotional pain of various forms, pain the recovery movement has attributed entirely to the families that bring us into this world. In this book we will be looking at what biology brings to the table, at the role biology plays in the myriad problems we have until now thought were entirely psychological.

Families (and workplaces, schools, shopping malls, towns and cities) are run by people, and people are run, to greater and lesser degrees, by their biologies. When there is anger or grief or despair or disorganization in any system, these destructive patterns originate, in part, in people's biological makeups. The purpose of this book is to help people recognize, and understand, that biology.

With understanding comes forgiveness: we hope this book will allow people to be kinder to themselves and to others, and to understand that often people are not doing the things they are doing because they are bad or uncaring or stupid. Perhaps we are doing the best we can; it is just that the best needs help. This book is intended to provide some of that help. This is a book about living well.

AUTHOR'S PROLOGUE

Catherine's Story

FOR ME THIS BOOK goes back to the birth of my son, Jimmy. In 1987, Jimmy arrived in our lives, a smiling nine-pound baby boy whom we—and our pediatrician—believed to be a perfectly healthy and normal infant. All seemed right with the world, and yet, somehow, I was not well. A year after Jimmy's birth I was sad, tired, chronically worried. I was functioning: I was taking care of Jimmy, writing a book, seeing friends, meeting deadlines, knitting Christmas stockings, mastering the art of low-fat cooking. By all appearances, I was living a life. But I felt bad.

In fact, I was depressed. But because I didn't *look* depressed, my husband and I didn't realize that that was what it was. We thought instead that something more sinister was happening to us. Because I had lost interest in sex, a common consequence of depression, we were terrified that something had gone wrong in our marriage. And so we spent many unhappy and tortuous conversations trying to understand what had befallen us. We analyzed everything. Had I withdrawn from sex because I'd become a mother? Did I feel competitive toward my husband because our little boy preferred him to me? Or was it my husband who was competing with me? Was he trying to be the favorite parent, thus provoking me to retaliate by withdrawing sexually? Our speculations grew more convoluted by the day. We were both so desperate to be happy once more that we would gladly have pled guilty to any or all of these possibilities if doing so could only put us back on course. But it couldn't: talking about our presumed unconscious conflicts did nothing to lift the gloom.

A small measure of relief came finally when my husband and I realized, rather suddenly one day, that I was in truth depressed. Not unaffectionate or uninterested or withdrawn—though certainly I was all of these—but *depressed*. There was a word for it. From time to time my coauthor and friend, John Ratey, reminds me about the drawbacks of labels, how a psychiatric term can box a person in. I know he's right, but I am here to tell you: when the label fits, it can be a blessing. As soon as my husband and I defined our problem as depression, the pressure lifted; instead of seeing me as a woman gripped by some mysterious toxic sexual reaction to motherhood, we could now see me as a depressed person who was not feeling a great deal of enthusiasm for anything, sex included. Seeing this, we felt better, and we were freed from the necessity to accuse or apologize. We could come together again in an effort to restore me to good spirits.

It was then that I saw the woman who was to become our family psychiatrist, Dr. Greer Sullivan of Los Angeles. She listened to my symptoms, asked me questions, and finally told me that I was suffering from an "atypical" depression (small wonder my husband and I had missed it) and that, furthermore, as depressions go, it was a mild one. That observation stopped me in my tracks: I remember thinking, If this is mild, I don't ever want to experience severe. She wrote out a prescription for Prozac, a drug that, she said, had been on the market for just a few months. She wanted me to try it because conventional antidepressants were not very effective in treating atypical depressions. Psychiatrists were hoping Prozac might be different.

They were right; it was. Within weeks I became one of the Prozac success stories that filled the media a few years ago: on day twenty-eight of the medication I was back. I was happy, alive, sexual (though to be honest, I should say that Prozac did not ultimately prove to be an unalloyed blessing for our sex life). I am not saying that suddenly, on medication, I had no more "psychology," no more unconscious conflicts or unhealthy attitudes toward sex and love—or that my husband and I never again disagreed or let each other down. Not at all.

But what I *am* saying is that Prozac taught my husband and me an invaluable lesson, and one of the fundamental lessons that underlie this book: we cannot, and we should not, underestimate the importance of sheer biology to a person's capacity to function. No matter what comes up in life—issues in a marriage, issues with children, issues with parents or in-laws—a person whose biology enables him or her to feel glad to be alive is better equipped to deal with these issues. That was what my experience with Prozac showed us: the drug did not alter my life history, but it did alter my biology. And when we change someone's biology, we may change his or her life. Certainly, medication changed mine.

This was my first object lesson in biology of the brain. We do not just have our individual psychologies; we do not just have childhoods or personal neuroses or unconscious conflicts. We have brains. And our brains, like any other organ in our bodies, can be in better shape or worse. As John would later tell me, the brain needs care and feeding, too. At that juncture in my life the care and feeding of my own brain meant taking an antidepressant medication, which a caring psychiatrist had wisely prescribed.

As it turned out, it was a good thing Dr. Sullivan came into my life when she did, because though we did not know or even suspect it at the time, my husband and I were only one short year away from embarking upon the darkest period of our lives. When I took our son to the pediatrician for his second birthday, our doctor told me that Jimmy's language was not developing as it should. We were to "wait and watch" for six months, he said, then see a speech therapist for an evaluation.

This did not particularly alarm either my husband or me, since my own brother had suffered a serious language delay: he had not been able to speak fluently until age six. Since my brother is fine today, we thought that was what would happen with our son.

But it was not to be. Jimmy's language did not catch up to that of his peers, and as the months went by, he fell behind in other ways, too. He wasn't interested in the things other children liked; he didn't watch *Sesame Street* on television, he didn't play with toy cars or blocks, he wasn't scared of monsters: videotapes that would terrorize the other preschoolers in the neighborhood produced no response in Jimmy at all.

When he turned three, a speech therapist told us she believed Jimmy was a "high-functioning" autistic child—he was, she said, "mildly" autistic. We were stunned; what could "mild" autism possibly mean? Was it like "mild" cancer? We read everything we could find on autism: head-banging, rocking, children biting their hands and arms, children who showed no affection, children who could not be touched. None of it applied to our boy. Jimmy did not bang his head or rock in a corner, and he was one of the most affectionate children we knew. He'd taught himself to kiss us well before his first birthday, and he insisted upon eating every meal sitting on his father's lap. He was a hugger and a cuddler, and had been from birth. He could not be autistic, we thought.

But he was. A year later, when Jimmy turned four, we received the official diagnosis. High-functioning autism.

Devastated, I returned to my psychiatrist. This time she saw my husband, too, and she helped both of us cope with the searing pain we felt. But more than that, she taught us. She taught us about autism, about the range of possibilities for an autistic person, about how to deal with the myriad experts and authorities who would now be part of our lives once and for all. There was no aspect of the enormous problem we faced that she did not address.

And she introduced me to the notion that would become the heart of this book: *forme fruste*. I heard the term first in Dr. Sullivan's office; then, two years later, from John. Over the course of writing this book we have come to use the phrase "shadow syndrome" in its place. All of the serious mental disorders of humankind, Dr. Sullivan told me, occurred in mild forms, as well. Florid, full-color mental illnesses like ma-

jor depression and manic-depressive illness come trailed by gray and sil-
ver shadow versions of themselves, the same thing in outline, but indistinct in detail; not easy to recognize for what they are. She herself had
made a specialty of working with schizophrenia, and a number of her
patients, all schizophrenic, were living and working independently.
They were *mildly* schizophrenic. I will always remember what she told
me: "In some ways it's harder for them," she said, "because they know
what's wrong and they have to fight it every day."

There was such a thing as mild autism, too, she said, and indeed,
since our son's diagnosis we have discovered that there are people in the
world with far milder cases of autism than his. There are autistic people
who go to regular school as children, attend college as young adults,
hold jobs, even marry. They *are* autistic; they are always different, and
they face severe challenges the rest of us do not. But they seem a great
deal like us. They can "pass."

This was my second, and most profound, lesson in the power of the
brain. People do not appreciate what the brain does until they've seen
what happens when something in the brain has gone wrong. The simplest of things, perceptions and actions we take for granted, are hard for
a person whose brain is not normal. One forty-two-year-old autistic
man we met, a man who had diagnosed himself after seeing the film
Rain Man, told us that to this day he could not read body language. A
college-educated person, he could not comprehend something so seemingly basic as when, in a conversation, it was his turn to talk.

This handicap made him sometimes awkward to be with, and if you
did not know he was autistic, you would chalk up his awkwardness to
psychological factors: a difficult childhood, a bad mother. It is easy
enough to see how Bruno Bettelheim arrived at his now infamous "refrigerator mother" theory of autism: if you don't know anything about
the brain, the brain's problems look like emotional damage. Certainly,
you would see our friend's social awkwardness as *his own fault,* a character flaw he could do something about if he wanted to.

But in fact, he can't. Once you come face to face with a case of mild
autism, you see clearly the limits our brains place upon us. This mildly
autistic man could not read nonverbal cues no matter how hard he

tried; the part of his brain that processes pauses in conversation simply was not working. (Whether or not, through extensive therapy and retraining, he could learn to enlist another part of his brain to carry out this function is another question. In any case, for him human conversation is never going to come "naturally.") It made me think: When we analyze someone's behavior solely in psychological terms, aren't we leaving something out? What about people who seem perfectly "normal" but are eternally awkward in social situations? People who never talk about feelings or who, when they try, don't know where to begin? Mightn't they, too, have some small glitch in their brain's functioning that makes it hard for them, normal though they are in every other respect, to interpret body language and feeling?

Which brings me to John. I met John through Jimmy, really. Within a year of the diagnosis I had begun to establish a circle of special-ed friends, other moms whose children had disabilities. One of them, Teri, whose daughter had learning disabilities and severe hyperactivity, gave me a file of material she had collected on attention deficit disorder. I was interested because I'd come to believe that autism was the ultimate attention deficit: an autistic child, I sometimes thought, was what a hyperactive child would look like if he couldn't pay attention to anything, ever.

Among Teri's papers was an interview with Dr. John Ratey, who was described as an authority on the subject of attention deficit disorder in *adults*. I had never heard of attention deficit disorder in adults, so I was curious. I began to read, and by the second column I was in shock: here was something that had been staring me in the face most of my adult life—and yet I had never seen it.

John was talking about men. Difficult men in particular. The kind of men who can't be intimate, who don't talk about their feelings, who don't seem to have much interest in their partners' feelings. And he was saying that many of these men were suffering from an unrecognized, adult form of attention deficit disorder. They were struggling in love for the same reason they had struggled in school: they could not sit still long enough to pay attention. Their problems with attention stemmed from problems in the brain's metabolism. They were difficult, in short, not because they were bad people, but because they had "bad" brain chemistry. Brain chemistry with a *difference*.

Given what I had just spent ten years of my life doing, this observation hit me with the force of epiphany. As a contributing editor to *New Woman* magazine, I had published countless articles on difficult men in one form or another: a fair amount of women's magazine time and energy, it must be said, goes into trying to figure out why men do the things they do. And invariably, when you write about why men do the things they do, the topic of intimacy arises. I had interviewed countless experts on the subject of men's "fear of intimacy"; I was well versed in elaborate "object relations" theories tracing male fears of intimacy back to the fact that it was largely mothers, not fathers, who raised baby boys. I knew all about men trying to suppress their "feminine sides" and men who suffered from homophobia. I had bought *Iron John* and *Fire in the Belly* in hardback, and was planning to tackle both the minute I cleared my desk.

But here, in John's interview, was something completely different. John was saying that problems in intimacy could stem from problems in biology: problems that looked strictly psychological in nature could actually grow out of minor malfunctions in the brain. Of course, the notion of intimacy being connected to biology was hardly foreign to me; I was living with a little boy who struggled daily with biologically based problems in intimacy and communication. But Jimmy's case was so extreme; Jimmy was *autistic,* after all. I had never thought that men who seemed perfectly normal might also have problems relating to people that were biologically based.

But now I realized that it was entirely possible. It is possible to have all kinds of minor flaws in the brain's functioning. Thinking back on our own experience, my husband came up with an analogy that made sense to us both: you can have a walking depression, he said, the same way you can have a walking pneumonia. You're up, you're around, you may not even know you're sick. But you're not feeling *good.* That was what I had had, a walking depression. A shadow syndrome.

And I was far from alone. The more you look at people through the lens of the shadow syndromes, the more you see it. People can have—

John believes most of us do have—mild, walking-around forms of mental disorders that, if they were serious, would be unmistakable. But when disorders are mild, people miss the connection. They don't think they're depressed; they think they've fallen out of love. They don't think they are suffering from a mild intermittent rage disorder; they think instead that their spouses and children are deliberately making them angry. They don't think something is happening in their brains; they think only that something is happening in their minds.

After my own experience with a mild mental disorder, I have come to believe that whenever people experience stubborn, recurring problems in life they should consider what role the neurochemistry of their brains may be playing. How much time do we spend blaming ourselves, each other, and our parents, for behaviors that originate in our biology? Behaviors like not being interested in sex, shouting at our mates and children, feuding with neighbors, firing insults at the boss, feeling too anxious to ask for a raise—all of these mundane, everyday events can have their roots in biology. They are strengthened or weakened by our psychology; one of the themes of this book will be the ways in which we can use our *minds,* our understanding, to compensate for minor problems in our *brains.* The field of psychology is essential, and knowing what role childhood plays in adult life will help. But it is one of the premises of this book that we should know as much about our individual biologies as about our individual psychologies. Because biology is never absent.

That is what this book is about: the mild, biologically based problems in the brain's functioning that we all experience some of the time—most of the time, for some people. It is about the shadow syndromes that affect our lives: how to recognize them in ourselves and in those we love, and what to do about them.

Ultimately, this book is about the care and feeding of the brain. The brain, I have come to believe, is the most underappreciated organ in our bodies. Walk into any bookstore and you'll find dozens of books on how to take care of your heart, but little on caring for the gray matter our hearts sustain. We take the brain, and the gift of life it gives us, for granted.

And yet proper nourishment of the brain is essential to a loving and productive life. Today the field of biopsychiatry is exploding with new research into the care and feeding of the brain; more and more, that is the direction the field is heading. But very little of this work has filtered out to the rest of us.

This book is a beginning. Our purpose is not just to offer readers a new batch of disorders to diagnose in themselves and in the people who are making their lives difficult, a fresh set of mental weaknesses to which the flesh is heir. Our hope instead is to share what is known today about how to escape the pain and confusion these unrecognized disorders create. Psychiatrists speak of achieving "optimal experience"; the rest of us say the same thing in different ways. Live life to its fullest, we tell ourselves; today is the first day of the rest of your life; don't worry, be happy. The quest to elude our shadow syndromes is the stuff of everyday proverb.

This book is for all of us.

AUTHOR'S PROLOGUE

John's Story

WHILE I'M NOT SURE what it says about me, my life's direction was set when, during my senior year in high school, I read Dostoyevsky's novel *Crime and Punishment*. Suddenly, in its pages, I discovered my life's work. I was gripped by the novel's themes of right and wrong, and of the emotional consequences of having to live with acts of right and wrong. When Raskolnikoff murdered a miserable old woman for her gold, reasoning that he, a struggling young writer with important ambitions, deserved the money more than she, I was hooked. While my newborn identity as a philosopher of good and evil may have been grandly adolescent, that was the moment that determined the course my life would take. Dostoyevsky's novel put me in a world I loved.

So in college I studied philosophy and religion. My subjects were God and love and choice and existentialism; I studied depth psychology through the works of Hegel, Nietzsche, Kierkegaard, Shakespeare, and, always, the Russians. What is the root of our being? These writers struggled with that question.

The times were ripe for my quest: it was the late 1960s, and I was caught up in the passion, in the brief renaissance when young people believed they were going to create a better life for all mankind. I was a card-carrying member of that era, and I meant my studies of God and life to be the grounding for a career of helping others.

After graduation from Colgate I moved to Boston, a city I had always loved. I applied for a job at the Massachusetts Mental Health Center because I wanted to work with the most severely disturbed of patients, and that was where you found them. I had my copy of R. D. Laing in my pocket; I believed, as so many of us did back then, that the severely ill patient possessed a wisdom denied to those of us who were merely normal. I didn't quite idealize these patients, but my view of them was certainly more romantic than it is today.

In this I was a typical citizen of the times. In the late 1960s many of the men and women we saw as heroes were essentially crazy people. Abbie Hoffman, Grace Slick, the SDS: whatever you thought, or think, of their politics, today they would have to be seen as suffering from disorders of mood and impulse. These were certainly not "normal" people; in fact, most of my friends and I weren't too impressed with the wisdom of the merely normal. Normal people, we thought, were dull and conventional. Irrationality was the ideal, and so I did not see Mass. Mental Health Center's severely disturbed patients as being as severely disturbed as they really were. I arrived at their ward wet behind the ears, ready to read poetry and sing songs, and generally follow the "Let It Be" philosophy of the Beatles, and of my hero Heidegger, who had written, "Whatever is, let be."

In true *Cuckoo's Nest* fashion, my sixties' impulses were instantly checked by the head nurse, a crotchety, conscience-driven Irish-Catholic woman who had been, and would be, the teacher of many psychiatrists. Here I was, a young orderly just out of college wanting to save lives, and there she was, a middle-aged nurse telling me, "No, you've got to make sure the chairs are straight."

Thus my entry into the adult world of reality. Although I did develop a more realistic view of severe mental illness under the tutelage of my new boss, my idealistic spirit remained undimmed. Soon I found new heroes. In those years the Health Center was a vibrant place; there was plenty of money for research, salaries, and patient care, and up until the 1980s most of Boston psychiatry was trained there. Some of the staff were extraordinarily talented. For a young person just out of school, it was an amazing educational opportunity.

The big influence on everyone's life then was Elvin Semrad. He was the director of training at the Massachusetts Mental Health Center, professor of psychiatry at Harvard, and president of the Boston Psychoanalytic Society. Medical students revered him because he was able to get even the sickest of patients to talk about their heartaches. The most disturbed, the most entrenched patients, people living with voices and shadows all the time: these people could relate to him as they had not been able to relate to anyone else. I came under his spell, and I wanted my own life to follow the shape of his.

But at the same time, the new era of biopsychiatry was dawning, and I wanted to merge my psychological and philosophical interests with a pursuit of some kind of research into the biological aspect of mental illness. Psychoanalysts, most of whom are M.D.s, had always acknowledged the importance of biology in mental illness, but for the most part they had simply genuflected before neurology and then lost touch with it in their daily practice. But now change was in the air. This was the period when the first powerful neuroleptics (or antipsychotics, used to treat schizophrenia) were being discovered; lithium, too, was essentially brand-new when I was starting out. It was a heady period, and I wanted to be analyst and neurologist both.

So, after two years in Boston, I started medical school at the University of Pittsburgh. I thought my life plan was set. I would use medical school to learn everything I could about every aspect of human biology that affected our lives: neurology, biology, genetics, neuropathology, neuropharmacology, hormones, everything. I wanted to have it all in my pocket. And, by the end of my years at Pittsburgh, I did.

But the second part of my plan was to prove far more difficult, for reasons having to do with my own biology (although I would not understand this for some years). My ultimate life's wish was still to become a psychoanalyst like my hero Dr. Semrad. All of my study of biology was to be prelude to my life's work as a psychoanalyst.

When I had the good fortune to be offered a residency back at Mass.

Mental Health Center, I knew I was in an ideal position to pursue my dream. I would be living in the midst of a thriving analytic community, and I would be able to study four months of neurology and to work with the brand-new CAT scan technology that had just become available. I was saddened to learn that Dr. Semrad had died only months before my return, but his legacy was still palpable in the halls as I set about achieving my goal of becoming an analyst as great as he had been.

To become an analyst in your own right, you must first undergo an analysis yourself. I was very excited by this prospect, and determined to be a model patient. I showed up on time for all my sessions (I even came early); I happily took my vacations when my analyst did; I free-associated for all I was worth.

But I was a failure as a patient. I could not free-associate properly. In truth, I could not free-associate at all. Somehow my brain did not work that way. While it is difficult to explain to people who have not undergone psychoanalysis, the process of free association is fairly passive. The patient is asked to let his mind drift from thought to emotion to memory and back again. But my brain was too active; I had no capacity to drift—to this day I still don't. Instead, a thought would cross my mind and I would pounce: I would latch onto it and pursue it to the furthest corners of reason. I would analyze, appraise, dissect—anything but drift. My mind was too active to let itself go in a free flow of thought and feeling. Finally, and with a tremendous sense of loss, I was forced to agree with my analyst's assessment: I was simply not cut out to be a psychoanalyst.

It is from this first critical life disappointment that a great deal of the impetus behind this book is drawn. What was happening to me then, as I watched my dream of becoming a psychoanalyst slip from my grasp, was the same thing that has happened to many of the people in this book—and that has happened to most of us at some time or another in our lives. My brain's biology, my basic neurophysiological makeup, was interfering with my ability to do what I wanted to do. I wanted to be an analyst; I wanted to be a good patient. But I could not because my brain was too driven, too active, too obsessed.

In fact, my brain was a classic example of the brain of an adult who suffers from attention deficit disorder, or ADD. Though I did not know it at the time, though I was only gradually to realize the truth as I worked with patients who had problems similar to mine, I was a hyperactive adult. And a hyperactive adult is the last person who should be attempting to free-associate with a psychoanalyst. ADD adults can't let things flow. They tend to focus from point to point, and when they hit a topic that draws them in, they will seize it and not let go (we call this hyperfocusing). Within the analytic session, this means that the ADD person's attempt to free-associate quickly becomes linear and goal-driven instead of free-floating and watchful. From his analyst's point of view, when a patient like me seizes one thought and runs with it, he ends up missing the next several associations waiting there in his unconscious to be made. But that is the way the ADD brain works. Only I didn't know it then.

Ironically, at the same time I was struggling with my ill-fated analysis, my dawning career as a psychiatrist was thriving. One of my turning points came with a patient the orderlies had nicknamed "Jaws" because of the many biting attacks she made on the people trying to care for her. She was a twenty-six-year-old autistic woman who banged her head so constantly—upward of four hundred times a day—and with such ferocity that she had detached both of her retinas. Now she was blind. She was so violent that she had *nine* full-time "specials" assigned to her alone: three staff members for each eight-hour period of the day whose entire job it was to protect other patients from her, and her from herself.

A friend of mine was looking after her, and he asked me what I thought. Trying to think of something that might help, I remembered an interesting paper I had read about the use of Inderal, a heart medication used to lower blood pressure, in treating patients with brain damage. Probably somewhere in the neighborhood of 20 to 30 percent of brain-damaged patients can become extremely aggressive; a once normal, calm, and loving person who suffers a severe head injury can emerge transformed, violent for life. The authors of this paper had found that Inderal quieted the aggression of some brain-damaged patients. Remembering that study, I suggested that my friend give his autistic patient a trial of Inderal.

It worked magically. Over a three-month period she stopped biting and banging her head *completely,* and my career as an investigator into the nature of, and treatments for, aggression was spawned. At the same time that I was having to relinquish my goal of becoming a psychoanalyst, I had almost serendipitously become an authority in a new and significant field—a field that had everything to do with the brain's biology. (It is probably no accident that, having begun my interest in psychiatry with a novel entitled *Crime and Punishment,* I made my first real mark in the area of violence and aggression.)

Now I continued to work on the psychiatric treatment of aggression, once meeting with a young prisoner in jail who gave every indication of being a born murderer. His family was functional enough, he had not been abused, and his brother had turned out fine. But from birth this man had been different. He was severely hyperactive; in fact, he was one of the most hyperactive people I have ever seen. As a tiny baby he was in constant motion. He never slept, he cooed twenty-four hours a day, he needed constant stimulation; there was no break for his parents at all. By the age of nine months he would rock his crib across the length of his bedroom to the window, which he would smash open with his head. When he grew strong enough, he would climb through the shattered glass onto the roof and run wildly around until his parents discovered him missing or a neighbor spotted him and alerted the household. Even as a baby he was always looking for the next high.

It was in this spirit that he finally committed murder: not out of rage or vengeance, but out of a need to create yet another high-stimulus situation. He was always looking for thrills; he was the kind of person who would drive against traffic on a six-lane highway just to see the cars scatter (he especially liked doing this when there was a cop around, because the policemen never knew what to do); he would provoke high-speed police chases just for the stimulation. He literally craved excitement. Diagnostically speaking he met the criteria for antisocial personality as well as for ADHD (attention deficit hyperactivity disorder)—he was the most hyperactive person I have ever seen.

On the night of the murder he had been picked up hitchhiking by a gay man whom he planned to rob. That might have been excitement enough for one night, but then the driver stopped for a second hitch-hiker. It was the presence of a third person in the car, an audience for whatever wild thing he might do, that set him off. He "had always wanted to kill somebody," as he told me, and now he had been presented with a golden opportunity to kill the driver with a witness there to watch. So he did.

As I interviewed him, I discovered he was so completely impulse-ridden that he was driven purely by the need for stimulation. After the murder he did not think of hiding the evidence or getting away; he did not think for one instant of self-preservation. The second hitchhiker had run off into the night and he was alone, so, when he got tired, he took the car and drove over to the murdered man's apartment which was closer by than his, and spent the night. That was where the police picked him up the next day. Nor did he fear the death penalty. Being sent to the gas chamber was simply going to be one more high-stimulus situation, gratifying at that level.

It was a horrifying story, horrifying especially in terms of what it said to me about the sheer power of biology. This young man had been headed down this path since birth; he was biologically *driven* to violence. His parents had done what they could to save him. He had had special classes, and people to help him. But nothing worked.

At the same time that I was becoming more and more involved in the pathology of violence, I was also establishing a private practice with the "worried well": the everyday Freudian "neurotics" like most of us whose problems are light years away from head-banging or committing murder for kicks. And yet as time went on, I saw parallels between the truly disturbed population of the criminally violent and the normal population with everyday problems who came to me for psychotherapy. In working with criminals I had been struck by how often the capacity to pay attention was an issue for them. In any highly aggressive population you will find that 80 percent have had symptoms of ADD and learning disabilities (often the two go together) in childhood. But the more sensitized I became to attention deficits in the chronically aggressive, the more I began to see traces of these problems in my everyday patients—and, ultimately, in myself.

My colleague, Dr. Ned Hallowell, and I began to talk about the ways in which ADD seemed to affect psychiatric patients in general. Ned was attuned to the issue because he himself suffered from the disorder although he had never been given that label; he had self-diagnosed in medical school. Reading an assigned chapter on attention deficit disorder in children, he had suddenly realized that all of the symptoms on the page applied to his own childhood.

Traditionally, child psychiatrists have assumed that children outgrew the disorder, and that is what we were taught in medical school. But now Ned and I began to see that many of our patients showed clear signs of difficulty concentrating today, as adults. While they were no longer *physically* hyperactive, *mentally* they were just as scattered as ever. In fact, as I thought about it, it became clear to me that my own brain worked this way. More startling yet, I began to see that my problems in trying to free-associate had been exactly what you would expect to find in a person with an attention deficit. My essential problem in free association was that my mind was both too active, leaping wildly from one subject to the next, *and* too obsessive, which meant that, again, I could not float along on a stream of associations. I would either drop an idea too quickly, or latch onto it too intensely. Nothing flowed. That is the mind of ADD: the ADD sufferer is plagued both by difficulties in staying with a topic, and by difficulties getting back off a topic once he has become locked in. That, I now saw, was me.

As Ned and I made these discoveries, we became aware of how widespread, and how thoroughly unrecognized, the problem of attention deficit is in adults. While millions of people have brain-based problems with concentration, impulsivity, and focus, ADD is rarely diagnosed in adults; until a few years ago, it almost never was. Instead, patients whose basic problem was hyperactivity would be diagnosed as depressed, or anxious, or addicted (since many untreated ADD sufferers self-medicate with alcohol or stimulants). All of these labels might be true, but all were secondary to a basic problem in paying attention and controlling impulses. They became depressed only after their hyperactivity had done a great deal to damage their lives, after they had lost jobs and marriages to the problem afflicting their brains. The hyperactivity came first, the depression or addiction second—which meant that we were seeing dozens of patients who were not being treated for what really ailed them.

Interestingly, none of these patients was doing very well in talk therapy, for the same reason I had not thrived in psychoanalysis. Their brains were too jumpy to benefit from a sustained hour of therapeutic exploration of their problems. Ned and I wrote our book *Driven to Distraction: Recognizing and Coping with Attention Deficit Disorder from Childhood through Adulthood* to try to encourage patients, psychiatrists, and psychologists across the country to think about the problems they were seeing in new ways.

It was around this time that Catherine called, wanting to do an interview on the topic of attention deficit and love. She had been struck by a short piece I had written about how difficult it is for a hyperactive man to be intimate, and had convinced her magazine, *New Woman,* to do a story on the subject. It was a meeting of minds: Catherine had already been introduced to the concept of what we came to term "shadow syndromes"—mild and usually unrecognized forms of otherwise serious disorders—by her own psychiatrist. So to her, the idea that a man might have trouble talking intimately with his wife or lover not because he was a bad person but because his brain could not stay focused made sense. More than made sense: it was a whole new way of looking at the things that go wrong in relationships. Catherine and I had a second area of interest in common, too, since her young son had been diagnosed with autism. I had written several articles on the subject, and we kept in touch. Within a few months we had decided to write this book.

Our goal is to help people, and their therapists, think about their problems in new ways: to discover the effects their biology may be having upon their psychology. I have always been bothered by the way in which the diagnostic process can close down a professional's sensitivity to the patient. Once the patient is labeled "depressed," he or she is depressed and that is the end of it. There is no need for further investigation. That works well for a patient who is suffering from a classic clinical depression, which is well delineated by the *Diagnostic and Statistical Manual of Mental Disorders*, Fourth Edition (DSM-IV) and highly treatable. In clear-cut cases the diagnostic manual gives doctors a powerful and effective tool.

But what about the patient who does not fit any of the established diagnostic categories, or who fits bits and pieces of several? For that is where most psychotherapy patients actually fall: most people who ask a therapist for help do not have one clear, well-defined, psychiatric difficulty. Perhaps a patient is sometimes depressed, sometimes anxious; perhaps he sleeps well but doesn't eat, or eats well but doesn't sleep; perhaps he has no physical manifestations at all, but his mood is dark and he tells you that his marriage is miserably unhappy. This patient cannot be found in the pages of the DSM. And yet this patient, like my ADD patients, may well have a difference in the brain that is affecting his ability to function—and that would respond to treatment. Because these patients do not fit the received diagnostic categories, they end up being categorized as simply people with "problems in living," and are given months or years of talk therapy delving into their pasts in search of clues to their present dilemma. The contribution their *brains,* their basic biologies, are making to their problems goes unrecognized, and untreated.

We want to help you understand what your own biological strengths and weaknesses are—and what those of those people you love may be. Knowledge is power: when you know how your brain works, you can take whatever steps you need to anticipate problems, and to play to strengths. And we hope, too, that as you read this book you will come to see that biology is not destiny. There is a tremendous amount we can do, through natural or medical means, to influence the neurochemistry of our brains.

One note. While some critics question whether a mild version of an otherwise serious disorder ought to be treated medically at all, we feel strongly that any condition that interferes with a person's capacity to reach his or her full potential is important. True, the mildly depressed person can limp along in his job and his marriage; he can be responsible, loving, and steady. He, or she, can *function.* All of the people described in this book function well enough to get by, most of the time. Perhaps they change jobs more often than other people; perhaps they end up divorced for a second time when they thought this was the marriage that would last; perhaps they quarrel with their grown children. Still, as the critics of biopsychiatry say, all of these things are normal enough: all of these things are part of life.

But the truth is, the "normal" disappointments of life are more normal for some of us than for others. A person with a mild case of ADD is far more likely to have a spotty job history and a troubled marriage than a person who can tune in and remain calm at will. The same goes for a person who suffers from a chronic but mild depression. Yes, that person can be stably married, but how vital is that marriage going to be when the mildly depressed partner is only minimally interested in sex and never seems to be having any fun? I know that in my life my own mild case of attention deficit disorder hurt my first marriage. My wife and I both would have been better off knowing what was making me tick.

Ultimately, the question is: why should the person with a very mild disorder accept his problems as simply his lot in life? If it is possible to treat a mild and hidden disorder by means of natural or medical interventions, then it is desirable. Even a mild disorder, given time, can damage a life, can drain away joy and hope.

This book will help you discover whether you have a mild difference in the brain that is affecting your capacity to live and love. Just as important, it will allow you to see the signs that the people you care for, your children, your spouse or lover, your parents, may be struggling with their own differences in the brain. And it will describe some of the current treatments that will help. While we do not want to stoke the media hype concerning the miracle cures of the new psychopharmacology, the truth is that minor miracles are happening, every day. And they are happening for people who thought their only problem was the inevitable pain life brings to us all. People who can't stay in a job, people who can't stay in a relationship, people who feel chronically angry at the world: so many of these people, when they begin to look at their biologies *as well as* their childhoods, have begun to find an answer at last.

We believe that this book will give you some answers, too.

1

THE NOISY BRAIN

WHEN WE ASK OURSELVES what minor flaws in the brain's functioning may be affecting us or someone we love, one of the most confusing issues is how many of the shadow syndromes normal people may fit. Sometimes depressed, sometimes impulsive, sometimes manic, sometimes obsessed: we may find aspects of ourselves, our families, and our friends in every chapter of this book.

That is why we begin here with the concept of *noise*. The one characteristic every shadow syndrome has in common is noise: an internal, biologically based, mental white noise. When we are mildly depressed, or mildly hyperactive, or mildly anything else, our brains cease to function as the quiet, reflective center of an ordered world. We become noisy *on the inside*. All of the syndromes result in a state of mental noise. No matter what their particulars, all of the syndromes have noise in common.

In this way, mental illnesses are much like physical illnesses. Every illness to which the body is prey has its specific symptoms—fever, joint pain, cell loss, muscular degeneration—whatever the case may be. But every physical illness also has *nonspecific* symptoms, symptoms that are universal to every disease we know. And the one universal in physical disease, the one symptom common to each and every malady human beings suffer is: the state of "just being sick." All sick people, no matter what is wrong with them, are just plain *sick*.

Though this may seem obvious, in fact for many years medical science failed to grasp the implications of this universal truth. It was Hans Selye who first introduced the "just being sick-ness" of sick people, back in 1925. He was nineteen years old, fresh from his studies in medical school, and meeting patients for the first time. The book *Tapping Hidden Power: Journey Through the Mind and Body* tells Selye's story:

> When his professor presented [him] . . . with patients in the earliest stages of various infectious diseases, Selye was struck by a curious fact: Although the patients as yet manifested few specific symptoms of disease, they all appeared exhausted, dispirited, and drawn. However . . . the professor regarded these symptoms as unimportant. "Since these were my first patients," Selye later wrote, "I was still capable of looking at them without being biased by current medical thought. . . . I could not understand why, ever since the dawn of medical history, physicians should have attempted to concentrate all their efforts upon the recognition of individual diseases . . . without giving any attention to the much more obvious syndrome of 'just being sick.'"

Later, Selye would go on to formulate the theory of what we to this day call *stress*, which he defined as "the nonspecific response of the body to any demand made upon it"—any demand including the demands of physical illness. As Selye learned, all sick people are physically stressed by their ailments.

What Selye's stress is to the body, noise is to the brain: noise is the brain's nonspecific response to the demands made upon it by difficult life circumstances, or by difficult (or flawed) biology.

John and his colleague, Steve Sands, of the Boston Psychoanalytic Institute, first developed the idea of internal noise a number of years ago when they were seeking a way to grasp the interior life of patients struggling with severe mental illnesses such as schizophrenia. "Noise" offers us a metaphorical way inside their experience, because all of us have experienced the disorganizing nature of real-world noise in its normal, everyday sense. The noonday rush hour, a jackhammer outside the window, the neighbor's stereo booming through the walls: while most of us will never hear voices, all of us have had the experience of being blasted by sounds and stimuli we cannot block out. We know how disorienting noise can be. We even have an expression for how we feel when the world is too loud: we say we "can't hear ourselves think."

The noise inside the brain of the severely mentally ill is not a literal noise, except in the case of schizophrenia, where a patient does in fact hear voices. It is a figurative noise; it is metaphorically akin to the very low signal-to-noise ratio of a radio channel filled with static. Inside the noisy brain, nothing is clear. The noisy brain cannot separate out stimuli or thoughts, either incoming or outgoing; everything is happening at once.

In terms of its consequences, brain-noise affects people in precisely the same way real-world environmental noise does. Overwhelming noise of any kind is profoundly aversive. Looking first at real-world noise, there are reams of data available on what happens to people attempting to recall lists of nonsense words, or add long columns of numbers, when bombarded by loud, unceasing noise. Invariably, people overwhelmed by noise make mistakes; their processing capacity falls apart. Inescapable noise is very stressful—so stressful, in fact, that when researchers investigate stress they typically choose noise as their means to *induce* stress in the people they are studying.

Thus we can begin to imagine what it must be like to live inside a brain that is itself the source of inescapable and incapacitating noise. This is the lot of the severely mentally ill: they must live out their lives inside a brain filled with noise, a brain that cannot settle itself down, cannot soothe its own chaos. The mental life of the severely mentally ill is a vicious whir; their minds cannot think about one thing at a time, but instead spin out wheeling masses of thoughts, feelings, sensations. Nothing coheres; thoughts are detached from feelings, and feelings are detached from bodily sensations.

This disconnect can lead to the bizarre reasoning that is the hallmark of the severely mentally ill. John remembers a patient, a thirty-one-year-old man with a thirteen-year history of schizophrenia, who arrived at his doctor's office complaining about his thighs. His thighs were bothering him; that was all he could say. Psychiatrists affectionately call this type of schizophrenic patient report "having the heebie-jeebies," because that's exactly what it is: the patient is not actually experiencing any real, diagnosable problem with his thighs. He has the heebie-jeebies.

In the case of this particular patient, he and his psychiatrist were eventually able to figure out that what he was actually feeling was a sexual attraction to one of the nurses at the hospital. But for him the channels that connect a physical sensation like desire to the mental emotion of desire were so filled with static—so noisy—that he remained completely in the dark as to what was actually going on inside himself. Deafened by his own interior din, he could not hear himself think; he could not feel himself feel. So he flailed about for a satisfactory explanation of the inchoate sensation engulfing him—which his mental illness readily gave him: the problem with his thighs, he told his therapist, was that someone had put implants in them while he slept! For the schizophrenic, a noisy brain leads to massive distortions of reality.

For the rest of us, reality—both the reality of the external world *and* the reality of our internal sensations, thoughts, and feelings—comes in far more clearly. Even so, the static produced by the shadow syndromes can lead to wounding distortions of fact and fancy, as we will see. For different shadow syndromes, of course, noise may come from different sources. Because of his oversensitivity to touch, for example, the mildly autistic person may be thrown into a noisy state by signals coming in from his own body. Such a person is defenseless against his body because he cannot let bodily sensations stream across his consciousness the way the rest of us do. Most of us have had quasi-autistic experiences from time to time: the experience of getting stuck on some bodily sensation we ought to be able to ignore—like the person who cannot get his glasses adjusted correctly on his nose. A person in this predicament cannot stop feeling the frames on his nose. Or, in another example: A patient once reported that she had suffered hours of insomnia the night before because she could not get comfortable in her bed. Wherever the sheets touched her body, they felt wrong. For hours she shifted about, trying to find the spot on her leg, the spot on her shoulders, the spot on her back, where the sheets would magically feel right. But she could not. A person who continually had this experience would be in the same predicament as the young autistic child who refuses to wear his clothing because he can't bear the feeling of the label brushing against the back of his neck.

Another example: The person with a mild form of attention deficit disorder may arrive at a noisy state via a slightly different route. People who suffer from ADD cannot filter stimuli from the environment; they tend to see everything there is out there to see, all at once. As one of John's patients describes it, "When I'm driving in traffic, I can't just see the car in front of me, and the car behind me. I see all the cars in front of me and in front of them, too; I can't *not* see them. I'm seeing dozens of cars, all at once. It wasn't until I started taking medication that I could actually look in my rearview mirror and just see the cars I needed to see." While the stimuli throwing him into a noisy state are technically coming from the environment, it is the faulty filtering mechanism of his brain that is the problem. He is continuously being thrown into mental chaos by his brain's incapacity to filter out the environment's irrelevant stimuli.

The person with a mild panic disorder will develop his mental noise in yet a different way; the person with mild depression will grow noisy in still another. But for all of us, no matter what the particulars of our shadow syndromes, a shared state of noise will be the result. And the results of a too-noisy biology will ultimately be painful.

■◻ TRAUMA FROM WITHIN

To understand what harm noise does to us we can turn to the large body of research, stretching back some twenty years, concerning "sensory overload." Noise is a form of sensory overload, albeit a sensory overload generated from within. Research into sensory overload began when psychologists became interested in the question of what happened to people when they were forced to take in too many stimuli too fast. Monographs like David C. Glass and Jerome E. Singer's *Urban Stress: Experiments on Noise and Social Stressors* were the result. What researchers found was that in fact stimulus overload is devastating to the brain's—to the self's—capacity to maintain itself. Entirely normal people who are severely overloaded, especially by unpredictable and uncontrollable stimuli, can show impaired functioning, raised physiological stress, internal chaos, impulsive actions, and a "lower level of adaptation" to life's challenges. A person on overload, in other words, is a person operating at the far low end of his capabilities.

Probably most of us have had this experience at times. Anyone who has had children can attest to the personality changes that ensue when we confront, say, a tiny infant with colic. The grating shrieks, the helplessness to do anything about the baby's distress, the utter mystery as to when the screaming is likely to stop: a colicky baby satisfies all of the criteria for "catastrophic" stimulus overload, and the parent's character suffers accordingly. If a baby cries long enough, parents eventually find themselves snapping at each other, shouting at the older children, swatting the dog. In short: faced with the sensory overload that is the colicky baby, parents rapidly regress to the lower level of adaptation Glass and Singer found in their stressed-out urban dwellers of the early 1970s.

Noise differs from sensory overload in one vital way: we cannot *escape* a noisy brain, as we can a noisy room. In normal life most of us can count on an eventual end to the environmental stressors that throw us into sensory overload. Sooner or later, the freeway commute comes to an end, the neighbor turns his stereo off, the crying baby falls into an exhausted sleep. But when our own brain is the source of the overload, there is no way out. For the schizophrenic patient with the heebie-jeebies in his thighs, the source of overload is his own scrambled brain. He is besieged from within, bombarded by a psychic noise whose source he can neither identify nor evade. Because research shows that prolonged states of sensory overload (or noise) are actually traumatizing, we can conclude that patients suffering from severe mental disorders are actually being traumatized *by their own brains.*

■

What professionals did not realize until recently is that an individual does not have to be schizophrenic to become traumatized by a noisy brain. Mark, another patient of John's, knows all too well the damage that results from too much noise within. A member of Mensa, Mark is one of those highly intelligent people who somehow never quite puts it all together. His business inclinations, like his father's, are entrepreneurial, but thus far his ideas have not panned out—largely due, he feels, to his own chaotic mind.

> My ex-wife used to say, "You have so much potential; I'm just waiting for that potential to kick in, and then we'll have a wonderful life."
> I figured life isn't that hard, but I seem to get to the one-yard line and something happens, I never get over the goal line. I either walk away, or I quit, or I say something totally off the wall.

And that is the end of that.

Exactly why Mark has hit the snags he has may be overdetermined, to use a Freudian term. But one of his problems, he himself feels, is a chaotic—or noisy—brain. Mark describes the noise he endures as a chorus of internal voices: highly critical, ultimately paralyzing voices.

> It's like the little man on my shoulder that will never shut up, but keeps chattering away. Even when I go to sleep, there's always that nagging voice in the background that's never ending. It's not my voice, and it's not my parents. It's like I have these advisors that are there, standing back and passing judgment on me. It doesn't really seem a part of me, and I've spent a lot of time trying to run from these voices. I've moved a lot. I went West, out to California.

Needless to say, all of these voices are uniformly negative; Mark does not have a host of angels perched on his other shoulder whispering, "Great idea!" or "Go ahead!"

Mark's "voices" are simply more vivid versions of the internal voices we all hear. He is not schizophrenic; he is not hearing voices in the classic sense of the term. Instead, his is a brain that is unable to turn off the internal critic most people develop as they mature. Worse, Mark harbors more than one critic. Where a "normal" person might hear just one unified voice of doubt, Mark hears dozens of negatives, coming from all directions at once. He hears a cacophony.

For many years, in an effort to silence his internal critics, Mark relied upon alcohol, and until his late thirties, when he joined Alcoholics Anonymous, he considered himself a functioning alcoholic. Interestingly, he reports that the concept of "noise" is completely familiar to his friends in AA; they discuss it at meetings. "We talk about having a monkey on our back," Marks says: a *chattering* monkey. For Mark, as for his fellows, alcohol soothes a tumultuous, and troubled, mind. "I always have a feeling of impending doom," he says, "even when things are going well. It's a gloomy feeling on the horizon." His partners at AA describe the same feeling, and for most of them a certain level of drunkenness dispels the fog. "One of the big reasons that I drank," Mark says, "was to try to numb those feelings. I'd get to a point where I'd be loaded, and then would sip the liquor to maintain that point. And once I was there, the voices would subside."

It is easy enough to see why a multitude of internal critics would paralyze a man's business life. But even a chorus of fans can be fatally distracting as well, as anyone who has had too many good ideas all at once (a condition known as hypomania) can attest: just the sheer noise level, bad *or* good, defeats action. As Mark observes, "There's a whirlwind of activity going on inside my head, and it's easy for me to get distracted and get out of control."

■□ THE CONSEQUENCES OF NOISE

Once in a noisy state—and a person who suffers from mild disorders may spend a great deal of time in an entirely unrecognized state of noise—certain consequences follow, none of them good. Most of these consequences fall under the rubric of a bruising tumble into Glass and Singer's "lower level of adaptation": noise diminishes a person's capacity to function. This is true in every realm, from the cognitive to the physical to the emotional. But it is particularly, and devastatingly, true in the realm of the social. A noisy brain invariably affects a person's capacity to deal with other people. That is why it is so important for people to become aware of the brain and its biology. If noisy states resulted in poor fine motor coordination, say, or in minor problems remembering small details like where we put our keys, they would not be so destructive. But the shadow syndromes strike us in the very heart of life, in our ability to live happily in a world filled with people.

There is a biological factor at work in this social decline. If we think of the brain in terms of its architecture, the set of behaviors and perceptions we call social skills occupies the very topmost, cortical level. Noise affects this top level, causing the person afflicted to fall back to a more primitive, "lower" level of brain functioning that corresponds to the social strategies of the adolescent or child. (Or lower still: internal noise may push us even further down the evolutionary scale to the level of the primate, or of the "reptilian brain," where we respond reflexively instead of thoughtfully.) All of us have witnessed this regression, as Freud called it, in ourselves or others: consider how quickly a marital argument can degenerate into childish name-calling, how rapidly two angry adults can metamorphose into two angry adolescents.

In some of the most interesting research on marital success and failure today, John Gottman, professor of psychology at the University of Washington in Seattle, has actually captured this connection between noise and social deterioration on videotape. Professor Gottman has looked at what happens to the *bodies* of married couples as they argue. He invites a couple into his laboratory, connects them to numerous sensors, and asks them to discuss a subject about which they disagree. As they argue, monitors measure cardiac interbeat interval, pulse transmission time to the finger, finger pulse amplitude, skin conductance level, and general somatic activity. And Gottman finds that every one of these measures registers an increase in arousal. Because skin conductance operates through a different biological system than do pulse and cardiac intervals, Gottman believes that the various systems affected by marital conflict are so widespread throughout the body that he has termed this state "diffuse physiological arousal." In other words: noise. When multiple measures of physiological arousal rise, a person has entered a noisy state.

The consequences of this state for a married person's functioning, Gottman has found, are uniformly negative. For one, a state of diffuse physiological arousal, or noise in our terms, impairs a person's capacity to process information. To put it bluntly, once in a noisy state, people are simply not as smart as they are when calm. Memory declines in this state, disrupting our ability to respond effectively to all of the data before us. And it becomes difficult to hold a thought; reactions become automatic, instantaneous. Finally, beyond both of these difficulties, intense physiological arousal also impairs reasoning ability, a phenomenon psychiatrists describe as becoming *concrete.* Once we have become concrete, we take things at face value; we are no longer responding to the subtle cues and subtext of social interactions, no longer able to think well abstractly, less able to conceptualize or project into the future. In the concrete state, conversations between spouses will take on the flavor of tit-for-tat. If a husband complains for the umpteenth time in one day that there is no food in the house, his wife fires back at once with the pointed observation that perhaps in that case he should go out and buy some. The fact that he may be alluding to something else: their sex life, say, or his worries about work, soars over both their heads. This is not to say that all communication between mates is always about "something else": sometimes an argument about groceries is an argument about groceries. But what happens when people become concrete is that they have no way of gauging the depth, the possible subtexts, of any particular exchange.

Gottman's work is fascinating because he can actually show, in videotaped transcripts, the point at which a marital argument breaks down into pure defensiveness, hostility, and insult. This decline corresponds directly to changes in each partner's pulse rate. As the pulse rate rises, the capacity to argue reasonably falls. It is a direct and striking correlation—so clear-cut that Gottman actually advises troubled couples to take their pulses in the midst of battle. In his experience, when a man's pulse reaches eighty beats per minute, on average, and a woman's pulse ninety, there is little point in going on. For both sexes, he writes, a pulse rate that has soared past a hundred is reason enough to end the discussion. A person whose heart is pounding away at one hundred beats per minute—due to anger, not aerobic exercise—is no longer capable of taking in, or responding intelligently to, what his or her mate is trying to say.

Other social skills falter as well, Gottman finds. As our processing skills decline, noise throws us back upon what psychologists call overlearned behaviors (again, the phenomenon Freud knew as regression). Overlearned behaviors are the behaviors we know all too well. These, not coincidentally, are the "lower order" behaviors, the behaviors we learned, and practiced, as children. We all know how to scream, shout, and cry; we know how to sulk and call names. We know these behaviors so well we do not have to think to do them, and that is the point. As the noise in our bodies and brains closes down our higher-order processing capacities, we lose access to the higher-order social skills we developed as adults. We regress to the cranky skirmishes of childhood.

Again, there is a biological substrate to this loss: overlearned behaviors are better laid down in the neuronal circuitry of the brain. Higher-order social skills, the skills we acquire with maturity, are the most recently acquired connections, and hence the skills supported by the weakest synaptic connections. Our more primitive behaviors and associations, the behaviors and associations of childhood, are actions we have done over and over and over again, resulting in synaptic connections that are stronger, more robust, more *fit* than those supporting our more recently acquired, mature behaviors. Internal noise shuts down the higher levels of the brain, the weakest synaptic connections, and throws the sufferer back upon the overlearned, synaptically robust behaviors of his early years.

■ THE PERSONALITY OF NOISE: ENVIRONMENTAL DEPENDENCY SYNDROME

What does a noise-shaped personality look like? As we will see, depending upon the source of the noise (mild depression, mild hyperactivity, whatever the problem may be), it can look like any number of things. But one of the most common results of a noisy brain will be an increase in self-involvement. Self-absorption rises with noise for the same reason it rises with physical pain or illness: a person who is struggling internally has less energy to invest outwardly, in the lives of other people. Just as a person suffering from the stomach flu is thinking mostly about himself, a person with a noisy brain is more self-focused, as well.

Apart from this seeming "selfishness," the noise-inflicted person may also demonstrate a mild form of a fascinating phenomenon we have long noted in the severely disturbed population: he may show a "pull to the stimulus." The standard example of a pull to the stimulus is the patient who, when shown a classic black-and-white Rorschach blot with a red splotch in the middle of it, can see—and associate to—only the red. He *must* look at the red; he is compelled to see red, and red alone. He is, in short, pulled to the stimulus that is the red splotch.

This happens in part because his processing is impaired; he has become concrete in his thinking and so is seeing only the most immediate and compelling stimulus in the field. But it also happens as a means of *defense* against the whirring of his brain, as a means of focusing down, of quieting his mind. Things can feel a great deal clearer, a greater deal calmer, when all we have to do is see red! Thus in essence, what looks like a personality quality is actually both a signal that a person is not operating at full capacity *and* a coping mechanism.

Though it may seem intuitively obvious that all of us would be drawn to the lone splatter of crimson in a sea of black and white, in fact there are very real differences between the kind of person who must zero in on the red, and the kind of person who can easily see the card as a whole—white, black, and red together. The person who sees the whole may have more choices in life, more emotional autonomy. The college student who can stay home studying on a Saturday night, instead of going out to drink with his friends, may enjoy a distinct advantage in life because he is not pulled to the stimulus of his friends. Thus, individuals who are not pulled to the stimulus possess far more ability to delay gratification, to work for a future reward rather than succumb to the pleasures of the moment. In sharp contrast, the person who has no choice but to zero in on the red may be environmentally dependent: his life is run by his environment, by whatever is the most compelling stimulus that presently lies before him.

The everyday version of this person is, often, the social chameleon, the person whose mood depends entirely upon what is going on around him at the moment. The environmentally dependent person may also practice situational ethics; it is very difficult for a person who is controlled by his environment to maintain an internal set of moral standards that transcend the immediate situation. This is the classic case of what we might call the traveling-salesman syndrome—a man who is a faithful partner at home but who, once he is on the road, loses all concept of marital fidelity. He observes one code at home, set by his wife, another altogether away from home, set by the people he meets in hotel bars. Environmental dependency can also lie at the heart of the deadbeat dad: it explains why a divorced man may be a devoted father while his children are actually around, yet fail to send the support checks once they are not. "Out of sight, out of mind" might be the environmentally dependent person's life motto.

Women may also struggle with noisy brains, of course (though, as we will see, women's relatively greater linguistic skills may mean that women have a better time of it when they do). But women's difficulties with noise may take different forms than men's if only because their lives have traditionally taken different forms: until very recently we simply did not see traveling saleswomen, or deadbeat mothers. Instead, the woman with the noisy brain might fall victim to the "mad housewife" syndrome of the 1960s novel and film of the same name. As we soon discover when contemplating the shadow syndromes, so many of these very mild disorders are already familiar to us in the guise of various cultural types. While we are rightfully leery of stereotyping large segments of the population, the truth is that certain stereotypes contain more than a grain of truth. The shadow syndromes explain why.

The mad housewife perfectly illustrates a destructive pull to the stimulus. She is environmentally dependent to the nth degree, the environment in her case being her house and its many imperfections.

Thus she is the woman who cannot walk through a room without dusting it. She *must* see the dust, *must* see the dirty sock crumpled on the bedroom floor. As in the more sensitive portrayals of this cultural type, more is going on with her than a simple cleaning fetish. At heart, and whether she realizes it or not, she is a noise-filled human being, a woman who, as the saying goes, cannot "get her act together." She may want to return to work, but can't seem to write her résumé. She may want to plan a family trip to the mountains, but the plane reservations don't get made. Her brain is spinning, and her irresistible pull to the stimulus of the dust mice under the bed is both a result of a decline in her processing abilities and a defense against the noise inside her mind. *Having to see* the dust is a signal that she is not seeing the larger picture that is her life.

■ WHEN SOCIAL SYSTEMS ARE NOISY

Entire families—entire social systems—may also demonstrate a pull to the stimulus. Here again, the template for what can happen in everyday family life can be found in the alter-world of the severely disturbed, in this case the chronic inpatient ward of the psychiatric hospital, better known as the back wards. On the female wards, often there is a patient therapists call the "alpha female." She is invariably a high-intensity actor-outer, a woman who disrupts everything, all of the time. She is a problem for all, patients and staff alike, and she is the cause of many, many IAs (staff terminology for "industrial accident," meaning the injuries—broken noses and arms, black eyes—doctors, nurses, and aides sustain trying to deal with a violent patient).

The rest of the ward population—patients *and* staff—are pulled to the stimulus that she provides. The entire social nexus of the ward revolves around the alpha female; living out their days in profoundly noisy surroundings, the staff reacts by focusing upon the compelling stimulus that is the alpha female. Everyone thinks about her, talks about her, asks after her when the workday begins.

They do this in part because they have become concrete, and thus find themselves absorbed by the particulars of the alpha female's behavior rather than by the meanings of those behaviors for the patient and for the ward. But they also fixate upon her because in fact focusing upon one raucous patient soothes the noise. The social matrix of the back ward turns out to be similar to the primitive brain, the brain challenged by overwhelming noise. The residents', and the staff's, need for the alpha female, for her vitally organizing existence, becomes poignantly apparent should she chance to improve. When the alpha female abandons her post, depression results for those she leaves behind—depression and often an increased sense of confusion. Very soon there is a subtle and unconscious attempt to promote another patient to alpha-female status. Whatever being the alpha female has meant for the patient herself, for the people around her she has been an essential defense against the din of their workaday lives on the ward.

It is easy enough to see how the pull to the stimulus, translated to family life, might play itself out. Family systems theory has for many years viewed the "problem child" as simply the person in the family who agrees to embody all of the problems the rest of the family wishes to deny: the problem child, to this way of thinking, is merely the *symptom* of trouble within the larger system that is his family.

Often enough, this may be so, but the concept of noise allows us to see the families of problem children from a different angle, and with a bit more empathy. The fact is, biology can have as much to do with the creation of a problem child as poor parenting: some children really are, for reasons having nothing to do with bad mothers or bad fathers, *difficult.*

And for parents, as well as for other siblings, a child with even a mild shadow syndrome is a noisy person, a maker of noise within the family system. This is one of the few chicken-and-egg questions that we can actually answer in some cases: for some troubled families it was the child and his problematic makeup who came *first.* Once a difficult child has been born into a family, its members, under stress, become more concrete in their thinking—growing paradoxically less well equipped to deal with the child than they would be if that child belonged to someone else. (That is why it is far easier for most of us to see what other families are doing wrong—because other people's children do not create noise in *us*. Other people's children do not impair our own processing abilities.) At the same time, the family, trying to quiet itself, is pulled to that child and his problems—in the process often making those problems worse. An intensive focusing upon the problem child organizes the family and, paradoxically, soothes. it. But because the family is not thinking well in the first place, the kind of attention they shower upon the child will be all wrong. The difficult boy or girl, now elevated to the status of alpha child, escalates his "bad" behavior and all is woe.

This brings us to one of the more striking, and, for those who must live with them, confusing, aspects of mental disorders: their fluidity. Mental disorders, even mild mental disorders, can become much worse in response to a noise-filled environment, a noise-filled family. This is an important reason why we have always blamed parents for their children's problems: because the parents' level of functioning *always* affects the child's—biologically based problem or no. The hyperactive child will become more hyper, the depressed child more depressed, the autistic child more autistic, when the family is not functioning at its best.

■□ COPING WITH NOISE: OTHER DEFENSES

Not everyone who is struggling with a noisy brain will feel a pull to the stimulus, of course; there are myriad ways we can respond to internally generated stress. Among these are:

The escape into rage. Anger can be a strangely soothing emotion. As we will see, rage is *organizing*: when we have worked ourselves up into a fury, we are completely focused, involved, and unified in violent sentiment against whatever it is that has moved us to wrath. Anger is so organizing that John's patient Mark consciously uses the emotion to get his day going:

The worst thing for me is if I'm allowed to float. It takes a Herculean effort for me to get out of bed in the morning, even though I'm not depressed. I'll float and say my prayers and drift in and out of sleep, and sometimes when I'm lying there the voices will be trying to get me focused, and get me up and running. So I might start thinking about sex with a woman, or fear and anger—maybe a guy who cut me off in a car. Then the voices will start urging me, they'll kick in to get me into fight or flight, to get me motivated. Anger and sex are the two big motivators that get my eyes open in the morning.

What anger and sex have in common is that both are physiologically aroused states—and biological arousal enables the brain to focus itself. That is exactly the strategy Mark has developed over many years of coping with a too-noisy brain: as soon as the day has dawned, he deliberately uses anger to get himself up and going—to halt the floating state that can drain away his day.

The escape into action. More dangerously, noise-filled people may also escape into action. When a lover's quarrel has escalated to violence, the very act of striking one's mate can be organizing and, thus, soothing. Any compulsive activity is focusing, and when we strike someone, we are temporarily at one with ourselves, with the violence of our action. This is one reason why cinematic images of violence are so compelling: in the lone hero battling the forces of evil, we see a purely focused human being. We see, paradoxically, *quiet.*

The escape into meaning. And finally, commonly, the escape from noise may take the form of an escape into meaning. The noisy state produces an almost unbearable pressure for explanations, for labels. We want to know *why;* we want to call our condition by its rightful name. We feel better just understanding what is wrong with us, even though understanding may do nothing to actually change the problem. Talk therapy often works according to this principle: simply developing a coherent explanation of, for instance, our childhoods, can be amazingly soothing.

We call this defense an escape into meaning when the meanings we embrace are neither a true nor a wise vision of our own life histories but merely an escape into a meaning that is premature. We see the escape into meaning most vividly at work in the lives of schizophrenic patients. The schizophrenic escapes into meaning on a daily basis: the unnerving voices coming from behind him signal that the FBI is having him followed, his thighs feel funny because they have implants.

For those of us grappling only with minor glitches in the brain's chemistry, the flight into meaning often takes the much more mundane form of a flight into blame. We feel noisy within, and we conclude that it is our parents' fault, or our mate's. This is one of the most destructive aspects of our struggle with internal confusion: we mistake its source. We explain the basic, biologically given chaos that accompanies any of the shadow syndromes not as the natural result of our own chemical and physical makeups, but as the fault of the people and events that surround us.

This flight into meaning can and does happen in therapy as well as in daily life. Therapy is often about dealing with noise, for client and therapist alike, and the pressure to assign an instant meaning to the patient's chaos can be fierce. Thus the therapist whose patients routinely "recover" memories of child abuse may be seizing upon a premature, and false, meaning in order to soothe himself as well as his patient. The patient has felt angry or frightened or lost for years; suddenly all is explained by one simple image. The jumble of feelings are organized for patient and therapist both, the noise quieted. What neither therapist nor patient has been willing to do is to tolerate the chaos within, to hold these feelings, share them, extend them longer and longer until patient and therapist can see what they truly do mean. The bad therapist jumps to meaning too quickly.

Here again, we see what havoc the noisy state can wreak upon the social world. And while colluding with one's therapist to invent an incest narrative is obviously going to be socially destructive, the smaller mistakes we make in assigning meaning can do damage as well. A woman whose brain is made noisy by a very mild form of obsessive-compulsive disorder may blame her husband for the chaos she suffers. Aided and abetted by protofeminist discourse in the media, she may tell herself that he is sexist, uncooperative, unfeeling, that the fact he does not clean the house to her (mildly obsessive) standards betrays his lack of respect for her. Thus an escape into meaning is going to create all manner of further problems with her by now resentful spouse, wounding the marriage.

■□ NOISE AND WORK

For most of us, a psychological condition like noise that diminishes social skills will also threaten our effectiveness at work. Most jobs require that we know how to deal with people, and coping mechanisms like an escape into anger will almost inevitably get in the way. And of course, a decline in processing abilities will harm our ability to perform any work that involves abstract thinking or higher-level organizational skills.

Certainly, the environmental dependency syndrome that some shadow-syndrome sufferers develop will pose obstacles to a successful career. The man or woman who is pulled to the stimulus is a person who may have tremendous difficulty formulating a plan and sticking to it. Goal-directed behavior, one of the bases of any kind of success in life and love, depends upon being able to organize one's thoughts and hopes, and act upon them in a direct and timely fashion. But the person who is pulled to the stimulus is constantly distracted—ambushed even—by the red spot.

Internal noise affects our ability to work efficiently and well in other ways too. For one thing, many people in a state of noise cope by "focusing down"—by drastically narrowing their field of vision. Biting fingernails can be a way of focusing down: when an individual becomes absorbed in the act of biting his nails, his brain feels, for those moments, calmer, more organized. He is focused upon a very small field of action. Pacing offers the same organizing, noise-reducing effect. (Hobbies, too, are often a highly adaptive way of achieving the same result. Collecting, gardening, knitting, cooking, tinkering with the car—all are productive and soothing ways of focusing down to one narrowly defined activity.)

For those who have learned to harness this defense, focusing down can be helpful: it can be a way of priming the pump, of gathering one's attention before the challenges of the day. But unfortunately, all too often the need to focus down can shanghai a day. Take the case of compulsive desk-cleaning. Many white-collar workers have had the experience of feeling that they cannot embark upon any productive activity whatsoever until their desk top resurfaces. The truth is, of course, that a person who is not in a noisy state to begin with can write memos or perform market analyses or negotiate contracts in the midst of a hurricane. We have all heard tales of authors who began their writing careers sitting at the kitchen table with children, pets, and repairmen swirling at their elbows. The writing progressed nonetheless. The conviction that we cannot work in the midst of chaos may well reflect a chaos *within*. And while it is true that a frenzied bout of desk-cleaning can soothe the soul, it can also get in the way. The person who misses critical deadlines because he feels *compelled* to clean his desk before doing anything else has been reduced to a lower level of functioning by the psychic noise he is trying to still.

Employees living in a state of noise can also become mired in obsessive rounds of "internal sequencing." Probably all of us have experienced the oppressive sensation of feeling so overwhelmed that we do not know where to begin. This feeling, again, grows out of a state of noise. Some of us will respond with an all-consuming process of internal ordering that does nothing actually to begin the work at hand. The hapless employee sits at his desk laying plans: "I'll write the memo first, then file the reports, then call the client." This plan sounds reasonable enough but cannot take hold in his spinning brain. Within moments this sequence feels all wrong; the call must come first, *then* the memo, *then* the files. But then the call can't happen because it will take too long; back to the memo first. Or maybe the best plan would be to tackle the files first thing and them move on from there. . . . The noisy brain cannot *settle,* cannot make a plan and stay with it. Meanwhile, as the sequencing process spins on, no actual work is getting done. The noisy brain is the biological reality behind the saying that a person is just spinning his wheels.

Finally, and most poignantly, the state of noise can diminish our capacity to *wish.* For many years popular wisdom has extolled the virtue of getting "in touch" with ourselves, and the concept of noise tells us how it is that we can be out of touch in the first place. In the noisy state we cannot know what it is that we truly want. We are too consumed by the noise, too absorbed in the effort to quiet the inner whir, to be able to see clearly our heart's desire. The saddest proof of this can be found in the stunted wishing of the chronic schizophrenic: these are human beings who can muster neither ambition nor desire, who do not wish for even so small a thing as a picnic in the woods, so overwhelmed are they by the commotion within. Indeed, the capacity to wish is so blighted in the chronic inpatient that his family and keepers rightly take even the smallest expression of a wish, perhaps a desire to watch television, or to venture outside the hospital for a ballgame, as a sign of improvement. The ability to wish is fundamental to being well.

For all of us noise degrades wishing. Certainly, the state of noise may be highly emotional. We may feel angry, anxious, sad, furious, defiant, afraid, or vengeful; we may feel all of these things at once. We may be suffused with longing; we may desperately wish our lives to be different. On the surface of things, the noisy state may look to us as if it is filled with wishing.

But simply being overwhelmed by unhappy emotion, and wishing it away, is not the same thing as knowing what it is that we want in life. It is not the same thing as true wishing. And in the world of work, knowing what we want lies at the heart of the capacity to commit to a lifetime of discipline, effort, and showing up on time. Probably many of us have known emotionally chaotic people who cannot seem to settle into a career: the problem, here, may be noise. Mark's career history doubtless has been marred by his own noisy brain; while he has had many business "interests," he has not, in his quarter century as an adult, formed a clear vision of what it is he hopes to achieve, what it is he might be remembered for after he is gone. And the need to combat his internal noise each and every morning as he tries to rouse himself from sleep prevents him from looking to the future. As the AA saying goes, for Mark it is one day at a time. While living life one day at a time has saved many an addict, when we can *only* live life one day at a time, the future dissolves.

Ultimately, all of the shadow syndromes threaten the future tense, threaten our capacity to wish for the rest of our lives. When we must struggle with a chronically noisy biology, it is almost impossible to be focused or directed; it is almost impossible to embrace a genuine and heartfelt ambition.

The loss of wishing hurts us in love as well. If we are fighting the chaotic noise of the moment, we may flee a marriage, a family, a love, when our true wish, the wish we cannot make contact with amid the din, would be to stay. The trauma of noise is that it takes our selves away from ourselves; it breaks the connection. Only when we quiet the noise within can we experience true need, true want, true desire. Only then can we know that this place, these people, are where we want to be.

2

THE BIOLOGY OF
BEING "DIFFICULT"
Masked Depression

ON THE FACE OF IT, "mild" depression sounds like a quiet problem. We think of the slightly depressed person as an unassuming soul: melancholic, perhaps shy, a meek and retiring figure standing on the sidelines of life's parade. A person who is more trouble to himself than to anyone else.

But in fact, the very mildest forms of depression may manifest themselves in an altogether more vivid form. Very mildly depressed people are often stressed, frazzled, angry. They feel overwhelmed and fed-up; they are the people who have "hit the wall." They bark at their children; they snap at their mates. They are chronically irritable, and they are having no fun.

In spite of all this, they may *not* be particularly "neurotic," in the conventional sense of the term. Where major depression can be—and usually will be—a severely warping experience, toxic to self and to love, the very mildly depressed come of age under an altogether lighter pressure from within. A person who is biologically inclined to be only mildly depressed over the years may have a perfectly happy childhood, and even a happy enough, or certainly tolerable, adolescence. If the mildly depressed adult was blessed with a family that believes in him, he may well have developed as secure and solid a sense of self as the most sanguine of natural-born optimists.

He is helped along in this process by both biological and psychological aspects of depression in its soft form. As to biology, researchers have found, interestingly, that the shadow syndrome of depression often does not come mixed with a great deal of anxiety—as severe depression almost invariably does. Of course, some mildly depressed individuals are also quite anxious; we do not mean to minimize this. One study found that approximately one-third of mildly depressed individuals are clinically anxious as well. But this leaves a large majority who, though mildly depressed, are not particularly worried or afraid.

For the mildly depressed, this is a source of strength. At its simplest, "anxiety" is simply a code word for "fear"—and fear is a corrosive emotion indeed. It is the anxious or fearful person whose image is conjured by the now almost quaint term neurotic: the person who is flustered, fearful, seized by one worry after another. In contrast, the person who is only mildly depressed is not preoccupied with fears of unseen dangers, or with an ominous future. As a result, he can be clear about who he is and what he is doing; he may lead an unreasonably constricted life due to his lack of pleasure and expansiveness, but he knows what that life is about. The sheer level of confusion, then, may be lower in shadow forms of depression than it is for those wrestling with other mild disorders.

The psychology of mild depression also confirms him in his sense of self. This is so because in fact mildly depressed people are often *right*. Their perceptions, their opinions, their view of the world—the mildly depressed person, sad to say, tends to be confirmed in his somber vision of life more often than not. But the natural-born optimist sees only happy things before him, and thinks happy thoughts; he glides through life in a floaty state of benign oblivion. In her book *Positive Illusions,* Shelley E. Taylor, professor of psychology at the University of California at Los Angeles, delightfully sets forth the million-and-one ways in which cheerful people delude themselves. One of the most touching is the belief, held by 90 percent of all automobile drivers, that they drive "better than average"—a statistical impossibility. As Taylor shows, the mildly depressed person tends not to harbor such gratifying illusions:

> Normal people exaggerate how competent and well liked they are. Depressed people do not. Normal people remember their past behavior with a rosy glow. Depressed people are more evenhanded in recalling their successes and failures. Normal people describe themselves primarily positively. Depressed people describe both their positive and negative qualities. Normal people take credit for successful outcomes and tend to deny responsibility for failure. Depressed people accept responsibility for both success and failure. Normal people exaggerate the control they have over what goes on around them. Depressed people are less vulnerable to the illusion of control. Normal people believe to an unrealistic degree that the future holds a bounty of good things and few bad things. Depressed people are more realistic in their perceptions of the future. In fact, on virtually every point on which normal people show enhanced self-regard, illusions of control, and unrealistic visions of the future, depressed people fail to show the same biases. "Sadder but wiser" does indeed appear to apply to depression.

Sadder but wiser applies specifically, as Taylor goes on to remark, to *mild* depression. Where the severely depressed do distort life to the negative, the mildly depressed are quite possibly the most accurate observers of life in our midst. They perceive with crystal clarity the truth that, when the glass is half-full, it is also half-empty.

Perhaps somewhat paradoxically, the result of this perceptual accuracy can be a stronger sense of self. While the mildly depressed person might prefer to be wrong once in a while (certainly those around him would prefer it!), in fact being right is highly reinforcing. The mildly depressed person learns, if nothing else, to trust his perceptions, to trust *himself.* Life may not be what he wishes, but he experiences himself as a person who knows what is what. He is clear about things. In this sense he is the opposite of his anxious, fretful cousin from the anxiety division of the DSM.

Thus, as with all of the shadow syndromes, the mildly depressed personality has its strengths. And, as with so many of the shadow syndromes, these strengths are often more compatible with the requirements of the workplace than with the requirements of love and family. The story of Caroline Rose shows us this.

■□ THE SUPERWOMAN

Caroline Rose was not a person who thought of herself as being depressed. She was a product of the roaring eighties, a committed careerist who was ambivalent at best about the prospect of having children one day; for years she and her husband remained childless by choice as both concentrated on progressing in their fields.

Finally, outnumbered by an older and a younger sister who had both had babies, Caroline made up her mind: she stopped taking her birth-control pills and, within the month, was pregnant with her first child, a daughter whom she named Laura. Now she was a working mother.

She fell in love with her baby at once, realizing instantly, as do so many women who have come late to childbearing, how much she would have missed if her decision had gone the other way. She and her husband filled hours and hours of videotape of their newborn daughter just lying on a blanket, doing nothing: to them the new baby was magic.

Caroline handled the responsibilities of parenthood with her usual competence. She leafleted every house in the neighborhood, and by her eighth month of pregnancy had found a nearby mother who would take care of Laura along with her own three-year old grandson. The situation was loving and stable, and Caroline now had in place the support system she needed in order to function at work. She thought of herself as happy.

But as Caroline's life sailed along, her sister's lives were falling apart. Both had had babies before Caroline; both were now learning that their babies had serious problems. One child, now two, was showing signs of a developmental delay; the other child, now three, had grown from a severely colicky baby who had once cried for forty-eight hours straight into a severely difficult two- and then three-year-old. This child's challenging behaviors were well outside the range of normally difficult behavior, and by the age of four she would be diagnosed as manic-depressive. Both sisters, reacting to their children's problems, had fallen into clinical depressions and begun taking antidepressant medication.

Her sisters' depressions were to have a major impact upon Caroline's life because, just as with the baby issue—when both sisters had been united in the view that Caroline should have a baby—the sisters now began to agree that Caroline was in fact not doing as well as she thought. Caroline's sisters had had the not unusual experience of finding themselves, on Prozac, better than well—of realizing that although neither of them had been severely depressed for years on end, neither had they been the largely cheerful and patient people they now became with their brain chemistry altered by an SSRI. In short, Caroline's sisters were experiencing the sea change in their view of themselves that can happen to a person who is successfully treated by psychopharmacology: both women came to see themselves as biological beings. And, seeing themselves as biological beings, they began to see Caroline as one, too.

Caroline's older sister remembers this period well:

I had always had mild depressions from time to time, usually in the winter, that went away on their own after a few months. I had even thought about taking medication because a friend of mine had done very well on it. But I hadn't come to that point. Then when I finally had a real clinical depression because of my son's learning disabilities, I saw a psychiatrist who put me on Prozac. It was brand-new then, and it was a miracle. Not only did my depression completely disappear, but my whole outlook changed. I had always been kind of fraught; I was angry a lot, tense, extremely obsessive. And on Prozac all of this just *went away.* It was amazing. It wasn't a personality change, exactly; it was that on Prozac I felt as I normally felt on my very best days. On Prozac I was at my best practically every day.

Naturally this made me think differently about my emotions,

about how much of my emotional tone throughout the day was actually coming from my biology rather than from my life. Before Prozac I had spent *years* being angry, twenty-four hours a day, over the plight of women. I was a classic raging feminist. On Prozac, I was still politically a feminist, but suddenly I could see that nobody in my position in life, with a good husband and a happy marriage, needs to be spending twenty-four hours a day being angry because women are oppressed. It's not natural. And I wasn't just angry because women are oppressed, I was angry—constantly angry—at my friends, too. This friend said this, that friend said that, and I would obsess and fume for days. I was an angry person. The change with Prozac made me see that.

The medication made her see her younger sister differently as well:

Caroline and I were close, but we had *always* argued. Always. There was never a moment of calm and getting along; we were constantly sniping. And a lot of it was Caroline sniping at me. For years we both thought this was about sibling rivalry. I was older and thinner and got better grades in school, and Caroline resented me; that's the way we both saw it.

But after I took Prozac, I started to see Caroline differently. I started to think: Wait a minute. This is *all* sibling rivalry? The fact that my sister can't spend two seconds with me without getting angry and tense and competitive? And I started to realize that she was pretty angry and tense and competitive a lot of the time; you never really heard Caroline *laugh.* She wasn't lighthearted, she was never up. She was negative. Not depressed, but negative. And to be honest, while I loved her, I also found her a difficult person to deal with.

Soon Caroline's sisters began to press her about the possibility of taking Prozac herself. As so often happens when one member of a family has found an answer, Caroline's sisters believed they had found an answer for Caroline, too. The problem was, it was an answer to a question Caroline had not asked.

Both my sisters were on the medication and were constantly berating me, telling me I should take it—I think because of my explosiveness; I wasn't really sure. I could see character differences between Jane and

Debby and me. They had more blues, more ups and downs, things I just didn't have. And they had both had real breakdowns when they were going through the diagnoses with their kids. My only problem was getting pissed off a lot. I remembered blowing up as a child, just taking on the world, arguing with my father when my sisters were too shy to do it. And I remembered the neighbors down the road talking about how they could always hear me yelling; they were always saying, "That Caroline sure has a good set of lungs." My mom could hear me yelling all the way from our friend Mary's house, and they lived clear across a cornfield. Who knows if it was just me playing; the story was she could hear me yelling. But I was never blue.

But after the birth of her second child, a daughter whom she named Elaine, Caroline's mood faltered. The baby looked different to Caroline, a dark brunette in a family of pale blonds, and not a pretty baby either, or not, at any rate, to Caroline's eyes. Overwhelmed and exhausted by the demands of two small children and a full-time job, Caroline found herself now feeling precisely the way her sisters experienced her: flat and joyless.

With Laura, I couldn't keep my hands off her. I wanted to hold, hold, hold my baby every single second. But with Elaine I didn't care. I held her, of course, but it was easy to put her down. Something just seemed wrong. I guess the first year went by—I thought maybe it was a postpartum thing. I thought she didn't look right, she didn't look like my daughter. She wasn't the miracle the first one was. And I never really pulled out of that.

Although life with the new baby was not what Caroline had hoped, in fact she was not depressed in a clinical sense. She would not have qualified for a diagnosis under the DSM; she was not even dysthymic—the clinical term for mildly depressive—according to the conventional usage. Nor did she think of herself as depressed, or even sad:

I was doing fine, but what made me think I should see someone was the comparison to Laura. I knew how wildly great everything had been the first year with her, and I knew things were not that great with Elaine. Intellectually, I understood that with the second baby there would be more work and it would be harder to get everyone dressed in the morning and out to day care and the office. Everything would be more intense. But I still expected to feel that warm, fuzzy mom thing. And I didn't.

With Elaine everything seemed more—not a chore, exactly. It wasn't depressing having the two kids and the house and the job, it was that life seemed flat. You had your schedule, you followed your schedule, and that was it. It was so mild that I told myself it wasn't really a big depression, and I was accomplishing everything, so I just thought, It's going to be this way for a year.

Since her health care was provided by a health maintenance organization, Caroline did not have the option of simply checking in with a competent psychiatrist. One of the problems with HMOs, in terms of mental-health care, is that the gatekeeping function of the primary-care physicians can pose a serious obstacle to a patient's receiving the help— or even the information—that he or she needs.

So Caroline turned to her gynecologist instead. He diagnosed her problems as a case of late-onset premenstrual syndrome, telling her rightly that PMS, a condition that had never been a problem for Caroline, can first appear in a woman's late thirties. "I remember telling him, 'Great, I have PMS and menopause to look forward to in the next ten years,'" Caroline recalls. "And he said, 'Yes.'"

Her doctor gave her a diet that he said could diminish PMS; she was to limit caffeine, additives, and chocolate. And he told her to begin a serious program of aerobic exercise. While Caroline had exercised for most of her adult life, the thought of adding an aerobics routine to an existence already devoid of down time was daunting to say the least. If Caroline had not been depressed coming in to his office, she was now: "I remember I started weeping in his office. I said, 'I get up at six A.M. already, and you're telling me to get up at five A.M. so I can get in the exercise?' And he said, 'Yes I am.'"

Caroline did. A working, commuting mother of two small children, she set her alarm for 5 A.M. every morning, got up, dressed, and rode her exercise bicycle for forty minutes, faithfully. Those forty minutes were the only period of personal time she had all day; by the time she and her husband had the children bathed and in bed at night, and the supper dishes cleared away, it was 9 P.M. and time to sleep if she was to have eight hours before rising again at five o'clock. Still, Caroline found the new regimen soothing in its way:

> For the next year I was exercising five days a week, ten miles on a bike, forty minutes of exercise every morning. But it turned out to be OK, because that was my quiet time. I would read and read and read; it was pitch black when I got up, and I would watch the sun rise. I ended up loving it, and I lost a bunch of weight and looked great. I'd go to work feeling great, and I loved my job.

If Caroline's workday had spanned only nine to five, the exercise regimen and the PMS diet might have been sufficient to restore her to good spirits, and her story would have had a happy ending. But Caroline was coming home each day to a second shift, and it was here, at home, that she was falling apart.

> I felt pretty good, but what was happening was at night and on weekends I'd explode with the kids. I sounded just like my dad, who always had a terrible temper; I'd be shouting about just minor things, like maybe the kids might be making a mess in their room, which kids do. One time I got so mad that I actually threw Laura's tape player against the wall, and I really wanted it to break into a million pieces. I don't even remember what prompted that, it was just anger.
>
> And then I had an altercation with Laura that made me go running in for help. Laura had taken a ball from Elaine, and I grabbed it from her and then she grabbed it back—it was absurd, like two little kids grabbing—and then I slapped her in the face! And I was horrified. You just stand there and go, What the hell am I doing? Slapping someone over a ball? This wasn't even something big like a child drawing on the walls; this was an ordinary childhood squabble between sisters. And I had lost it.
>
> The next day I had an appointment with Laura's doctor about some medication she had been taking, and I said she's doing great, but I was like a crumpled paper sack sitting in the chair. He immediately went next door and got a counselor and brought her in.

Within days Caroline would begin a trial of antidepressant medication.

■□ STRESS AND THE HIDDEN DEPRESSION

Caroline's problem was every working parent's problem: she was over-whelmed. At age thirty-eight, Caroline was now a woman severely over-taxed by her life; held together by a rigorous program of diet and exercise, she was making it through the day, but collapsing at night. The stress of dealing with small children was, after long hours on the job, long hours commuting to and from the job, and long hours running errands and shopping for groceries and cleaning the house and cooking the meals, simply more than she could handle with good cheer. She could physically do it; she could power through the towering to-do list that greeted her each morning at five o'clock. But she could not do it with a happy heart. She was burning out, and her children were reaping the consequences.

Caroline's problem, in short, was her life. It was not her "brain chemicals" in any simple, genetic sense; it was not her *particular* destiny to be a screamer and a yeller, though screamers—and yellers—did have a long and memorable pedigree in her family. At most, Caroline came to working motherhood with an inborn disposition toward a quick tem-per. But it was the conditions of her life that pushed her over the line.

But however she had gotten there, she recognized that she was now in fact over that line. While her problems had stemmed from stressors in her environment, those stressors had done their biological damage, and Caroline's brain chemistry now fell into the mildly depressed range. For Caroline, a woman who still did not truly think of herself as depressed, antidepressant medication was to work beautifully. She re-members her first weeks taking Prozac:

> It was a funny experience, because you take the medicine and you notice, really, nothing. Though at the same time for some reason I felt I wanted to be taking it. So all that effort and burden must have been lifting some, but it's so subtle that you can't put your finger on it. It's hitting you at a subconscious level.

Interestingly, the changes this subtle medication were to make in Caroline's life showed up most clearly at first in her work, the place where she had perceived herself as functioning the best.

I was doing my yearly budget, which takes a month and a half and is extremely stressful. And a staffer came in and said: "I can't believe it, you're so different. This year no matter when I come in, you give me a smile, where last year you were so tense I never quite knew when I could come in."

The budget season has always been hard, because people will come in and interrupt you in the midst of calculations, and it's very burdensome because you lose your train of thought. But your staff has to come in; life can't stop for a month while you do a budget. And after Prozac, I would put my pencil down and chat for ten minutes. Before Prozac, I would talk while still staring at the screen and typing. I was still empathetic and still listening, but after Prozac, I would turn around and look at them. I got the same performance reviews, both from bosses and from peers, either way; and because I have an empathetic side, people had always rated me their favorite boss. But everyone liked the change.

Finally, one day one of the other managers came in and he was practically babbling; he kept saying, "You're just so different this year." He knew there was a difference, but he didn't know what it was. And I said, "You know, I'm on Prozac." He was amazed because he had had major depressions—we'd know when he was having one—and I'd encouraged him to take Prozac because of my sisters' experience. So he was shocked to hear I was taking it.

The major subjective change that Caroline experienced, and that her staff was perceiving in her, was a startling drop in her felt level of stress. Caroline's reaction is interesting in light of psychiatrist Michael Norden's claim, in his book *Beyond Prozac,* that Prozac, rather than being primarily an *antidepressant,* is essentially an anti-stress medication. Certainly Caroline's experience fits Norden's hypothesis; while she did not have anything less to do, she felt dramatically less overwhelmed by life and its many responsibilities. For Caroline, Prozac treated stress:

I had a Day-Timer I carried with me everywhere. That was very reinforced by the company; we were given seminars on how to organize time. And all the higher executives were promoting something called the Franklin Planner. That's the buzzword right now at the companies. The Planners are in all the shopping malls, and they teach whole-life classes on them.

With the Franklin Planner the whole gimmick is that they're selling for the chaotic lives we have. They hold seminars and give videotapes, and you're supposed to schedule all your objectives. At meetings people come out like these born-again organizers. You have all these executives sitting around tables now with these Bibles, and the Franklin Planners are the exact size of a Bible, which is a bit of an off-size, and you've got a grocery-shopping insert, and a menu-planning insert, and a medical-planning insert—and it tells you a lot about what two-career families are up against these days.

So my company was encouraging me to go to the Franklin seminars, but I had this Day-Timer that I could not, would not, let go of. If I left it at home, I would have to turn around and drive twenty miles to get it. I would go to the movies and have to have it in my car; I put it in my diaper bag; I was never without it. It began to dawn on me that that was a little odd: why do you need this calendar every second? And of course you explain that away, too, because your brain is so full you cannot remember to get a gallon of milk after work; you have to write it down. So you have all these struggling moms and dads saying I know there's something I'm supposed to do—and it's, Oh right: take the kids to school.

In short, everyone else whom Caroline knew was in the same boat. Overtaxed, overextended, incapable of remembering even a minor errand without attending a seminar on organizing one's time. But now, taking an antidepressant medication, Caroline felt her tensions dissolving.

I noticed my calendar was suddenly just as planned—it still had all that stuff in there—but if I forgot it, I forgot it. I'd just say, "Oh damnit, I don't have my Day-Timer, I wonder what I was supposed to do today?" And that was it. It *is* a bit unnerving having back-to-back appointments and not knowing who is going to walk in the office next, but I wouldn't worry about it, and I definitely wouldn't drive twenty miles back home to get my book. I'd just take the day as it came.

Interestingly enough, now I find that I don't forget the Day-Timer as often as I did before—and that if I do, I can somewhat remember what's going to happen that day without it. I have a sixth sense that I didn't have before.

Caroline's family life was changing as well. A superwoman is not necessarily a fun person to be—nor to have as one's mother. Certainly Caroline was not running her home with a light touch:

> The way I was handling our home life was, Friday night I would make up the menu for the week, so I'd have the grocery list ready by early morning Saturday. Then I'd shop before the crowds were there and before the kids were too wired. So then I was set with groceries for the week. Then I would do precooking during "dull" moments, so we would have home-cooked meals waiting for us every day of the work week. This used to swallow every weekend, I couldn't do anything Saturday mornings, ever.

From the most positive point of view, Caroline was successfully managing to have—and do—it all: the career, the two children, the house, the husband, the husband's career, the tasty home-cooked meals. Everything was happening, and it was happening on time. But in fact, Caroline was operating out of the biochemistry of depression. Now, with Prozac, the burdens of working motherhood felt lighter.

> I noticed I was actually going to the pool with the kids on a Saturday and saying, "Screw the pre-cooking." The other amazing thing was, I started deviating from the menu. I started buying one extra thing that could be the screw-the-menu thing, like hamburgers or something, and I even allowed macaroni and cheese to be the screw-the-menu thing. And I noticed the quality didn't really suffer. The two-hour precooking technique still took just two hours, but I could do it whenever I wanted. I had the mental freedom to do it whenever I wanted. We were still eating the same good menus, but everything was more relaxed.
>
> So instead of being home Saturday working from my Day-Timer, I'd be at the pool, playing with the kids, buying Popsicles. One day I ate five or six Popsicles and I thought they were *great*!

These were the moments that moved Caroline to see herself differently, to see herself as perhaps being a person who *had* suffered for some time from a touch of depression, a case so mild she had not been aware of it until her mood darkened after the birth of her second child. When winter arrived and Caroline, for the first time in her adult life, did not feel her spirits drop, she became convinced of it. She had been mildly depressed for some time, and had not known it.

> I'd been having that flat feeling for quite a while, and my husband would say, "You're not fun anymore." I always pooh-poohed him because I felt it was a case of: Yeah, you're not having sex every day, so I'm no fun. It's easy to dismiss the husband.
>
> But in retrospect, I realized that he really did mean that we didn't do things like sit on the couch and watch TV and laugh; we weren't having *fun*. I was driven from dawn to dusk and then got to bed so I could get up the next day—I was on autopilot; I had a mission. And I couldn't go anywhere without organizing every single moment. Sometimes I would even write out what I was going to do in the morning: I was going to get the kids up, give them breakfast, dress them, etc.

It is well known that depression can be very damaging to relationships (the decline in sexual appetite alone can devastate a marriage), and in fact Caroline's marriage was showing the characteristic signs of wear clinicians see in marriages in which one partner is depressed. Caroline's loss of pleasure in life, a condition called anhedonia, was silently draining the life out of her marriage.

But if her marriage was suffering, her children were far more vulnerable. Children depend not only upon their parents' love and guidance, but also upon their parents' good cheer. Researchers have found that within six months of birth, the babies of depressed mothers show a pattern of electrical activity in the brain completely different from the babies of happy mothers: the brains of babies whose mothers are depressed show a pattern of intense activation in the right frontal cortex, precisely the neurochemical profile shown by their mothers. As a general rule (though as we will see, the brain is more complicated than this), heightened levels of activity on the *right side* of the brain spell trouble; activity on the left side is "good." Happiness, cheerfulness, euphoria: all of these treasured states correlate with heightened electrical activity on the *left side* of the brain. (The mnemonic device for remembering this concept is the phrase "Right is wrong." If the right side of the brain is boiling over, that is "wrong," wrong in the sense of being neither a good nor happy state of affairs. The left side is "right"; it is the side we want to be dominant, at least when it comes to mood.) Interestingly, research has also shown that infants *come into* the world with a predisposition toward a more active right brain or a more active left brain; it appears that a temperamental inclination toward the sunny or the dark side of life may be, as many parents suspect, inborn. Tiny infants whose left-brain activity exceeds that of the right are active, bubbly, sociable; babies whose right brains are highly charged are shy, anxious, fearful.

At this point we do not know why the babies of depressed mothers show greater right-brain activity. Certainly, a depressed mother is less sociable and smiley, and it has been shown that social stimulation sparks firing in the left brain. At the very least, it seems fair to say that the depressed mother is doing little to *help* her baby stoke up his left brain, whatever his innate makeup. All babies, regardless of temperament, need cheerful parents to help them develop their own good cheer, and openness to the world.

For Caroline, these lessons came hard.

> I had always believed that Elaine was so different from Laura, my first. Laura was a cuddler, and Elaine wasn't. And all of a sudden with the Prozac Elaine was in my lap every second, and it broke my heart because I realized I wasn't letting her be a cuddler. My husband doesn't agree with this; he says Elaine actually became more cuddly as she got older. He never saw me as rejecting her because I was in a bad mood. But I felt horribly guilty about it.

The ability to "have fun," while important to a marriage, is vital to a child, and it had been a long time since Caroline had simply had fun with her daughters. She was a good mother in the technical sense; her children were well fed, well clothed, well tended. The house was picked-up and clean; the dinners healthy and served on time. But those weightless moments of sheer joy between mother and child had disappeared. Now Caroline found herself singing in the car with her children; more than this, she found herself *wanting* to sing in the car with her children. Everything seemed brighter, up to and including night-time TV:

> One night *America's Funniest Home Videos* was on. My husband always would chuckle and laugh out loud when it was on, and I would sit there and think, What a stupid guy. I felt irritation when he laughed. All of a sudden, I realized I was sitting and watching this stupid show and laughing loudly, and both my kids and my husband were looking at me. It was so other, coming from me.

This is precisely the kind of moment children draw sustenance from: sometimes children need to sit with their parents and laugh at stupid television shows. We will not hear this from child-rearing experts, of course, who universally frown upon the centrality of television in American family life. But the gaiety of moments like these is vital to a child's sense of walking lightly in the world.

Perhaps even more important, as Caroline's sense of pleasure in life and in her children flooded back, her temper ebbed.

> That was the element where I knew there was a change, where the Prozac wasn't subtle. Before I took it, I would jump up from the table and be screaming at the kids, and suddenly this just melted away, and I could use all the nonsensical advice from the mom books about talking so children will listen and so on.
>
> I had been able to be patient and calm with one child, but not with two. I notice that I still have moments where I have explosions and I will think, Oh my God, this shouldn't happen on Prozac. But I find that when these moments occur I can accept guidance from a psychologist or a book or my own better self and get put right back on track.

For Caroline, learning that she was suffering a mild and hidden form of depression was a life-altering event. From now on, Caroline will judge her life not only by what and how much she is getting done, but by the tone she is setting for the people she loves. Mood, she now sees, matters very much.

■ THE SLIPPERY SLOPE

For most of us even a very mild depression can do harm; what is "mild" in a mood disorder may not be mild in terms of living our lives. Thus any mood issue, no matter how minor, deserves to be taken seriously. But with depression in particular, it is important to attend to the sub-clinical forms, because mild depression left untreated can progress to full-fledged clinical depression. This is the flip side of the genetic coin: the fact that depression is the least genetic of all the mental illnesses means that anyone can develop it. If we are not (necessarily) doomed by our genetics to suffer severe depression, neither are we protected from it by "happy" genes. Mark George, a psychiatrist and neuroscientist who has performed PET scans of the brains of clinically depressed individuals, cites research showing that virtually anyone can become depressed—severely depressed—given a life blow of sufficient force. As he says:

> People who've lost their spouse after longer than a fifteen-year happy marriage—the loss is severe, profound, not conflicted, involving major adjustments in lifestyle—a year later half of those people will be clinically depressed. And this is excluding all of those people who've ever suffered depression before.

In short, fully half of a group of newly widowed individuals so resilient they have made it to the mid-century mark without *ever* experiencing a major depression will fall into grief so dark that they descend into clinical depression. These are people who may even be genetically disposed *not* to become depressed; and yet half will develop a true depression when wounded deeply enough.

Recent suggestions that a genetic "set point" exists for mood—analogous to the set point for weight—do not contradict this finding. It is doubtless true that some babies come into the world genetically disposed to be happier than others, just as some babies are destined to be plumper than others. Nevertheless, severe trauma can and does affect brain biology in even the most innately cheerful of people. In short, a set point for mood can *change* over time, just as the set point for weight

can change in response to illnesses such as thyroid deficiency or diabetes, or simply to the normal processes of aging.

There is no question that aging affects the brain as well as the body.
Few of us weigh naturally at fifty what we did at twenty; when it comes
to weight, the set point marches over onward up the scale. By the same
token, the fifty-year-old who has sustained a major life trauma—and
whose state of normal grieving has been allowed to progress unchecked
to clinical depression—may find that his ability to spring back to his
accustomed state of well-being has been compromised. Research has
shown that the brain's production of stress hormones increases with
age, and stress hormones can significantly worsen the damage done by
neurological insults such as strokes and seizures or severe life traumas.
That is, major life stressors, such as the loss of a beloved spouse, will be
more dangerous to the older brain, with its naturally elevated levels of
stress hormones, than to the younger brain. Thus for some of us, mood
set points are destined to decline over the course of a lifetime.

Further evidence that emotional set points can change over time is to
be found in the data showing that depression is rising in countries
around the world. Only 1 percent of Americans born before the year
1905 had suffered a major depression by the age of seventy-five but 6
percent of Americans born since 1955 had already fallen into a clinical
depression by the young age of *twenty-four*. These statistics are not simply the result of better reporting, or of a greater willingness on the part
of the depressed to speak openly of their mental state. The rise is actually happening, epidermiologists agree; it is real. (There has been no
comparable increase in other commonplace disorders such as social
phobia, for instance.) Strange though it may seem, Americans who sur-
vived the Great Depression and two world wars are far less depressed
than Americans whose major historical life traumas were the Kennedy
assassination and Vietnam.

Some authorities attribute the greater vulnerability of younger generations to the breakdown of social supports: the rising divorce rate
(suicide rates parallel divorce rates), the disappearance of extended families, the widespread loss of faith in church, school, and government.
(Black Americans, for instance, have a suicide rate half that of whites,

which many attribute to the centrality of religious faith in black culture.) The rising divorce rate may be a particular problem for the adult
children of divorce, because traumatic events in childhood—and divorce is often traumatic for children—can damage neurons, creating a
susceptibility to depression in adulthood.

Others speculate that rising rates of depression, like rising rates of
cancer, may have an environmental cause: polluted air, workrooms
without windows, positive ions saturating the atmosphere. It is entirely
possible, this group argues, that the contemporary urban environment
is just as toxic to the brain as it presumably is to the rest of the body.
Michael Norden's *Beyond Prozac* provides an excellent summary of this
view. Whatever the explanation, the striking rise in depression over the
course of just one generation tells us that genetic set points are not im-
mutable. Although the emotional timbre of our lives is often remarkably stable, it can, and does, change.

The groundbreaking work of Dr. George may tell us why and how
normal grieving can become clinical depression. George, formerly of
the National Institute of Mental Health and now with the Medical
University of South Carolina in Charleston, has performed a series of
PET (positron emission tomography) scans of the brains of clinically
depressed patients. PET scans measure the presence of radioactive glucose in the brain. The brain feeds on glucose; sugar is its fuel. A PET
scan can show how fast the brain's cells are burning glucose. In essence,
the PET scan gives us a picture of how active the various regions of the
brain are at the time of the scan. If a region is taking up a great deal of
glucose, it is more active; if it is taking up less glucose, it is less active.
(In determining what is more and what is less, researchers draw two
types of comparisons. With right brain/left brain studies, some researchers compare left and right hemispheres within the same person's
brain; others compare one hemisphere in a group of depressed subjects
to the same hemisphere in a group of nondepressed subjects.)

George's PET-scan findings for depression and sadness are fascinating because they reveal a difference—and possibly a causal, developmental link—between normal sadness and true clinical depression.
That is, a momentarily sad person looks different, on the PET, than a

clinically depressed person. The merely sad person will show greater glucose metabolism—greater activity—on the left side of his brain than he does when he is feeling emotionally neutral. The left side, specifically the left cerebral cortex (in shorthand, the higher, thinking brain) and the left limbic region (the evolutionarily earlier, emotional brain—sometimes called the reptilian brain) are "lit up."

This is a fascinating discovery for many reasons, not least of which is the fact that on the surface of things it contradicts the widely held view, mentioned above, that negative emotions are a function of the *right* brain: that a "negative" baby, or a depressed adult, will show far greater activity on the right side of the brain than the left. George is well aware of these findings. In fact, according to George, there are now nine separate studies confirming this finding:

> The level of activity in the left prefrontal cortex correlates with how depressed you are. It is a linear relationship: the less activity the more depressed.

So why, in George's scans, do we see sadness firing up the *left* side?

While neuroscience cannot yet resolve this inconsistency in the data, George speculates that the overactive left brain in sad-but-healthy people may in fact be the brain's effort to "back-regulate" an overactive *right* brain: the left prefrontal cortex has gone into overdrive in order to counterbalance the right brain's new state of overactivity. Thus what researchers like George may be seeing on their scans of transiently sad normal subjects is the brain's effort to bring itself back to true. It is not the overactive left brain that makes us feel bad; it is the overactive left brain that helps us to *stop* feeling bad.

While this reading of the data can only be speculative at present, the scans do strongly support the perception that there exists a difference, at the biological level, between ordinary sadness and clinical depression. In fact, one of the most important felt differences between everyday sadness and clinical depression may be a relative lack of true sadness in the severely depressed: when George and his associates asked depressed subjects to induce a state of sadness in themselves, they could not do it—a finding eerily compatible with the longstanding psycho-analytic insight, first developed in Freud's famous essay "Mourning and Melancholia," that the severely depressed patient must be *helped* to mourn, helped to experience his sadness and loss. George describes what happened:

> We would do an interview where we would ask subjects about events in their lives where they were very happy or very sad. We'd get actual historical events. Then, if we were looking at sadness, we'd try to find out when they were actually saddest, what they were wearing, where they were standing, and so on. We'd get the details. Then on the day of the PET scan, we would say, "You're standing there by the grave," and you're remembering how you felt . . . try to feel that way now."

Depressed people could not do this. Happy people could; happy people could come into the lab, spend a few moments thinking about the loss of a loved one, and become very sad indeed, sad enough to produce a functional difference in their brains. They could also summon a state of happiness or even euphoria by remembering very happy moments in their lives. But depressed people could do neither. They could not make themselves transiently happy (small surprise there); neither could they make themselves transiently sad. They could not feel the way they felt beside the grave. Their emotions were dulled, lopped-off, and they complained of being blunted. (An interesting finding, as George remarks, in view of the fact that antidepressant medication can have the same effect. Some patients find that on medication they do not possess the same emotional responsiveness—the same range of emotion—that they enjoyed off the medication, between depressions. This flatness is one of the better-known reasons people stop taking their medication.)

But although ordinary sadness and clinical depression look very different on an initial scan, down the road, George argues, the two converge. Perhaps the most creative aspect of George's thinking is his hypothesis concerning the way in which sadness becomes depression: the *over*active left brain of the sad person, he believes, eventually burns itself out, becoming the *under*active left brain of the clinically depressed. George speaks of the left brain, in sadness, being "hyperactive." If nothing happens to raise the spirits of the chronically sad person, eventually he exhausts his left brain, turning it, now, hypoactive. This, then, is what clinicians find on the scan: the depressed person with the sluggish left brain. Researchers take their pictures at one point in time, thus missing the high activity on the left that preceded—and caused—the low activity they find in their studies. (Of course, this hypothesis does not explain the anxious newborns with the high-right/low-left profile, since presumably these babies have not been alive long enough to move from hyperactive "sadness" to hypoactive "depression." The effort to reconcile data concerning anxious newborns with the scans of anxious and depressed adults will doubtless produce fascinating new insights into sadness, depression, and their many variations.)

Whatever may be going on with "depressed" newborns, the clinical implication is clear: people should take even very mild depressions seriously, because a mild depression can—and as often as half of the time will—develop into a severe depression. What is more, mild depression is quite treatable, which is all the more reason to attend to it when it occurs. In the study of grieving spouses researchers found that when the newly widowed receive professional help, either in the form of talk therapy *or* in the form of antidepressant medication, the number who go on to develop clinical depression falls dramatically, from 50 percent to the 10-to-20-percent range, depending upon the study. When it comes to depression, prevention, it seems, *is* nine-tenths of the cure.

The ultimate lesson of mild depression, as with all of the shadow syndromes, is that people must begin to think of their brains differently. Normally, we *don't* think of our brains; we don't think of preserving and protecting our brains in the way we might think of, say, preserving and protecting our hearts. When the subject is heart health, it is clear to all that the proper course in life is to head off heart disease *before* it develops. This is why we are flooded with articles, in every service publication, on heart-healthy diets and heart-healthy exercise and heart-healthy lifestyles and so on. Prevention is the message.

But with brain-based troubles, people assume that the thing to do is to struggle along and hope for the best. A person might seek talk therapy if he is feeling bad enough, but most of us have to be feeling dark indeed before we consider even so much as asking a friend for a referral. We assume that, sooner or later, brain-based problems will take care of themselves.

But in fact, the brain is like any other organ in the body: the brain, like the heart, needs care and feeding, too. People should address small problems in the brain's functioning before they become large problems. Apart from the sheer misery and destructive force of a full-blown clinical depression, reason enough in itself to practice prevention, research shows that a serious depression actually leaves its mark upon the brain even after the depression has lifted. The most disturbing of these findings is that one clinical depression can "set us up" for a second in much the way that one sprained ankle leaves the ligaments more vulnerable to another. While for many years professionals drew a distinction between reactive depressions (depressions in reaction to painful life events) and endogenous depressions (depressions growing out of a person's depressive biology rather than a reaction to a stressful reality), that distinction is now breaking down. When they look at the "natural history" of depression, researchers George William Brown of the University of London and Ellen Frank of the University of Pittsburgh find instead that almost all *first* episodes of depression are reactive: they happen in reaction to painful life events. But after that, for many people, depression becomes ever more organic in nature. The second depression will happen in response to a much smaller trouble, the third depression will be sparked by something even milder, and so on. Eventually, depression takes on a life of its own, seeming to strike at will; at the very least, it becomes increasingly difficult to say what in the environment has happened to provoke a recurrence. At this point clinicians will perceive the patient as endogenously depressed, when in fact what has happened is that that person's brain has been sensitized to endogenous depression by previous bouts of reactive depression.

Researchers liken this developmental sequence to the kindling phenomenon long known to clinicians in the field of epilepsy. The kindling effect has to do with the brain's response to electrical current.

Normally, our brains can handle a fairly substantial jolt of electricity without going into seizure. But it turns out that what our brains *cannot* handle is repeated, low-level jolts. Given enough small shocks, the brain will begin to "seize" and, more to the point, ever-smaller shocks can begin to cause major seizures. Small shocks that would not faze the never-before-shocked brain can send the often-shocked brain into violent spasm. The analogy to depression is obvious, and may be biologically sound. Previous depressions leave a person shaken and vulnerable. Once we have been hurt often enough, it becomes easy to plunge into depression over a problem that would barely register upon the happy person with the heretofore serene existence. Eventually, as the brain becomes more and more reactive to smaller and smaller problems, the "initiating" trouble becomes all but imperceptible. More intriguing yet, Dr. Brown also reports that endogenous depressions often occur six months to one year *after* the precipitating event—making that moment even less identifiable by clinicians and patients alike. By the time a person's reactive depressions have progressed to endogenous depressions, he has developed a "delayed reaction" to stress that may make his life and emotions bewildering to him and to his family and friends. Depression, even mild depression, is a slippery slope. Once we are on it, a stoic soldiering on is not the answer. As Caroline discovered, depression must be addressed.

■ THE SOCIAL DEFICITS OF DEPRESSION

Even if depressions did nothing to harm our brain's biology, their impact upon the quality of life is devastating enough that they are not a state to be taken lightly. There is a rich literature spanning twenty years of inquiry that shows the social deficits of depression; as early as 1974, Peter M. Lewinsohn proposed what he called the "social skill deficit theory of depression." Invariably, researchers find that depression is an unattractive disorder; as a general rule people do not like people who are depressed. (This finding holds true for anxious people

as well, and for those with bipolar disorder.) As researchers Chris Segrin and Lyn Y. Abramson put it, in the stark language of the academic
psychologist:

> A review of [the] research indicates that depressed people reliably ex-
> perience rejection from those in their social environment and that de-
> pression generally is associated with impairments in social behavior.

Certainly, any condition that causes a person to be "reliably" rejected by
friends and loved ones bears looking into; for this reason alone even the
mildly depressed person would do well to seek help. Being rejected by
the people we love and need, including our children (one poignant
study found that children avoid eye contact with depressed parents), is
no way to live.

Segrin's and Abramson's contribution to this issue has been to study
exactly what it is that depressed people are doing to elicit the rejection
they experience. And, as it turns out, the problem with depressed people truly is a social "skill" issue; their troubles do not stem from what
is called mood contagion. In other words, the problem with depressed
people is not that they cause those around them to feel depressed as
well; it is not an issue of depressed people being what we call downers.
The problem is that depressed people, for whatever reason, behave in
ways that cause them to be perceived as, in essence, rude. Depressed
people withhold the social positives people want and need: they smile
infrequently, seldom gesture, answer questions only after long and
uncomfortable pauses. They show a "poverty of speech": if one were
to perform a simple count of the number of words a depressed person
uses in conversation, and compare it with the number of words
the nondepressed person uses, the sum would be lower. Their
"nonverbals" are poor as well: they make scant eye contact, their tone
of voice is often flat, and their speaking voice is pitched too low. In
conversation they nod their heads far less often than do the nondepressed.

Taken together, all of these behaviors, or nonbehaviors, read as a lack
of responsiveness. And, as Segrin and Abramson point out, people like

people who respond to them with a convincing display of animation, enthusiasm, and attentiveness—precisely the qualities the depressed and withdrawn individual lacks.

Segrin and Abramson argue persuasively that, when it comes to social ability and depression, the chicken-and-egg question may be answered both ways. Evidence exists to show that poor social skills can cause depression (always a danger in mild forms of autism, and in many cases of attention deficit disorder as well), *and* that depression can cause poor social skills. Interestingly, the researchers reason that the socially skilled person who develops a temporary deficit in social skills due to his depression may have the better prognosis, because as his depression lifts a bit, he will be able to reclaim his normally proficient "people sense," and thus regain the positive responses from others that will help him to continue his climb out of despair. Meanwhile, the depressed person who suffers a lifelong deficit in social skills will simply continue to create situations in which people reject him, giving him ever more reason to remain depressed. And indeed, research by D. F. Klein shows that in fact, chronic depressives differ significantly from recurrent depressives in terms of social difficulties. His study finds that people with chronic, unyielding depression are not only worse off in terms of current social relations, but showed poorer social adjustment in adolescence as well. In short, chronic depressives often have social problems dating back for many years. What this means in terms of treatment is as yet unclear. Not surprisingly, at least two studies (one conducted by the NIMH) have found interpersonal therapy (which focuses upon relationships) to be more effective in treating depression than cognitive therapy (which focuses upon the patient's negative thoughts). But other studies have shown the opposite, and one group of researchers came to the conclusion that cognitive therapy works better for depressed patients with an intellectualizing style of coping, while interpersonal therapy works better for depressed patients with a predominantly emotional approach to life. Opinion varies. But in any event, when it comes to social relations, the lesson is one of form over content: we do not lose friends by "thinking" negatively, by giving expression to negative thoughts and topics, we lose friends by "acting" negative, withholding the smiles and gestures and gazes that make others feel welcome.

On the face of things, it would seem logical that the social deficits of depression are secondary to the disorder: that depressed people can be unresponsive and rude simply because they feel so bad. While no one has looked into the eye contact of people suffering agonizing back pain, it is probably safe to assume that if anyone ever does we will find an eye-contact deficit in this population as well.

However, Mark George's work with the clinically depressed raises the unsettling possibility that the social deficits of depression may in fact be primary, biologically based, symptoms of the disorder. Most strikingly, George has found that clinically depressed subjects have trouble matching faces by emotion: a depressed person often cannot match a sad face to a sad face, a happy face to a happy face, anger to anger, or fear to fear—a task any nondepressed person can perform quite easily. Moreover, clinically depressed people consistently skew their interpretations of emotion downward, reading happy faces as neutral, neutral faces as sad, and sad faces as agonized. George calls this tendency a graying down. While it is easy to see how a depressed person might "gray down" the world for purely psychological reasons, it is more difficult to imagine how purely psychological factors could interfere with a person's capacity to perform a simple matching task. If deficits in social matching skills are biologically based—and we have no reason to assume that they are not—they raise the possibility that clinical depression, like autism and in some cases attention deficit disorder, may impair social functioning in a fundamental, and primary, way.

Whether or not we are eventually going to find that innate social deficits also exist among the only mildly depressed, we cannot say. The disorder we are calling mild depression may be in fact a significantly different disorder from clinical depression, a psychiatric entity unto itself. As George observes:

All of these imaging studies are really helping us to take this term "clinical depression" and realize it likely does not cover just one disease. Depression is probably going to turn out to be like epilepsy. There are fifteen different epilepsy syndromes—some due to genetics, some due to trauma, and so on—and they respond to different medications, and have different prognoses. We're at this point with depression. With these new tools we're teasing out different subgroups. It may begin to make more sense to talk about the *depressions*.

Still, while the subtypes of depression remain to be sorted out, it is entirely possible that all forms of depression reduce social intelligence, at least while the depression is running its course. And even the possibility that mild depression may impair social functioning in subtle, biologically based ways argues in favor of taking subthreshold depressions very seriously indeed.

■□ A DAUGHTER'S STORY

For most people a full-blown clinical depression is unmistakable. The physical symptoms alone, the loss of appetite and energy, tell the sufferer that something is very wrong. Moreover, it is the very nature of the disorder to make a clinically depressed person feel that something is wrong with him, and not just with the people and events that oppress him. But with the mild depressions things are different. The great danger in the mild depressions is that their victims will *not* self-diagnose; they will not define themselves as depressed. They may not even see themselves as being different from anyone else. Mildly depressed people often tell themselves that everyone feels the way they do; that they, like 90 percent of the universe, are merely "stressed," or "burned out," or burdened by uncaring friends, employers, and mates. They feel fully justified in feeling (and often, in behaving) the way they do, and they are not inclined to subject themselves to psychiatric scrutiny.

While it is certainly true that it is life that produces many a mild depression, to think this way is to miss the point. Once we have developed a mild depression, we have entered a different biological state, and not a good one. To argue that one is perfectly justified in feeling irritable and blue because of bad life circumstances is directly analogous to arguing that one's arm is perfectly justified in aching because of a hairline fracture: of course the pain is justified, but that does not make it any the less physical in nature. With the mildly broken arm, one goes to the doctor—and a mild depression that persists may very well mean a trip to the doctor, too. That is what is admirable about Caroline's story: she is a woman who took her symptoms in hand. She addressed the biology of her condition, first through exercise and diet, and then, when that approach proved insufficient, through medication. She assumed responsibility for her mood and behavior, and gave her children happier lives as a result.

Other children are less fortunate. As the child of a mother with chronic, and unacknowledged, mild depression—interspersed with the occasional severe episode—Jane Walker believes that she and her two sisters sustained a great deal of psychological damage during their childhood:

> I would say that my mom wavers between periods of severe depression and then milder depressions that last for a couple of months, but aren't the type where you think she's going to drive off a cliff. The bad ones can last six months to a year, and since I was fourteen—I'm thirty-five now—she's had three of them, though one lasted for four or five years. But during the years in between those depressions, she is not really a well-functioning person.

As a girl, Jane virtually never saw her mother happy or relaxed. She was always dark.

> It has struck me ever since I was a child that my mother has no friends. She does have this one woman who is supposed to be her best friend; she is the only person of her own age that my mother ever hung out with. But she only sees her once a year, and she is extremely gossipy and critical of her when they are apart. She is like this about everyone; she'll malign my brothers to me all the time. She will blacken the reputation of anyone who steps out of the room, and she assumes others are doing the same to her. Whenever she did have a friend, she would have a big falling out sooner or later; she would tell us, "She's no longer speaking to me."

If Jane's mother had no gift for friendship, she possessed even less talent for motherhood. Jane and her sisters brought no friends to the house; their friends were not welcome. And her mother allowed no after-school projects: no Play Do sculptures, no papier-mâché, no sewing lessons or model cars. When the children were babies, they were left alone in their cribs to cry; Jane's mother believed that to cuddle a crying baby was to spoil it. She followed a strict schedule, picking up her babies once every four hours, on the hour. She was a stern disciplinarian, and a fierce critic of her children's clothing and manners. And she built character by assigning a chore load that, certainly for upper-middle-class America, bordered on the Dickensian:

> By the time I was in high school I'd have one or one and a half hours of chores to do every day after school, then four hours of chores on Saturday morning that we had to do before we did anything else. The first thing my mother would do when I got home from school was call me from her job and give me the list. That's all she would say to me, just what she wanted me to do.
>
> My mother was a neat freak, so a lot of her control over us would come from her controlling my cleaning. I would wash cushions for the porch not once, not twice, but three times. Maybe I forgot the underside of the zipper on the cushion.
>
> Then when she got home, the first thing she'd do was put her hand on the TV to see if I'd had it on. If it was warm, she'd know she hadn't given me enough chores. And once she got home, I wasn't allowed to talk on the phone.

Of course, a lengthy chore list does not an unhappy childhood make, but as with many people suffering from the shadow syndrome of depression, Jane' smother was not just joyless, but critical as well. She could be cruel.

> My mother was extremely critical. I was very skinny as a child, but she was always telling me I was a "butterball." When you look at the pictures of me when I was eight, I was a stick. That's when two-pieces came in and everybody had to have a two-piece. So we went shopping for two-pieces, and these were brutal experiences for me

because I was standing in front of the mirror and my mother just took apart every aspect of my body in an extremely abusive way; she'd tell me that fat was hanging over my bathing suit. I was *eight!*

Then when I was in high school I did gain weight, I think because I was depressed; I didn't know why I had gained it. It was the weirdest thing to me, because I'd been skinny as a bean to the point that people commented on it, and then boom I went on the pill and gained twenty pounds. And my mother was so horrified by this that I once went to my mom's office and my mom hissed at me that I was an embarrassment to her and I was never to show up in her office again. Then she made me walk to and from school in the hopes that it would make me lose weight, and that lasted the whole spring.

Obviously, you would worry about a child who had a big weight gain like that, but there was no discussion, or consideration of my medication or anything. It was totally punitive; the whole focus was on no-boy-will-want-to-go-out-with-you. It was almost as if she had set up a self-fulfilling prophecy by telling me the whole time I was a kid that I would be too fat, and then I became too fat. And I stayed chubby until I was twenty-eight.

Jane remembers distinctly the point at which her mother's difference from the other mothers became clear to her. She had just turned nine.

After my birthday I realized there was something about my mother that was different.

I saw her as not fitting into my concept of motherhood. I was very analytical as a child; I would write things down, lists of things, comparative lists of things. So I compared my mother to the mothers of my friends, and she was so different that what I concluded was that I couldn't remember being a baby, but I thought I'd been a happy child (and I do think my mom got worse as she got older) and I had two concepts that were profound to me at the time: my mother is not my friend, so eight was the happiest I'll ever have been because I didn't know then what I know now.

I once asked her, "Could you be my friend like my cousin Bobby's mother is his friend?" And she didn't speak to me for two days. I said, "Bobby's mother will look at his projects"—and my mom's anger was so intense, she would literally foam at the mouth. Foam would come out of the corners of her mouth, and we three would call it, "Oh, she's foaming at the mouth." We'd never heard the cliché; we made it up before we ever heard it.

Jane developed a child's imaginative understanding of her plight:

My two older sisters watched *Star Trek,* and I developed an entire working theory that my mother had been taken by aliens and they had left a fake mother in her place. And I didn't know what to do with the information, I didn't know who to tell. I was like a little adult; that's how people used to describe me. Kids like that do a lot of adult thinking even though they're way off base, and my thought process was very intense. I couldn't tell my father because if it was true he would be undone, and he had medical problems and I didn't want to do it to him. And the other possibility was he wouldn't believe me and that would be awful.

So I told my sisters, and they laughed at me and said, "You're just adopted and she doesn't love you." And I tinkered with that idea, but I realized it wasn't true because I looked so much like my father and my sisters. So I stuck with the alien idea, then eventually outgrew it the way you outgrow Santa Claus.

After that I had more of an acceptable concept, which was that I was my father's child but not my mother's, and that this had been an elaborate secret that had been kept from me.

The public image of depression has been sympathetic, with articles and books focusing upon the private suffering of the depressed individual. But the children of depressed men and women often tell a different story; the true face of depression can be rejecting and cruel. While some mildly depressed people may suffer only sadness and a loss of pleasure in life, many others are chronically angry, blaming, and oversensitive to the point of paranoia. Kathy Cronkite, author of *On the Edge of Darkness,* a book of interviews with people who have experienced depression and professionals who have treated it, and herself a mother who has suffered severe clinical depression, asked her nine-year-old son, William, "What do you think it would feel like to be depressed?" He told her:

Extremely overreactive and angry. Rage. Jumping and screaming at someone for making an ordinary small mistake that anyone could make.

This is a typical experience of children raised by parents who are depressed.

Jane's mother has been no more successful as the mother of adults than she was as the parent of young children. Jane's classic tales of the "toxic" mother show the all-too-familiar human toll of depression:

I dated a guy who was older than I was, and was powerful and had a high-profile position and was the kind of man who would need a real glamour gal on his arm. We broke up many times, and my mother was always coming up with reasons why we had broken up, and it was always based on my appearance—"You wore *that?*" she'd say. One time she was visiting me in Los Angeles and I was wearing an old robe, and I slept in it that night. Now you would think that a mother's worry would be "Are you sleeping with him?" or "Do you have birth control?" But instead she said, "You are *not* wearing that robe to bed with him are you? No wonder he broke up with you. Have you seen yourself in that robe?"

If I was in a negative place, she was four steps deeper in the mud; if I thought someone was dating other people, it wasn't just that they were, it was "What did you do to make them date other people?"

Or she might call me at work, and I might say, "It's empty in here, nobody's here" and she would say, "They don't like you? They left without you?" That would be her first thought. Any situation where a normal mom would give you a positive reality check, my mother would take the opposite view: Your friends hate you, you're going to be fired.

I have an anxiety problem as an adult and I think she created it. My relatives don't have anxiety problems; they weren't anxious, depressed—nothing. My mother is the depressed one and she never got help, and I am an anxious, anxious person, and my older sister is so anxious that she is about to explode all the time and has been on blood-pressure medication since age thirty-five.

This is the mother we know so well from countless novels, self-help books, and confessionals: the mean and wounding mother who undermines her children's sense of self at every turn. Many of these mothers have problems other than depression: some have personality disorders, others simply bad character. But many are suffering from unrecognized, and mild, depression. Happy people do not act this way; the first thought that crosses a happy woman's mind when she sees her grown daughter wearing a T-shirt to bed is *not* "No wonder he dumped you!" The happy person sees the world through the rose-colored glasses of myth; the happy mother sees a beautiful daughter in a cute T-shirt whose affections any man would be lucky to win. But Jane's mother looks at her children and sees only troubles. Children who are too fat, or too lazy, or about to be fired by bosses, or left by lovers.

And she sees children who do not care enough about her. Sadly, about this she is right.

> I guess the biggest thing I want to say is that my mother has lost the true spiritual love of her children for her. The heartbreaking factor here, speaking as a mom myself, is that her children don't wholeheartedly love her. We "love" her, but we don't want to be with her. And when you have three children, as she did, that's a lot of kids who don't want to be with you.

Once, when Jane's mother had descended into a more serious depression, Jane and her sisters staged a family intervention, confronting their mother about her condition, and insisting that she see a therapist. Reluctantly, she did. But the effort was to no avail.

■ □ THE SHRINKING HORIZON

Clearly, depression, even mild depression, is bad for the people we love. But beyond this, it is bad for us. Leaving aside the potential for mild depression to grow into clinical depression, even the mildest of depressions is bad for the person in its grip because depression profoundly limits growth. The mildly depressed person reacts to his pain by battening the hatches, by drawing inside himself and shutting out the world and its stresses.

But the trouble is, stress is essential to the thriving brain. In order to grow or to change, the nervous system requires a certain degree of "noise" or "stress" to activate it; there must be some disturbance within. A fascinating body of research dating back to the 1960s, none of it well known to the public, demonstrates the positive aspects of stress. Researchers did not always understand this; for many years psychologists defined any situation that taxes our resources—including good situations, like earning a promotion or falling in love—as being "stressful." Thus were born the many life quizzes that appeared in popular magazines some years back, in which readers awarded themselves points for stressful events ranging all the way from death to winning the lottery. The happiest of events were seen as being just as likely to lead to stress-related diseases and problems as the most devastating. But careful research has not borne this out, and today psychologists define stress as a situation that is challenging *and* threatening. In fact, positive stress— like the challenges associated with being promoted—is enormously good for us, and good for our brains.

Interestingly, even negative stress, like feeling afraid, or jumping into an ice-cold swimming pool, turns out to be good for us if it is intermittent. Intermittent negative stress in fact "toughens" us, makes us more resilient: apparently "suffering" does build character, as people have long believed, so long as our suffering does not go unrelieved. How it does this is not known precisely, but physiological differences between mice who have been toughened through exposure to intermittent stress and mice who have not are well documented. A mouse who, for example, is handled intermittently by experimenters as a baby—a highly stressful experience for baby mice—grows up to be far "tougher" in adulthood, far less fearful. His behavior in frightening situations, like being dropped into a tank of water, is measurably different from that of his nontoughened brothers.

His biology differs as well. Putting it simply, mice—and people—possess two biochemical responses to stress: they emit large quantities of the neurotransmitter adrenaline, and of the stress hormone cortisol. Although cortisol is essential to many bodily functions, in the context of disorders like mild depression it can be thought of as the "bad" hormone, with adrenaline (and noradrenaline) working entirely to the good. High levels of adrenaline correlate with better performance on math tests in sixth-graders, with higher scores on six-hour matriculation exams in high-school students, and with superior performance on choice-reaction-time tasks and two-hour radar-screen monitoring tasks in college students. Army recruits training to become paratroopers fare better in written tests, jumps from training towers, and jumps from airplanes when their adrenaline levels rise.

Intriguingly, these advantages extend to the social realm as well. According to their teachers, the high-adrenaline schoolboys with the good math test scores mentioned above were also "more satisfied with school and had better social adjustment and emotional stability." Subjects who show large jumps in adrenaline in response to stress also show "lower neuroticism and day-to-day stress scores." In all, it seems that when it comes to coping with stress, adrenaline levels cannot be too high.

The picture is quite different with cortisol. Essentially, "toughened" individuals show very low rises in cortisol in response to stress. When their cortisol does rise, it returns to base level faster than it does in nontoughened individuals. (As do their adrenal levels, intriguingly. Although it does not seem possible to have too much adrenaline in the first moments of confronting a challenge, subsequently toughened people's adrenaline levels fall more rapidly than do those of nontoughened, emotional, or neurotic—terms researchers in this field use interchangeably—individuals.)

In terms of mild depression, what is important about this data is that individuals *become* "tough" through *repeated* experiences of stress. We are not born tough, we become tough (though no doubt there are temperamental differences in the point from which we start). And to become tough we must be toughened by experience, by repeated episodes of "stress." But in a state of depression cortisol is elevated regardless of what is going on in the environment: one of the biological facts of depression is that a depressed person can and does show elevated cortisol levels just sitting quietly alone in a chair. Clinically depressed people secrete elevated levels of cortisol even in their sleep. While no one knows why, the oldest and best theory is that depression creates a chronic state of stress in its sufferer. Stress spurs cortisol production; therefore, the reasoning goes, depression increases cortisol by increasing stress. (Antidepressants, then, lower cortisol via the same roundabout route. Antidepressants do not act directly upon cortisol production, but by lowering an individual's stress they eventually result, downstream, in cortisol reduction, as well. This is one of the happy lessons of psychotropic medication when it works: a good drug can unleash a cascade of positive events. When a medication improves one neurotransmitter system—serotonin function, say—that one lone effect then ripples out through the rest of the brain's chemistry, causing further changes for the better. This is the "effect of the effect.")

Unfortunately, what this cortisol connection means in terms of everyday life is that the mildly depressed person is in no position to seek out more stress; he is already biologically stressed. What is more, he is chronically stressed; his cortisol levels are high at all times of the day. By definition, he cannot seek out, or even experience, intermittent stress since he is not able to return to a nonstressed hormonal level between episodes.

Thus does depression breed depression: the mildly depressed person cannot embrace the stress he needs in order to thrive. Rather, the depressed person must constantly seek ways and means to relax, to soothe his system, to still his mind and its spinning ways. Learning and development slow to a crawl as the depressed person grows ever more avoidant, turning his back upon the people, places, and commotion that bring color to our cheeks.

And that, ultimately, is the reason we must alleviate depression by whatever means we have at hand: depression is antilife. That depression has been implicated in women's infertility is poetic symmetry; depression brings with it a closing down of possibility, a dimming of the light. Depression, even the mildest of depressions, silences the soul.

3

THE PATHOLOGY
OF ELATION
The Hypomanic Personality

FOR PEOPLE WHO have never witnessed it firsthand, a manic episode does not sound, on the face of it, all that mentally *ill.* People in the grip of mania are suffused with confidence, energy, positive thinking, and a sexual vitality that would put the early James Bond to shame. Better yet, in the manic state the afflicted individual suddenly develops the personal magnetism and outright charisma required to make his wildest dreams come true: manic individuals are exciting, compelling, sexually electric, and alive. Mere mortals are drawn to them like moths to the flame.

Many of us are aware of the attractive side of mania, which seems to have had good press, and so it can come as a shock when we read accounts of what mania is truly like. The truth is: a person in the grip of a full-blown manic episode is mad. As more than one authority on the subject has pointed out, just one severe manic episode can destroy a life. It is not uncommon for a person who is manic to end up in jail; it is very common for a person emerging from a manic episode to discover that he has lost everything—home, car, business—in just one uncontrolled spending spree. And, of course, manic states are not, reputation aside, pure highs. Kay Jamison, the well-known authority on manic-depressive illness who revealed her own manic-depression in her memoir *An Unquiet Mind*, speaks of white and black manias; she has suffered both. The words black mania are far more evocative than the official terminology used to characterize highs that are also lows: the "mixed state." Jamison vividly describes the dark side of mania, the mixed state of agitated depression combined with soaring energy and sexuality:

> . . . my manias . . . had violent sides to them. . . . Being wildly out of control—physically assaultive, screaming insanely at the top of one's lungs, running frenetically with no purpose or limit, or impulsively trying to leap from cars—is frightening to others and unspeakably terrifying to oneself. In blind manic rages I have done all of these things, at one time or another, some of them repeatedly; . . . I have, in my psychotic, seizure-like attacks—my black, agitated manias—destroyed things I cherish, pushed to the utter edge people I love, and survived to think I could never recover from the shame. I have been physically restrained by terrible, brute force; kicked and pushed to the floor; thrown on my stomach with my hands pinned behind my back; and heavily medicated against my will.

True mania is devastating to all. Devastating to the sufferer, devastating to friends and family, devastating to property and career. One full-blown manic episode is a life disaster.

That said, there is no denying the positive side of the manic experience, and manic-depressive individuals will often resist taking the lithium they need to become well. A white mania is a difficult state to relinquish:

> I simply did not want to believe that I needed to take medication. I had become addicted to my high moods; I had become dependent upon their intensity, euphoria, assuredness, and their infectious ability to induce high moods and enthusiasms in other people. . . . I found my milder manic states powerfully inebriating and very conducive to productivity. I couldn't give them up.

And in fact, all of this is true: in the mildly manic state—the state we call hypomanic, *hypo* meaning "below" or "less than"—people are *better than normal.* They think more rapidly than people who are not hypomanic, they are more creative, their IQs are higher. They are more productive. They are more attractive in every sense: sexier, friendlier, more fun to know. Here again, Jamison's account of hypomanic reality is eloquent and affecting:

> My family and friends expected that I would welcome being "normal," be appreciative of lithium, and take in stride having normal energy and sleep. But if you have had stars at your feet and the rings of planets through your hands, are used to sleeping only four or five hours a night and now sleep eight, are used to staying up all night for days and weeks in a row and now cannot, it is a very real adjustment to blend into a three-piece-suit schedule, which, while comfortable to many, is new, restrictive, seemingly less productive, and maddeningly less intoxicating. People say, when I complain of being less lively, less energetic, less high-spirited, "Well, now you're just like the rest of us." . . . But I compare myself with my former self, not with others. Not only that, I tend to compare my current self with the best I have been, which is when I have been mildly manic. When I am my present "normal" self, I am far removed from when I have been my liveliest, most productive, most intense, most outgoing and effervescent. In short, for myself, I am a hard act to follow.

Not surprisingly, for many manic-depressive patients, the central question is always whether it is possible to take just enough of their medication to become hypomanic without progressing to florid mania.

Usually, the answer is no. True manic-depressive illness, or bipolar I, as it is now called, is an all-or-nothing proposition. The patient must either take enough medication to stabilize completely, giving up hypomania as well as mania, or he continues to cycle between increasingly dark highs and often suicidal lows as the disease worsens over the years. And make no mistake about it, bipolar illness does progress, as Jamison describes:

> My manias were occurring more frequently and, increasingly, were becoming more "mixed" in nature . . . my "white manias" were be-

coming more and more overlaid with agitated depressions; my depressions were getting worse and far more suicidal.

Thus the answer for the bipolar-I individual seems clear: for most if not all, there is no choice between mild manias and severe manias. The choice instead is between life and death.

But those individuals fortunate enough to have surfaced in the bipolar-II category may be able to live out their lives in a wider safety zone. Interestingly, manic-depressive illness is one of the few psychiatric categories for which the existence of a shadow syndrome is well established, and has been for decades. This is undoubtedly due to the fact that, as we will see, soft mania is in so many ways an advantageous—and often highly attractive—temperament to possess. Thus doctors and patients have long been able to speak openly of soft manic-depression, with little shame or stigma attached. As well, the difference between the severe form of the illness and its soft forms is so stark—with classic manic-depressives ending up hospitalized, or dead by suicide, while their milder cousins use their soft mania to conquer worlds—that the reality of a shadow syndrome for this disorder simply forced itself upon psychiatric consciousness early on.

Much is known about the disorder researchers call soft bipolarity. Simply put, bipolar II is essentially bipolar I without the mania. So long as a bipolar-II patient remains bipolar II, he may suffer depressions severe enough to cause him to be suicidal, but, on the upswing, he will not progress to full-blown mania, but will stop short at hypomania. He does not become paranoid or delusional; he is not psychotic. People in the midst of hypomanic episodes are never hospitalized; by definition, hypomania does not destroy a life. That is the good news.

Unfortunately, individuals who belong to the less dangerous categories of bipolar disorder *are* at risk of becoming severely manic-depressive in time. Fully one-third of cyclothymics—a milder form of the disorder still—will eventually come to qualify for a diagnosis of bipolar I. Even people who suffer winter or summer depressions may, in the worst-case scenario, become manic-depressive as their brains react to years of repeated depressions followed by repeated elations. (Many experts believe that seasonal affective disorder is in fact a form of mild manic-depression, and some have suggested that postpartum depression—as distinct from the postpartum blues—also reveals a bipolar tendency or vulnerability.)

Cyclothymic temperament is, as we say, less severe than bipolar II: individuals of this type suffer only mild depressions, combined with mild manias. Softer yet is the hyperthermic personality; these individuals possess the least negatively affected make up of all. Hyperthermic personalities enjoy (and "enjoy" is the correct term) frequent hypomanias, with virtually no episodes of depression at all, mild or otherwise. Hagop Akiskal, one of the foremost authorities on soft manic-depression, has produced one of the most complete descriptions of the hyperthermic temperament: these are people who spend most of their time in a hypomanic state, only occasionally dipping down into the euthymic state—which is the normal, nonvariant, and balanced mood of people who do not suffer from mood disorders. Hyperthermic personalities sleep little; they spend less than six hours a day in bed, even on weekends. They favor denial as their defense mechanism of choice; for them bad things simply do not exist. And they come to be this way before the age of twenty-one.

In terms of personality, Akiskal offers a list developed by Kurt Schneider as far back as 1958. Hyperthermics, Schneider wrote, are: "irritable, cheerful, overoptimistic, or exuberant; naive, overconfident, self-assured, boastful, bombastic, or grandiose; vigorous, full of plans, improvident, and rushing off with restless impulse; overtalkative, warm, people-seeking, or extroverted; overinvolved and meddlesome; uninhibited, stimulus-seeking, or promiscuous."

Clearly, from this inventory, the hypomanic state is not all good, as we can see from psychoanalyst Bertram Lewin's classic profile in his book *The Psychoanalysis of Elation:*

> . . . these persons are characterized by the immense enterprise they show in daily affairs, overfilling their time with inconsequential doings, throwing themselves vigorously into hobbies, sexual affairs, or

business deals, to drop them all abruptly with a striking sudden loss of interest.

Still, there are worse things in life than immense enterprise, and it is easy to see why a person who has experienced hypomania might feel wholly positive about the experience: a person in the midst of a hypomanic episode is a whirlwind of high mood and soaring productivity. People in hypomanic states are suffused with a sense of purpose; life is filled with meaning, and the hypomanic is gripped by the conviction that *there are things to be done!* Often the hypomanic feels he is on a Mission from God, and being on a Mission from God is, undeniably, an agreeable state to be in. (At the biological level, the religious tinge to hypomania is likely linked to temporal-lobe issues. Temporal-lobe epilepsy often moves its sufferers to religious ecstasy, and, as Jamison and Frederick K. Goodwin point out in their definitive text, *Manic-Depressive Illness,* manic-depressive illness and temporal-lobe epilepsy overlap in ways we do not yet understand.) Whatever the "biology of religion" may be, the hypomanic feels himself suffused with a moral purpose that may be frankly religious in character. But regardless of whether or not he experiences a heightened sense of connection to God and faith, he is propelled by the conviction that he is a *good person.*

Better yet, the hypomanic person also possesses the energy to make his blue-sky dreams come true: as we will see, a housewife in the midst of a hypomanic episode pretty much *can* paint the entire exterior of the house, on her own, in one weekend, if that is what she takes it into her head to do. Hypomanics are extraordinarily productive; they are people who can leap tall buildings in single bounds.

The self-confidence of hypomania may be even more intoxicating than the exploding energy: people in hypomanic states simply do not know self-doubt. There is some realistic justification for this: in psychological testing hypomania has been shown to raise IQ and to "facilitate creative problem-solving"—people probably *are*, in reality, smarter and more creative when they are in hypomanic states than when they are not. And hypomania can increase one's charisma (though, as we will see, the opposite may occur as well).

And last but far from least, the heightened sexual responsiveness of hypomania is nothing if not pleasurable, though of course this alteration in mental state can lead to trouble as well. At least one researcher has found the highest divorce rate on the entire affective-disorder spectrum, including major depression, to be among bipolar II's. Patients in the bipolar-II category have a 33 percent rate of separation and divorce, compared to a 21 percent rate for bipolar I's and 17 percent for unipolar depressives. The hypersexuality of mania, in many ways the mirror opposite of major depression, which deadens sexuality, contributes to the high rate of divorce among married bipolars.

Marital strain aside, manic-depressive illness in its shadow form can be so beneficial that even the authorities of Nazi Germany, in their quest to eradicate all mental defects from the race, decided to spare it. Goodwin and Jamison tell the story of a study commissioned by the Nazi administration to settle the issue: when the report found that manic-depressive illness was "far overrepresented in the higher occupational classes," the author of the report recommended against forced sterilization of manic-depressive patients, particularly when the mentally ill individual did not have siblings who could pass on the positive aspects of the disorder. Socioeconomic data throughout Europe and the United States bear out this association between manic-depression and higher social status. At the very least, we do not see the downward drift in a family's social status that we would expect to find when a major mental illness strikes successive generations, a finding that supports the argument that manic-depressive illness in its shadow forms may confer certain advantages.

■ JOSEPH RAMIREZ: HYPOMANIA AND THE AMERICAN DREAM

Joe Ramirez's rise from child refugee of Castro's Cuba to psychiatrist in Boston's medical mecca dramatically illustrates the—at times—supreme survival value of the mildly manic personality. Sent alone to America from his home in Havana at the age of eleven (no other member of his family having been granted a visa) he thrived in the New World. There was no certainty that his parents or siblings would ever be allowed to follow him to the United States; there was no guarantee that his father, who was a member of the Cuban underground movement, would remain a free man in his native land. Still a boy, Joe was alone in America. For many if not most of the children of Cuba's middle and upper-middle class, being sent to the new land with neither family nor friends to care for them was traumatic. But for Joe, buoyed by manic energy and confidence, it was an adventure.

After he reached the United States, Joe was sent to a refugee camp in Florida, where he stayed for two months:

> It was an Air Force base barracks with twenty people living in one room. The beds were triple deckers, three beds on top of each other—it was like twenty people living in a one-bedroom apartment. We had to schedule bathroom times.

From here he was moved to an orphanage in Iowa where he lived in suspense for a year and a half, not knowing whether his family would be allowed to follow:

> One day the sister superior said we want all of you kids to write a let-ter to Jacqueline Kennedy saying you're here and alone and you need your parents . . . and there were eight or nine of us who were Cuban in the orphanage and there was going to be one last boat, a boatlift, and after that they were going to close the migration down. And all of our families came in the last boat.

None of this fazed the eleven-year-old Joe. As a psychiatrist today, he attributes his resilience to the hypomanic qualities he already possessed as a boy:

> I think the hypomanic qualities I have as an adult were already there, because to me the whole thing was an adventure. Most others were wrecked by it. The orphanage was right by the Missouri River, so you could read *Huckleberry Finn* and *Tom Sawyer* and it was all right there. And in the orphanage there were a few Indians who formed an

alliance with the Cubans, all of us being minorities, so that was kind of interesting, and you had to learn English and that was a new language, so I was busy—and you had to keep your eyes open.

Hypomanics crave stimulation, and for Joe the experience of being shipped to a brand-new country at age eleven met his need for novelty and excitement. Even the possibility that his family would be lost to him forever seems merely to have provided him with fresh opportunity for a new escapade:

> I didn't necessarily assume my family *was* going to get to America, because during the missile crisis all communications were broken off. So I and some of the other kids had escape plans from the orphanage; I figured I'd go with the Indians to the reservation.
>
> These qualities put me in a leadership position, so that I've always been a leader without seeking it. I would just say, "I'm going to do it this way, I don't care how you do it." I would feel very confident, and that attracts people.

Already, in Joe's young life, we can see the magnetic pull hypomanic personalities exert upon their fellows. Suffused with energy and high spirits, Joe was the boy to whose side the young lost children rallied.

The child is father to the man, and while Joe himself, reflecting upon his past at age forty-four, is surprised by the many unexpected turns his adult life has taken, he is in many ways the person today that his adventurous youth would have predicted. Once reunited with his parents, he became a sports maniac (this is how he remembers himself) nicknamed the Warrior by his friends in high school; propelled by the same high energy and confidence that carried him through his early refugee days, he far outperformed his actual physical abilities. A skinny kid playing middle linebacker, he became the star of the team. He almost fell in with the wrong crowd, and was popular with the girls; once or twice he came close to breaking the law. Though intellectually gifted, he did not apply himself to his studies; he was the kind of adolescent who skated on thin ice. But adversity had not hardened him and he was alive to the possibilities of the world. He once led a food strike, and later on he started his own janitorial company. He remembers his teenage self as a dark horse.

In college, as he matured, he found himself drawn to the idea of becoming a psychiatrist:

> Psychiatry allowed me to be very eclectic. I could read philosophy and that could be useful in psychiatry, I could read religion and that could be useful, I could read chemistry and humanities. . . . Psychiatry was the one thing in medicine that overlapped all the other, nonrelated fields.

To the hypomanic all subjects are interesting, and all subjects exert a pull on one's potentially limitless ability to be fascinated. Jamison's memoir has a wonderful passage on this aspect of the manic state, in which she attends the UCLA chancellor's garden party at the beginning of what was to become her first florid manic episode:

> I . . . had an extended and rather odd conversation with the chairman of my department [who had once headed a research project involving elephants] . . . we started a long, dendritic discussion about doing research on elephants and hyraxes. . . . I cannot begin to remember the detailed arguments and common interests underlying this strange and extremely animated conversation—except that I immediately, and with great gusto, took upon myself the task of tracking down every article, and there were hundreds, ever written about hyraxes. I also volunteered to work on animal behavior studies at the Los Angeles Zoo, as well as to coteach a course in ethology and yet another one in pharmacology and ethology.

Needless to say, Jamison, a young professor at the beginning of her career, had not been hired to teach courses in animal psychopharmacology—and would put her chances of earning tenure in jeopardy if she allowed herself to be sidetracked by such wildly left-field enthusiasms. Certainly, no one is awarded lifetime employment for looking up countless hundreds of articles on hyraxes in the college library. But in the grip of an escalating manic episode, Jamison found such calculations beyond her, and the episode reveals much about the hypomanic experience. The hypomanic's appetite for sheer information can be insatiable.

For Joe, medical school fed this appetite:

> I thought med school was great because of the wealth of information; it was like being in a candy store. Everything was fascinating—you got to see brain surgery, you got to amputate, you got to deliver babies. . . . It was exhausting but exhilarating. Most people hate med school, but I loved it.
>
> I probably loved it even more because of the sleep deprivation, which is one of the things that precipitates hypomania. I would be on call, and so the very nature of my job made me hypomanic.

Sleep-deprived and wired, Joe was now launched upon a life of manic adventure. Once, inspired by a lecture on neuropsychiatry, he took off for MIT, the home institution of the lecturer, and met the speaker in his office. The lecturer proved to be at least mildly hypomanic himself, and the two men spent a supersonic hour revving each other up with their mutual passion for neuroscience, the lecturer typing furiously away the entire time, taking notes on this historic meeting of minds. By the end of the hour Joe had been hired. Only a first-year resident, fresh out of medical school, already working a sixty-to-eighty-hour week, he left MIT that afternoon having been assigned an office, a personal assistant, and even a parking space for his car.

Then, in typical hypomanic fashion, he forgot all about it. He certainly did not have the time to join a research group at MIT, and he never went back. The whole episode just dissolved.

It was during Joe's second year of residency that he began to reap the potential financial benefits of the hypomanic nature. During his first year he had been assigned to an extremely intense, *E.R.*-like hospital floor. The building was ancient and decrepit, there were sixty patients crammed into one ward, and emotions ran high. Joe loved it.

But the following year he was moved to the basement of the hospital, a silent and empty scene that was extremely difficult for him. He experienced this change as an emotional loss and, as can be the case with people on the bipolar spectrum, the challenge of the loss tipped him up rather than down. Trying to fill the void, Joe soon hatched a plan no even-tempered second-year resident could have possibly conceived:

> I went to interview for a moonlighting job, to do some psychiatric coverage for another hospital. They needed someone to work three or four hours a week in their clinic, but the guy mentioned he needed emergency services, too, because he couldn't get his people to cover.
>
> So I said, "How much money do you have in the budget," and he said, "A hundred thousand dollars," and I said, "I'll take it." It was spur-of-the-moment. He said, "Do you have the people to do it?" and I said, "Yes."
>
> I was prepared to do it by myself if I had to until I gathered other people, and this is the other thing about hypomania: you underestimate what you're about to tackle. To me the worst scenario was I would have to do it all by myself, which meant I would have to be on call every single night of the week while working all day as a resident—and this didn't bother me.

On the way back home he stopped to call his close friend and fellow hypomanic, Bob.

> We moonlighted in similar kinds of places, and I said, "Bob, I got this contract, let's go in on it," and so we did. And now we had two people to share the call.

Rapid decision-making, instantly formed partnerships, an easy assumption of risk: all are hallmarks of the hypomanic state. And in this case, all were to pay off. On a roll, Joe returned to his deserted basement and set up headquarters.

> I sent out three hundred letters, to every single mental-health provider in the state, and told them, "We have this organization . . . and we can supply your needs better and cheaper. . . ."

For a couple of months, until Joe could get the legal work done, he and Bob covered whatever calls they had; after that everyone wanted to be part of it. The company took off, becoming the largest vendor of psychiatric services in the state of Massachusetts within two years. It is still in operation today, sixteen years later, although Joe, bored and stressed by the bureaucratic detail of having to deal with state agencies, scaled back his involvement less than one year after the company had succeeded so brilliantly. This is hypomania at its best, its most productive, and its luckiest. It is not surprising that the demographics of manic-depression show a distinct list toward the upper socioeconomic strata, when a person on the mild end of the spectrum can so easily create a thriving company in just two years' time, essentially on impulse.

On the other hand, the risks involved in hypomanic decision-making should be obvious to all, and today Joe faces a potential bankruptcy proceeding for all of the same reasons that made his first venture a brilliant success. Like many another hypomanic before him, Joe was soon bitten by the real-estate bug. It would be interesting to know how many vast real-estate fortunes are owed to the genes responsible for manic-depression, speculation in land being to the hypomanic what a ball and hoop are to the natural athlete. Action, movement, the easy ability to *score:* once Joe was introduced to real estate, he was hooked.

> I bought up a whole bunch of real estate and again some of the decisions were impulsive. If I was on a vacation, I would be looking for things; I'd pick up the local paper, get to people, try to make a deal. One day I walked into a shopping center, looked at it, and said, "This is fine," and a year later I made a hundred thousand dollars on the deal. And I just saw the place once. I felt I was on a roll. It was a euphoric sense; it was risk-taking on a grand scale for somebody of my means.

All went well until the tax law changed, and Joe's empire came crashing down. His partner declared bankruptcy, and Joe may soon be forced to follow suit:

> All of the properties that I bought in the town where I lived made money; the ones that lost money were out of state. Without the hypomanic aspect of things, the prudent thing to do is to stick close to where you are so you can keep an eye on your investments. In each

state you have a new set of rules, a new set of lawyers; it's not the way to do it—if you were giving a seminar on business, that would not be the way you would tell people to work. But wherever I went, I bought something.

Following the rules is not a strength of hypomanics; nor, often, is the simple practice of common sense. Joe's partner Bob, himself a mild hypomanic, still recalls the time when their accountant, reacting to yet another financial scheme of Joe's, said to him: "You are the kind of person the tax code is made for." Still, common sense or no, Joe appreciates his disorder on the whole:

> I like my hypomania. It wrecked my first marriage, and it probably cost me a couple of million bucks. But other than that it's fun. And it's made me a better person. It's not for everyone, but darkness accentuates light; it makes for a clearer, sharper picture. And hypomania enhances my creativity.

It is the hallmark of the hypomanic that he can remain blissfully unscathed in the midst of financial disarray. Of all those with shadow syndromes, it is the hypomanic who sees the glass not only as half-full but as destined soon to be full to overflowing. To the hypomanic, the bounty of life is vivid and real.

■□ THE LOVE OF A GOOD WOMAN

It is not easy to understand precisely what went wrong in Joe's first marriage, and how his hypomania contributed to its demise. Joe himself views the marriage as having been happy much of the time. His wife attended law school while he developed his medical career, and they were together for ten years. Trying to explain how the relationship soured, Joe traces the problems back to a dark period in his own family's life:

> As I was in my training, I had a lot of family deaths. My father, my grandmother, and my grandfather all died in a year. And that

changed my view on the importance of getting a degree; I saw a different kind of reality. I wanted to live, start enjoying the world.

To Joe, as perhaps to many or even most hypomanics, "living" meant breaking out of the conventions of everyday society, and bending the rules that governed social conduct:

> I would be running an oncology group for nurses who were dealing with dying patients, and when you walk out of that experience, whether you're a few minutes late to a social gathering or whether you're wearing the right tie—or all of those little things—they mean nothing. But to my wife, she was detail-oriented and all of those things meant a lot.
>
> She was more day-to-day and practical. She was a bright woman who was going to law school, and the way they teach lawyers to think is, you have to prove things and have quid pro quo—and to me that was abhorrent. I couldn't take it; I felt like, "It's all protocol. I don't want to live my life this way."

At that point in his young life everything—his chosen profession, his family's losses—was conspiring to put him into a continual, heightened consciousness of life and death. It was a realm into which his practical lawyer-wife could not follow him, and he felt betrayed.

> I was depending on her when my family was dying, and she was caught up in the law and that to me was not right. That precipitated a lot of the trouble. The stability was gone, and for me a stable relationship has to keep my keel more even.

This is as much as Joe will say about the unraveling of his first marriage, although he hints at hypomanic attractions to other women as another source of tension. In any case, the marriage came to an end.

But Joe's second marriage, which began in his thirties, has been a success. Much of the credit for this, Joe feels, goes to his wife:

> My wife is a very strong character, meaning she has a good heart, and integrity. She's also someone who is willing to accept me. She was willing to go to California with me, and take the dive. I finished working in Cambridge on a Friday night and I had to be at work in

San Francisco on a Monday morning, so she and I drove forty-eight hours straight. I went to work on Monday and we stayed in a bed and breakfast until we found a place. Then when we came back, we drove back with the baby across the desert. She's not hypomanic, she's pretty even-keel. She likes travel and adventure, but she is pretty even. She can tolerate the fact that I'm not conventional, that sometimes I am unpredictable.

Today Joe is a person who has won for himself what therapists call a "therapeutic marriage": a marriage that is good for his psychological functioning. His wife is a profoundly stabilizing influence in his life, and the four children they have brought into the world have transformed Joe into a person who thinks before he acts. Of course, the decision to have four children in the first place was, in some respects, yet one more hypomanic leap into the unknown:

> I've had four kids in ten years. It's interesting because at one point I didn't think I was going to have any kids because I thought that would be akin to being Prometheus Bound, and sometimes I feel that way now. But relationships are anchors, and there was a part of me that felt that this was what I'm here to do, this was part of my biological mandate, . . . to pass on to the genetic pool that which had been given to me. Life requires leaps of faith, and then improvisation. You create your own shot, then follow through. And I figure that again, I was confident that I would come out standing; I'm like a cat, I always land on my feet—so four kids, what the hell?

This is bipolar philosophy at its best: hypomania can give a person the confidence he will need to take the grand risks in life, without sapping him of the discipline to see his commitments through.

■ THE BIOLOGY OF ELATION

Bipolar disorder is genetic. It is transmitted from parents to children, and from children on to their children. Of all the psychiatric disorders, manic-depression is the most genetic, even more genetic than schizophrenia. Mark George, the psychiatrist and neuroscientist who has become well-known for his PET scans of the clinically depressed, tells a little-known story from the annals of psychiatric research that starkly illustrates just how genetic bipolar disorder is:

> Here at the NIH [National Institutes of Health] in Washington a group of researchers, years ago, took identical twins where one twin was schizophrenic and the other twin wasn't, and they were clearly able to show the effects of the disease on the brain. They got a lot of mileage out of that one study.
>
> So then people wanted to do the same thing with bipolar disease. And they were unable to find *any* identical twins where one had the illness and one did not. These were NIH researchers; they could tap the entire world's population of manic-depressive patients, and they could not find one set of identical twins who was not concordant for the illness.

Schizophrenia, a highly genetic disorder, shows a concordance rate of 50 percent, meaning that when one identical twin is schizophrenic, the chances of his sibling also being schizophrenic are fifty-fifty. But with manic-depressive illness, when one twin was found to be bipolar, the other twin was *always* bipolar (though other researchers, as we will see, have found a small group of discordant twins): this is a striking and, frankly, shocking result to contemplate. Geneticists agree that a 50 percent rate of concordance is more than sufficient to establish the fact that a given disease has a genetic basis: it is virtually unknown for a genetic disorder to show a nearly 100 percent rate of concordance among identical twins. (Unipolar depression is far less genetic than manic-depression, although there is a significant genetic component to unipolar depression as well.)

Precisely which genes are involved in the transmission of manic-depression from one generation to the next is not known, though researchers are fast closing in upon their quarry. Several genes will probably be involved, with the severity of the disorder in any given individual depending upon how many of the genes he has inherited, with which mutations. A mildly affected person like Joe, for instance, might be born with just one or perhaps two out of a possible total of five genes for the illness. A severe and unrelenting case, like Kay Jamison's, might require that all five genes be present (if five it is).

The question of gene mapping, of course, raises the issue of prenatal screening: what will happen when pregnant couples are able to test their fetuses for the genes that cause manic-depressive illness? Jamison argues that we should not, as a society, embrace a practice of systematically rooting out all DNA that codes for bipolar disorder. We would lose too much, she believes. At least one study supports Jamison's position: Ruth Richards's investigation of manic-depressives, cyclothymics, and their unaffected relatives. Richards decided to study the healthy parents and siblings of bipolar patients, reasoning that it was quite possible that the relatives of manic-depressive individuals show the true benefits of the genes for the disorder. Presumably the healthy relatives do inherit some of their afflicted relatives' tendencies toward manic-depressive illness without becoming ill themselves. This phenomenon, whereby a "bad" gene also endows some among us with certain desirable, or even highly desirable, qualities, is well known in the field of genetics. The gene for sickle-cell anemia, for instance, also protects its carrier from contracting malaria.

Looking at the dimension of creativity—an obvious place to start, given the very high rates of manic-depressive illness found in major poets and musicians—Richards found that all three groups, bipolar I's, cyclothymics, and unaffected relatives, did indeed show greater creativity than did people who had no manic-depression in their family trees. But she also found that it was the unaffected relatives who were most creative of all. Being related to a manic-depressive person, while not being manic-depressive oneself, is in all likelihood a significant advantage in life. Attempting to root out all bipolar genes, whatever those genes ultimately prove to be, is probably a mistake. As a society we will lose too much.

Joe's own family tree supports Jamison's view. Like Joe himself, Joe's paternal grandfather, who was in all likelihood moderately manic-depressive, largely benefited from the disorder:

In a lot of ways I'm repeating my grandfather's history. He was a guy from Spain who left when he was eleven and went to Cuba and was an entrepreneur and made a lot of money and lost a lot of money, and had a large family. . . . And he always had this grand aura about him, a bigger-than-life image.

But for Joe's uncle, the son of this larger-than-life grandfather, the bipolar streak running through the bloodline was to prove devastating:

> My uncle has manic-depressive illness. He went on a marrying binge and married two or three women at the same time, and at one point he wanted to kill my grandfather. He was finally hospitalized and had shock treatments.

If parents of the future choose to abort fetuses with the genes for bipolar disorder, they will certainly prevent tremendous suffering; that much is true. But they may also destroy tremendous talent, vision, and will.

■□ THE BRAIN IN FLUX

The basic biology of manic-depression remains a mystery. There is some evidence of structural differences in the brains of bipolar patients: brain scans reveal the famous unidentified bright objects (UBOs) that also show up in MRIs of people with Alzheimer's disease and multiple sclerosis. UBOs are bright white patches on the screen; hence the name. In anatomical terms, a UBO is a lesion, or damage, to the brain's white matter. Mark George explains:

> The brain is made of grey matter, which is the nerve cells, and white matter, which is the "cables" that connect nerve cells to one another. When a nerve cell up at the top of the skull wants to communicate with the cerebellum it sends a signal down through a cable covered with *myelin*, which is white—white matter. The UBOs are interruptions of that myelin. They're sometimes seen in normal aging, with people developing one UBO per decade. So if you have three UBOs in your thirties, that's normal. And you see them in people who have a first episode of depression later in life.

The unidentified bright object is a place where the cable has been "cut" or somehow damaged; the white mass on the screen is probably water. The fluid that bathes the brain has flowed into the lesion or wound, leaving water where there should be tissue. On the screen this fluid reads as a UBO.

Typically, mania is associated with lesions of the right hemisphere. We should mention here that, as is often true in the still-young field of brain-scanning, some researchers have not found this to be the case. But enough have replicated this finding that it is safe to assume researchers will eventually reach a consensus that right-hemisphere damage *is* involved in many cases of mania.

This makes sense: it is the right brain that is responsible for normal negativity. Damage to the right brain harms the brain's capacity to process and to feel bad things, producing a person—or animal—who is inappropriately happy. A person who is *too* happy. And while the notion of being too happy is counterintuitive, in fact it is quite possible to be inappropriately cheerful. The expression "grinning like an idiot" conveys this truth: certain forms of mental retardation, for instance, result in a very impaired individual who smiles and giggles throughout his day, regardless of what is actually happening around him. Mark George remembers seeing a patient, very early in his career, who had sustained damage to the right hemisphere of his brain:

> I'll never forget a patient who had very advanced multiple sclerosis, where the immune system attacks the brain and there are multiple small regions of the brain that have scars and are not functioning. And in some of the end stages of multiple sclerosis, there seems to be almost an inappropriate euphoria. This patient was bedridden, with bad bedsores and no family or friends, totally dependent on others for everything, a very sad case . . . and he was just happy. I'd walk onto the ward and he'd be cracking jokes and asking me to come over and chat with him. It is very striking when you see it because these are terminally ill people. Ten or twenty percent of the end-stage patients have this.

Thus it is certainly possible to experience an excessive form of happiness that is the result not of a happy life or a good attitude, but of damage to the right brain. Such damage may be an important biological source of mania.

Further evidence that mania may involve damage to the right brain can be found in the work of neurologist Vilayanur Ramachandran of the University of California at San Diego. Ramachandran studies the results of right-brain damage in a group of stroke patients who display a condition known as anosognosia. These patients, who have sustained damage to the right side of the brain—and who, as a result, are paralyzed on the left side of their bodies—will deny, in the face of all evidence to the contrary, that they are in fact paralyzed. The denial persists for only the first weeks after their strokes; eventually, they recognize the obvious. But for those few weeks, these right-brain-impaired patients flatly deny that anything untoward has happened to them.

Dr. Ramachandran believes he has found a biological basis for the defense mechanism of denial: a suppression of the negative right brain that allows the rosy worldview of the "happy" left brain to reign unchallenged. Because the left brain is also the language side of the brain, Ramachandran further links denial to the faculty of speech. It is the job of the left brain, he believes, to write the story of our lives, and to keep it consistent, which is what a good storyteller does. When some detail does not fit, the left brain smooths things over by denying that detail's existence. In the case of anosognosia the detail that does not fit is the fact that the patient has become paralyzed, and the left brain, free of the right brain's negativity, simply decides that the paralysis has not happened. Thus the left brain is the locus of the normally useful self-deceptions we all employ virtually every minute of every day.

Completing the picture, Ramachandran argues that, in essence, the right brain's function is to look for signs of trouble: the right brain scans the environment for anomalies. If the anomalies it finds are serious enough, the right brain somehow overcomes the left brain's ability to create a consistently positive view of the world. Sustain damage to the right brain, then, and the left brain is set free: the left brain can simply insist that no paralysis has occurred, that *everything remains the same.* This, in Ramachandran's view, is the message of the left brain.

Speculation aside, Ramachandran's theory clearly supports the find-

ing of UBO damage to the right brains of manic patients. To a significant degree it also supports, as is often the case with emerging findings
in the field of neuroscience, the classic psychoanalytic view of manic-
depression. Psychoanalysts have long interpreted the heedless elation of
the hypomanic personality as a massively effective form of denial, as we
see in Lewin's classic discussion of this question:

> A suffusion of the whole personality by the mechanism of denial led
> [psychoanalyst] Anny Angel (1934) to refer to two patients as
> chronic optimists. Despite only too much evidence to the contrary,
> these women believed that everything would inevitably come out
> right in the end. Disregarding extraordinary frustrations in fact, they
> were able to think only of unavoidable happy endings and preserved
> an entirely unwarranted, even dangerous, cheerfulness. In both cases,
> in the unconscious, the happy ending meant the ultimate acquisition
> of a penis.

While a quaint explanation of the hypomanic personality by today's
standards, Lewin's discovery of penis envy at the root of manic joy nevertheless captures the sense of absolute possibility of the person whose
left brain has soared to dominance: for the hypomanic, anything is possible.

■□ ENVIRONMENTAL PSYCHIATRY

Although manic-depressive illness is widely recognized as the most genetic of the mental illnesses, there is a great deal of data attesting to its
high degree of relatedness to the environment—both the social environment of family, friends, and work—and the physical environment
of light, temperature, electromagnetic fields and the like.

In terms of the physical environment, some authorities believe that
seasonal affective disorder, or SAD, is in fact a form of bipolar disorder.
Certainly, many manic-depressives, including Kay Jamison, cycle according to the season, some having manic episodes routinely in the
summer, others becoming manic in the winter. Although the popular

press normally associates the spring light with feelings of well-being, summer depressions can and do occur quite often, and, when they do, are typically more severe than winter depressions. Serotonin levels are at their lowest in late winter and early spring, the time of the year that produces the highest rate of suicide as well. Summer heat is also bad for depressives; one severely depressed woman was successfully treated by keeping her air-conditioning turned to the low sixties throughout the summer months. (This approach proved so unpleasant as a lifestyle, and so difficult for the patient's spouse, that she eventually abandoned this "natural" approach for the simpler strategy of taking an antidepressant each morning. The medication worked, and she and her husband returned to normal life.) As to electromagnetic fields, while no one knows how these may affect the mood swings of bipolar disorder, there is evidence of an association between EMFs and suicide. (Jamison and Goodwin suggest that exposure to very low frequency electromagnetic fields may accelerate the bipolar individual's internal clock by disrupting circadian rhythms. This remains to be investigated in the future.)

As to the social environment, in the future, when the genes responsible for manic-depression are fully isolated, we will see even more emphasis upon the social environment's role in "triggering" the disorder. It is widely believed that not everyone with the genetic vulnerability to manic-depression actually develops the disorder; factors in the social (or physical) environment must help matters along. Of course, this perception may prove to be overly optimistic, given anecdotal evidence like Mark George's story about the impossibility of finding even a single set of twins who were *not* concordant for the disorder. The lowest figure cited for concordance between identical twins is Goodwin's and Jamison's 80 percent, which is extremely high—and which raises the question of what the remaining 20 percent of "healthy," presumably nonbipolar twins actually look like in real life. If these healthy twins suffer soft forms of bipolar illness themselves, they would still be classified by researchers as nonbipolar, and thus nonconcordant. Yet for all practical purposes the concordance rate would actually approach 100 percent. (Researchers in the epidemiology of autism report having tripped over this artifact of experimental design themselves only recently. For years the concordance rate for autism was believed to be 50 percent. When one identical twin had autism, the chance that his sibling would also have autism was 50-50. But later, when researchers returned to these nonconcordant twins as adults, they found that the nonautistic twins were in very poor shape. The presumably normal twins had no friends, no lovers or spouses, oftentimes no jobs. They were obviously not normal, and in fact suffered shadow forms of autism—thus bumping the concordance rate up to at least 90 percent, and probably, realistically speaking, to a full 100 percent.)

In short, anecdotes like George's and concordance rates like Goodwin's and Jamison's 80 percent make it difficult to believe that a person who has inherited the genes for manic-depression can do much in the way of environmental manipulations to avoid developing the disorder. While it may take a trigger from the environment to set the disease in motion, an 80 percent concordance rate tends to imply that, one way or another, a trigger is going to appear.

Still, we can turn to the example of other polygenic (meaning many-gened) disorders such as diabetes as a guide: although diabetes is highly genetic, researchers do believe that many people with the genes for Type II diabetes can avoid developing the disease by keeping their weight low in mid life. Such patients would carry the genes, but would avoid the triggering mechanism necessary to put those genes into play. By analogy, it is entirely possible to imagine that a person who has inherited, say, four of the five genes for manic-depression (and again, we do not know how many genes are involved—this is hypothetical) *could* in fact turn to environmental strategies to lower his odds of actually becoming bipolar.

Thus, once we are able to identify children who possess some or all of the genes for manic-depression, we will certainly devise ways to cushion their passage through adolescence, the period during which bipolar illness often develops. These might be the children, for example, whose parents *should* be encouraged to "stay together for the sake of the children." Or, because research shows that moving to a new neighborhood and school is highly stressful to most children, parents of children bearing the bipolar genes might make a commitment to remaining in the same home throughout the adolescent years. Whatever path parents in this situation were to take, the goal would always be to give their child as much support as possible during this dangerous period.

As to the children, they would need to receive a form of life counseling—advice concerning career and marriage—that took their genetic vulnerability into account. Certainly, all individuals testing positive for the genes, regardless of age, would likely need—and want—to follow a strict policy concerning the degree of social stressors they allow into their lives.

Most important, anyone with a genetic vulnerability to manic-depressive illness would need to understand what the concept of kindling—which applies as much to bipolar illness as to clinical depression—means in terms of his own life. As we have seen, the term "kindling" refers to the biological truth that a mental disorder can, and does, take on a life of its own: that where a person's first depression may take place in reaction to a negative life event, the second one may take place in reaction to a much less serious life event, and the third may happen simply because it happens. At this point in a genetically vulnerable person's life, the brain has been so battered by its previous bouts with depression that it can now set itself off, with little or nothing in the environment to provoke it. The same phenomenon holds true for manic-depressive illness. As we have seen, fully one-third of manic-depressive patients report having experienced mood swings long before they developed the disorder. Thus anyone with a history of unstable mood is well advised to take care before plunging headlong into the next risky relationship or business opportunity. The price in terms of biology may be too high.

Often the wisest strategy for such individuals is to create, or to embrace, a life that does not pitch them an inordinate number of curves. While none of us can choose to lead a life free of calamity, we can choose to commit ourselves to mates, and to careers, that offer less drama rather than more. It is a fundamental message of this book that we all must respect our own biologies, and if one's biology tends toward the bipolar, then it is right and self-respecting to separate ourselves from people who would clearly push us further down this path.

Unfortunately for the bipolar personality, who delights in the tumult and glory of life, this is not simple advice to heed. The sober truth is that the bipolar character has not been built to withstand the stress of continual life dramas: he must pace himself. Describing the normal brain, Jamison and Goodwin offer the image of the suspension bridge, a marvel of technological design that allows a massive structure to sway with the wind but not collapse. The bipolar brain, they write, is a bridge without give. And the bipolar personality is best advised to stay free of life's gales. Temperamentally drawn to the earth-shattering forces of life and love, the bipolar personality has not been designed to sway gracefully with their force.

■ MARY ELLEN: THE MAD HOUSEWIFE ONCE MORE

Of course, even those mildly bipolar individuals who fully recognize their need for a soothing life will not necessarily be able to create one. This is the case for Mary Ellen, a woman whose life would test even the calmest of souls. Mary Ellen is the full-time mother of two very difficult children, premature twins diagnosed by age two as having severe forms of attention deficit disorder accompanied by learning disabilities. Both boys are aggressive toward their parents and toward each other; at age six they cannot have play dates because other parents will not allow their children to spend time with them. Mary Ellen has been told by professionals that whether or not they will be able to lead productive or independent lives as adults is an open question. For Mary Ellen and her husband the chaos of living with their children—just the grinding, unrelenting *noise* of living with them, combined with the uncertainty about their future—is a chronic environmental stressor of a major order.

Given her own unstable brain chemistry, Mary Ellen is not the person for this job. Prone to mood swings, she is herself at risk of developing a full-blown bipolar disorder—a condition, her psychiatrist has warned her, that can appear at any point in a person's life. There is no age at which people are safe, no age after which it is too late to become manic-depressive. For Mary Ellen there were danger signs early on:

> I think I had mildly manic episodes in college, where I'd stay up all night and memorize whole books—*entire books*—and then write wonderful essays. I'd be wide awake, I didn't have to take drugs to stay awake the way all my friends did when they needed to pull an all-nighter. The deadline would just suddenly hit me out of the blue, and I'd be up all night, and I'd get A's on the exams and essays I stayed up for. It was a weird way to go to school. The aftermath would be exhaustion, and I would get sick after finals. And the material was just in short-term memory; I'd forget everything I learned.
>
> I think I had one truly hypomanic episode when I was taking philosophy. I was having trouble in the course, because I had tried to write papers that proved the existence of reality—that a chair actually existed, in reality, as a chair, and not just as sense data—and I kept getting creamed on them; I was getting B's and C's. The professor told us there was no way to prove the existence of things. And this really unnerved me; it was a very upsetting idea. Finally, I got incredibly overloaded, and I remember walking home one night where I started having visual images in my head of books infinitely stacked up in these huge piles. . . . And I was thinking that if I just kept going faster and faster, getting through all those books I could see inside my head, I could find the *answers*, because philosophy triggers the idea that everything can be proven. I had this feeling: "I have to go faster."

While an experience like this is not mania, it is close enough. Certainly, it is a prelude to mania. Mary Ellen was losing her felt connection to reality; she was experiencing a near-hallucination accompanied by an urgent need to do something that made sense only to her: *to go faster.* To churn through mile-high stacks of books, to find the answers: to prove that reality existed! And while it is one thing for a professor of philosophy to argue that the existence of reality cannot be logically proven, it is quite another, psychologically speaking, for a nineteen-year-old undergraduate to be gripped by the urgent need to do just that. A healthy person simply feels the reality of things, whether or not that reality can be proven by logic. Walking home to her dormitory,

Mary Ellen was in danger of losing her felt connection to the solidity of life, a connection her professor no doubt fully enjoyed.

As we would expect, Mary Ellen suffered frequent mild lows as well; she had been a timid child, and she had grown up to become an anxious adult. She worried constantly, and fell in love with a man whom she now believes, looking back, to have been a true, albeit undiagnosed, manic-depressive. Her relationship with him, she says, was a roller coaster, and she lived in constant suspense over whether she was currently in or out of favor with the man who was the love of her life.

Eventually, Mary Ellen was able to break with her boyfriend and move to Minneapolis, where she met, and within the year married, Stan. Stan was a good choice, steady in his affections and ambitions. Life with him was quite radically not a roller coaster; he called when he said he would call, and came to fetch her for their dates on time. If, in the famous formulation, 80 percent of life is showing up, Stan was a person who showed up. He was the right man for Mary Ellen, and for several years she lived happily with him. Though she was frequently anxious about her work teaching first grade under the eye of an overbearing principal, she was never clinically depressed, and certainly never manic.

All this was to change after the birth of the twins. The pregnancy did not go well. Mary Ellen went into labor at twenty weeks; repeated hospital stays, bed rest at home, and continual medication prolonged it only to thirty weeks, when her water broke and the boys were born by cesarean section.

They were not in good health. Though neither suffered an intracranial hemorrhage, a grave danger to micropreemies like Jeremy and Joe, they remained in neonatal intensive care for many weeks before coming home on monitors. Soon Mary Ellen and her husband discovered that both boys had developed the hyperactivity and associated learning problems that are also a risk in children born so young. The twins were so difficult to deal with that the crisis period surrounding their birth essentially never ended, and the family lurched from the catastrophic situation of caring for very sick babies to the equally catastrophic situation for caring for behaviorally disordered toddlers and preschool-ers—for whom, in this country, day care is not available. After the twins were born, life never returned to normal.

Within the field of psychiatry, Mary Ellen's family situation is known as a severe environmental stressor. And while there is probably no person on this earth who would thrive in this situation, Mary Ellen was precisely the kind of person who should not be doing what she was doing, caring for severely challenging children on her own, twelve hours a day. She soon developed a severe, suicidal depression, sparked by a scene in which, at her wits' end, she had shaken one of the boys. When, that night, her son complained of a fever and a stiff neck she be-came convinced that she had injured his spinal cord and caused him even more brain damage. In fact, he was coming down with a virus, but she would not know this until the next day. Stunned, Mary Ellen lay in her bed, unable to move or cry, unable to think of anything but the wish to die.

But she did not die. At age thirty-six she made her first appointment with a psychiatrist, and began a course of antidepressant medication.

The medication worked. All thoughts of death left her, as well as much, though certainly not all, of her daily sadness over her children's condition. And, as Michael Norden has discussed in *Beyond Prozac,* she found herself feeling less stressed as well. While we are not accustomed to thinking of stress as an emotion, in fact the feeling of being stressed is just that: it is a feeling. Antidepressant medications like Prozac treat not only the grief of depression but also the emotion of stress.

Mary Ellen and Stan were greatly encouraged by her improvement. But the relief came with a cost: for people who have an unrecognized and subtle tendency toward a bipolar makeup, as Mary Ellen did, anti-depressant medication—and in particular the drug Prozac, which Mary Ellen was taking—can tip them into hypomania or even, in some cases, a full-blown manic episode. By virtue of her subtly bipolar makeup, Mary Ellen was at risk.

Over the course of the next two years, Mary Ellen found herself plunging into frenzied home-improvement binges—mad but produc-tive bursts of homemaking activity that in and of themselves were, like Joe's impulsive real-estate purchases, not all bad:

While I was taking Prozac, I would have these house-painting spells where I was painting and wall-papering, and I would do it all night long. One time I came home from a trip back home with the kids. It was hideous; my dad had gone completely nuts with the twins, and both of the boys had been awful every second, and I stepped in my front door and put down my luggage and boom, it hit. And I started emptying closets—this is after unpacking, I unpacked *real* fast—and I emptied two closets from two different rooms and I switched all the furniture in two rooms back and forth without any help, and I painted both rooms, all in twenty-four hours. I was up all night; I can't remember if I slept at all. . . . I remember feeling like, "Oh, I have to do this house *now*," and I was furious with Stan for sitting down relaxing and watching TV. I felt like "My house is a dump, I have to do this today!"

For Mary Ellen these episodes were a clear case of environment and biology merging to produce the beginnings of mania, as Mary Ellen's psychiatrist saw at once:

My psychiatrist felt that what triggered it was being back home after having both my children and my father out of control—the house was the one thing I *could* control. And I don't really dislike the house-painting sprees; I find them useful. I think people do get stuff done when they're hypomanic; I don't think you can sit around being hypomanic and not get anything done.

But while for Mary Ellen these initial episodes were in many ways satisfying orgies of productivity, Stan found them difficult at best.

He couldn't stand these times, because I wasn't available, and because usually they cost money. He would feel like, Oh my God, what is she doing now? He'd come home from work and it would be a total surprise, everything would be torn up, and I'd want his help and make him feel bad for not helping. It used to piss me off how he could sit there and not care if the rooms were repainted.

Stan's reaction is a common one: hypomanic episodes are generally far more enjoyable for the person having the episode than for the person along for the ride. Counterintuitive as it may seem, the depressed side of bipolar disorder is less damaging to personal relationships than the hypomanic or manic side. Goodwin and Jamison cite a key reason for this disparity: put simply, people tend to be more critical of themselves when depressed, more critical of others when manic. Thus while the manic person may experience soaring self-esteem, unfortunately this generosity of judgment does not extend to those he loves.

Relationships may also be damaged by the hypomanic's lack of insight, a fact of bipolar life Mary Ellen was to learn firsthand. Goodwin and Jamison describe a classic study to this effect, an experiment in which both staff members and manic-depressive patients at a mental hospital were asked to describe the patients' behavior and outlook during depression and mania. As it turned out, when bipolar patients were depressed, their self-assessments largely coincided with staff members' perceptions. Staff members described depressed patients as flat, unsociable, rejected, and rejecting, and the patients agreed. But when patients swung up into mania, their self-perceptions veered radically far afield from the perceptions of staff members; manic patients possessed virtually no ability to see themselves as others saw them. Where the manic patient looked in the mirror and saw a person who was "sociable, trusting, moderately impulsive, . . . cautious and not at all stubborn or aggressive," staff members saw instead an individual who was "only moderately sociable, somewhat distrustful, extremely impulsive and aggressive, quite rejecting of others, and completely incautious and unafraid." Goodwin and Jamison conclude:

> These facts imply that the self-critical judgmental process is severely impaired in the manic state but not in the depressed state. This is consistent with the well-known fact that manic patients do not usually admit to any illness, or that they deny the maladaptive nature of their behavior. This is also why it is difficult to detect the presence of manic states by means of self-description type inventories; these usually show that the manic patient is normal.

Self-descriptive inventories show that the manic patient is normal because the manic patient thinks he *is* normal: he does not see himself through another's eyes. While a person who is depressed usually knows that he is depressed—or at least recognizes that he is not feeling at all well—the person who is manic, or hypomanic, thinks that he is *perfectly fine.* And thinking that one is a perfectly fine individual in all respects can be a recipe for disaster in almost any intimate relationship. When a person loses the self-critical faculty, love and friendship suffer.

While Mary Ellen's wild house-painting sprees were unmistakable red flags, they were still quite mild and harmless compared to the real thing, which Mary Ellen, now carrying the dual risk factors of antidepressant medication and chronic environmental stressors, was well on her way to experiencing. By the time the twins were five, she had had her first true episode of hypomania.

It was set off by the even more severe stress of the twins' entrance into kindergarten. During their preschool years they had attended separate classes in a Montessori school where the teachers and staff were so patient that the boys had made it through the day. One teacher, who had befriended Mary Ellen, did remark to her that in public school the boys would probably be tracked into special-education classes, and naturally that idea occupied Mary Ellen's thoughts as fall approached.

The twins' entrance into public school was a disaster. Neither boy could sit in a chair, or on the rug for more than a few minutes; they could not take part in circle time; they were destructive of property and aggressive toward other children. In a classroom setting they were extremely challenging little boys.

The school was no help. Because both boys' IQs tested in the normal range, they were classified as "normal" and thus undeserving of special resources or aid other than a couple of hours a week of tutoring in basic academic skills. To the teachers in Mary Ellen's conservative small suburb, her twins were simply bad boys. They were forever being pulled out of the classroom and sent to the principal's office; Mary Ellen could not get through a school day without a call from the principal asking her to come in and pick them up. Trying to relax in her few hours away from her children—blessed hours of quiet for the mothers of normal children—Mary Ellen would cringe every time the telephone rang. The silence of her house now became ominous and oppressive.

Just a few months into the school year the twins had learned nothing at all, administrators and teachers were angry with Mary Ellen and hostile to the boys, and other parents in the class were beginning to make their resentment felt. Mary Ellen felt like a trapped mother animal fighting vainly to protect her young.

Very depressed now even with her medication, Mary Ellen raised her dose. Within weeks she was launched into her first hypomanic episode.

I found out about this private school for emotionally disturbed children two hours from my house. So I pulled both boys out of public school, and put them in the new school, and at first things were much better because all the children were SED (severely emotionally disturbed) there, so Jeremy and Joe didn't stand out. And I felt incredible gratitude to the director of the school; I started to almost worship her, to think she was saving all these children's lives.

So then she asked me to teach at the school because I had been a teacher before I had the twins, and I said yes. My class was all emotionally disturbed or severely learning-disabled kids, or both, so I had kids ranting and raging at me six hours a day, my own twins ranting and raging all night, plus I was driving four hours a day, and I was having to prepare my class late at night. It was all way too much, and I started talking way too fast. I started thinking God had sent me to that place to cure all those kids, turn their lives around—and of course I couldn't settle for mediocrity, so I was collecting all the horrible books the director had bought and putting them away, and trying to make individualized lesson plans for every single child in my class, and I was exhausted. I stopped sleeping; I was only sleeping a few hours a night.

I was very up, I didn't have any negative feelings at all, and I was flirting with this ugly teacher at the school who I never would have been attracted to normally; I was very pleasant and confident and well-dressed and I had a great sense of humor. . . .

But it couldn't last forever. I got exhausted, and meanwhile both of the boys were going crazy because they weren't seeing me at all. I had them in an after-school program until six, and then we drove two hours home, and then I had to cook dinner and prepare for the next day. I started crashing, realizing I couldn't do it. I could only do it if I was up most of the night; I could only do it if I was hypomanic. It took me three weeks to realize this, where a normal person would have said, "This is going to be over my head, I won't do it."

The soaring self-confidence, the quick-wittedness, the flirtatiousness, the lack of sleep: all are signs of a hypomanic episode. And, like most hypomanics, Mary Ellen felt suffused with purpose and drive:

It was like God had directed me to do this, and I remember telling our minister, "Oh, I got this job, I have found my calling in life." And he said, "What a good answer to prayer." . . . And two weeks later I had to tell everybody, "The calling is off."

The entire episode, start to finish, lasted only three weeks. Frightened by what had happened, Mary Ellen immediately saw her psychiatrist, who felt that although Mary Ellen was at risk for developing bipolar illness, she did not now qualify for the diagnosis. In her view the episode had not lasted long enough to be an episode of true mania. But both Mary Ellen and her doctor were now concerned about where Mary Ellen's life was heading.

Within the year, Mary Ellen became hypomanic for a second time. It was summertime, and she and another mother had planned a camping trip for the twins' Boy Scout troop. As the mother of children with behavioral challenges, Mary Ellen was forced to play a large role in any and all activities they pursued so that she could be on hand to control them. Thus she had signed on to serve as den mother to the troop.

I was at camp for the weekend, and it was very, very hot, close to a hundred degrees. There was no air-conditioning anywhere, and we had to cook all our meals over open fires and take care of all these boys. Everyone was severely stressed, and they all went home and got bad backs. But I went home and got hypomanic.

It started on the trip home. I was driving, and I started planning the next camping trip in my mind, figuring out how to make it work, how we should do it in early spring instead of waiting until August, when it was so hot, and I was planning so rapidly that I got lost three times.

Mary Ellen was on a roll, but the upshot of her dawning hypomania was not to earn several hundred thousand dollars on hypomania-driven real-estate purchases, as Joseph Ramirez did. Instead, Mary Ellen's experience shows the toll hypomania can take upon relationships:

> I was planning, planning, planning—and I overstepped my boundaries because I kept bugging Debbie, who had just become the new den mother, since my term as leader was up. I practically ran her over and was very annoyed with her when she was not going along with my ideas. I was rude to her—maybe not rude, but it seemed like it to her—it was "This is it, we have to do it, and I have the way to do it," and I was completely oblivious to the fact that I was making her incredibly angry. Finally, things became so bad that she wrote me a letter.
>
> And all of a sudden I realized she couldn't even talk to me. I realized she felt afraid of me, or threatened, and couldn't even come to me. She was a very good friend, and when I got the letter, I realized I was totally out of line; it was a major red flag. I knew I had been way over the edge, because Debbie is very easy to get along with. So I knew that if I was feeling angry with her, I was probably the one who was out of line.

By that point Mary Ellen's whirring brain had sailed on from point A to points B, C, D, and beyond, leaving a valued friendship in ruins without Mary Ellen's even being conscious of having given offense. This is the terrible danger of hypomania: while the hypomanic state can make a person more intelligent in terms of cognitive skills, it may also lower social intelligence. Mary Ellen, normally a sensitive person and a loyal friend, was devastating an important relationship without even being aware of what she was doing. Suffused with the rightness of her own thoughts, and the wrongness of everyone else's, she had in fact ceased to be a friend.

But as friendships were falling unnoticed all around her, Mary Ellen was on to new adventures:

> There was a week's period before I got the letter where I had been thwarted by Debbie and I stayed mad at her, but I went off in another direction; I thought, Well, if she can't use me then boom: I got

a job at T. J. Maxx! I was driving along in the middle of all this, and there was a brand-new T. J. Maxx with a sign out front asking for employees, and I just pulled in, parked the car, and walked right in. And I was bullshitting with the manager, and there I am, this suburban den mother in a room with all these illegal immigrants and low-income black women; hypomania can really lead you in funny directions sometimes. And the manager was going nuts, he couldn't believe I was there. He said he'd be calling me the next day, I could have whatever hours I wanted.

I called my mother, and she didn't think it was a great idea, she thought it was a little much. Stan just said, "I don't care what you do." He saw it as another one of my whims, like the painting; he didn't think it was that great of an idea to be running out of the house for minimum wage, but he was hands-off. If that's what you want to do, fine.

Fortunately, this escapade was over by the next day; Mary Ellen managed to come to her senses in twelve hours' time. She called the manager and told him to take her name off the list. But in the meantime, she had completely forgotten the Boy Scout situation.

By the end of the week—it was less than seven days—when I got the letter from Debbie, I had almost forgotten about the Boy Scout incident. I opened the letter, and I realized Debbie was still upset, and it hit me out of the blue. I thought, "Why is she still mad about this? *I'm* not mad about this!" But she was still perceiving me to be mad. She was on a completely different time scale. Everything was moving so much faster for me than it was for everybody else.

Fortunately for all involved, Mary Ellen was not so manic that she could not calm herself and analyze where things stood. Unlike a person in the grip of full-fledged mania, she still possessed insight, in both the common and the psychiatric sense of the term: when she tried, she was able to see herself as others saw her.

It really hurt my feelings, a whole letter over this Boy Scout thing. I immediately called Debbie and apologized, but even after the apology I could still feel this distance. She didn't understand.

She didn't know anything about my problems, so I told her all about my hypomania. I named it, and I told her I'd had it before. She understood and said she was sorry she wrote the letter, and she was very glad to have the hypomania explained. She said she'd never thought of that. Her perception had been that I was completely competent and self-confident, and she felt like I thought she was an idiot. The state I was in was a real take-charge thing, it wasn't "Let's see what we can do together." I was taking over because I was driven to do things the best way, which was my way, even though I had turned leadership over to her.

Information really helped. Once she understood she was OK.

Happily for Mary Ellen she was to find an easy answer. Although she was genetically prone to bipolar disorder, the factor tipping her over the line was not her children but her medication. Antidepressant medication is always a bit risky for those prone to mania, because in the process of lifting the bipolar person out of a depression it can push him or her on up into a manic episode—overshooting the mark, so to speak. This was what was happening to Mary Ellen. Now her physician prescribed a different antidepressant, one she felt might be safer, though all antidepressants can cause mania in some patients. She was right; Mary Ellen has remained stable since beginning the new medication.

Mary Ellen and her psychiatrist have agreed that if she experiences another hypomanic episode she will take lithium, because, as her doctor has stressed, an individual can develop manic-depression at any age, and Mary Ellen is at risk. This is one of the most important messages of the shadow syndromes: prevention can be nine-tenths of a cure. When it comes to mild versions of severe disorders, it is important to intervene sooner rather than later.

■☐ HYPOMANIC PERSONALITIES; OR, THE HAPPY WARRIORS

The soft forms of bipolar disorder have fascinating ramifications for personality and character formation, because a person who is even mildly bipolar is used to living life as two people, or perhaps even three: a fully developed depressed self, a fully developed euphoric self, and a solid and grounded evenly balanced self. This is important because most of us experience ourselves as one person, with one identity. Although in fact all of us are riddled with contradictions and inconsistencies, that is not how we *feel*. We feel like the same person across very different situations, and with very different people.

For bipolar individuals this is less often the case. Bipolar people can feel like a completely different person from one day to the next: they can, frankly, *be* a completely different person from one day to the next. And bipolar personalities often know this about themselves. The result is that, for them, character is less likely to "wrap itself around" the disorder. Bipolar individuals may be freer than, say, unipolar depressives, to reject the dictates of their biology, once they find the means to do so.

Soft bipolars enjoy a second advantage over their more one-note brothers: a person who swings from low to high and back again can profit both from the realism of depression and from the soaring self-confidence of hypomania. This is a remarkable combination; remarkable and, when it comes to the social world, formidable. The person who knows both depression and hypomania can, when depressed, *remember* what it was like to be suffused with grand thoughts and conviction. And, by the same token, the hypomanic person who is having one too many good ideas concerning real-estate speculations or rescue missions at schools for the emotionally disturbed can learn to say to himself, sooner rather than later: I am getting carried away. In short, where most of us are captive to our emotions, the mildly bipolar person can develop a capacity to step back a pace from even his most powerful emotions and observe. He becomes both the star of his own movie, and the director—a crucial distinction.

Because of his "split personality," a person with bipolar shadow syndrome may ultimately be happier than are many of us with the other shadow syndromes; he or she may be a happier person even than the "normal" folks among us. Certainly, bipolar individuals appear to fare well in comparison to their close relatives, the pure unipolar depressives. The high self-esteem of the hypomanic state seems to persist during periods of calm, and Goodwin and Jamison report that "the personality profiles of remitted bipolar patients are more normal than those of remitted unipolar [depressed] patients." Translated, this means that when he is neither manic nor depressed the bipolar individual enjoys, overall, a better attitude and better life functioning than does a unipolar depressive when he is not depressed.

The bipolar patient possesses one further strength: he is less wedded to his darkest thoughts. It is a truism of psychiatry that patients resist change, and that, when patients do change, they mourn the loss of their symptoms. Thus the depressive does not freely "give up" his depression. But the bipolar patient is all too happy to abandon his depressive self. He does not see his dark moods as fundamental to his identity; he experiences depression as an aberration, not as part and parcel of his character.

Unfortunately, since depression bestows the gifts of insight and an all-too-realistic modesty, which hypomania steals away, the hypomanic is not entirely well served in the ease with which he disavows his passing sorrows. As a result, the hypomanic may follow a different life course than do those with other shadow syndromes; it may take him longer to discover the value of his many moods, and to integrate their lessons into one self and soul. In practical terms, what this means is that the hypomanic personality may find the decade of his twenties rough sledding indeed.

But eventually most hypomanics begin to learn from their mistakes. Sometime in the decade of his thirties, the hypomanic personality, if he or she is lucky, learns to modulate; he learns to step back, to put his impulses on pause. It is at this point that the true advantage of a bipolar nature emerges: where the pure depressives among us can be ground down by the hard realities of life, the hypomanic can always draw upon his good nature—and his capacity for denial—to take bad times in stride. At forty the hypomanic may be just hitting his stride; being older and wiser is a state that suits him. In middle age the hypomanics among us become the happy warriors of life, the seasoned men and women of vision who lead the way.

4

ADULTS WHO TANTRUM

Intermittent Rage Disorder

MOST OF US ARE accustomed to hearing people say they are going into therapy because they feel sad or anxious, or because their marriage is breaking up, or they have lost their job, and they need a few weeks of help. But not often does a friend or family member confide that he has entered therapy because he is too angry.

Although John first made his reputation as a specialist in violence and aggression, his patients, too, arrive at his door for the same reasons they arrive at any other therapist's door. They come to him because they are sad, alone, anxious, frightened—because they are anything but angry. Given the toll anger takes on human relationships, this is disheartening but not surprising. Anger as an emotion is often what psychiatrists call ego-syntonic: it is an expected, and acceptable, part of the way to feel. Anger, in short, is a descriptor of the self people do not mind having. Depression we reject: "I'm depressed" is neither a good way to feel, nor a good thing to say about ourselves. But "I am angry" sounds strong, righteous, justified.

Thus when people do come to therapy for help with anger, it is often because someone else in their lives—not uncommonly a beleaguered mate—has made them do it. Which brings us to the crux of the difficulty in defining anger as a brain-based problem deserving attention: while none of us enjoys being the object of someone else's rage, most of us quite like, cherish even, our own angry thoughts and feelings. Anger can feel very good indeed; anger can make us feel full inside, while depression makes us feel empty. Probably most people would rather be angry than terribly sad, and many have discovered the conversion of sad feelings into angry ones as a formula for alleviating despair. Therapists, too, have long understood that one way to spark a patient out of depression is to help that person to become angry. Angry feels more powerful than sad; angry feels strong and masculine, while depression feels weepy and feminine. Anger, we think, is active; depression passive.

The "masculine" feel of anger as opposed to depression may have influenced the course of psychiatry and psychology when it comes to dealing with what professionals used to call disorders of rage. Psychologist Rosalind Barnett, senior research fellow at the Wellesley Center for Research on Women, argues that once the media publicized, in the 1970s, the link between women and depression, "mental illness" tended to be equated with the sad emotions rather than the angry ones. (General interest in the anxiety disorders may have ebbed at this time as well. Where the most famous psychiatric medication of the 1960s and 1970s would certainly have been the tranquilizer Valium, today that honor would go to Prozac.) Overwhelming feelings of sadness and despair, which women do suffer in greater numbers, came to be seen as the quintessential emotional problem, while overwhelming feelings of anger and rage, which men suffer in greater numbers than women, attracted little or no attention from the popular press.

Those of us who lived through the rebirth of feminism in the 1970s can recall what came next: the discovery, and subsequent glorification, of *women's* anger. By the seventies not only was intense anger not considered a disorder (at least not by the public at large), it was considered a positive sign of mental health. In that decade and since, feminist leaders and women's magazines alike have urged women to "get in touch" with their anger: Get in touch, then "let it out." Apart from the psychologist Carol Tavris, whose book *Anger: The Misunderstood Emotion* was a lone voice in raising doubts about the essential goodness of anger, the culture reached a collective decision that it was time for women to express their rage. The time of Mary Tyler Moore had passed, the day of Roseanne had arrived. Thus the identification of mental illness with depression and anxiety, not rage, was reinforced.

The result of this cultural shift is that it is difficult to move people today to entertain the possibility that their *own* anger may be a sign of a difference in the brain that is not doing them much good. Most of us experience anger—even chronic, unyielding, borderline tantruming forms of anger—not as an emotional problem, but as a valid response to life's many injustices and difficult people.

And yet when we examine the biology of anger, we see that anger and depression are intimately linked. Depressed people are all too frequently angry people as well, certainly irritable if nothing else. A volatile temper may be part of disorders as severe as manic-depression, and as mild as attention deficit disorder; in fact, unreasonable and unreasoning anger is a symptom of many of the syndromes listed in the DSM.

Ironically, the very pervasiveness of anger as a symptom may also have contributed to the neglect of anger per se as a mental state in need of attention. Because anger is part and parcel of so many varying and diverse conditions—and because we value anger in a way we do not value sadness or anxiety—no one looks at anger as a thing unto itself. Intermittent explosive disorder, a self-explanatory diagnostic category that appeared in the DSM-III, does not appear in the DSM-IV; it was removed because no one used it.

But the time has come to breathe new life into the concept of a rage disorder. When we speak of the "angry young man," or of the "adult who tantrums," we may be speaking of a shadow syndrome of an intermittent rage disorder. These people are suffering from subtle differences in the brain that result in an explosive emotional makeup. This is the kind of person who "blows up," "flies off the handle," or "explodes," and we are accustomed to explaining his behavior as the result of selfishness, narcissism, immaturity, or all three. But in fact this person is the way he or she is at least in part due to differences in the brain.

We'll present a fuller discussion of what these differences are later; at this point we want to note simply that, at heart, problems with rage are problems with impulse control. Impulse control is one of those fundamental psychiatric concepts you can go all your life without stumbling across until the moment you become a parent. Anyone who has struggled to raise a well-behaved child he can take out in public knows the crucial importance of impulse control to a child's life, and most parents have also noticed the very different levels of built-in impulse control children seem to bring with them into the world. For some children, quite simply, being good is a great deal easier than for others.

Impulse control is exactly what the phrase implies: it is the capacity to control one's impulses. The child who has an impulse to run into the street or kick the dog, but who can control those impulses, is a lucky child indeed, beloved of teachers, neighbors, and elderly relatives alike. All children—all adults—have negative or destructive impulses, and the capacity not to act on those impulses is critical to a happy life.

Doctors, teachers, and parents most often confront problems in a child's impulse control when a child suffers from attention deficit disorder, a mental disorder now known to be biological in origin. In adult life, problems in impulse control may be more subtle, but adult tantruming would certainly be one. A grown-up person who has an impulse to scream obscenities at his boss or spouse, and who then proceeds to do just that, has not managed to block his impulse.

■ THE ANGER ATTACK

Although most people do not seek therapy for mild to moderate problems with anger (as they might for mild to moderate problems with, for instance, anxiety or depression), there are signs that our feelings about the value and meaning of anger may be changing. At the personal level, the soaring divorce rate of the past twenty years has dampened some of our enthusiasm for the notion that anger is always and inevitably a noble and empowering emotion in men and women. The chronic irritability of urban life further challenges the belief that being in touch with one's anger is an unalloyed good.

Meanwhile, the medical profession has weighed in with its own grim news concerning anger: "Anger kills!" proclaims Redford Williams, in his book of that title. The text, with its graphic account of the physiological changes that accompany bouts of rage—adrenaline pouring into the system, heart beating furiously, slender veins being stretched to the limit by pounding bursts of blood, fats surging into the bloodstream— is enough to give the most unrepentant plate-smashers among us pause. The history of Williams's work also suggests that our feelings about anger, as a culture, are changing. Williams is an intellectual descendant of Meyer Friedman, the originator of the notion that Type A personalities were at greater risk of dying by heart attack. When Friedman first published his discovery, he did not view the Type A person's anger as the problem. Type A's were angry, yes, but they were also competitive, ambitious, always in a rush, and Dr. Friedman thought it was the whole package that produced the greater risk of death.

But Williams further defined the concept by discovering that it is *only* the angry and suspicious attributes of Type A's that put them at risk. Competitiveness, ambition, obsession with time: these qualities are apparently benign. Hence the title of Williams's book, *Anger Kills*. It is the Type A person's hostility, distrust, and aggression, he has found, that pose the true risk to the heart. That Williams would even think to narrow the Type A person's problems down to anger pure and simple may be a reflection of a different cultural *Zeitgeist* that has come into being. Anger per se may now be a more likely target of medical scrutiny than it was in Friedman's era.

Finally, the epidemic of violence in America that we have seen in the past twenty years inevitably casts a new light upon the value of anger. Assaults, murders, kidnappings, rapes: these crimes are not committed by people in calm and sanguine frames of mind. If we were to subject every prison inmate to psychiatric scrutiny, the category of intermittent rage disorder would begin to look very real indeed.

Evidence that anger may be emerging as a significant psychiatric category unto itself can be found in Maurizio Fava's original work on anger attacks. Fava has identified a group of patients, all of them clinically depressed at the time of his studies, who also suffer anger attacks which consist of, in his words, "sudden, intense spells of anger associated with a surge of autonomic arousal including . . . tachycardia (a rapidly beating heart), sweating, flushing, and a feeling of being out of control." An attack might be spontaneous—seeming to come out of nowhere—or provoked, but 66 percent of the time the person having one experiences it as "uncharacteristic" and "inappropriate to the situation." After it is over, a nearly unanimous 93 percent feel guilt and regret for their behavior during the attack. In other words, these experiences are true *attacks* in the way heart attacks are attacks: an anger attack feels like something happening *to* you rather than something you are *doing to* the people around you.

But as they are well aware, people in the throes of an anger attack are likely to be doing a great deal to the people around them: 63 percent of Fava's group reported attacking others either verbally or physically, while 30 percent said they threw or destroyed property. Anger attacks are not, generally speaking, something a person is able to sit out quietly in a corner.

Anger attacks, Fava found, are common in depressed people: nearly half, 48 percent, of the clinically depressed patients he studied reported having them. Interestingly for our purposes, Fava also found that 21 percent of nondepressed people suffer anger attacks as well, a startlingly high figure when you think about it. One in five normal, everyday, nonclinically defined people experiences bouts of rage so intense that their heart races and their skin breaks out in a sweat. One in five normal, everyday people experiences violent *attacks* of rage he or she cannot control.

A figure like this opens up a different angle of vision on the problems that afflict our daily lives: if one in five people suffers from out-and-out anger *attacks,* this means that most of us have experienced anger attacks at close range, either in ourselves or in the people we love and depend upon. And Fava's one-in-five figure raises the question of anger management to new prominence. While the popular press floods the reading public with books about self-esteem and intimacy, what we may really need are more books, like Williams's, on how to cope with anger.

Having established the existence of anger attacks, Fava set out to discover what effect the drug Prozac might have on them. He chose Prozac because of data linking aggression to low levels of the neurotransmitter serotonin. Within the profession, psychiatrists speak of a low-serotonin syndrome, the theory being that the lower a person's serotonin, the more likely he is to be violent—the person with the lowest levels being the arsonist. Because Prozac raises serotonin levels, Fava reasoned that it might subdue rage attacks.

It did, dramatically so. Prozac reduced the incidence of anger attacks in all of the patients, and for 71 percent the attacks *disappeared completely.*

The implications of this discovery are profound. Few of us, when we are tantruming, or when we are being subjected to someone else's tantrum, stop to think that our biology may have something to do with the scene that is unfolding furiously around us. And yet the fact that an antidepressant medication could stop anger attacks altogether in 71 percent of a group of depressed patients implies that, certainly for these patients, their tantrums had a significant, brain-based component. Their lives had not changed; they were still coping with the same irritants and provocations they faced before. But their biologies were different.

How significant a change was this for Fava's patients? A great deal has been made of the capacity of medications like Prozac not only to alter psychiatric symptoms, but to change even a patient's core personality. While the philosophical question of what is a symptom and what is a personality is not something we can resolve here, suffice it to say that Fava did find evidence of changes not only in patients' passing moods, but also in the basic characters underlying those moods.

In thinking about symptoms versus personality, professionals have long relied upon the distinction between trait and state. A state is your present frame of mind; a trait is a personality characteristic that does not change with the mood or the moment. A trait is who you are.

Anger as a *state* would be the anger a person feels at a single moment.

Anger as a *trait* would be a chronic anger he or she always feels about all of the things that bother him or her. Anger as a trait is a kind of value system, a way of seeing the world as a hostile place that requires one to be on guard. When people say that someone is an angry person, they are saying that for that person anger is a personality trait, not just an occasional bad mood.

It makes sense that a serotonin-boosting medication like Prozac would treat anger as a passing state; that is what we would expect. The FDA-approved purpose of antidepressant medication is to relieve depression, which is considered a temporary disorder of state, not a permanent disorder of personality. ("Personality disorders" are classified as an entirely different and separate group of diagnoses in the DSM.) This is exactly what Fava found: when he asked patients taking Prozac to check off such items as "feeling angry," "feeling hostile," and "not feeling kind to people"—all descriptions of a *current* mental state—he found a dramatic 58 percent decrease in global feelings of irritability and anger. Clearly, his medicated patients changed their emotional states.

But they changed traits, too, at least traits as measured by the Cook and Medley Hostility Scale. Cook and Medley is a classic test, dating back to the 1950s, of hostility as a personality characteristic. It consists of a subset of items concerning hostility taken from the Minnesota Multiphasic Personality Inventory (the MMPI, which, to this day, remains the gold standard of personality tests): statements such as "I would certainly enjoy beating a crook at his own game," or, "When someone does me a wrong, I feel I should pay him back if I can, just for the principle of the thing," or, "I have often met people who were supposed to be expert who were no better than I." All of these items measure hostility not merely as a passing mood, but as a stable value system, an enduring point of view.

Fava found that in just eight short weeks, patients taking Prozac showed a 15 percent reduction in hostility as measured by the Cook and Medley Scale, a 15 percent reduction in anger as a lifelong character trait. It is a discovery that supports Peter Kramer's claim, in *Listening to Prozac,* that some of his patients responded to the drug with changes not only in mood but also in basic personality underlying mood. These patients underwent a very significant change indeed.

Ironically, of course, at the same time that psychiatrists were discovering Prozac's capacity to quell anger, the talk shows were filled with former patients claiming that the drug had actually caused them to become violent. In most of these cases Prozac probably had nothing to do with it. When you look at the psychiatric records of these patients, you find that often they were also taking several other medications at the time of their violent acts, and that many of them had been violent or suicidal in the past, long before their doctors prescribed Prozac.

However, it is entirely possible that Prozac *can* in some cases cause what psychiatrists call akathisia. A person suffering from akathisia is seized by an inner feeling of restlessness, a need to move around, and a proneness to action. For most of us that action would not take the form of lethal action, but for some it might. In that handful of patients for whom akathisia will lead to violence, a Prozac-induced bout of akathisia could in fact end in mayhem.

Apart from this, some of the apparently adverse reactions people have had to Prozac could be due simply to what psychiatrists have long known as a paradoxical effect. When you experience a paradoxical effect in response to a medication, you respond in exactly the opposite manner that most people respond. For example, the vast majority of people find Xanax to be a highly effective tranquilizer and sleeping medication. But a small group of people actually become more hyper and alert on the drug. Because any psychotropic medication can produce a paradoxical effect in some patients, it stands to reason that there may be a small group of people who respond to Prozac by becoming more angry and violent instead of less so. These may be the people populating the talk shows a few years back with claims that Prozac is a violence-inducing drug.

In short, whether or not any individual's claim that he became violent or suicidal on Prozac is true, the possibility that a few people will become more rage-filled on Prozac (or on any other antidepressant) does not contradict the reality that the vast majority of people will become far less so. Treating the brain is a complex art; that is why we require licensed physicians to prescribe medication and to monitor its effects. The fear and hysteria generated by a few well-publicized claims of Prozac-provoked murder and suicide are based upon a misunderstanding of the way in which a good medicine can or even should work.

■ THE ANGRY HUSBAND

Fava's work concerns patients with the very real, identifiable, and diagnosable condition we call clinical depression. He says that it is not clear how his findings relate to nondepressed people who experience anger attacks. However, given what we are daily learning about the brains of the worried well, it is likely that temper tantrums in people who are *not* depressed are going to turn out to be just as biologically based as anger attacks in people who are.

Gary Lansing first came to see John some years ago because he had heard of John's work with attention deficit disorder in adults. Having read an article about the disorder, he had recognized a number of the symptoms in himself. It would become clear later that the problems really worrying Gary were far more dramatic, and far more serious, than a simple case of difficulty in organizing his thoughts. But Gary withheld this fact from John in the beginning.

John confirmed that Gary was indeed suffering from ADD, and prescribed a low dosage of the antidepressant desipramine as treatment. Gary soon reported feeling much more focused and organized.

It was not until this point that Gary somewhat self-consciously revealed a side benefit from the medication: he had stopped tantruming at home. Before treatment, Gary said, he and his family had been severely affected by his chronic rage attacks: he had been averaging forty tantrums a month. His marriage was on the brink of collapse and his small daughter was terrified. Now, in the few weeks during which Gary had begun taking medication, he had gone from forty tantrums a month to none. It was a stunning, life-altering effect for which he had neither asked nor hoped.

Only now did Gary confess to John how profoundly destructive his temper had been—and how desperately he had tried to master it. By the time Gary saw John, he had exhausted every avenue open to him *except* medication in an effort to deal with his problems. He was an active member of Alcoholics Anonymous, which had helped him to remain sober for ten years; he regularly attended a men's group to discuss feelings and relationships; he had been a runner for years; he had religiously practiced the breathing, meditation, and relaxation exercises experts recommend as a way of calming oneself before the onslaught of intense emotion. He had done everything in his power to change.

None of it had worked. Although he was sober, his problems with other people had not diminished in the slightest. His first wife had left many years before; he had married again, but this marriage, too, was disintegrating under the pressure of his ferocious temper. The men's group could do nothing to help: the rest of the men in it were trying to experience more feeling, not less.

> They used to say they were trying to take their feelings out of their head and put them into their stomach. But I wanted to get my feelings out of my stomach and into my head.

He wished he *could* live more in his head, wished he could be cooler and less suffused with feeling every waking moment of his life. In short, he was struggling to achieve the very state his counterparts in the group were trying to overcome.

By the time he saw John, Gary was desperate to save his marriage. But he was even more anguished by the effect his anger was having upon his child:

> My daughter captured my soul. I have never, ever in my life felt the same about anything as I do about my daughter. And all the work I had done in AA, all the hours in the men's group, it wasn't enough. I was still acting out, I was doing all kinds of outrageous behavior at home. And I was scaring my daughter.

It took Gary as long as it did to turn to psychopharmacology for help because of the intensely negative ideology of Alcoholics Anonymous concerning psychotropic medication. To AA, a drug is a drug. Alcohol is Xanax is Prozac is BuSpar. The organization sees no difference. Because AA had brought Gary back from the depths of his alcoholism, his gratitude to the organization, and his need for it, were such that he felt he could not defy their counsel. Only the terror on his daughter's face could move him to break at last with the teachings of AA.

Gary's experience makes it clear that a person does not need to be clinically depressed, as Fava's patients were, to suffer from an anger problem that is biological in nature. Gary was not depressed. He was just too angry. The fact that a psychotropic medication, an antidepressant in this case, abruptly stopped Gary's anger attacks is evidence enough to conclude that his attacks were brain-based.

Looking back over Gary's life, the signs pointing to a biologically rooted problem are readily apparent. He tantrumed so severely as a boy, long past the age of four when normal children grow out of their tantrums, that his mother feared he would one day kill someone—a fear common among parents who are struggling to raise children with brain-based disorders of temper.

Gary's parents' own problems with alcohol and mood are further evidence that their son's difficulties have a biological basis. His father was an alcoholic, his mother a suicide at the age of forty-five. Gary inherited a double dose of "anger genes," alcoholics and depressives alike suffering from problems with rage.

And finally, the nature of Gary's anger attacks is further evidence that he was struggling not only with a difficult childhood but with a flawed biology to boot. Gary experienced his rages in much the way the patients in Fava's study experienced theirs: as out-of-control attacks, flash floods of emotion that washed over the dam separating impulse from act in an instant. In short, Gary *could not stop himself.* He describes the experience:

> It's automatic pilot, it's just happening. If you were outside your body watching it happen, you couldn't stop it.

In his years of trying to understand what comes over him in these moments—and of trying to describe this furious state in AA meetings—Gary turns often to a chilling experience he has recounted many times. During the Vietnam War, Gary was a flight instructor. It was a dangerous business; there were always many craft in the air, some of them piloted by students, and the fog could roll in without warning. Suddenly, the weather would close down, and the inexperienced pilots would have to switch, fast, from visual flight rules to flying by instrument.

On the day that has stayed with Gary throughout his life, he was coming into the landing pattern when he switched over to tower frequency. Suddenly he was plunged into the midst of a life-and-death drama playing itself out over the air waves. A student, flying solo, had missed the approach to the runway and been forced to climb back up into the sky to try again. The cloud cover that day was low, and within moments the student had lost all visibility.

The student panicked. He keyed the mike, pressing down on the button that allows the pilot to speak to the tower, and frantically called for help. But in his terror he did not let go of the button, which meant that the tower could not talk back. *No one could talk him down.* Everyone on the frequency listened in horror as the young pilot screamed for help; they could *hear* him panicking as he rolled his plane and flew it into the ground. He was gone.

Gary has long drawn a parallel between what happens to him in moments of rage and what happened to the young pilot in his panic:

> The awareness that gave me was that this student was looking right at his instruments and his instruments were telling him exactly what his airplane was doing. But he couldn't see it. What he was looking at was in the moment. But where his mind was, was that he had already crashed. I guarantee you, he was looking directly at the instruments and not seeing them. And that's what happens when I lose my temper. I'm there, but I'm not seeing it happen.

Gary's struggle has been to find a way to *stop* the panic—in his case the rage—in the moment, to look at what is happening, to see it, and to stop it. To change course.

But his anger attacks are as unstoppable, to him, as the young fighter pilot's fatal panic attack was to him:

> I've been so focused on meditation and on running. I run to try to train my mind to stay in the moment. I've noticed that I'll be in a conference and someone will say something that will spike a fear in me, and for a couple of minutes I will not be in the conference. Then two minutes later I'll be back and I'll respond to what the person said and people will look at me and say, "Where have you been?"

Nothing Gary has done to keep himself in the moment has worked. Not meditation, not running, not deep breathing, not AA, not the men's group. Nothing worked until John prescribed a medication.

■ WHO'S IN CHARGE?

No doubt some readers, certainly readers who have never experienced an anger attack, will be skeptical. After all, you might argue, Gary does not tantrum at work; he manages to keep his temper at least partially under control there. Why, you may ask, can't he control it at home?

Carol Tavris, a skeptic when it comes to biological explanations of bad behavior, has made the same observation vis-à-vis the tantruming of major sports figures—which, she observes, has risen dramatically in recent years. Although environmental psychiatrists might disagree, Tavris argues that it is unlikely athletes' "anger biology" can also have risen dramatically in the ten or twenty years during which sports like tennis have become so much less civilized. She concludes that for tantruming athletes something other than biology is at work:

> We are witnessing an increase in anger and aggression in contemporary sports not because of instinct, but because of rewards. In many cases, angry displays have become good business for management and successful strategies for players.

Tavris points out that even a famous tantrumer like John McEnroe knows when to hold his fury in; she cites his statement that, "Against Borg I'll always behave. I have to." As Tavris puts it:

McEnroe, in short, knows how to use his tantrums to his advantage and to control himself when *that's* to his advantage.

The seeming ability of people with brain-based problems like anger attacks to control those problems when they must makes them maddening to those who live with them. Parents of children with attention deficit disorder, who often—though not always—experience anger problems as part of the syndrome, invariably make the observation that their child "can pay attention when he wants to." The fact is, sometimes hyperactive children can pay attention as well as the next child. And sometimes they can't. Parents and teachers reason, like Tavris, that if a child is capable of doing it sometimes—as John McEnroe is capable of controlling his temper sometimes—he should be capable of doing it always.

Unfortunately, this is not the way biology—or self-discipline—works. One confusing aspect of the shadow syndromes is that while the person with a *mild* difference in the brain can "control" the effects of that difference to a large degree, doing so requires great energy and high, even fierce, motivation. In other words, not tantruming, for a person prone to anger attacks, is completely different from not tantruming for a naturally calm person who does not "have a temper." For the person who is biologically given to anger attacks, remaining calm in the face of aggravation is always an unnatural response. Sometimes he or she can do it. But it takes tremendous effort.

Speaking of this issue as it applies to children with ADD, Dr. Allan Phillips, assistant clinical professor in the department of psychiatry at UCLA, puts it this way:

> The child with an attention deficit *can* pay attention. But it takes that child 100 percent motivation to do what a normal child can do with only 55 percent motivation.

There's the rub. How many of us can maintain a state of 100 percent motivation all of the time? Few. To understand what it is like for a person with a brain-based problem to keep up this level of motivation, think of dieting. Probably every would-be dieter among us is capable of controlling his or her calorie intake—*perfectly* controlling it—for one day, two days, three days, a week. But two weeks? Three weeks? Three months? A lifetime? All dieters have off days—pizza, ice cream, and chocolate chip cookie days—which is why diet books and magazines invariably ask successful dieters to share their strategies for handling lapses. That is the problem for the person prone to anger attacks: a tantrum is worse than a junk food spree. The person given to anger attacks cannot afford to have any lapses at all; one slip for him (or her) has far more serious consequences than does one slip for the dieter. This is the challenge a person with a brain-based difference faces: to control his temper every day, all day, forever.

This explains, too, why people with brain-based differences tend to be at their worst at home with the very people they ought to be treating the best—the family who loves them. The essence of "home" is *not* having to police oneself every second, not having to perform. Home is where we go to relax. The problem is, when the person who suffers anger attacks relaxes his vigilance, his tantrums fly out of control.

There is of course a second reason why people tantrum at home: it is precisely the people we love who threaten us the most, because they make us feel ashamed of our ugly behavior. The psychology of the rageful person (as distinct from the biology) is the psychology of shame. Shame is not to be confused with the all too familiar notion of low self-esteem; shame indicates a state of self-loathing, or at the very least self-disgust. And shame demands concealment; the person who is ashamed hides himself from the eyes of others.

While most people who suffer self-disgust feel able to keep a shameful core hidden from colleagues and acquaintances, it is impossible to hide from the eyes of lovers and families, who know us so well. The people with whom we live "see through us," or so we believe; thus the mere sight of a family member who has done nothing at all to provoke a shame-filled tantrumer can cause him to feel *exposed*—and then, in short order, enraged (a sequence very apparent in Gary's relationship with his wife, as we will see). Since, as Tavris points out, even the worst of tantrumers do not tantrum 100 percent of the time (though there are certainly severely brain-damaged individuals who do just this), the psychology of shame helps to explain the psychological triggering factors that set off the tantrumer's vulnerable biology.

Thus the fact that a person like Gary *can* control his temper under certain circumstances and not under others does not mean that we are "gods within ourselves," that we exercise an ultimate authority, from on high, over our thoughts and our actions. That Gary could partially control a tantrum at work does not mean that he could have controlled his tantruming at home simply by choosing to do so; he could not. He had tried everything; he was highly motivated. He certainly did not want to be throwing fits. But he could not stop his anger attacks once they began.

■ THE FALSE SELF

Anger always has a target; angry people are angry *about something*— which means that a biologically driven anger problem *can* be addressed (if not always successfully) through psychotherapy, through cognitive therapy, and through classic psychoanalysis. One of the best discussions of the nature of uncontrolled rage, a discussion that explains not only how tantrums get started in the first place, but why tantruming adults may need and value their anger, can be found in the work of psychiatrist Howard Wishnie. Wishnie worked at Massachusetts Mental Health Center back in the glory days of the 1970s, when Cambridge was littered with brilliant psychiatrists and psychoanalysts. He worked with drug addicts and prisoners, and eventually wrote an important book on the subject called *Treating the Impulsive Person.*

Borrowing from Heinz Kohut, the father of self-psychology, Wishnie argued that people possess two selves: the internal and the external, or the "true" and the "false." This is a concept familiar enough to most of us: the shiny, confident—but false—exterior covering the decidedly less impressive, but real, person within. Wishnie went on to theorize that each psychiatric disorder created its own particular internal self. For the poorly organized person who was prone to aggression, the hidden internal self would be that of the helpless wimp: this is the classic makeup of the bully whose blustery exterior hides a coward concealed

within. The manic-depressive's shameful internal self would be a listless soul with no energy to act; the narcissist's internal self would be a nothing, a nonentity.

Wishnie believed that the more self-aware and self-loving we are, the better integrated are our two selves: in other words, when we are self-loving, the split between the internal and the external, the true and the false, is not great. But for the violent criminal the divide between the two selves is profound. The criminal is driven to aggression when reality "pierces through" his grand external self to his helpless internal self. Something happens to make the criminal feel small and ashamed— to make him come abruptly face-to-face with the internal self he is hiding—and he panics. He "disintegrates": he sees his internal self which, to him, is horrendous, and his choices are few. He can kill himself, or he can panic and act out aggressively—act out at a person who is causing him to come in contact with his despised inner self. That person might be a wife or lover who puts him down (or who seems as if she *could* put him down if she chose); it might be a driver who cuts him off in traffic; it might be anybody, anytime, anywhere. The violence comes from the criminal's panic at the sight of his true self, which something in his social environment causes him to meet head-on.

Wishnie, of course, was speaking of violent criminals. (Former prison psychiatrist and Harvard professor James Gilligan offers a brilliant and contemporary rendering of Wishnie's analysis in his book *Violence*. After a twenty-five-year career spent studying criminal psychology, Gilligan concludes that all acts of violence are motivated by profound and searing feelings of shame.) But in the same way that severe biological disorders of the brain can have milder versions, severe psychoanalytic disorders of the self can also have their everyday variants. In fact, Gary, our former tantrumer, describes his own experience of rage in terms almost identical to those used by Wishnie. All of his adult life, starting in late adolescence, he has been keenly aware of a searing divide between external and internal realities. This sense of division doubtless has its roots in childhood. Gary's was the classic alcoholic family, in which denial ruled the day: his father's drinking was never discussed.

Gary's role, as firstborn, was to make things right. Gary's father routinely left for work by 7 A.M., and returned at midnight after an evening
of after-work drinking in the bars:

> The firstborn is usually the hero. So with my dad never around very
> much, my mother put me in the male role of the family. I had to ac-
> complish all these things; I had to project the image that things were
> OK.

Gary was an all-American swimmer for three years in high school;
after college he became a decorated fighter pilot—he was literally the
family hero.

But inside himself Gary lived life in a state of chronic fear, fear of not
being good enough. His fear had everything to do with his own drinking, which was essentially a form of self-medication. "Drinking enabled
me to get through uncomfortable times, through low self-esteem." His
fear also had everything to do with his rages. Gary's description of his
rages at home perfectly illustrates Wishnie's theory:

> There have been times I didn't want to come home because I didn't
> think I was good enough, I couldn't be a father.

These feelings of inadequacy would then spark an explosion: just the
sight of his wife, as he walked in the door at night, could drive him first
to consuming feelings of inadequacy and then, in a flash, to rage. The
sight of his wife pierced through his competent, good-father external
self, throwing him into a panic that quickly turned to rage.

This is a good example of a somewhat different way in which character can wrap around biology, a subsidiary route by which a person's
character and biology can come together into a truly miserable whole.
Gary's character, formed by a childhood spent as the firstborn son of an
alcoholic father and a depressed mother, was such that he needed to be
the all-good father and provider who could make everything perfect.
That was his psychology; his biology made him prone to rage attacks.
The mixture proved devastating. The normal small failures of effort
and will that all parents experience could send Gary careening into a

tantrum, and the tantrum would then itself become further evidence of his abject failure as a husband and father. His biology, in short, made him feel more ashamed of himself than he already did. Gary did not become an "angry person" because of his quicksilver temperament; his character did not wrap around biology in the sense of causing him to develop an angry philosophy of life, the way the mildly depressed so often develop depressive philosophies of life. Instead, character and biology came together in Gary to convince him of the essential worthlessness of his being. His view of his own character, in short, was warped by his biology.

To understand better how toxic Gary's particular combination of biology and character has been for him, we can imagine another combination altogether: a middle-aged husband and father with the same childhood as Gary's but who was blessed at birth with an innately calm and cheerful temperament. Such a man would have just as strong a need to make life perfect for his family—but *his* biologically driven reaction upon walking in the door might be to think that everything pretty much *is* perfect in spite of whatever signs there may be that everything is not! There are plenty of left-brain people out there patrolling the suburbs whose biology points them up, not down: these are the constitutionally cheerful souls who inspired the saying "water off a duck's back."

Unfortunately, Gary is their polar opposite; nothing rolls off his back, ever. He is a right-brain sort of person; his biology makes him painfully sensitive to every sign, no matter how subtle, that he is failing as protector of hearth and home. Then his anger biology kicks in and the household explodes. He has no biological capacity whatsoever to override the negative effects of his childhood.

Because of his exquisite vulnerability, even the house itself could set him off. Some years earlier he and his wife had bought a classic fixer-upper which, truth be told, had turned out to be more than they could handle. It was still in a shambles, and his wife now wanted to move to a newer, less challenging house.

Before Gary's treatment with desipramine, his wife's attitude—just *knowing* her attitude regardless of whether she said anything about the house or not—would drive him to rage. He says today:

One of the big things that always set me off was that my wife wanted to sell our house when I've invested a lot of my emotions in it. Every time she would talk about selling I would get very angry about my failure to finish the construction, or to have foreseen all the problems before we bought the house, or to have understood the limitations on what I could actually do. It's a sense of failure, for me, that she hates this house.

Gary's tantrums would begin when this sense of failure pierced through to his vulnerable internal self. He would panic, then rage. Within moments he would be shouting, swearing, throwing dishes, punching walls. Although Gary has never read the works of Howard Wishnie, he describes a rage attack that could have been drawn directly from the pages of Wishnie's book.

Gary's experience of his anger is so intuitively psychoanalytic, in fact, that he speaks perceptively of the mirroring relationship between husband and wife. The point of love for him, Gary says, has been to find a woman who could reflect back to him the image of himself he so desperately needed to see. He tells a story of having lunch not long ago with the woman who was his first wife, and discovering that he had no idea who she was. What she wanted in life, her likes and dislikes, the things she found funny—all of these details had passed him by. To him, as her husband, her whole reason for being had been to reflect back to him the family hero he was trying so hard to be. For his entire adult life he had been consumed by a fear and self-loathing so intense that he could not see past his own pain and rage to the person sitting across the room. His emotional life was geared solely to sustaining the image, the family hero.

Here again, we see the havoc an undiagnosed disorder can wreak upon a life. Not understanding that his rage problems were brain-based, Gary blamed himself, hating the way he was. (We see, too, that at a certain level of intensity anger ceases to be ego-syntonic and becomes distinctly ego-*dys*tonic.) Gary's life shows how a difference in the brain can end up taking over a person's entire existence. Often a person like Gary will follow a tragic downward spiral. He begins by realizing something is "wrong," by experiencing himself as different, flawed.

Other people aren't exploding in rage the way he is; what is the matter with him? From here he moves on to self-blame and self-punishment, and from this stage it is just a short step to losing the capacity to relate to loved ones in any kind of truly giving way. The need for constant reassurance simply becomes too great to allow the afflicted person to spend much time focusing on other people. Eventually, such a person finds, as Gary did, that his sole requirement in a lover or mate is that she be his golden mirror. He needs to be told, continually, that he is a good person. And, as Gary found, a love relationship in which the only point of being there is to hear your lover tell you you're a hero is barely a relationship at all.

The psychology of shame and rage sheds light, as well, on the kind of angry couple who is said to "push each other's buttons." We all know couples who do this, couples who invariably choose to say exactly the one thing that will most enrage or devastate or humiliate their partners. What is happening here is that one partner is piercing through the other partner's external self, forcing that partner into brutal contact with an internal self he or she wishes forever to avoid.

Finally, the psychology of rage eloquently explains why it is that people so often value their anger even while feeling profoundly ashamed of it at the same time: anger belongs to the fiery, potent, and commanding false self. The adult tantrumer may feel that beneath his anger there lies a small and frightened child, a helpless being at the mercy of a harsh and violent world. Psychodynamically speaking, for such a person to give up rage is to give up strength, give up safety. That rage provides only a false strength makes matters no easier.

After the publication of Peter Kramer's *Listening to Prozac,* the media was filled with speculation concerning the possibility that people would soon be taking pills to change their personalities. The irony of this flood of articles was that in the rush to cover the new psychopharmacology, journalists lost sight of the fundamental psychoanalytic precept concerning people's profound resistance to change. The truth is, most people do not want to be all that different. They want to feel better;

they want their friends and family to love them more, their boss to appreciate their work. But they do not want to exchange their old personalities for new ones. Tell people you've discovered a pill that will alter their characters, and you'll have few takers. It is the hard, slow work of psychotherapy that makes it possible for a person even to contemplate taking such a medication in the first place. When it comes to disorders of anger, many too-angry people are not truly looking to change.

■ THE BIOLOGY OF RAGE

In his book *Emotional Intelligence,* Daniel Goleman gives us a useful way to think about the tantrums of people like Gary. Goleman uses the phrase "emotional highjacking" to describe their explosions into sudden fury. The connotations of the word highjacking are particularly fitting here, as people like Gary experience these tantrums as happening *to* them, entirely against their will.

In an emotional highjacking, an excess of mental noise throws the higher brain centers off-line, allowing deeper, more primitive structures to seize control. More specifically, once an event causes the brain to lose its rhythm, to stumble out of synch, the frontal lobes of the cortex decline in function, allowing the more engaged and enraged amygdala to take over. The cortex is the most recently evolved and thus "highest" part of the brain; it is the seat of reason. The amygdala belongs to the evolutionarily older limbic system; it is called the reptilian brain and is the seat of emotion. In a tantrum, emotion highjacks reason; amygdala highjacks cortex.

When this happens, we lose the ability to organize our thoughts; we do not consider the consequences of our actions, we just act. Rodin's sculpture of *The Thinker* is an idealized view of the pondering human who is able to consider life rationally. The statue is in many ways a celebration of what might be considered our highest evolutionary achievement, the most advanced capacity of our brains. But when anger takes over we essentially lose our thinker function. Unable to pause and ponder, we simply react, much like a hound dog when it catches the scent of game. Something automatic kicks to life, our instincts take over, and we are off.

This loss of the thinker brain occurs when we are overwhelmed with noise, either real-world or symbolic. In the face of too much mental noise, our older defense mechanisms react by propelling us into the fight-or-flight mode. This can happen for many environmental reasons, such as too much stress, too much physical noise, too much heat, too little blood sugar, and so on. Almost any type of excess or extreme—physical, mental, or social—can overwhelm the thinker brain.

Alexander Luria, the great Russian neuropsychologist of years past, described the way in which a poorly functioning or damaged frontal lobe could make a person more aggressive and impulsive. Today, PET scans have extended this observation further, showing that murderers and violent prisoners have frontal cortices that are normally underactive, a condition that is called *hypo*frontality. The violent criminal's control centers are simply not as engaged as they should be, and thus exercise less influence over other parts of the brain—which means that these men are far more easily highjacked by activity in the deeper, reptilian brain.

A person may be born with, or develop, a structural difference in this region of the brain. As well, frontal-lobe deficits may come and go depending upon what else is happening in the brain and body. The brain, like the rest of our physical selves, can have good days and bad: if you lose sleep several nights in a row, this change in and of itself can reduce frontal-lobe function. Because the frontal lobe is the chief executive of the brain, *any* deficit in frontal-lobe functioning can have serious consequences. In the evocative language of neuropsychology, the frontal lobes are the seat of executive function. The frontal lobes consider lines of action, inhibit certain actions as unwise, and decide upon—and execute—other courses of action as proper. When it comes to anger, the frontal lobe serves chiefly as an inhibitor; it is the seat of impulse control. Thus the frontal area acts as a brake switch upon anger. In the kind of anger attacks we understand best, this brake is malfunctioning; it is not strong enough to hold back the angry impulse. A person with a poorly functioning frontal lobe attacks first and regrets his action later.

Hypofrontality is one of the best-known vulnerabilities in the constellation of variables that leads to tantruming, and beyond tantruming to aggression and violence. However, adult tantruming is not a relatively simple biological problem like obsessive-compulsive disorder, for which neurologists have now isolated the precise brain structures involved. Rage disorders will doubtless prove to have a variety of causes, as Mark George predicts of depression: eventually we will speak of angers, not anger. In short, many different pathways through the brain will eventually be identified, all leading to the same endpoint: an out-of-control temper.

Hypofrontality has implications not just for a person's emotional makeup, but for his cognitive abilities as well. For instance, a significant finding in studies of murderers is that violent criminals typically have difficulty using language. In fact, this is such a prominent feature of this population that Hervey Cleckley, author of the seminal book *The Mask of Sanity*, published in 1955, claimed that a form of deep-seated aphasia (a profound difficulty using and understanding words) was typically present in psychopaths, the most aggressive citizens among us. The verbal expression of thoughts is, of course, primarily a left-frontal function, and it is the frontal lobes that are "down" in many rage disorders. It is not surprising that we should find language disabilities in violent people: the deficit in frontal-lobe function results in twin deficits in both impulse control and language ability.

Distressingly, if the language function of a tantrumer's frontal lobes is compromised, he or she lacks yet another essential anger-management tool beyond the basic capacity of the frontal area simply to ride herd upon impulse. Language, words, and symbols all act to capture and objectify our inner experience; language serves a natural delaying function that helps us to grasp what we are experiencing and formulate what we are going to do about it without resorting to blind rage. A language disability deprives the angry person's brain of an important tool to manage his anger, and he or she may quickly regress to physical action.

Other research confirms this finding of a link between poor impulse control and language deficits. Recently, the Project for Gender and Violence at the Ackerman Institute in New York City reported finding that verbal communication problems are a significant contributor to the violent tendencies of men in spouse abuse cases. Statistically, the violence-prone man is likely to have a history of some kind of language difficulty, either in the form of dyslexia, attention deficit disorder (which often involves language issues), brain damage or alexithymia (a disorder in which a person cannot label feelings). Therapists at the Ackerman Institute are now focusing on training the language-disabled man to use words to express himself as a step in controlling his anger. At the biological level, these tantruming spouses are trying to use language to introduce enough of a delay into their behavior that their frontal cortices can resume some measure of self-control and thus stave off potential highjackings.

A third, and fascinating, finding among those with deficient frontal-lobe functioning is that they show abnormally low levels of serotonin throughout their brains. The serotonin system inhibits neuronal firings in many areas of the brain, and it is particularly essential to regulating the limbic regions that are key to our emotional life. It has been well established that there is an inverse relationship between serotonin levels and the degree of aggression in any given individual: people and monkeys with low serotonin levels are more violent than people and monkeys with high serotonin levels. In fact, serotonin has been called the brain's "police force." It is an ever-ready chemical restraint system that, when bolstered with Prozac or other serotonin-increasing agents, may bring about the desired result of lowering violence and aggression.

The serotonin system, then, acts as an interdependent and parallel system helping the frontal cortex to stop, ponder, and sculpt our final brain-directed conclusions or actions. Fortunately, the interdependent nature of neurotransmitter systems gives us an opening: we can attempt to treat frontal-lobe function by specifically targeting the serotonin systems that indirectly influence frontal function. In other words, when we use a serotonin reuptake inhibitor to treat anger or aggression, the medication directly affects serotonin levels, which then in turn affect frontal-lobe function. Medications such as Prozac were not developed specifically to "treat" the frontal lobes, but they may in fact have the effect of boosting frontal-lobe function.

■ ANGER ADDICTS

The hypofrontality of many rage disorders brings with it another fascinating and counterintuitive implication. Poor frontal-lobe function means that there may be a biological reason why people hold on to their anger: a person can become *addicted to his rage.* Addictive behavior is addictive because it is self-medicating. That is, an addictive behavior (like compulsive gambling, compulsive shopping, compulsive rage) makes the person acting that way feel better because it positively affects, at least for a time, specific states in the brain.

Anger may make a person feel better because it affects the brain at a purely biological level. Anger may function in much the same way stimulants such as Ritalin and Dexedrine do: anger can bring sluggish areas in the brain up to speed. While we will discuss this theory in detail in our chapter on attention deficit disorder, suffice it to say here that psychiatrists working at the National Institute of Mental Health have discovered that hyperactivity may come not from a brain working too fast, but from a brain working too slowly.

Psychiatrists have long known that there is a group of patients who respond well to stimulants. These include people with ADD, but they also include people suffering from depression and other disorders. The person who responds to stimulants may respond in exactly the same way to explosive rage. Violent expressions of rage may actually make that person's brain work better for a brief period.

Evidence for this hypothesis exists in the work of psychologist Michael Jacobson of UCLA. In studying the physiology of emotionally and physically abusive husbands, Jacobson has discovered a subgroup, twelve out of his group of fifty-seven men, who become not *more* aroused by a marital battle, as you would expect, but *less* aroused. In the midst of a raging battle, their heart rates actually show a deceleration: they are physically calmer during the fight than before or after. Speaking of these men to a reporter, Jacobson's comments are revealing:

> The only other known state in which there is a deceleration in heart rate is focused attention. These men look like they are being very attentive and focused.

Of course this is exactly how a hyperactive person *should* look when being effectively medicated by Ritalin—or effectively self-medicated by rage. (It is entirely possible that this subgroup might also respond positively to the emotion of fear, and for the same reason. Like rage, high fear can be an organizing state when one or more parts of the brain are underaroused. Fear brings the sluggish brain up to speed. This may explain those cases of abusive or tantruming spouses who *are* able to control their outbursts when they are threatened by the serious and real prospect of losing their mate.)

In any event, we can see how essential anger might become to a person whose brain is so chaotic that he or she feels organized and focused only when he is screaming at other people. If anger makes you better— and it looks very much as if anger does make this particular subgroup of men in Jacobson's studies better—then you are going to seek out more and more opportunities to be angry. You are going to become an anger addict. And weaning someone from an addiction, whether that addiction is to alcohol or to gambling or to rage, is not easy.

■☐   **OTHER ANGERS**

Anger is not just a frontal-lobe problem, although every rage attack does involve the frontal lobes. It is theoretically possible to possess normal frontal-lobe function and yet still suffer rage attacks due to problems in other areas of the brain. Essentially, the frontal lobes are the final, common pathway for all anger states originating from any cause.

Any noisy state within the brain can produce a state of frustration that builds to anger and then rage. If hyperarousal in other parts of the brain becomes severe enough, these emotions can overwhelm an otherwise normal frontal lobe, resulting in a highjacking. In this case the frontal lobes fail to stave off the rage attack, but not because the frontal lobes are themselves malfunctioning. Rather, a sound frontal lobe is simply overwhelmed by the level of impulses coming to it from other regions.

Gary's rage attacks (which probably did involve some deficit in frontal-lobe function) very likely developed in part from overarousal in posterior regions of the brain called the brain stem. The brain stem lies at the bottom of the brain, leading down into the neck and connecting with the spinal cord. It is the very oldest part of the brain. Desipramine, the medication that worked so remarkably for Gary, treats neither serotonin nor the frontal lobe; instead it primarily raises the levels of another neurotransmitter, noradrenaline. Thus desipramine may act to reduce random, noisy brain-stem firings, whose overactivity prevents the frontal lobes from getting a chance to step in and mediate. By quieting these posterior areas, desipramine may then permit the frontal lobes to act as they should.

John has generally found desipramine, officially an antidepressant, to be a useful drug when it comes to treating ADD adults who have significant problems with anger and aggression. It has an all-day effect (thus allowing the often forgetful ADD type to take just one pill and be done with it), and John has discovered that these patients respond to doses so low that they don't even show up on a standard blood test and would be considered sub-therapeutic as a treatment for clinical depression. At these low doses, the risk of side effects is much smaller, and the onset of effect upon ADD and aggressive symptoms is usually reported to occur in the same day. While the medication works in only a relatively small percentage of adults, for those people it can have a powerful and life-altering effect.

While the image of being thrown into rageful states by an overaroused brain makes intuitive sense, it is also possible to end up in rage states due to chronic underarousal. This is the passive, underactivated sort of person; a person with the brakes stuck "on." Sometimes these people will use anger to try to arouse themselves, to wake themselves up. At worst, these are the vicious murderers in our midst; Gilligan offers chilling interview transcripts from killers who describe committing their murders purely in order to try to feel something—*anything*. (One prisoner, a man who raped and murdered a fourteen-year-old girl, then buried her body in his backyard, told Gilligan: "From the time I entered military service I always wondered what it'd be like to kill someone. I wanted to do it. What I wondered was, whether I'd have feelings or not.")

More often, the underaroused tantrumer is the mild-mannered person who "blows up" once or twice a year. What happens here is that this person is chronically underaroused; but then, when his brain finally does rev up, it overshoots the mark. The frontal lobes (which are usually slightly underaroused as well in this person) give way, and a full-scale rage attack ensues.

In the years to come, we will know more about the different angers and how to treat them. Anger is highly responsive to psychotropic medications in several categories: antidepressants like Prozac; blood-pressure medications such as the beta-blockers (Inderal, Corgard) and clonidine; mild tranquilizers such as BuSpar (not related to Xanax and Valium, which belong to the benzodiazepine family)—all can have dramatic effects. And none is dangerous. For many tantrumers, medication supported by behavioral-cognitive therapy, which teaches thoughts and behaviors that can head off a tantrum before it has begun, will prove the best approach.

While our culture harbors a prejudice against psychiatric medication, we feel strongly that people whose lives and functioning are substantially improved by medication should be able to receive the treatment they need and be supported by friends, family, and media pundits as they do so. Too often, they are not.

There is a Calvinistic sentiment in our country that people should earn their happiness, that emotional well-being should not come so easily as the act of swallowing a pill. Under certain circumstances, and with certain problems, this view has its merits. But severe and chronic anger is too significant a problem to justify a refusal to medicate as a moral stance. As anyone who has lived with adult tantruming can tell you, uncontrolled rage attacks are profoundly destructive—destructive to the person having them and destructive to the people witnessing them. A parent's rage attack is devastating to his or her child. This recognition was what drove Gary, a man who was completely convinced by the AA prohibition against consuming any kind of drug at all, to reject his own deeply held belief that all medications are bad and wrong. "With my daughter," he says, "I could see in her face how frightened she was."

It is to Gary's credit that he has done everything in his power— everything up to and including breaking with AA doctrine—in order to seek out a medical doctor and follow his advice. He is a man struggling to do right by his family.

5

PRISONERS OF
THE PRESENT
Mild Attention Deficit Disorder

IN AMERICA, "hyper" people have always had their appeal. We belong to the New World, after all; and the sheer energy and pluck it took for our immigrant forebears to pick up and move across continents is a quality we cherish. It is a quality not unlike the high-energy, slightly manic behavior we know as part and parcel of attention deficit disorder.

Where a florid case of ADD will almost certainly handicap its sufferer, a mild case may have its advantages. Certainly, the ability to abandon old lives and start fresh, as the immigrants did, can be one. As one descendant of Russian Jews put it after a journey to the impoverished countryside surrounding Moscow, "The main thing I learned going to Russia was that I was glad my ancestors got on the boat." We can be certain that those boats hold more than a few hyperactive adventurers.

By now the broad outlines of attention deficit disorder are familiar to many: ADD is believed to be a flaw in the attentional system that makes it difficult for a child, or a grown-up, to pay attention on command. "On command" is the critical phrase here, because the ADD child can and does hyperfocus at times: he can become locked into a subject or activity (a video game, for example) and be unable to pull himself away. Because the individual with an attention deficit veers from one attentional extreme to the other, from too little attention to too much, some professionals are dissatisfied with the label "attention deficit," which they rightly feel to be a misnomer. The problem is an attentional inconsistency rather than an absolute deficit.

Less well known to the public is the fact that ADD children fall into at least two distinct camps: those with ADHD (attention deficit hyperactivity disorder), and those with ADD-without-the-H. ADHD children are the classic wild-and-woolly little boys (though, of course, some of these children are wild-and-woolly little girls): the children who can't sit still, who blurt out answers in class and show off for the other kids, who get into tussles on the playground, who get all C's and D's when their parents and teachers *know* they're capable of A's and B's. They are the children who do not work up to capacity, and their report cards over the years could practically serve as diagnostic manuals for the syndrome: "Michael could do so much better if he'd try"; "Michael has trouble staying in his chair"; "Michael talks in class"; and so on, down through the years. This is the classically hyperactive little child whom no one can fail to notice. Parents and teachers alike have long complained that these children bounce off walls, and they do.

But people can and do fail to see the attentional problems plaguing this child's dreamy peer, the ADD-child-without-the-H. These are the daydreamers, the children who cannot be seated next to a window. Quietly out of it, they do not jangle the nerves of their teachers, and thus escape the professional scrutiny that rains down upon the head of the noisy little boy in the next row.

But these children may be just as impaired in terms of their ability to thrive in school, and in life outside of school. Often they are girls, who may be underdiagnosed for the disorder. ADD boys outnumber girls by five to one, but these are figures for diagnosed children only; little girls may be slipping through the cracks. Evidence for this can be found in the fact that little girls are demonstrably underdiagnosed for dyslexia, which is often accompanied by ADD. And some theorists of ADD believe that because of brain differences between young boys and girls ADD does not reveal itself in girls until puberty. The calm little girl who abruptly runs wild at adolescence—with eating disorders or promiscuity or a sudden rejection of her studies—may in fact be a child whose ADD has only now broken through. If so, this child will almost certainly go undiagnosed during her grade-school years.

ADD was long thought to be a disorder of childhood, a problem children eventually outgrew sometime in adolescence. But recently that view has changed. We now know that 40 to 60 percent of children do not leave their problems behind; they simply become less visibly restless. Their minds remain frenetic as their bodies calm.

In order to understand the shadow syndrome of ADD, it helps to look at the disorder in its full-blown or frank form. In a florid case of adult ADD, people suffer from a trio of symptoms:

Impulsivity. This is the hallowed developmental concept of "impulse control," perhaps the single most important characteristic distinguishing the child who will be beloved by all from the child who will not. The ADD child simply cannot control his or her impulses as other children can. He runs into streets, blurts out answers without raising his hand, hits the little boy next door. When an impulse to do or say something enters his mind, he does or says it at once, without reflection. For the ADD child, life is a matter of shoot first, ask questions later.

The adult with poor impulse control may have learned to look before crossing, but he continues to suffer from verbal spillage. If it comes into his head to tell his boss he's a jerk, he does; if the words "I can't stand the sight of you" pop into his head during an argument with his spouse, out they come. Precipitous, un-thought-through actions tumble forth as quickly as do his impulsive words: the ADD adult may jump in and out of jobs, relationships, projects, commitments. And, of course, in the worst-case scenario the adult who suffers a frank case of the syndrome can be violent. For the ADD person the reflecting, filtering, censoring mechanism all of us require in order to function in the world is impaired.

Distractibility. Again, this is the little boy or girl who can't sit by the window. ADD children are profoundly distractible; it is very difficult for them to stay on task because *everything* distracts them and throws them off.

The ADD adult suffers from this problem just as fiercely; it can be impossible for an ADD adult to get anything done in a normal work environment, with its ringing telephones and gossiping colleagues. A distractible person may have to go to extraordinary lengths to create an environment that will allow him to concentrate: one woman, a professor with a Ph.D. in history, found she was forced to do all of her writing in the dead of night, while the city slept. Even then she found the hum of her refrigerator intolerably distracting.

Paul, a thirty-eight-year-old real-estate developer diagnosed with an attention deficit only as an adult, describes the scattershot thought processes of ADD in this way:

> It's like being in the TV section of a department store where you're surrounded by thirty-six-inch screens, all playing a different show, all with the volume turned up too high.
>
> Then imagine that on one set they're talking about an assassination attempt on the president's life, and they're not sure whether he's going to live or die, and on another screen there is a boring sitcom. The out-of-control feeling is that your mind will go back and forth between the two even though you're trying to concentrate on the significant event. Your mind is just as likely to focus on the unimportant thing. I feel helpless to make myself focus on what's important.

This happens to people like Paul every hour of every day. They can be in the middle of a life-and-death discussion with a lover or a spouse and suddenly find themselves thinking that they need to wash the car. Not surprisingly, these frequent lapses in interest do not go over well with the long-suffering spouse.

The severe distractibility of the adult with an attention deficit is probably responsible for two other hallmarks of the syndrome: the ADD adult's trouble getting organized, and his tendency to forget whatever it is he or she was doing, thinking, or saying just moments before. The classic ADD adult may live life in a swirl of forgotten errands and obligations as he swerves from one activity, person, or thought to another, unable to alight long enough to bring his efforts to a proper close.

Physical or mental hyperactivity. We all recognize physical hyperactivity: this is the adult who paces, or jiggles his leg, constantly doodles, or bites his nails. Mental hyperactivity is the internal correlate of leg-jiggling. It is the noisy, whirring brain: the person who constantly interrupts; who, in conversation, changes the subject before anyone else is ready to move on; who cannot fall asleep at night because his brain is churning.

Finally, one not-well-understood facet of ADD is that some, though by no means all, of its sufferers show specific deficits in social skills. ADD children may have trouble making or keeping friends, often because they read other children incorrectly, or because they fail to read them at all. A little ADD boy engaged in a pretend fight, for instance, will not take in the cues that say his friend has had enough, and so will not stop when he should. Soon the friend is furious, and the fight is real. The relationship is imperiled.

Why ADD-ers should show a problem reading social cues is not clear, though many assume that this is just one more consequence of the whirring brain: ADD men (and women) may not read body language because they cannot tune in long enough to fully *observe* body language. And because the ADD adult's childhood has passed him by in a whir of activity, this line of reasoning goes, he did not receive the same schoolyard training in reading others that the rest of us did.

However, it is also possible that the ADD person's deficits in social skills are primary, not secondary; that a problem with "social intelligence" is part and parcel of the syndrome. This line of thinking flows directly from the work of cognitive psychologist Howard Gardner who, in *Frames of Mind: The Theory of Multiple Intelligences,* argues that people possess not one general intelligence but many separate intelligences. Social intelligence, the ability to read and comprehend ourselves and the people around us, is one intelligence among at least six, according to Gardner. A person could be relatively "low" in social intelligence yet brilliant in another intelligence, such as the intelligences underlying mathematics or music. Given that biologically based deficits in social abilities may be involved in depression—and are certainly involved in shadow forms of autism—it is entirely possible that some forms of attention deficit disorder also involve differences in the brain's ability to process the social world.

■ THE MILD ONES

In the frank case of adult ADD, these core symptoms can unravel a life. Like their childhood selves, adults suffering from severe ADD do not live up to their potential. When ADD is severe, the wait can be forever, and its sufferer is left feeling bewildered. The classic story of full-blown ADD is the intelligent person who cannot get his life together, and who becomes increasingly demoralized, anxious, and depressed as the years wear on.

But the person with mild ADD may look quite different. The mild ADD-er is not simply the slightly less chaotic twin of his more severely afflicted brother. The mildly ADD person may seem, at first glance, nothing at all like the forty-year-old Mensa member who is still trying to put his intelligence to practical use. Hyperactivity does have its advantages: high energy, high enthusiasm, and the ability to hyperfocus, all of which can take a person to great heights in some realms. Emergency-room physicians, high-risk commodities traders, movie moguls: all of these "types" show symptoms of mild hyperactivity, and many may in fact have subtle forms of the disorder. When a job requires that workers spring from one high-intensity situation to another at lightning speed, a little bit of hyperactivity can be a good thing. And his or her penchant for risk-taking may lead to great success as an entrepreneur or a venture capitalist—or in any career that requires a love of high-risk undertakings. In earlier centuries these people might have become military adventurers or explorers. Thus the mild ADD-er may be a brilliant success in life—at least in his work life—when he makes a good match between his job and his mind's skittery ways. He will doubtless suffer from pockets of disorganization, of course; he may be the top salesman who never gets his paperwork done, or the financial executive who cannot file his own taxes. But for the mild ADD-er these limitations are not crippling.

Beyond the fact that the mildly ADD adult has, by definition, milder problems, he enjoys a further advantage over his severely ADD counterpart as well: an advantage in his ability to perceive and assess those problems in the first place. A disorder like ADD affects thoughts as well as emotions; it strikes at basic cognitive processes. In the case of the ADD adult trying to come to terms with his disorder, the disorganization that afflicts his *thinking* may cause him to look in the mirror and see a globally flawed human being. This is "noise" in the mirror, noise interfering with the coherent, detailed, and nuanced sense of self. The mildly hyperactive adult, in contrast, enjoys the good fortune of being able to survey himself and see something far more precise, and real: a hard worker, say, who misses deadlines, and who needs to find ways to compensate for this flaw. In other words, the mildly ADD adult is able to form a coherent and integrated self-image, consisting of coherent strengths and weaknesses. But for the severely hyperactive person, thoughts and perceptions can be so blurred that it is difficult for him to organize anything, including his own sense of self.

Thus the mildly ADD adult is, for instance, the disorganized person who can purchase a book on how to organize his life—and then actually use that book to go ahead and organize his life. He, or she, is able to compensate for his failings in ways that elude the severely ADD person. Having better control over his "attentional apparatus," he can pay attention to his weak areas, and to his strategies for self-improvement, long enough to make his life work. Thus the mildly ADD executive might deliberately cultivate a virtual obsession with his datebook, checking and rechecking it many times throughout the day. While the mildly ADD adult has a great deal of difficulty remembering all that he is supposed to do, the mildness of his attention deficit does allow him to "remember to remember"; his memory works well enough to keep him coming back to the memory aids without which he would be lost.

■□ A THERAPIST'S STORY

But while the mild ADD-er can often excel in work, his private life may be a different matter. As with so many of the subsyndromes, the real trouble can register in the social realm. Debby, a fifty-year-old former therapist, perfectly captures the fine-at-work/miserable-at-home dichotomy mildly ADD professionals may confront.

For many years, Debby was a wonderful therapist. She had excelled in her training throughout school, and when she began her own analysis, quickly became the darling of the analytic community. She was a rising star in her city's therapeutic community.

One reason for her success was her ability to focus upon other people's problems. As she puts it, she was not only a good listener but an intense one: she could concentrate fully, and profoundly, upon her clients' lives. She offered the same rapt attention to her friends, and spent many years of her life deeply engaged in their troubles as well.

Unfortunately, her extraordinary ability to empathize with other people's lives, while a boon to her clients, was destructive to her: "They got better, and I got worse," as she puts it. The problem was that her capacity for listening grew out of her undiagnosed ADD. As is true of most ADD-ers, mild or not, Debby tended to be environmentally dependent. Like the textbook "stimulus-bound" patient who can see only the red splotch in the Rorschach blot, Debby was riveted by the problems her patients and friends brought to her. For Debby those problems were the red splotch, and she had no choice but to see them, think about them, *live* them. As she says:

> We who have ADD find other people very contagious. I would sit with clients and take problems in at levels I didn't even know. I became my clients, the way we become our children.

In terms of the architecture of her life, this meant that Debby was ricocheting from one life crisis to another not so much because therapy was her chosen profession but because other people's life crises so powerfully ensnared her attention. In essence, Debby could not stop plugging in to other people's lives. While she wanted nothing more than to develop a second career as a writer, she simply could not get her writing done in the downtime between sessions with clients and friends; the life dramas were too compelling, her control over her "attentional apparatus" too weak. She could not focus her attention at will; she could not sit down at her desk in the morning, before her day's work as a therapist began, and write a page of polished prose. For Debby the result of her irresistible pull to the stimulus of other people's lives was a growing demoralization that would ultimately become a major depression.

And, as the years went by, her private life worsened steadily. Shortly after she had finally stopped seeing patients in order to devote herself full-time to her writing, she met and married a man who, she now sees, was himself suffering from the syndrome, and a full-blown version of it at that. He was wildly ADD in both the best and the worst senses of the term: flamboyant, energetic, and an enormous amount of fun, but completely irresponsible and unable to see any project through to its end. He always had schemes up his sleeve, but in reality what he was doing was sitting around the house, smoking marijuana (marijuana being the drug of choice for many hyperactive adults, and a particularly destructive one). (Generally speaking, when individuals with ADD abuse drugs, they will choose either marijuana—which calms them down—or stimulants such as cocaine and amphetamine—which, as we will see, bring sluggish areas of brain metabolism up to speed. All three provide temporary relief, but ultimately they create more problems than they solve.) None of his big dreams came to pass, and Debby's savings supported them both.

Not surprisingly, the marriage did not work. And, during the years that it was not working, Debby slid into a torpor. Technically diagnosed as being clinically depressed, she was so unhappy that she very nearly reached a condition of retarded depression, meaning a person who is, quite literally, not moving. "I did nothing for my entire marriage," she says today. Thus her marriage spanned six years of profound passivity, years in which the most activity she could muster was to lie in her bed, reading. Needless to say, nothing came of her writing during this period. When she was finally referred to John, he saw a woman sitting in a chair, looking dead.

■□ PAYING ATTENTION TO ATTENTION

It was John who first suggested a diagnosis of attention deficit disorder to Debby. This was a leap, since Debby was so obviously, manifestly, *depressed.* But while her previous doctor, a friend of John's, had been valiantly attempting to treat her depression, nothing had worked. Antidepressant medication, the obvious choice, did not touch her suffering and in fact seemed to make matters worse.

Her doctor referred Debby to John because he had begun to wonder whether another angle of vision might be what was needed: specifically, a way of seeing that looked at Debby's cognitive, or thought, processes as much as at her affective, or emotional, processes.

In this sense, attention deficit disorder is not simply one more diagnosis on the books; it is a new kind of diagnosis, a diagnosis that stands the usual psychiatric hierarchy of emotions first, and all else second, on its head. In "paying attention to attention," ADD researchers challenge one of the most fundamental orthodoxies of contemporary psychiatry: the primacy of mood in determining who functions well and who does not.

For most psychiatrists mood is the primary category in assessing a patient; when a new patient arrives in his office, the psychiatrist will automatically look for problems in affect, as his training has taught him to do. He is unlikely even to suspect problems in the brain's thinking and perceiving apparatus. But psychiatrists with a strong working knowledge of ADD are looking for something different: they are seeking the flaws in basic mental processing capacities that may *result,* secondarily, in painful affect.

The ramifications of this reversal can be profound, and were for Debby. With John the question now became whether beneath Debby's obvious and undeniable depression there lay a different problem altogether, a problem with attention that was creating her all-consuming mood disorder. And indeed there was: Debby was a mildly hyperactive adult. But even her mild variant of the disorder had been sufficient to stymie her writing ambitions for many years, and to produce her over-involvement in other people's problems. This combination, the writing lifeless on the desk while the writer tends to her woe-ridden comrades on the telephone, was lethal, a certain recipe for the severe depression she would go on to develop.

John's diagnosis of ADD offered Debby a very different explanation of her problems. Like most patients in therapy, Debby simply assumed that her depression had its origin in her childhood. She attributed her problems to a poor relationship with her mother, a rigid and control-ling woman who had pretty much devoted herself to snuffing out the spirit in her boisterous teenage daughter. This analysis seemed logical enough; certainly, a bad relationship with one's mother has produced many a depressed adult daughter.

And yet for Debby the process of working through this relationship in therapy, which she had been doing for some twenty-odd years when she met John, had produced no relief at all. For John the most signifi-cant sign that a diagnosis of ADD might be justified in Debby's case was her lifelong inability to see long projects through to their end. In-stead of setting reasonable goals and meeting them, she would jump into a writing project with both feet only to find her initial energy and enthusiasm fading as yet another idea or writing project was aban-doned. Her environmental dependency was no help in this realm, as it was in her work as a therapist, because virtually all of her writing was self-motivated. (This is not to say that you can't be a writer and have ADD, but if you do have ADD, and want to write, you will probably do best working under tight deadlines imposed by an editor—a situa-tion in which you have strong environmental demand.) And, spending most of her time offtrack, Debby was profoundly bored as well as de-pressed. In short: she was not functioning well intellectually; she was not showing the kind of commitment to work, to a life's ambition, with which a person of her abilities would normally be blessed.

And, as the two went further in their talks, John found that while Debby was physically very quiet—hypoactive, even—she was mentally frenetic. Outwardly, she presented as a person suffering from a retarded depression. But inwardly, her brain was constantly churning, searching continuously for a focus. Mentally, she could not sit still for a moment, except when hyperfocused upon the life stories of her patients and friends.

Taken together, the inability to complete a project and the internal hyperactivity were sufficient to establish the diagnosis. For Debby, herself a psychoanalytically trained therapist, this way of seeing her life and her problems was nothing short of revolutionary. For the first time in forty-odd years, she was going to therapy and *not* talking about her mother. Now Debby began the work of taking a second look at her life, of seeing it all—her work issues, her marriage issues, her childhood issues—through the lens of her brain's basic thought processes. And, as she suspended her assumptions about her mother's all-pervading influence, she began to understand her depression differently.

To begin, as she saw more clearly how her attention deficit had thwarted her life's ambition of becoming a writer, she began to understand her depression as a reasonable response to a hidden handicap. Just as a blind person might grow depressed over being blind, Debby now saw that she had grown depressed over being blocked by her brain's difficulties in sustaining focus.

Beyond this she began to realize that her experience of depression was different from the classic depressive's experience of depression. In clinical depression the depressed mood is pervasive, and unremitting. A clinically depressed person stays depressed, no matter what the circumstances; clinical depression is not responsive to environment.

But an attention deficit depression is highly responsive to environment, so much so that when something in the environment captures his interest, a depressed person with ADD can actually forget that he was depressed just minutes before. In attention deficit disorder, mood is enormously changeable. This was true of Debby. When she began to think about how her black moods actually worked—as opposed to what may have caused them in the first place—she saw that in fact her depressions lifted quite easily under the proper circumstances. Environmentally dependent, she could be thrown into utter despair by a bad environment, lifted back out by a good one. As she explains:

Part of ADD is being field-dependent, meaning you merge with the environment. I began to see that the depression was not as severe as it felt, because if you threw me into a different environment, I wouldn't have been depressed.

Locked into a bad marriage, Debby was an environmentally dependent woman in love, which meant that she was profoundly affected, in every possible way, by her bad marriage. She was *more* depressed by her flawed marriage, in short, than a non-ADD woman would have been by the very same marriage: more depressed because she had no mental or emotional independence from whatever drama was going on around her. Unable to separate herself from her marriage in any way, she had lapsed into severe depression.

Worse yet, she was pushed even further down by the ADD person's tendency to hyperfocus: she had hyperfocused on her own depression, becoming, in a real sense, addicted to her despair. She was obsessed by her depression, could think of nothing else—not only because of the pain, but because, for the scattered ADD soul, a powerful depression can be a uniquely centering condition. For Debby, it was.

Thus, whatever role her childhood had played in her grown-up pain, the *processes* of Debby's mind, far more than the content of her childhood, were now driving her breakdown. And it was these processes that needed a therapist's attention.

Convinced, Debby accepted a prescription for Cylert, one of the stimulants which, like Ritalin, is highly effective in the treatment of ADD:

It didn't work at first. I felt totally wired and my brain froze even more. I think in some ways the medication makes the ADD worse; I'm a little more chaotic, my room's a little messier. But two months after I was on it, I could sit down in the morning and write for five hours. I had my attention span.

And, almost miraculously, her depression lifted:

The medication definitely lifts my spirits, though I'm not sure whether that's because it just lifts my spirits, or because it allows me to write and *that* lifts my spirits. I'm fairly certain it lifts my spirits because it lets me write.

This was a revelation to her: nothing had changed about her childhood, a topic John did not encourage her to discuss at great length in therapy, and yet here she was, a new woman. A new woman because of a change in her capacity to focus. The mood followed her thought processes. Within a very short time after beginning to take the Cylert, and learning various methods for coping with ADD, she had at long last launched a highly visible and successful career as a journalist. It was a startling, and lovely, second act.

And, we might add, it was a career launch that was quintessentially ADD: she began her new life's work by flying to a war zone halfway across the globe and setting herself up as a freelance war correspondent. The ADD brain seeks stimulation, and there are few human experiences more stimulating than war.

Today, three years after having received the diagnosis of attention deficit disorder, Debby has given a great deal of thought to the miracle bestowed upon her:

> I'm an unusual version of a hyperactive person in that I had tons and tons of psychoanalysis. And in psychoanalysis there was the concept of the observing ego, of the therapist and client working together to build the observing ego. I started analysis at nineteen and finished at twenty-nine, and I did build that ego. So I think for me psychoanalysis was in a way a treatment for ADD, even though that was not what we were working on. I think a lot of people with ADD are not quite so self-aware as psychoanalysis made me be; I had had this intensive training in being able to observe myself. Without those ten years I would look very different today; without them I would have been far more chaotic, far less conscious and less observant, much more dictated by moods.
>
> But at the same time analysis was bad because the introspection made me more depressed. I tend to get riveted by the dark side of life, which then gets called depression. But in my case my obsession with the dark side is actually, I now believe, a cognitive thing. It's part of my deeper problems with focus. So for me self-observation was a double-edged sword.

Today, with the diagnosis, the medication, the analysis, I've gained an emotional intelligence I didn't have before. For the first time, I have a sense of the context. If I'm in the country and a bleak feeling is coming upon me, I don't say "I'm a terrible person" and then start ruminating about everything bad that ever happened to me. Now I can just say "It's a gray day" and know that I need more stimulation in order to cheer up.

Debby has also given thought to the nature of a *mild* case of ADD, as opposed to the frank case that derailed her ex-husband's life.

I think most people with florid ADD can't make a decision. Life decides for them, and they're so stimulus-bound that the problem child or the difficult husband becomes *it,* becomes the whole day. They can't fight it off. With mild ADD you can make a decision about whether something is going to be central.

I think, too, that there is something about form. The fully ADD people I know can't achieve form—in the work itself, in the day, in not letting the negative stimulus throw them completely. And the confidence that you can structure your day or your mood or your life, or your words on a page, is everything.

■ WHAT DO WOMEN WANT?

One of the themes that rapidly emerges in thinking about the milder forms of ADD is the question of women. Sooner or later, when you talk to women who have been diagnosed with the disorder, you experience a shock of recognition: so many of the problems they describe, problems stemming from their attention deficits, sound so familiar. The woman who only falls in love with married men, the woman who is brilliant at her job but miserable in love, the mad housewife: all of these cultural types may, sometimes, evolve out of an undiagnosed and unsuspected case of mild attention deficit disorder.

To start with the effects of ADD upon romance, the love life of the mildly ADD woman (and certainly of the frankly ADD woman) is fraught with difficulty; there is just no way around it. Though here she may enjoy an advantage over her male counterpart. Because the left brain is more robust in little girls, they are better able to compensate for the basic disorder of ADD, particularly for any deficits in social intelligence. (The phenomenon of women having milder versions of disorders that are quite serious in males occurs with other disorders as well, fragile-X syndrome being a notable example.)

Thus for the mildly ADD woman, her problem may not be alienating people she wants to attract: she may have figured out, as a child, how to make and keep friends in spite of her ADD. She is probably not going to be a social klutz, and her ADD-ish energy levels and enthusiasm can give her a high-voltage appeal. But she may still have problems in the subtler social realm of deciding whom to approach and whom to avoid. She may choose the wrong man to love, and may do so repeatedly, in part because she is in fact not absorbing all the social cues other women see right from the start.

Or, in another variant on the ADD constellation, she may actually be picking up too many cues. With her difficulties in filtering, she may simply be getting too much information about everyone she meets. She finds herself unable to parse the essentials, a skill the non-ADD woman may take for granted. When you have a sea of data on any new prospective date, at least some of it will be good, just as some of it will be bad. Drowning in dating semiotics, the ADD woman ends up not being able to tell the home team from the visitors.

But beyond whatever problems she may face in terms of social intelligence, she may actually select *for* trouble in her choice of mate. Here the ADD woman's tremendous need for stimulation can reap a whirlwind. Perhaps the single most important reason why a mildly hyperactive woman will choose men who are bad for her is that they hold her interest in a way that the "boring" (and this is the term she will employ) nice guy does not. Some women know this about themselves; they will say that they need a man with "edge." Depending upon the woman, edge might mean a rock star or an entertainment executive or a brooding poet, but whatever form it takes, these women know quite precisely what they do not want: They do not want Ozzie Nelson. They do not want a calm and steady presence who leaves them feeling starved for stimulation.

Aided and abetted by the voluminous self-help publishing industry in this country, such women may believe that their "bad" preferences come from having had bad childhoods, or from being too ambitious and creative to "settle" for the nice guy, or from being smart women who make foolish choices. But what they will not suspect is that their romantic choices may stem from a biological source, namely a defect in their brain's attentional apparatus.

One of John's patients, a highly successful career woman who had spent twenty years falling for the wrong man, finally came for help when she found herself in danger of alienating the one good man whom she had finally been able to love. She told John about her most recent unhappy evening with this man, the kind of evening, she was coming to see, that happened to her more than to most.

After she had endured a very stressful week at work, her lover had fixed her a wonderful meal: wine, good food, candlelight; all this to be followed by a massage. It was a fantasy production, the kind of evening about which most women can only dream. It was her dream, too, she thought, and so she was horrified to find herself subtly, but stubbornly, sabotaging the mood. She could not relax, could not unwind; she could not feel good about this man's obvious love for her. Soon she began to pick at him, challenging little things he said, replying a bit sharply to benign remarks, failing to respond at all to others. And she kept at this until she had provoked a fight. The evening was ruined.

She came to John for help. For all of her trouble relaxing into a loving relationship, she did not want to return to the turbulent loves of her life thus far; she wanted to stabilize in love, at last. If she destroyed this relationship, she knew it would mean a swift and certain regression to the men who didn't call, the confirmed bachelors, the recently divorced. And she knew that in the troubles that now threatened her present relationship, it was she who was stirring the pot.

The diagnosis of ADD came as a revelation to her, although she was certainly no stranger to its symptoms: she had always thought herself hyper in the ordinary sense of the term. But she had not made the connection between being hyper and falling in love with men who were not good for her. What she was to learn was that for her, as for many mildly ADD women, "bad" men were highly stimulating in every way, up to and including her brain's biochemistry. She was a woman, in short, who was self-medicating not with cocaine or amphetamine, but with the drug of a bad relationship. This is why people with ADD marry other people with ADD, as Debby did: they choose each other for the high stimulation a person with ADD will reliably provide.

Life changed radically once she received a diagnosis and began treatment. Now, for the first time, she could sit still; she could tolerate a calm day in the presence of a benevolent love. She could do more than merely tolerate a calm relationship with a good man; she could actually enjoy quiet time in love. The difference was so startling that she took to calling the medication she had been prescribed her "love potion." Without it she could not love a man worth loving.

■□ THE MAD HOUSEWIFE

Turning from the world of dating to the world of marriage, even a very mild case of ADD can take a serious toll on a woman's capacity to live with the role of wife-and-mother. Put simply, the hyperactive woman is likely to find the low-stim life of naps and diapers difficult in the extreme. It is not just that the hyper woman will tend to grow bored when tied to the house. She will also find her mood, as well as her internal sense of mental acuity, declining as well. This is so because the mildly ADD woman who stays at home with children has essentially given up her medicine of high stimulation in the larger world outside. Because an unmedicated ADD-er cannot focus well, the ADD housewife's focus slips, confusion results, and anxiety inevitably follows. Confusion breeds doubt, which in turn breeds worry.

And, too, the distractions inherent in full-time motherhood are extremely difficult for the woman who is even mildly ADD. Looked at from the perspective of ADD, children are full-time distraction machines: their needs are never predictable, and one of their main functions in life is to interrupt their parents.

People with no attentional problems can weather this aspect of parenthood; they can remember where they were before each interruption. But the ADD mother is going to find herself continually, ongoingly, chronically not remembering what she was doing, where she was going, what she was thinking. Worse still, the role of homemaker requires tremendous organizational skills. When you have an attention deficit—even when you do not have an attention deficit—a house quickly becomes one big barn of a place for things to be lost in. Toys, bills, remote controls: to the ADD brain, the amount of sheer stuff to keep track of is overwhelming. As the ADD mother finds herself chronically searching for the application forms to summer camp, or the bottle of prescription cough syrup she thought she locked up in the lockbox, or the keys to the car she thought she put back in her purse, she can skid into a state of perpetual aggravation. And of course, the irritability that can also be an intrinsic part of even mild ADD does not help when it comes to withstanding the daily annoyances of running and maintaining a household.

And last, but far from least, the life of the full-time homemaker can play hell with a mildly ADD woman's environmental dependency. She is likely to feel a grating "pull to the stimulus" each time she sets foot in a messy room, and with children and pets (perhaps we should add husbands here, too) underfoot, rooms are always going to be messy. As one woman describes this phenomenon:

> I'll walk in the kitchen and I'll see the dirty dishes and I'll think, "Oh, I *have* to do those dishes, but then on my way out to the garage to get some more dish detergent, I'll pass the laundry basket and think, "Oh, I *have* to do the laundry," but then I'll start sorting laundry and I'll see a torn sock and I'll think, "Oh I *have* to mend this sock". . . and I feel so bad all the time that I'm not getting any of it done.

This woman, suffering from an acute case of ADD, actually felt so overwhelmed by her house that she could not speak of it without crying. While a mildly ADD woman will probably not be driven to tears by the demands of her physical surroundings, she, too, is going to have trouble walking through her house without feeling bombarded by *things that need doing.* For the mildly ADD woman, being somebody's lover may be a far sight easier than being somebody's wife or somebody's mother.

Finally, for the married woman with ADD, the need to nurture her family can easily consume her every waking moment, just as it did for Debby during her years as a therapist. As one of John's patients, a woman who was not diagnosed with attention deficit until her midforties (and only after both of her children were in treatment for the disorder), wrote:

> I inherited, was apprenticed and indoctrinated into, the role of the caretaking, sacrificing female. My liberated friends have always told me that I do too much. For my husband and children. And my mother. Even my friends who work seem to manage their own lives and families with room left over for themselves. I have none.
>
> I have devoured over one hundred self-help books, from John Bradshaw to Norman Vincent Peale, and have not felt any happier about myself or managed to make my own life any smoother. Counseling and therapy were fairly useless, basically a means of weathering the current storm. But always, my frenetic return to the business of caretaking took the first priority. Like an addiction!

This woman, like many ADD-ers, is controlled by cues from her environment, driven by her environment rather than by her internal sense of self. And because her environment is so rich in other people's problems, she organizes around those people and their needs. Her friends are right: she *is* doing too much, but not (entirely) because she has been raised in the doctrine of female sacrifice. As she herself notes, her friends have been raised with the same teachings, yet all are managing to find time for themselves. More than that: her friends experience themselves as having lives of their own, rather than living for and through the lives of others.

Thus the giving part of motherhood can be problematic for the ADD mother because of her tendency to become, as this patient says, addicted to the drama of others. As with all addictions, of course, an addiction to other people's problems does offer its pleasures: the ADD mother's overinvolvement in her family's lives may help her to feel calmer, better organized. In short, her environmental dependency can be both a primary symptom of her disorder *and* a defense against its chaotic force. This is precisely what John's patient discovered when she finally received a diagnosis and began treatment. As she writes:

> After treatment, I understood that my role as wife and mother helped me stay focused, kept me from boredom, and let me channel my enormous energy into everyone else's projects and daily emergencies.

Her complete immersion in the role of caretaker served the same, self-medicating purpose a chemical addiction can. Just as an addiction to cocaine can calm and organize the hyperactive person, an addiction to the highly stimulating drama of a loved one's problems has calmed and organized many a hyperactive mother.

■□ THE SLUGGISH BRAIN

For most people, of course, a drug like cocaine, or a behavior like overinvolvement in other people's problems, would be far from calming. For the "normal" brain both cocaine and family problems are stimulants pure and simple: things that work you up, not soothe you down.

But the biology of the ADD brain is different. In the most famous inquiry into the neurobiology of ADD to date, researcher Alan J. Zametkin of the National Institute of Mental Health discovered that, in attention deficit disorder, the problem lies in the brain's metabolism. Interestingly, his results run counter to what we might expect: in the frontal lobes of the brain (the same general region involved in rage disorders) the hyperactive person's brain metabolism is not faster than other people's, but slower. In other words, the brain's frontal-lobe metabolism, in ADD, is sluggish. Thus, for many of the adult hyperactives Zametkin studied, the area of the brain that controls attention, motor impulses, and the capacity to inhibit impulses was discovered to be metabolizing sugar—sugar being to the brain what gasoline is to the car—at a rate 10 to 12 percent slower than that of a normal person's. The brain needs energy to keep mind and body focused. Without that energy, thoughts and actions spin out of control.

Zametkin's discovery may explain why stimulant medications like Ritalin work to control the symptoms of attention deficit disorder. It now seems likely that Ritalin, Dexedrine, and Cylert work by bringing the brain's metabolism up to speed. They do this by boosting levels of the neurotransmitters dopamine and norepinephrine—which explains why certain antidepressants can and do treat ADD as well. Norpramin, Effexor, and Wellbutrin—all antidepressant medications that also affect dopamine and norepinephrine levels—are also established treatments for attention deficit disorder. Not surprisingly, a street drug like cocaine, which raises dopamine, can work in the same way—and indeed, Dr. Walid Shekim, chief of child and adolescent psychopharmacology at the Neuropsychiatric Institute at UCLA and an authority on ADD, cites a calming effect from cocaine as an indicator that a diagnosis of ADD is warranted. He recalls one young man who told him: "When my friends take cocaine, they get high. When I take cocaine, I get serious." (Of course, cocaine is not, in the long run, a good treatment for ADD. Apart from the fact that it is illegal, it affects too much of the brain, going far beyond the dopamine system in its effects. And it is extremely addictive; it is as addictive as nicotine, another drug of choice in ADD. Surveys show that the rate of smoking among ADD population is three times that among the non-ADD population. In contrast, although Ritalin is federally classified as a controlled substance, it is virtually nonaddictive.)

By the same reasoning, a mild ADD-er might well find ways to self-medicate through stimulating behaviors. Adults with frank cases of ADD are notorious risk-takers; they are attracted to any situation that shocks the brain, whether it be race-car driving or corporate deal-making or shouting matches with loved ones. Always, the intensely ADD among us feel calmest and most organized during these high-stakes moments. Mildly ADD people may self-medicate with milder dramas, of which, within marriage, the daily micromanagement of a family's needs and troubles would certainly be one, or, outside marriage, the choosing of difficult people as lovers. Either life choice will produce for the ADD adult a necessary jolt, a biologically soothing life drama. Either will focus the ADD brain.

■ MEN, LOVE, AND ADD

Of all the shadow syndromes in this book, it is entirely possible that ADD causes the most trouble between the sexes. The connection between ADD and romantic problems first occurred to John a few years back, when he met with a male patient who opened by saying that he had read all the books on men who can't be intimate. "I am that man," he told John. "I can't be trusted, I can't develop an intimate connection." He felt tremendously guilty over his inability to sustain intimacy either with a woman or with his children, and he had come for treatment of this problem.

In fact, his real problem was a frank case of adult hyperactivity. He could not be intimate because he could not sit still long enough to achieve intimacy. He could not bear quiet time in a room, and found it intolerable to sit with his children or his wife because he literally could not do it, just as a hyperactive child cannot sit still to do his schoolwork. This man was failing in his personal life for the same reason a hyperactive child may fail in school: he could not pay attention.

From this fundamental deficit in the ADD male flow numerous failings we may attribute simply to his being a man: not listening, not tuning into feelings, not remembering to put the dishes in the dishwasher. But not all men have trouble listening or tuning in to feelings or remembering to bus their dishes, and a man who does have these problems may need a second look. The problem may lie not in his maleness, but in the workings of his brain. The fact is, a man who has a neurological problem with attention is not going to be any more "attentive" when it comes to love and marriage than he was to school as a little boy. And when the disorder goes undiagnosed, the ADD adult's lack of attentiveness looks like a lack of love and consideration. It looks like a character defect: a specifically *male* character defect.

It is not that the male ADD-er is unaware of the problems. Dave, a pharmaceutical sales manager who was diagnosed in his forties, is acutely aware of his own problems with intimacy:

> Say I'm here in my office and I'm thinking about my life because that's what I'm focusing on at the minute and I want to share my realizations with my wife. Yet when I'm home in bed with her, I'm probably already thinking about something going on in the office, so to her there's this cold, unfeeling person she's married to next to her in bed. She's talking to me and it's going right over my head.

Add the ADD male's forgetting problem to his intimacy problem, and you quickly uncover a group of thoroughly exasperated wives. Dave says,

> I'll tell my wife I'm going to the store to pick up a few things, and she'll say get some Philadelphia cream cheese, a loaf of bread, and a gallon of milk. Maybe even just walking out the door I've forgotten one item, and by the time I reach the store I've forgotten all three. You have to survive on notes.

Needless to say, where distractibility, restlessness, and impulsivity can be difficult qualities within a marriage, in the dating world they can be outright fatal. And any couple, married or not, struggling with undiagnosed ADD can quickly be sucked into a cycle of recrimination and guilt that does nothing to alleviate the situation. Without a genuine understanding of the disorder driving these behaviors, neither partner can take the steps they need to work around it.

■ THE BIKER WITH THE HEART OF GOLD

To some degree, what form a shadow syndrome—or a full-blown case—will take depends upon a person's upbringing and background.

A blue-collar boy with ADD, either mild or severe, will tend to look different from an upper-middle-class boy with the same difference in the brain, because their respective cultures channel their problems and energies differently. And the blue-collar boy with ADD will grow up to become a different "type" than the white-collar boy with ADD.

Rick Walker, an electrician living in New Jersey, grew up as the mildly ADD child of blue-collar workers. Like so many adults with ADD, especially those with relatively mild cases, he was diagnosed only after one of his children—his second daughter, a little girl born very prematurely while Rick and his wife were stationed in Germany—was diagnosed. "She was two pounds, fifteen ounces when she was born," he remembers, "and we had to take her for physical therapy all the way through her early years. Then when she got to school, she had problems in kindergarten and first grade. She was very distractible, she was in her own little world." Nicole was extremely bright: her language scores were very high and her IQ tested at 148. But she was faring so badly in school that her teachers recommended she repeat first grade.

Rick was able to argue his child's way into second grade, but there her problems grew worse:

> So the evaluators suggested we take her to the Children's Hospital in Boston, where they deal with lots of preemies and kids with emotional problems. And as the person there was talking to my daughter about her problems, I'm getting all these little zaps in my head, thinking this happened to me as a kid.

Nicole was given a diagnosis of ADD, and from that day on, Rick wondered whether the ADD label might apply to him. He could see how important the diagnosis was to his daughter's functioning:

> We put her on Ritalin and the first night she seemed very wired— she had dilated eyes—and I sat with her all night, just watching her eyes. My wife got all nervous, but I said let's give it a shot. In two

weeks she seemed to get used to it, and then her marks started to improve. Right now her grades are unbelievable, and without it her teacher will tell you she bounces off walls. She hums to herself, she's giggling.

And I'm thinking to myself, I'm still doing these things! So I went to my doctor, and him and I always bump heads. I have high blood pressure, and he'd always take my blood and I hated that, and he'd tell me to stop smoking and I didn't listen. I said to him my daughter was diagnosed with ADD and I think I might have this. And for me to admit this to anybody was amazing.

Rick asked for a referral to someone who specialized in ADD, and eventually landed in John's office, where John did indeed diagnose him with a mild case of ADD. (His daughter's severe prematurity probably made her case worse.) Rick's problems were mild in that they did not prevent him from holding a job, or from marrying and having children. Although school was a struggle ("I had very good potential, but I was an underachiever; I was told that all along"), he made it through, graduating from high school and joining the army at eighteen.

He also stayed out of trouble for the most part. Although his father had died when he was seven, and his working mother had little control over him, he managed to avoid serious difficulty with the law. Nevertheless, he did manifest even the mild ADD-er's love of rule-breaking:

> In fifth grade I skipped school for two weeks, stayed home, and made keys to get into buildings; I could use a file to make the keys fit the lock, and I had an oatmeal can full of keys.

Rick's dedication to this kind of activity cost him friends:

> I never could hang out with the kids who were smarter, because I acted childish and they saw me as a child. So the normal kids would shun me off, so I had to hang out with the not-normal kids, and I got along with them because they were always up to something. Let's go get a fake ID, let's go buy some beer, that kind of thing. They'd call the cops on themselves so they could get chased, tell the cops they were raising hell.

Not surprisingly, Rick was a fighter, too: "I would pick a fight with anybody," he remembers today. "I used to focus on the fighting and like the excitement of it." For Rick, fighting wasn't about revenge or status in his teenage community, it was about mental stimulation. It was a rush.

In Rick's life we can see the influence of culture: While Rick's after-school life would shock many an upper-middle-class parent, within the boundaries of his world he was never truly over the line. For all his rabble-rousing he was doing no more than flirting with the law; he was, and was seen as, at heart a good kid. Being a good kid, he attracted the help he needed. There was the grade-school teacher who believed in him and "could get me to do things"; there was the principal who sat him down and talked sense to him about his attempt to enlist in the Army before the age of eighteen ("He'd been in the Marines," Rick says, laughing, "and he told me, 'You're out of your mind—you don't want to see your friends getting killed.' And I'm saying in my mind, *Yes I do!* It sounded like an adventure"); there was the teacher who ran the STEP program that allowed Rick to attend school half a day and work the other half. "It was kids like me," Rick says of the program, "all hoods, always up to something. I loved it. He took us under his wing."

After high school Rick got his wish. "It was 1972," he reports, "and I figured I could still catch Vietnam if I hurried." So he enlisted. Of course, the fact that Rick wanted to go to Vietnam when so many of his peers were devising every conceivable strategy to stay out is probably reason enough for a differential diagnosis of ADD: Rick was driven by the ADD-er's need to see *action.*

His career in the military was also typical of a mildly ADD recruit. Always, he did his best under circumstances of high pressure, high stimulation. His tour of duty in Germany was the peak of his Army experience for that reason:

Over in Germany it's a whole lot different than in the states because you actually have a mission there—the Wall was there. I was really gung-ho: Kill Russians. Be prepared. You'd have alerts at two in the morning—I loved it. When we'd get alerts, they'd call up on the phone and give the code, and I'd slip in the tape *Apocalypse Now* with the Doors singing. Jim Morrison's letting it go and this would psych me up, I was pumped. I loved my job.

Rick's work involved solving field problems:

The field problems were a challenge to see how far we could push the artillery pieces without them breaking down. If you have four guns and two break down, you don't have enough. So we drew a field problem where if a gun broke down I had it fixed before a twenty-four-hour deadline. We'd enter the field problem with four guns and come out with four guns because I could fix them so fast.

But if Germany was to be the pinnacle of his Army career, the backwaters of Texas were to be the nadir.

I finished my tour and got orders for Texas, Fort Hood. I didn't want to go. I started hearing about stateside duty: you don't want it because it's all show and pony. So right off the bat I'm saying, Oh man, here we go. In Texas, the minute I get there, I meet the sergeant and the guy says this is not like Germany, forget everything about Germany, this is Fort Hood now. Get your uniform straight, cut your hair—it was show and go. People coming to visit, make sure the guns are parked in line, all this menial stuff. Other guys said, "If you leave here with the same rank you came in with, you're doing real good."

Show and go being just about the last form of human activity with which the restless ADD soul is equipped to deal, Rick attracted trouble like a magnet:

I didn't fit in. They looked like ass-kissers there. "Let's go and sit in the first sergeant's office and kiss butt and say yes to everything." I'm not like this. I feel I should be able to do a job and not have to kiss your butt to get by.

I could just tell this was going to be it for me. To get promoted to E-7 you have to take a photograph and they look at it with a microscope to see if your mustache is right, and your ribbons are straight.

And I never did it. I started to get counseling statements. If you do something wrong, it gets written down and you have to agree or not agree to it and it goes in your record. One officer said, "I can ruin your career"—a West Point kid—and I said, "Is that right?" and he said, "That's right," and I knew someone was gunning for my blood. I wanted to be the rough-tough NCO I was in Germany and get the job done. Here I was back in high school where I had to fit in.

We had a gun breakdown, and I disobeyed an order to use a wrecker to pull the engine because I knew it wasn't safe. I used the A-frame, which takes longer, but it's certified for that poundage. That was my attitude: We're going to do it my way.

So my commanding officer takes me aside and says it's your fault these guys are working late—it's nighttime and we're working with flashlights—so he's going to counsel me. I said, "Do what you want," and here I go with a counseling statement. I had never gotten a counseling statement my whole time in Germany; I was a good soldier.

Things went from bad to worse. Rick nearly threw a punch at a lieutenant involved in the counseling statement: he was saved from himself only by the intervention of an older sergeant who had taken a liking to him.

My battalion motor sergeant liked me. He was an old sergeant, had twenty-eight years in, just trying to wait for his retirement, didn't want any problems. He yelled out his window, "Walker, can I talk to you?" And when I got inside, he said, "You were going to hit that man—you're crazy."

But kindly battalion motor sergeants or no, Rick was not temperamentally suited to stateside duty, and he knew it. He was impatient, he was restless, he was looking for action. The field exercises in Germany had contained and channeled all his wild ADD impulses, but at Fort Hood his frustrations drove him to the point of blurting out to his first sergeant, who was Hispanic, that "the only mission we have here is keeping the Mexicans from crossing the border":

I didn't mean to say that, but I did. So then we had Sergeant Walker the rebel, not going to listen to anybody. Which is true, but in other units I did that and they liked it. So I said, "When my time comes, I'm out." I let my time expire before I reenlisted. People said, "You're crazy, you've got twelve years in active service." You have to be in twenty years to retire, but I left. I could have stuck it out, but I couldn't deal with it. People to this day can't believe it.

Rick's married life has suffered from the same issues: hotheadedness, impatience, impulsiveness. When he and Mary met, Rick was between stints in the Army, working at a well-paying city job his neighbors, who admired his military service, had helped him to get. Nights he spent hanging out at a local biker bar.

I couldn't believe that Mary liked me. She was a nice girl from the right side of the tracks, and I was from the wrong side. I was in love; I used to pick her flowers and put them in beer cans. She loved it.

We dated for a year and I asked her to marry me. I got off my motorcycle and got down on one knee and proposed. Here was someone who would accept me for who I was. Her mom didn't want anything to do with me—she wanted me to park my Harley behind the house.

After the wedding they discovered that "accepting someone for who he is" is easier in courtship than in marriage:

My wife and I were seeing a marriage counselor prior to my seeing Dr. Ratey because it was like I was in my own little world. I wouldn't include my wife in any decisions. When we bought this house, I thought we needed a deck, so I said, "We need a deck," and the next thing you know I'm putting up a twelve-by-thirty-two-foot deck, and there was no talking to her about it. I drew up the plans, then threw them away and built the deck. And I changed all the heating. Normal people would sit down and talk about it.

This kind of behavior is ADD-driven: making decisions on the spur of the moment (impulsiveness), being out of touch with the rest of the world (distraction), not thinking to include his wife in household decisions (social deficit). And while events like sudden deck-building can be irritating to a spouse, other actions Rick took under the influence of his ADD-ish brain were more damaging. The birth of his second daughter was severely traumatic for the entire family, and Rick did not handle himself well.

My wife had placenta previa, but it wasn't diagnosed. We were stationed in Germany, and only the officers' wives could see doctors. Mary was telling the midwives she was having cramps and spotting, and they kept saying, "Don't worry about it." So finally the bleeding got so bad, we had to take her to a German hospital by ambulance, and the doctor said, "The baby's coming, you're dilated, but we're going to put you on this medicine that will try to keep the baby in." So there was my wife in a German hospital, she can't speak the language, and she starts going into labor.

After twenty-four hours the German doctor is telling me the baby doesn't look good, she has a fifty-fifty chance of living, my wife may die. My wife was in labor twenty-four hours, twenty-six hours; I was very worried about her, she was really cramping up, shaking, totally out of control. So they had her prepped for the cesarean, but the German way of thinking is to keep the baby in as long as possible. But after twenty-four hours the doctor says, "Look, it's time, I'm going to do my best." He had to break the water, and it was real hard to break, and Nicole came feet first. . . . I was completely fried, I needed to get away from there. Nicole cried as soon as she was born, and I had tears streaming down my face, and I backed up behind the curtain and I didn't want anybody to see me. I'm thinking, I gotta get out of here, I'm too keyed up. I went home and I bought a case of beer and I drank almost the whole case. And I left my wife alone.

I woke up in the morning, and I went back to the hospital, and my wife is still mad at me today. I left her, I just had to get out of there, I couldn't handle it.

While a shadow syndrome of any kind is not an excuse for disappearing from the hospital after your wife's wrenching labor and delivery, in fact even a mild case of ADD can "drive the behavior." While almost any man in Rick's position, having just witnessed a catastrophic delivery that has culminated in the birth of a three-pound baby, might well be seized by an impulse to flee, a man with no trace of ADD in his brain's workings would have a far easier time of it forcing himself to stay. This is why knowledge of the shadow syndromes matters: one of the surest paths to doing the right thing is knowing what it is about you that will make you do the wrong one. Once you know that you have a problem with impulse control, as Rick now does, you have a better chance of staying the course. You know the enemy.

But while Rick has had difficulties conforming to the role of husband, after the early preemie days in the hospital were over he connected easily, and profoundly, with the demands and responsibilities of fatherhood. His ADD was part of this: for Rick, fatherhood has been like a return to Germany; fatherhood has given him a mission. The demands, and the perils, of parenthood are stimulating and organizing for him; and he is a very good father to his little girls.

In the early days, of course, there were health scares. Rick rose to the challenge of all of these:

> Three or five months after Nicole came home, she had some kind of respiratory thing that the doctors were saying wasn't anything. I walked the floor all night, paced with her for twenty-four hours. The only way she could breathe comfortably was if I patted her on the back. The next day she turned blue, she couldn't breathe. And again the Americans didn't diagnose her, so I threatened the captain; I said she had to go to a German hospital. It turned out she had double pneumonia, so she was back in the Kinder Clinic again.

Now Rick's ADD was allowing him to fight a different kind of fight, a fight for his child's life. Later he would fight for his daughter's schooling, and for her medical treatment; he has been her fiercest advocate. The former high-school boy who loved to fight for the thrill of it now has something real and important to stand up for in his children's needs.

Beyond defending his children he was good, too, at simply interacting with them on their level:

> After my first daughter was born, all of a sudden, boing, I'm hitting it off with kids. I can sit down and play blocks with little kids for

hours. I just relate real well to little kids, something I never thought I'd do. At a family function I would hang out with kids because I couldn't participate in a conversation on politics. I wouldn't be listening.

In this, Rick was characteristic. To non-ADDers the ADD personality often reads as immature: ADD-ers often have the boundless enthusiasm and open faces of the young, partly because of their high energy, and partly because they are so forgetful that they tend to see every experience as brand-new. Here again, Rick has profited from a positive side effect of his disorder: relating well to children, for whom life experiences are by definition happening for the first time, because his ADD has kept him in touch with what it means to be a child.

Rick's success as a parent is one of the signs that his ADD is mild; as we have seen, more intensely ADD parents can have tremendous difficulty focusing on their children. It is also a sign of the benefits the disorder can bestow. Rick's energy, his intensity, his need to live life with a mission—all make him the good father that he is.

■ WALL STREET COWBOYS

Had he been raised by upper-middle-class professionals, Rick's life would undoubtedly look quite different. Different not only due to more money and greater opportunity, but due also to the fact that the white-collar world may be less forgiving of behaviors the blue-collar world views as the normal activity of boys going about the business of being boys. The sons of doctors and lawyers and teachers are never taught to use their fists; many are forbidden to own toy weapons of any kind. Thus a little boy with an attention deficit disorder may attract a great deal more intervention if he is the son of the upper-middle class than if he is not. And he may learn to channel his hyperactivity differently as a result. A few years back, in a news story on aggression (which is closely linked to ADD in some children), someone suggested that, depending upon his upbringing, the very aggressive little boy will grow up to be a football player, a criminal, or an executive. In the world of ADD there is a great deal of truth to this perception.

With the mildly ADD son of professionals what you may see is an adult like Robert, an entrepreneur now in his mid-thirties. Robert lives with the classic split between work and love to which so many mild ADD-ers fall prey: his work life has thrived while his relations with women can only be described as stunted. In popular parlance, Robert is a living exemplar of the Peter Pan syndrome: he is the grown man as little boy. And, to an important degree, both his success as a businessman and his failures as a potential husband and father, flow from the workings of his brain.

In the business world, his energy, enthusiasm, and ADD-driven creativity, combined with his native intelligence, have allowed him to create businesses that, over the years, have thrived: software consulting firms, paralegal services for the masses, real-estate assessment services that landed fat government contracts. At age thirty-four he has just sold his third business for several millions. In the entrepreneurial realm, his restless drive to start something, set it up, get it rolling, and then move on, has brought him wealth and standing. Culturally speaking, he is a cousin to the Wall Street cowboys of the 1980s, to the takeover artists who spent that decade vaulting from the high of one deal to the next. During those years it was an op-ed commonplace that deal-makers like Robert were more interested in the quick money to be made in the buying and selling of corporations than in the long, slow process of building a business in the first place, and Robert's career would certainly confirm these laments. He has always moved too fast to make a long-term commitment to anything—person or business.

Nevertheless, the fact that he can see a project through to fruition—at least far enough along to create a sellable entity—is a sign that his ADD is mild. It is also, in Robert's case, a result of his brush with obsessive-compulsive disorder: once he has hyperfocused upon a goal, his obsessiveness overrides his distractibility. Obsessive thoughts and behaviors are common in the ADD population: ADD authority Walid Shekim estimates that one-third of all people with ADD also show obsessive-compulsive features. While obsessiveness can be difficult to live with, for the mild ADD-er it can also be a help. In Shekim's words:

Although not living up to one's potential is a standard description of the ADD adult, quite a few of them are very successful, especially those who have the obsessive-compulsive aspects, because they become workaholics. If a person is hyper and gets obsessed with making money and is compulsive about it, he can do very well. But it's often at the expense of other things.

Other things being, commonly, love and family. And that is Robert's story: he is a man who, in theory, wants love and commitment in his life, wants to "settle down." But, apart from a brief engagement that disintegrated shortly after college, he has not been able to make a commitment to a life partner. And his romantic history throughout his twenties was so tumultuous that he has virtually withdrawn from the sexual realm altogether. In the past two years he has had sex with only one woman, and with her only once, after meeting for the first time at a friend's wedding:

> I gave her a ride back to the hotel, and when we got there we decided to stop at the bar for a drink. And we talked for hours. It was the most intimate conversation I've ever had with anyone; we told each other things we'd never told anyone else. It was as if we were soulmates, we just felt totally connected to each other.

In the early morning hours they made love, and, when Robert flew back to New York, they kept in touch by telephone. But nothing developed. "She will always be a unique person to me" is all Robert can say about this encounter. He doesn't understand it himself.

The path from hyperactive child to confirmed bachelor (the same process can be seen in women) is complicated. It is easy enough to understand the problems married ADD-ers encounter: sooner or later, and probably sooner, the ADD-er's problems with forgetfulness, distractibility, and impulsiveness become problems for his beleaguered spouse. But it is less obvious why ADD might block the way of a person's marrying in the first place.

Some of the problems ADD causes in the search for love are more apparent than others, of course. At the simplest level, the adult with ADD may bring to any romantic encounter an expectation of failure.

Lacking in social skills, he may come to the dating scene with a history of not quite getting the world of other people, and precious little confidence that he will be able to figure it out this time around. More, the sheer number of scoldings and punishments he experienced as a child may also have left their mark. As Dr. Allan Phillips, assistant clinical professor in the Department of Psychiatry at UCLA, notes:

> If you follow these children around throughout an ordinary day, the number of nos and stops and donts they hear is astronomical.

For the ADD male the fact that the scolding voices of childhood are so often female (since so much of his time is spent in the company of mothers and female elementary-school teachers) cannot help. And it is axiomatic that a man who enters a relationship expecting to be disapproved of soon will be.

Finally, and as we have seen, the unattached ADD male must grapple with that perennial stumbling block for ADD-ers everywhere: his brain's fierce need for constant stimulation. The high of falling in love with a new person may be significantly more organizing, and more soothing, to the ADD brain than the everydayness of a twenty-year marriage.

Any or all of these well-known problems associated with ADD may unite to create the confirmed bachelor. But the perennially single ADD-er's problems may run deeper than this. Robert offers this sense of what troubles him:

> I am the man people mean when they talk about getting in touch with yourself. When I meet a new woman, I don't know what I want; I don't feel like I have an inner self guiding my moves. I *feel* that there is a real me, deep inside somewhere; I feel that my real self sends out messages to whoever I'm pretending to be, and guides me. But I don't feel that my romantic partners can reach that part of me any better than I can.

For Robert, and for many sufferers of ADD mild or severe, the disorder has affected not only his thoughts, his emotions, and his behavior; it has shaped his very sense of identity. Put simply, the ADD child, mild or severe, may arrive at adulthood with a sense of self much more tenuous than that of the normal child. Difficulties in finding someone to love flow from this. A fragile identity does not necessarily hinder business or career success, since it may be possible to "fake it" in the world of work forever. But a tenuous sense of who one is can make marriage, or even a semicommitted live-in relationship, an impossibility. What happens with Robert is that he constantly feels that he is putting on a performance:

> At work I'm always on, I'm like the comedian working the crowd. I'm watching every second, gauging the audience, always figuring out exactly what to say, the right timing, the right tone of voice. It is work. But outside business I will actually cross the street rather than have to speak to a colleague or an acquaintance. I dread running into people, because I'm so tired of figuring them out, figuring me out. So tired of keeping up the act.

Part of the problem, for Robert, is his internal noise: he is besieged by his own chorus of inner voices. "The voices are always going," he says, "judging, advising, assessing, questioning." It is, clearly, exhausting. For the rest of us social encounters are far less thought-ridden. We meet someone, we like them or we don't, we talk. We go on from there, or we don't. It is that simple—or at any rate our subjective experience of the encounter is that simple. To enjoy socializing we need to feel at one with ourselves; we need quiet within.

Robert is rarely quiet within, and the voices distract him from himself; more troubling yet, the voices may have interfered fatally with his development of a self in the first place. He is not fully formed, or, at least, he does not *register* as fully formed, either to himself or to others. At its most destructive, ADD can disrupt the developmental process of establishing an identity. The sheer volume of mental sensations and impulses produced by the disorder is difficult to bind into one unified soul; being besieged by interior voices most of one's waking hours will certainly work against anyone's subjective sense of unity.

Beyond this the twin forces of forgetting and environmental dependency may radically interfere with the creation of an unassailable sense of self. Even the mildly ADD person forgets so much: not just what to pick up at the grocery store after work, but what he was thinking just moments before, what his wife told him over breakfast this morning. It is not hard to see why chronic forgetfulness would be disabling when it comes to getting things done, or to keeping loved ones happy and well tended. But at a deeper level forgetfulness also affects the self. The chronic forgetfulness of ADD means that each new experience is just that: *new.* Too new. Ultimately, we build our sense of identity through recognition, through apprehending an experience as something we have seen or heard or done before, and remembering how we felt about those things then. Through memory, wisdom is born.

But when we constantly forget, life fails to register; everything seems shiny and new. We live life without history. The ADD adult is buffeted by the newness of things, overwhelmed by his own unbridled excitements. He cannot become a fully unified self because in some sense he remains at the ego level of the small child with the big round eyes, seeing the world for the first time.

And if he suffers at all from environmental dependency, he is pulled to that brand-new world with a force sufficient to erase his center: thus Robert, falling in love at a wedding, for one night. Each new woman he meets is too new; and in the context of a wedding he finds himself pulled to the stimulus of the couple exchanging their vows. After the bride has thrown her bouquet, he has one of the most intimate encounters of his life in a hotel bar, courtesy of the wedding-day surround.

And so, forgetful of his own history, helplessly pulled to an environment that re-creates him in its image, Robert exists in the here and now; he lives life in the moment. Not because he wants to, but because he must. The end state of the symptoms ADD adults know so well, the impulsivity, the distractibility, the restlessness, is a state of mind most ADD adults do not recognize in themselves: they are prisoners of the present.

And being a prisoner of the present, the ADD adult loses the capacity to wish. For wishing always assumes a future tense, and a self without history cannot project itself into the years to come. Robert, the classic prisoner of his own present, cannot truly wish. He can want; he can yearn; he can long. But he cannot *know* what it is that he wants. And, not knowing what it is that he wants, he becomes a man who falls in love for one day.

6

AUTISTIC ECHOES

WHILE ALL OF THE shadow syndromes strike at the heart of social life, in most cases this is so because the world of work can be easier to negotiate than that of love and friendship. Structured employment offers even the most chaotic souls among us just that: *structure*. Schedules, routines, deadlines; work gives us rhythm and rhyme, and the daily cycle of early to bed, early to rise soothes the unquiet brain. Any psychiatric hospital worth its salt relies upon structure as a primary treatment for the severely afflicted souls within its walls; often doctors give their patients strict schedules to follow outside the hospital when they are discharged. Structure saves; it is a primary weapon in the arsenal of treatment options. And, in the real world, paid employment, not love, provides the main source of structure for the rest of us. For this reason alone, work is a tonic.

Thus it is that the shadow syndromes more often flourish in the open spaces of our private relationships. Mild depression, mild mania, mild ADD: all can sabotage the bonds of love and friendship. But

with the disorder we know as autism, things are different. In autism—
full-blown and mild—social difficulties *are* the disorder; they are not
the side effect of being scattered or depressed or anxious or hypervigi-
lant or whatever it is that any given shadow syndrome causes us to be.
The autistic person suffers a primary deficit in the ability to form and
sustain relationships with other people no matter who they are: friends
or colleagues, lovers or mates. The autistic person fares no better
with strangers: people passing on the street, clerks in supermarkets, policemen on patrol. More than one autistic man has been beaten by
policemen who interpreted his lack of response to their commands as a
sign of drug use or worse. A person who truly lacks social ability is at a
terrible, even life-threatening, disadvantage in dealing with the world.

In the words of Ivar Lovaas, professor of psychology at UCLA and a
man who has spent thirty years studying autistic children, "Social in-
eptness is the definition of autism; it's the one thing all autistic children
have in common. They don't have IQ in common, they don't have
problems with emotional attachment in common. But they all have social delays." Thus the social problems that grow out of the mildly autistic brain are hard-wired in: autistic social deficits are primary, stubborn,
and unyielding.

Until very recently parents, teachers, friends, neighbors, spouses,
colleagues—all of us, in short—have viewed social awkwardness as entirely a matter of character. Bad character, we assume, or bad upbringing. We speak of social "skills" as if social niceties were easily acquired
and simple abilities, like riding a bicycle or driving a car: capabilities
any reasonably well-put-together person can readily pick up.

But the example of autism proves otherwise. Autism is not caused by
bad parents; it is not caused by early deprivation. And yet the autistic
child is profoundly ill equipped to make his way in a world filled with
other people. He suffers overwhelming troubles with communication;
it is difficult for him to ask or answer questions, difficult for him to use
the word "yes." Even if he possesses language (and children diagnosed
with Asperger's syndrome, a very high-functioning form of autism, do
speak very well), he only rarely grasps the back-and-forth of a conversation; instead, he monologues, or sits silent as a stone while others

speak to him. He cannot read body language or facial expressions; if he can, he cannot do so as well as other children his age. He cannot play games unless he is painstakingly taught every step involved.

One mother tells the story of enrolling her extremely high-functioning daughter, a little girl so intelligent and expressive that she was not diagnosed with Asperger's syndrome until the age of eight, in soccer. The little girl obligingly tramped out onto the field with the rest of the children—and then stood there. She did not chase the ball; she did not run when the other children ran. This is the kind of mysterious behavior in an extremely high-functioning, unrecognized autistic child that *looks* like defiance, or slow-wittedness, or both. But in fact, this little girl, who spent her time at home reading long novels several grade levels above her own, did not grasp the fact that she was supposed to chase the ball. The fact that all around her other children were doing just that told her nothing. When her mother asked why she had spent the game standing still, she replied that she thought she was supposed to wait until the ball came to her.

This quality of being "out of it," as we say, is pervasive in autism. Even if the autistic child does learn how to play tag or hide and seek, he does not understand why he should. Other children's absorption in games is a mystery to him. He does not *get it*. The litany of social oblivion goes on: the autistic child does not, for example, understand the concept of sharing, from either side of the fence. He does not realize that others expect him to share with them, nor does he appear to feel any measure of distress when someone else refuses to share with him. A normal child can take a toy away from an autistic child with impunity; the autistic child will not react. Perhaps most shockingly in a small child—in a person of any age, for that matter—autistic children seem to possess no natural instinct for self-defense. Parents tell heart-wrenching stories of running to the aid of their sobbing autistic child only to find him standing passively with big tears rolling down his cheeks as another child pulls his hair, or twists his arm. The autistic child does not fight back.

In all of this the autistic child differs from other mentally challenged children; a mildly retarded child without autism will possess far better social abilities. The psychologist Howard Gardner, author of *Frames of Mind: The Theory of Multiple Intelligences,* has pointed out that children with Down's syndrome are actually fairly able socially; other researchers have contrasted autism to Williams syndrome, which results in children who are mentally retarded, but socially aware and capable. The ability of the human genome to produce children who are cognitively retarded but socially able, or cognitively brilliant (as in certain autistic savants) but socially deficient, shows that social intelligence is a separate intelligence dependent to a significant degree upon brain structure and chemistry.

Autism, of course, is no longer considered a mental illness. It is now known to be a developmental disability, a defect in the child's developmental process. (Mental retardation is one of the most common and best-known of the developmental disabilities.) In autism certain expected childhood stages (waving "hi" and "bye-bye," developing shared attention, engaging in pretend play, and many more) fail to occur on time, or at all. Thus the idea of hidden, subsyndromal forms of autism may seem at first blush simply impossible, for the same reason that the notion of a hidden case of mental retardation would be impossible: mental retardation to any degree is just too obvious a deficit to go unremarked.

But in fact, very mild cases of autism do occur, though it has only been within the past ten years that researchers have discovered this. Edward Ritvo of UCLA was the first person to publish a paper concerning the existence of people with mild forms of what is one of the most severe of the developmental disabilities. In a letter to the editor of the *Journal of Autism and Developmental Disorders* entitled "Eleven Possibly Autistic Parents," Ritvo raised the possibility that a mild form of autism might indeed exist. "While none of our autistic patients has achieved independence in adulthood," he wrote, "it is our impression that some of their parents had early developmental delays and symptoms throughout adulthood pathognomonic of autism." In other words, some of the severely autistic children he diagnosed were brought to him by parents who looked a bit autistic themselves. (Which raises the interesting possibility that early investigators into autism, describing the "coldness" of some parents of autistic children, were actually describing not a character defect but a mild form of the disorder occurring in the parent. Was the "refrigerator mother" made famous by Bruno Bettelheim actually a woman with very mild autism?) In any event, it was to be through the parents of autistic children that Ritvo would first identify a hidden autistic population working and living normal—or at least seminormal—lives among normal people.

During the 1980s Ritvo and his colleagues Anne M. Brothers, B. J. Freeman, and Carmen Pingree undertook an epidemiological study of every autistic person then living in the state of Utah. The purpose of the study was to look for factors, such as prenatal influences, birth trauma, and so on, that might have caused the autism, and to gauge the risk to families with one autistic child of having a second or a third.

But as they spoke to the parents of children with autism, they stumbled onto an unanticipated result: some of these parents looked autistic themselves. Some of them hand-flapped, rocked, and toe-walked; some were social isolates; two of them actually said straight out that they were autistic just like their children. It turned out that they were. Independent examinations by other diagnosticians confirmed the diagnosis of autism in eleven parents—nine fathers and two mothers. While today the notion of an autistic parent may not seem so extraordinary, just a few years back the concept was revolutionary. As Ritvo remarked shortly afterward, "If you had told me ten years ago that there were autistic people who were married and had kids, I would have said, 'You're crazy, they're all living in institutions.' Now, in the wake of the Utah study, he changed his mind: "As with most diseases," he wrote, "there appears to be a mild form of autism that is compatible in adulthood with marriage, parenting, satisfactory heterosexual sexual performance, and gainful employment."

Who is the person with a hidden form of autism? He is the odd duck. His difference from "normal" people is readily apparent to all of us; we recognize him as being somehow off. It is only his kinship to the Rain

Man that we have missed. We should add that the word "he" is in all likelihood correct; while autism at the low end of the spectrum affects two boys for every girl, at the high end there are five autistic boys for each autistic girl. These are estimates for diagnosed cases only, of course; it is quite possible that as we move into the very mild, undiagnosed cases, the sex gap grows wider still. Mild autism may be overwhelmingly a disorder of men.

On the other hand, it is also conceivable that at the highest end of the spectrum we will eventually discover *more* females, not fewer, once we really look; perhaps the celebrated female advantage in language and social intelligence protects some women born with the genetics for autism, nudging them up out of the diagnosable category of "high-functioning autism" into the unrecognized and unsung shadow syndrome of the disorder. Perhaps in women mild autism, like mild attention deficit disorder (to which autism is probably related genetically), is masked by other strengths. We don't know.

At present the classic autism shadow syndrome is undeniably male. And, social stereotyping aside, the most recognized embodiment of this shadow syndrome is the nerd. He is the computer programmer hunched over his monitor at all hours of the day and night, a pocket protector lodged permanently in his rumpled shirt. He has few or no friends; often he has no wife. He is a geek.

He is called "geek" or "nerd" or "wonk" for one reason alone: he is socially awkward. Out of it. Techie types have long recognized this quality in themselves: MIT actually offers a January course in social skills that students call "charm school." One year Miss Manners spoke at the course's end. Nor has the connection between autism and computerdom gone unnoticed. *Time* magazine once ran an item comparing Microsoft's Bill Gates to the famous autistic savant Temple Grandin (Gates's reported autistic qualities included rocking, jumping on trampolines, not making eye contact, and not having the social skills necessary to enter a group conversation). And Douglas Coupland's novel *Microserfs,* about a group of Microsoft employees who leave the company in order to try to have a life, includes an extended passage on autism:

At lunch, Mom preempted all other conversation starts by discussing Michael. "Sometimes I think that Michael is ummm—*autistic*." She blushed. "Oh, of course, what I mean to say is—well—have *you* noticed?"

"Michael's not like other people," I said. "He goes off into his own world—for days at a time sometime. A few months ago he locked himself into his office and we had to slide food under his door. And so he stopped eating any food that couldn't be slipped underneath a door."

"Oh, so that explains the Kraft cheese slices. Carton-loads."

Karla, still low energy from the flu, broke in: "You know, Mrs. Underwood, I think *all* tech people are slightly autistic . . ."

Why exactly the mildly autistic person should be so drawn to computers—and so good at them—nobody knows. Some of the appeal is undoubtedly psychological in nature; as we will see, people with any degree of autism are oversensitive to stimuli, and do not tolerate change or spontaneity well. Computer programming may offer the ultimate in the way of a controlled environment, an activity in which the mildly autistic person can control every bell and whistle. But beyond this, it is likely that mildly autistic people do in fact possess a special talent for computer programming and its offshoots. They are right-brain types; they have good visual-spatial brains, and see the way things fit together. The infinite lines of code that go into the creation of a computer program may fall together for them naturally.

We could say that the microserf nerd is the ultimate exemplar of the man who doesn't get it, if not for the fact that the mildly autistic man so completely and profoundly does not get it that he transcends the category of obtuse male altogether to become simply—odd; different; strange. Where the mildly ADD man is the enemy of women's magazines everywhere, the mildly autistic man is simply a puzzle. He is beyond the pale.

■□ AUTISTIC ECHOES

Aaron is a thirty-four-year-old virgin who would never be thought of as autistic by any mainstream diagnostician. For one thing, he is far too successful to be seen as cognitively impaired in any way; by his early thirties he had already become extremely well-off working as a multimedia consultant for start-up computer companies. As well, he is too "normal" in manner; he is not shy; he is well spoken. A personable conversationalist, his vocal inflections are correct. (Even very high-functioning autistic adults usually speak somewhat differently from the rest of us: often their diction is formal, their affect somewhat flat. One high-functioning autistic reports that his colleagues sometimes call him "Mr. Spock," after the Leonard Nimoy character on *Star Trek*.) And yet Aaron is one of those people who excels at work (he is a computer specialist in high demand), but cannot construct a social life. He has been in and out of therapy for many years trying to understand his sexuality, trying to understand, too, his lack of connection with other people. His life is a puzzle.

Most of us, contemplating Aaron's life, would alight upon the familiar answers. Some of us would blame Aaron's childhood, as Aaron himself has done for many years. Aaron was born fifteen years after his next oldest brother, when his parents were older; his parents separated a few years later. ("I always joke that I was a save-the-marriage-baby," Aaron says, "and I failed at my first job.") Both parents were intrusive in the extreme; his mother always kept her things in Aaron's closet, and once, when the two of them traveled together to Israel, had him carry three packages of sanitary napkins for her in his suitcase. Even after Aaron became an adolescent his father routinely walked into his room without knocking, often catching Aaron just emerging from the shower. Once the marriage ended, Aaron had little life apart from his mother during the week and from his father on weekends. A lonely child of divorce, Aaron made few friends, a fact that, in his view, was of little concern to his parents: whenever he asked his mother why he didn't have friends, she would tell him if he had just one good friend in life he had "a lot." While as a homily this notion is reasonable enough, as a guide to childhood it is all wrong: a child who cannot make friends with other children is in trouble.

Thus the most tempting explanation for Aaron's social disconnectedness is the classic one: his parents raised him badly. An equally compelling alternative arises from the sexual aspects of Aaron's difficulties: Aaron, we might conclude, is simply a homosexual who has not been able to accept his orientation. There is evidence enough for this interpretation of his life as well: as a teenager, Aaron had a number of homosexual experiences with other boys, and to the extent that he does feel sexual desire, his focus is male:

> The way I describe it is that men can feel more hedonistic; with men it would be sex for pleasure's sake, but not emotionally satisfying. Women seem more compatible to me in an emotional sense, and yet there's just this large barrier sexually.

Reading this, some will have an "Ah-ha" experience: Aaron is a closeted homosexual, they will conclude, a closeted gay man with intrusive parents who did not respect his boundaries!

And yet, neither explanation quite fits. For one thing, Aaron's social problems extend beyond simply having been isolated as a child: he does not read people well. His problem as a child was not just that he was spending too much time with grown-ups; even the time he did have with children his age did not run smoothly. And the problem with other children was not that he seemed, as some gay men in childhood, effeminate or girlish. The real difficulty was that he did not know how to make friends, and other children teased him. To them he seemed odd. For the normal child, this would not be the case; even an overprotected only child can readily pick up social skills on the playground. Normal children breathe in the whys and wherefores of other children, like air. Aaron did not.

His possible homosexuality also falters as an explanation for such issues as to why Aaron, to this day, cannot make small talk. Being homosexual, even being a severely repressed homosexual, does not render a person incapable of functioning at cocktail parties. Closeted homo-

sexuality does not make it difficult for a person to recognize and respond to, say, tone of voice—a major problem for Aaron in all of his
encounters with other people.

The clue that Aaron's problems may stem from his biology as much
as from his social psychology came from something he mentioned in
passing in John's office. Aaron cannot dance:

> I can't dance, I just can't do it. When I was a kid, I went to a camp
> where they did Israeli dances. The way they teach the dance is to have
> you do three steps and name it, then another three steps and name
> that, and so on. Then in the dance they call out the names. And I
> could never follow the calls, I would totally fall apart.

More recently, Aaron had experienced the same problem while rehears-
ing for a play. At one point in the production he and the others were to
do a simple dance, and Aaron found that he simply could not learn it.

> We were a few days from dress rehearsal, and everyone else had
> learned the dance and I hadn't. I was saying, "Do it again, do it again,
> do it again." Finally, I said, "Will you humor me?" And I had the di-
> rector stand there with our bodies touching, my front to her back,
> my knee to her knee. I moved in her step and we walked through the
> whole thing, and then I could get it.

To the parent of an autistic child this means of teaching will be instantly familiar: it is called "motoring through." When a parent motors
an autistic child through an action such as opening the door, he first
tells the child to open the door, then he takes the child's hand, puts it
on the doorknob, turns, and opens the door. He motors the child
through. In order to learn a simple dance step, Aaron intuited that he,
too, needed to be motored through the movements involved.

For John, these seemingly minor idiosyncrasies gave him pause.
Physical coordination is a function of the cerebellum, and the cerebellum—as we will see—is one of the major areas of the brain affected by
the syndrome of autism. Thus when John heard Aaron's tales of cere-

bellar mishap, he began to think of Aaron as a patient whose problems might stem as much from an innate social deficit as from intrusive parents or repressed homosexuality: the biology of Aaron's brain might have decreed that Aaron would have difficulty making friends even growing up in the happiest of homes as an undisputed heterosexual. It is entirely possible that Aaron also suffers some of the same cerebellar damage seen in the full-fledged autistic, that his lack of coordination physically corresponds to his lack of "coordination" socially.

Certainly, Aaron himself responds powerfully to the notion of autistic child and parent meeting a disconnect when they try to share their experience of the world:

> Dr. Ratey was talking to me about social skills and how a parent trying to communicate with an infant looks at something and the infant follows the gaze and they share that object. But if the parent turns away and the kid doesn't get it, then the kid thinks, Why did my parent turn away from me?
>
> When he told me about this, I saw an image of the mother holding the child, and the mother looks at something, like a toy, and the reason the mother is doing that is to entice the infant to look at the toy as well so they can share that view—that can be a shared experience. But the infant is looking at the mother and the mother turns away and the infant just perceives it as mother turning away, and the infant doesn't get that he's supposed to look at the toy also. And so what winds up happening is that the infant just starts feeling distance and potentially abandonment. And I thought, Wow, that's what my photographs are about.

Aaron is an accomplished amateur photographer, who photographs children in states of isolation from the adults who surround them. One photo might show a small boy looking up at a group of adults, trying to see what they are doing; we can't see what it is, and neither can he. Another might show a small girl sitting on some steps beside her mother, whose back is turned to the camera and who is only partially captured in the frame. The children are separate, disconnected. In a metaphorical sense, they are autistic.

Interestingly, when her son was young, Aaron's mother invented a picture-imitating "game" that sounds like an elaborate version of the imitation-building exercises behaviorists have devised for autistic children:

> When I was a kid, my mother separated from my father. She would do something she called "playing picture." There was a Picasso print on her bedroom wall of a mother and child, and the game would be for the two of us to try to mimic the painting together, to get into the position of the mother and child in the painting.

Of course, classic psychoanalytic interpretation would view a scene like this as Oedipal in nature and symbolically incestuous, which is indeed the way Aaron has seen it for many years:

> It is an image that, as I look back on it, feels really invasive. The reason for her doing that was for support; it was part of her getting emotional support from me and the surreptitiousness was that it was a game when in fact it wasn't a game. It was her life force, her energy.

We are on classic American psychoanalytic terrain here: the devouring mother, the smothered son who will grow up to desire men. But in fact, when it comes to autism, the most effective parenting style *is* highly invasive, so much so that Clara Claiborne Park titled her now classic account of bringing up her autistic daughter Jessy, *The Siege*. Park describes laying siege to her daughter's unreachable self, forcing eye contact, forcing response, forcing connection. Being highly invasive, in other words. Aaron's mother may have been invasive and suffocating, *or* she may have been struggling to connect with a child who was different, a "puzzle child" (the phrase used to describe autistic children for many years) who could not make contact with her in the way that his two brothers could. The picture game addresses so many of the autistic person's limitations that one begins to wonder about Aaron's mother's experience of her son. Viewed from the perspective of the autistic disorders, her picture game is clearly an exercise in imitation (a gross weakness in the truly autistic but doubtless a milder problem in an autistic shadow syndrome), an exercise in human touch (so often a problem in autism), and an exercise in social relatedness all rolled into one. Was the picture game overbearing motherhood, or good therapy? Or both? Evidence that it may have grown out of a therapeutic impulse, however inchoate, comes from Aaron himself:

> As I look back on it, the image feels really invasive, and again, what I'm doing: I'm intellectualizing the past. At the time I think it felt really warm, really good. I *could* share the picture when we were doing this; my mother and I could share the experience.

Aaron's social deficits are subtle enough that most people would not suspect there was anything wrong. Where his problem manifests itself most clearly is in a tendency to monologue. Aaron recalls once being brought to task for this by a group therapy leader:

> I was telling a story of some sort, a high-school story, and she stopped me and said she felt really discarded by what I was doing. I asked her what it was, and she said she wanted to relate to me on that story and she was trying to get in and talk to me and I wouldn't let her. I wasn't allowing her to give feedback.

In other words, he was monologuing, not allowing anyone else to speak—something that came as a complete surprise to him. And, in keeping with the trusting nature of so many autistic and autisticlike people, Aaron was completely undefensive in the face of this criticism, which he viewed, simply, as useful information:

> I thought that her saying that was the greatest thing because if someone would just say that to me, I would say, "Oh, I'm really sorry you're feeling bad, please tell me." Or I would say, "Do me a favor, don't couch it, just severely interrupt me if you need to say something."

Most of us would feel wounded—at least initially—by such a criticism, openly declared for all to hear. Aaron's ability to welcome criticism as being merely useful feedback reflects the trusting nature of the high-functioning autistic person, who typically (except, as we will see, in the case of the "shy gorilla") does not intuit hidden motives. Aaron is an eager student. He possesses the lovely openness of the autistic soul.

Not surprisingly, Aaron has great difficulty picking up on the unspoken. He tells a story of his brother once saying to him, "Do what you want" which, as it turned out, actually meant, as it so often does in life, "Don't do what you want." Oblivious to subtext, Aaron went blithely ahead and did things as he saw fit, provoking a confrontation with his brother, who finally said to him in exasperation, "If I want you to do something, I'll just have to tell you straight." Where to his older brother the thought of having to spell things out for a fellow adult was exasperating, to put it mildly, to Aaron this seemed proper and correct: conversation without subtext, he feels, is what conversation ought to be.

If subtext between brothers is unreadable for Aaron, small talk with anyone is a disaster: "I cannot deal with small talk whatsoever," he says. He does not attend cocktail parties; he does not linger by the water cooler, shmoozing with colleagues. In fact, Aaron does not shmooze at all, under any circumstances. What is more, he sees this aspect of his character as an entirely positive trait. In his view small talk is a bad thing:

> It makes me sick, because it's pretense, it's not real. It's drivel, it's nonsense, it's a waste of time and energy. Of course, all of this may be rationalization because I don't understand small talk and I feel excluded from it.

Rationalization it undoubtedly is: small talk, and the ability to engage in small talk, is a basic social necessity. It is the glue that holds the group together; without it social life would dissolve into self-contained duos of one-on-one partners holding round-the-clock heart-to-hearts. This is in fact the form of communication Aaron vastly prefers:

> My best times with friends are when I can sit down with them and lock into a part of my brain where I can talk to them about emotional things or experiences.

Interestingly, researchers have found this preference to be characteristic of high-functioning adults with autism: as British researcher Helen Tager-Flusberg found, they do well talking about "desires and emotions," but poorly talking about "beliefs and ideas." For many of us, of course, this observation will come as a surprise given the autistic person's celebrated difficulties with empathy and emotion. But, in fact, high-functioning autistic people are often extremely articulate when it comes to describing their own internal states and symptoms; the many vivid and moving autobiographical writings by autistic individuals are testimony to this. That autistic people should have difficulty talking about ideas is not surprising as it is well-established that autism involves deficits in the ability to deal with abstractions. Autistic people are famously literal-minded; they will typically interpret a question or a remark in its most concrete sense.

But the fact that autistic people can be very good at describing their own feelings does complicate the classic picture of autism a bit. It is entirely possible that, as the work of multiple-intelligence theorist Howard Gardner suggests, there is a biologically based split between knowledge of self and knowledge of other. The autistic person's *real* problem may be not so much with emotion as with empathy—with perceiving and comprehending the feelings of others. Certainly, that autistic people lack empathy is an extremely commonplace observation routinely made by parents and professionals, and by autistic persons themselves.

But whatever the source of the shadow autistic's preference for personal revelation, the truth remains that nonautistic people prefer, and expect, a wider range of subject matter. More than once Aaron has put off a potential romantic partner by instantly giving her, on a first night out, a detailed account of his psychiatric history:

> There was a woman in the play group who was interested in me, and we went out to dinner a couple of times and I ended up sabotaging it. I made myself sound like an escapee from Bellevue, talking on and on about Zoloft. She lost all interest.

While the content of Aaron's conversation is clearly problematic here, no doubt his rhythm was off as well, as the well-known autistic savant

Temple Grandin has said of her own social rhythm. A first date usually requires some fairly brisk back-and-forth, and certainly a longish discourse on Zoloft will throw off the expected meter. To inaugurate a dinner date with the revelation that one is under a psychiatrist's care is a conversation-stopper in every sense of the term.

That Aaron's difficulties may stem from an inborn deficit in social intelligence is indicated by the fact that his problems do not begin and end with an aversion to small talk. While a person can lead a perfectly reasonable existence without ever attending a cocktail party, a life without any grasp of adult sexuality is a different matter altogether. Aaron's virginity cuts him off from far too much: from intimacy, from close companionship through the years, from the possibility of having children. And thus far at least, he has not been able to make headway with this issue. His sexual confusion is profound; it is so pervasive that he is not even aware of whether he feels attracted to a person or not. He does not experience crushes; not, at any rate, that he is aware of.

His one attempt to free himself of his virginity offers further evidence of a fundamental social disconnect. Not long ago, he hit upon the plan of traveling to Las Vegas with the intention of sleeping with a prostitute. Although he could not bring himself to summon a call girl to his hotel room, he did manage to locate a brothel on a handout map:

> I can trick myself into doing things I don't want to do, so I said to myself, If I can't make a phone call to the sex services, I can pick a destination on the map and drive there. And I knew that if I got there, I wouldn't turn back.

The brothel proved to be a cluster of motor homes encamped deep in the desert. There was a Harley-Davidson on display out front, gleaming behind red velvet stanchion cords. To a person of normal social awareness this would have been a scene that was bizarre at best; to Aaron it was entirely indecipherable:

> The Madame says the girls will be here in a minute, and then this parade of women comes out all dressed in Victoria's Secret underwear and she says, "OK, pick one," and I'm saying, "What? How do you pick?"

Bewildered, Aaron made his first social misstep: he selected the prostitute who seemed to have "the most character." Things deteriorated from there:

> She asked how I was feeling, and I said I was really scared and I was telling her about Zoloft, and she said, "I don't do no drugs."

Once again, Aaron was turning a first encounter with a woman into a therapy session, or trying to; though it might seem almost impossible to embarrass oneself in the context of an encounter with a prostitute, Aaron managed to do precisely that. Needless to say, the conversation did not go far, and Aaron's chosen partner quickly got down to work:

> She said she had to get me ready, and she gave me a back rub for a total of twenty seconds, then turned me over. It was like a doctor's office—she told me to take my clothes off, and she washed my genitals with Lysol.
> It was almost impossible to have an erection, and completely impossible to come, and she got really mad.

For all of Aaron's planning, the entire scene had deteriorated into yet another failed first date. Whatever psychiatric issues may have been involved for the prostitute herself, who had not exactly carved out a normal social life on her own behalf, she undoubtedly possessed a superior grasp of the social behavior required in this situation, which apparently involves doing what you've come to do quickly and efficiently and omitting any discussion of your psychiatric history.

The autistic, or autisticlike, nature of Aaron's social makeup has made it impossible for him to construct a love life. But the problems he encounters in trying to make sexual contact are ones that, again, you would not connect with autism unless you were intimately familiar with the disorder in its severe form. Aaron's description of his most recent close encounter will be affecting to anyone who lives with a truly autistic person:

> Recently, I dated one woman a little bit. I met her at a Jewish group, and she called me up and invited me to go to the esplanade. We had

a nice time, and I don't know how it happened, but we managed to start kissing some time much later on, and it was all very odd and very strange. That is my only real recollection, it was just strange. And she was commenting on it being strange.

I was working in technical sales support and we made a yearly goal, so we all got a trip to Bermuda and I asked her if she wanted to go with me. She said yes and it was just totally freaking me out. I didn't know if I should touch her, shouldn't touch her, what I should do.

I never wound up having intercourse with her, it was just mostly touching and that kind of stuff, masturbating.

I couldn't spend the night with her. One of the problems is I don't feel I have any kind of privacy from my parents or other people with that. I feel that if someone asked me a question, I'm obligated to answer, and that someone can just look at me and know what I'm thinking.

This is autism at its subtlest and, in some ways, its loveliest: Aaron is a man who cannot lie. More than that, he is a man who, suffering an autistic lack of empathy for the thoughts of others, concludes that other people *can* read *his* thoughts. He experiences himself as an open book, and, in his dealings with other humans, he has only one option, to be honest. It is here that the psychodynamic approach to Aaron's life falters. The socially adroit child of intrusive parents learns to lie, and lie again; such a child, faced with parents who keep their Kotex in his suitcase, and walk into his room without knocking after he has showered, will learn to deceive early and well. But Aaron, ever so slightly deficient in social understanding, has not acquired the social sophistication required to deceive. He cannot do it. And because he cannot lie, he cannot fall in love. He feels himself too open to all.

Perhaps he is right in this. Temple Grandin has said that she has no unconscious; all her thoughts and memories, as she told the neurologist Oliver Sacks, are fully conscious and retrievable at will. She does not— indeed cannot—repress bad things. She, too, is an open book.

In her often brilliant *Autism: An Introduction to Psychological Theory*, at one hundred and thirty pages a small gem of a book, Francesca Happé has written, "Autism is a disorder which fascinates because it seems to be so essentially a disorder of the human condition." In Aaron's life we find her meaning: autism is a fractured mirror reflecting back to us the odd truths that underlie the noblest of emotions. Lying and love, deception and intimacy. Small talk and genuine emotional connection. Those of us who are good at one are good at, or at least fully capable of, the other. (And indeed, research has shown that those autistic children who are best able to grasp what other people are thinking are also best at lying and cheating. A child who has no comprehension of the internal life of other people—no comprehension that different people think different thoughts—does not attempt to lie or to cheat, because it does not occur to him that lying or cheating is *possible*.)

Freud once wrote that there is a barrier between souls, that none of us wants to know what fantasies and impulses truly lie inside the other. We recoil at the sight of a naked unconscious, as he saw. Aaron lives on the other side of this insight. Operating with only an attenuated notion of what goes on inside the minds of other people, Aaron *feels* naked, open to the world. There for all to see. Incapable of protecting himself, incapable of lying when he needs to, Aaron cannot love another.

In many ways, Aaron has learned to disguise his difference. Although he is a bit nerdy in appearance, he works at being included, at not coming across as the space case he otherwise would. And for the most part, he succeeds. In terms of behavior, one of his main strategies, a strategy almost universally employed by high-functioning autistic people and their semiautistic cousins, is to mask the problem. Aaron's photography has always been extremely useful in this respect: "I used my camera to disconnect me; I'd walk around at family functions with the camera." It was a clever ruse: instead of lookingt like a person who could not carry his half of a conversation, Aaron looked like a busy photographer. He translated his social deficit into an activity that is socially acceptable.

But finally, what makes Aaron only an autistic "echo" rather than a truly autistic person who is extremely high-functioning, may be the fact that he *can* correct his behavior, to a significant degree. He possesses some genuine ability to see himself as others see him:

When the group leader told me she felt discarded, honestly I didn't view that as negative feedback. I'm grateful that someone would say that because they're just letting me know how they feel about something, and I can fix it.

Thus the larger social world, for Aaron, may be opaque, but it is not entirely unknowable. He needs things spelled out; he needs people to be direct. But when people *are* direct, he can get it. And that makes all the difference.

■□ THE CEREBELLAR CONNECTION

It is now known that autism results from neurological impairment; it is coming to be believed that many of the mild social deficits we see in the nerd or the geek may also result from milder forms of the same impairment. While the neurology is not as yet fully understood, separate studies undertaken by researchers Margaret Bauman of the Massachusetts General Hospital and Harvard Medical School, and Eric Courchesne of the University of California at San Diego, have pinpointed two major areas of the brain: the hippocampus and the cerebellum. Of these, the surprise is the finding of cerebellar involvement, since the cerebellum was traditionally seen as the region responsible for physical coordination. (The hippocampus, which is part of the limbic system or "reptilian brain," handles certain forms of memory, an ability obviously affected by autism.)

In magnetic-resonance scans of the brains of autistic people, Courchesne has discovered that 88 percent of his patients showed *hypoplasia* of the cerebellum; that is, the cerebellum of the autistic person is significantly smaller than the cerebellum of a normal person. In the remaining 12 percent he found *hyperplasia* of the cerebellum; the cerebellum was too large. Courchesne explains what is startling about this discovery:

> For over 200 years, the cerebellum has invariably been viewed by medical science as part of the motor control system of the human brain. For 50 years, infantile autism has been viewed as a disorder of

the highest forms of human mental function. Of all the theories of infantile autism over the last 50 years, perhaps the oddest is the one that links the cerebellum and autism.

The question is, how does a deficit in the part of the brain that controls physical coordination produce the incredibly varied and complicated deficits in socialization, in communication, and in imagination ("Wing's triad," after the British authority on autism, Lorna Wing) that we see in autistic people? After all, stroke victims who have sustained damage to the cerebellum do not become autistic. They develop cerebellar syndrome; they struggle with simple physical maneuvers like walking up and down stairs for the rest of their lives. Instead of being able automatically to put their foot down in the right place on the stairstep, they have to consciously *think* about putting their foot down in the right place on the stairstep. Physical life, after cerebellar damage, is filled with effort. But a cerebellum damaged late in life does not produce a Rain Man.

Nevertheless, Courchesne has discovered at least one area in which cerebellar and autistic patients do look very similar indeed, and that is in the ability to shift their attention quickly from one thing to another. Courchesne devised a study in which subjects look at a field containing two empty square boxes with a cross in between. The subject is asked to focus on the cross, and to press a button as soon as he sees that a light has been turned on in one of the boxes. Both autistic patients and cerebellar patients, Courchesne finds, take much longer to register the light than normal patients do. A normal person can pick up a new stimulus in the environment with lightning speed, and Courchesne concludes that this capacity is localized in the cerebellum. There is more to coordination than simply being able to put our feet where we want them without having to think about it; our ability to put our attention where we want it without having to think about it is apparently coordinated by the cerebellum as well. In autistic people, as in cerebellar patients, the smooth flow of attention has been severely disrupted.

Courchesne's stroke of genius was to ask what would happen to the infant who *comes into* this world with cerebellar damage, who embarks upon his lessons in the world and its ways saddled with a clumsy attentional apparatus. In this respect many autistic babies are far more challenged than the cerebellar stroke victim, since approximately 40 percent of autistic people show significant parietal-lobe damage as well, which impairs their ability to attend to numerous stimuli at once. When it comes to the issue of paying attention, autistic children are in far worse straits than children with ADD. The attention deficit of autism is profound. Because evidence from autopsies of autistic brains shows that in autism the damage occurs early in fetal development, the autistic baby will have tremendous difficulty tuning in to the world around him from the very beginning of his days on earth.

And the baby who cannot tune in, Courchesne reasons, will confront nearly insurmountable obstacles in making sense of the people and things that surround him. Rather than plunging into life headlong as a normal baby does, the autistic baby, as it is so often said by the people who love him, will seem to live "in his own little world." But it is not a world of his making; it is a prison. It is not, as psychoanalysts like Bettelheim once believed, a world into which he has "withdrawn." It is a world into which he has been pushed. What is actually happening to the autistic baby is that he is receiving the world in pieces, in fragments. Where the normal baby can shift his attention from a nose to an eye to a mouth in a fraction of a second, the autistic baby, Courchesne has found, may need as many as five to six seconds to make these shifts. (And quite possibly more: Courchesne arrived at the five-to-six-second figure through laboratory experiments using carefully controlled, and limited, stimuli. He rightly points out that a baby with such a deficit would be far more handicapped trying to process the complex colors, shapes, and shadows of the real world.) When we imagine ourselves in the position of the autistic baby, autism makes more sense: if it takes five to six seconds to shift from gazing at your father's nose to gazing at your father's eyes, you are not going to be seeing your father's *face*. You are going to be seeing parts of a face (parts of whose face?) and the parts are not going to cohere, in memory, into a meaningful whole. They are going to be stored, simply, as face-pieces.

Personal testimony supporting Courchesne's conjecture comes from high-functioning autistic people, many of whom have spoken of "visual dropouts," of not being able to see *all* of a tree, or to see the tree as a whole. An autistic adult might see simply a branch, or a leaf, or a bird perched on a branch. But the tree *as a tree,* as a coherent entity, does not jump out at him.

When it comes to social competence, this inability to shift attention, Courchesne argues, has devastating consequences. Social information, the look on a parent's face, her tone of voice, is fleeting; it happens in a moment and is gone. The autistic baby, locked into whatever stimulus has captured his gaze, cannot move his eyes up to his mother's face quickly enough to learn what she is thinking about that object. If the baby is staring at a puppy and the mother smiles, he will miss her smile. By the time he can attend to her face, her expression has changed. If he pulls the puppy's tail, he will miss his mother's frown. Her "No!" and his tail-pulling will not form a coherent whole in memory. They are separate pieces of reality, disparate fragments in a life that does not add up.

Thus the autistic baby misses a vital first developmental step: he fails to develop joint social attention. two people attending to the same thing at the same time. By the age of fifteen months a normal baby will look at something his mother is looking at, or ask her to look at something *he* is looking at; he will share that object with her. But the autistic baby does not do this; the autistic baby does not point. Nor is he drawn to look at something someone else is looking at. As a result, he is excruciatingly difficult to entertain. If his mother says "Look at the kitty," he does not look. Nor does he ever ask of his mother that she look at a kitty with him.

More than this, the normal baby engages in social referencing: he will scan an adult's face to see what he or she is thinking about whatever it is that is going on. If you watch a normal baby as young as eight months sitting on his father's lap at the dinner table, you will see him stare at his father's plate of spaghetti, then stare up at his father's face to see what his father *thinks* about this plate of spaghetti! Already, the normal baby is scanning the social environment, picking up clues.

The autistic baby, handicapped by a sluggish cerebellum, cannot do this. And, because this deficit afflicts the child at the very beginning of life, his developmental process is devastated. He cannot learn what he needs to learn about objects, which come into his head in pieces; neither can he learn what he needs to learn about people, who also come into his head in pieces. And of course, this same damaging sequence may hold true for all forms of attention, auditory and tactile as well as visual. From this one deficit, Courchesne believes, many characteristic traits of autism may flow: the need for sameness and routine, the limited interests, the repetitive behaviors. All of these might be strategies to make the world hold still long enough for the autistic person to form a coherent image of it. And for the autistic baby, the developmental blessings that flow from an intact attentional apparatus, the ability to imitate others and take turns and engage in make-believe and share, do not happen. The baby who cannot share attention at fifteen months grows up to become the four-year-old who cannot read a playmate's intentions written on his face.

If, for the genuinely autistic among us, nothing from the outside world is coming in smoothly, nothing is coming back out smoothly either: autistic people are awkward. Often, as the cerebellar anomalies would predict, they are physically awkward (though they may be highly coordinated in certain activities or sports), but certainly they are socially awkward. They lack rhythm. In her book *Thinking in Pictures,* Temple Grandin offers this wistful description of what it is to be out of step with the world:

> During the last couple of years, I have become more aware of a kind of electricity that goes on between people that is much more subtle than overt anger, happiness, or fear. I have observed that when a group of people are together and having a good time their speech and laughter follows a rhythm. They will all laugh together and then talk quietly until the next laughing cycle. I have always had a hard time fitting in with this rhythm and I usually interrupt conversations without realizing my mistake. The problem is that I can't follow the rhythm.

Temple's difficulty with social rhythm is a universal among autistic people, and it is true, too, of the autistic person's far milder cousin, the "social klutz." The socially awkward person can be seen in cerebellar terms: uncoordinated, out of step, lacking in social *grace*. Our language is filled with phrases and jargon that point to the connection between physical coordination and social.

It is a connection psychiatry has thus far neglected. In contemporary psychiatry, when a patient presents with social difficulties, the physician will round up the usual suspects: a bad childhood, a crippling mood disorder, a borderline personality, or any of the many psychiatric conditions that can impair love and friendship. What he will not look for is evidence of cerebellar dysfunction.

But in fact, in a significant subset of patients with social problems, such evidence is there for the asking. In John's practice, a pattern began to emerge once he had read the work of Eric Courchesne and had begun to think about social disabilities in terms of cerebellar function. Soon enough, he began to notice things that would have slipped past him before: a patient would remark in passing that he had never been able to skip as a child, or clap in time to music, or balance on his left foot. Where before these statements would have held no particular meaning for John, in the wake of Courchesne they leapt out at him. Time and again, he found, in patients whose social troubles did not seem to be due to a mood disorder or a painful childhood, there was also a history of problems in rhythm and balance, even in patients who had performed well in sports. Always, social awkwardness was accompanied by some form of physical awkwardness. The social klutz, the geek or the nerd, may in fact be the very mildest of the mild: he may belong on the very high end of the autistic spectrum.

And because his social awkwardness is wired into his brain, his only recourse is to recruit higher centers of the brain to compensate: he must use his cerebral cortex to perform work his cerebellum (and hippocampus) would normally do—just as the victim of cerebellar syndrome must use his cortex to tell him where to put his foot.

The result, of course, is a set of effort-filled social skills that are far from natural. Temple Grandin has written a number of fascinating accounts of how she set about teaching herself the ways of normal people. For many years she used the image of the sliding glass door to remind herself not to stand too close to people, and she read transcripts of the Begin-Sadat negotiations, which had been published in the *New York Times,* in order to study the art of conversation. Naturally, as she read she committed the dialogue to memory; then she played her mental tapes of the two world leaders in her head, over and over again.

For Temple, these strategies worked fairly well, though in manner and tone she is noticeably somewhat different. Other autistics have written of trying to acquire even less tangible social skills, such as a sense of humor. In the riveting book *There's a Boy in Here,* a he-said-she-said memoir by an autistic young man and his mother, each of whom tell their side of the story of his childhood, Sean Barron's mother describes her son's efforts to learn how to be funny:

> He gave up trying to figure out the joke books and started watching *Gilligan's Island* every day after school. It was the only television program he'd ever watched except game shows, which attracted him because of the flashing lights and repetitive noises. "But oh God, why did he have to pick *Gilligan's Island*?" we all wondered. He memorized whole chunks of dialogue and repeated them to [his sister] Megan . . . over and over and over, until she screamed with fury. I told him he had to stop.
>
> "She won't laugh."
>
> "Sean, you can't *make* someone laugh if they don't think there's anything funny. When you repeat it, she thinks it's even less funny."
>
> He used lines from the show at random, furious if we all didn't burst into guffaws, and he teased Megan mercilessly when she didn't respond. I told him that he had to stop teasing her or he could no longer watch the TV show. He kept on repeating the same lines over and over, to Megan and then to me.
>
> "Okay, that's it. You can't watch that show anymore."
>
> He argued violently. . . . I said I had warned him many times and that I wanted to hear no more about it.
>
> The next day he came home from school and, at 4:00, when *Gilligan's Island* was telecast, he sat in front of the television set without turning it on. For a half hour he watched the blank screen, chuckling to himself from time to time, sometimes laughing out

loud. At 4:30 he got up. "Boy, that was a really funny show today!" he said as he passed me.

After this, Judy Barron writes, Sean's ritual protest went on for a month. Every day he would come home from school, sit down, and pretend to watch *Gilligan's Island*. Finally this episode in the life of mother and son drew to a close, Sean having come no closer to gaining the much longed for ability to make other people laugh.

■☐ THE MAN WITH A SECRET

When Ed Ritvo first suggested the then-radical possibility that there might exist *married* autistic people, most professionals were initially disbelieving. But in the years since Ritvo's letter to the editor of the *Journal of Autism and Developmental Disorders* concerning his "eleven possibly autistic parents," the ranks of recognized autistics who are married have been growing. These people were here all along; they simply had never been diagnosed. Today fully grown autistics are receiving the diagnosis for the first time in middle age. For many, it can come as a terrible shock.

Susan and Dan, of southern California, are a married couple who, after twenty-three years of marriage, are dealing with the revelation of Dan's autism. It has been very difficult. Of her husband's social disability, Susan says, "Dan lives in fear all the time. He feels angst all the time." Dan's fear is the fear of making a social misstep, of offending others without intending offense, of humiliating himself before the people with whom he hopes to be friends. Dan poignantly describes the dilemma he faces:

It's scary when you do or don't pick things up correctly, and *you don't know*. You're either going to be dinged or complimented. And as far as I'm concerned, I did whatever it was exactly the same way both times. There's no predictability inside me that says I'm doing it right this time, or I'm doing it wrong that time. Even when someone reassures me that I'm doing it the right way, it doesn't help. The fear says:

I'm only OK until I screw up again. I have a friend who was in the Navy, and he says that in the Navy you can do the same thing exactly the same way, and one time you're having coffee with the captain and the next time you're in the brig. I feel like I'm in the Navy.

This is one of the most poignant aspects of Dan's problem: it is not just that his autism causes him to do things the wrong way; far more troublesome is the fact that he has no ability to perceive when he has done something right and when he has done something wrong. His autism, mild though it is, strips away the self-monitoring mechanism upon which the rest of us rely. He cannot *see*. He is like a blind woman putting on makeup: as far as she can determine, she has done it the same way today as she did yesterday, and as she will again tomorrow. But in reality, in other people's eyes, she comes out looking different. Dan has no ability to make himself "come out" the same way from one day to the next.

What this means is that, for Dan, autism has penetrated not only his basic character, but his ability to *observe* his basic character. With all of the other shadow syndromes, most of us, if we have had sufficiently good parenting, are able to construct an observing self that is somehow not ADD or obsessive-compulsive or dysthymic or whatever it is that we are. This is one of the things good parents do: good parents help their children to develop distance from themselves, learn to reflect upon their emotions and their actions. Parents teach children to observe themselves. Thus the child not only develops a strong and centered personality, he or she also develops a strong watcher personality. The mildly depressed person who has had good parenting can feel depressed and yet maintain a part of her brain that is not depressed, that can rationally assess what lies ahead and what can be done about it. And, if we have not had effective parents, we can turn to therapists to help us develop the watcher within as adults.

But with autism—even with very mild autism—the capacity to watch is limited indeed. Psychologists speak of mind blindness and the metaphor is apt: the autistic person is largely blind to the minds of others, blind to the social world the rest of us inhabit. Just as a good par-

ent cannot teach a blind child to see colors, neither can the good parent teach an autistic child to see social reality. The social deficit is too
profound, too organic.

In their marital therapy, Dan and Susan struggle with this issue.
How much change is realistically possible for Dan? Susan does not hold
out a great deal of hope:

> Dan will spend a session with his therapist talking about something
> like how to offer sympathy to me. And then he'll come home and pat
> me like a dog, or tug at my hair. He did this all through *Batman* last
> night, because I'd just found out I didn't get a job I wanted very
> badly and I was really upset. Dan just sat there and yanked on a tuft
> of my hair for two hours. This is after an agonizing session of de-
> tailed work with his therapist.

While Dan's therapist takes a more optimistic view, Susan's twenty-
three years with Dan have taught her that, with autism, change is un-
certain. Autistic people do change, but not permanently; instead they
cycle. They are more autistic some days, less so others (this is one of the
qualities of autism that makes it look more like the mental illness it was
long thought to be, and less like a developmental disorder). Susan has
observed this phenomenon for many years now; she speaks of Dan as
having connected days and disconnected days. And with autism, Susan
has learned, what goes up must come down. The cycling of autism is
extremely frustrating to parents and loved ones, of course, because what
looks like improvement or learning so often turns out to be only the
high point on a roller coaster you can't get off. Susan sums up her sense
of helplessness:

> That's a key thing with autism. It's whatever is going on in the chem-
> ical synapses that day, it's not learning from past experience.

In other words, Dan does not "learn." The good, connected days inevitably give way to the bad, disconnected days. He has no ability to
hold on to the good day; he has no ability, even, to tell the difference
between a good day and a bad day. On a good day he might bring his

wife fresh-cut roses from the garden (he has learned from his therapy that wives appreciate such gestures); on a bad day he might bring his wife roses from the garden that are dried up, shriveled, already dead. This difference means everything to his wife, and to his marriage, and he cannot see it.

■□ A MARRIAGE BLESSED BY THE CHURCH

Dan and Susan met twenty-four years ago in a church youth group. They were Pentecostal, and in the context of the Pentecostal Church, Dan did not seem especially strange.

> *Dan:* When I was a kid, there were two groups of kids who took an interest in me, the Mormon kids and the Pentecostal kids, and there were more of the Pentecostal kids, so that's who I became friends with. The Pentecostal Church has a lot of emotion and feeling and right-brain activity that is incorporated in the worship that was frowned upon by everybody else. They'll dance in the aisles with services that last three hours, with a lot of activity that would be socially unacceptable anywhere else; they'll sway their hands and there's lots of noise going on, language, speaking in tongues—anything where all kinds of sounds are coming out that are not mediated by cognition, and it's not understandable. It's a "heavenly language," lots of repetitive one-syllable words being uttered over and over.

In the alternate world of the Pentecostal, a religious practice self-consciously different from the wider world of liberal Protestantism, Dan's eccentricities were accepted. For his part, Dan could satisfy many of his autistic impulses in a socially acceptable manner within the context of a fire-and-brimstone religion:

> I sang in a black gospel choir. We had this one event in particular—we would go on a Saturday night to L.A. to sing in a rented theater,

and it went on the radio. The phrases were repetitive, because the soloist does all the complex singing, and the chorus does the repetitive stuff. This would go on for two or three hours, and I would feel real good afterwards.

From the perspective of an undiagnosed young man with autism, this must have been nirvana: the perfect verbal "stim"! Many small children with autism will spend hours chanting the same word or phrase or sentence over and over again. This is considered a form of verbal self-stimulation, or stimming, as it is called by parents and professionals alike. While Dan was not, to the best of his memory, echolalic as a child (echolalia being the child's echoing back either of language he has heard immediately or later on), in the choir he reveled in the pleasures of repetitive speech.

But, as usual for Dan, when it came to the social aspects of life among the Pentecostals, he was oblivious. Today he laughs, looking back at his experience in the choir:

> It didn't even occur to me that I was in a dangerous position; my parents probably would have killed me for going into South Central. It never even occurred to me that it was wrong to be out with black people—which, in my neighborhood, it was.

This is the sweet side of autism: while the autistic husband will have no concept of how to comfort his wife when she has suffered a setback, he will also not know how to hate another human being for the color of his skin. Autism offers the world its own purity.

Dan and Susan came together in the wake of Susan's tempestuous relationship with Dan's roommate, Mike. It is a story that now, in retrospect, is suffused with autistic leanings and traits. But at the time, in the context of an intensely fundamentalist church youth group, the pairing made sense:

> *Susan:* There was a lot of sexual tension between Mike and me, because neither of us believed in sleeping together before marriage. So we had enormous arguments, and Dan always

patched them up. He never got sucked up in the argument; he wasn't empathetic. He'd just say "Susan, shut up and sit over there, and, Mike, you shut up and sit over there."

Dan was intellectual, and I was very lonely intellectually. I had an IQ of 162, and I was a physics major, and the church considered me to be "out of the will of God" because being intelligent and studying physics were not womanly. The church brought in a psychologist to speak to the girls. His course was called "Soft, Warm, and Yielding," and he taught us that if you got up and turned off the TV, then you were taking authority away from your husband. I called the course "Hot, Tight, and Wild" and got hauled on the carpet. In the fundamentalist church, passion is not OK.

In this environment Dan seemed like the normal one. He was incapable of sexism, and he was incapable of making the kind of social judgments that defined Susan's IQ as too high, her physics major "out of the will of God." Dan was a friend. When Susan, nursing a broken foot, stayed up all night to write Mike's term paper for him, Dan was there helping, a gesture that rendered him all the more appealing when Susan discovered that Mike had spent the evening out on a date with another girl. She broke off with Mike, and rebounded to his sensible roommate Dan:

> *Susan:* I told myself, in the midst of all this insanity I have found a normal person who thinks like I think. He did not put any emphasis on my appearance—I literally could wear hair curlers and mudpacks in front of Dan and he wouldn't mind—and I was crazy about computers, and here was fresh meat from out of the sky who could really program. We could talk mainframe computers, and when I had a problem programming, Dan could just look it over and say, "There's where the problem is." Or I'd discuss boyfriends with Dan; he was safe, neutral territory. He thought it was normal that I had a high IQ and was busily preparing myself with career skills, and that I didn't speak French. All the girls in the church were beautiful, and had to learn French; knowing how to speak French was considered feminine. Dan didn't care about any of it.

In fact, Dan's utter oblivion to the sexual standards and appetites of his peers was a danger sign. But to Susan, a gifted young woman struggling to come of age in a fundamentalist church that prized neither intelligence nor ambition in a female, Dan was a breath of fresh air. He was the sane one in a sea of Bible-thumping pastors, youth-group leaders, and Christian psychologists; he was a man who did not even comprehend, much less embrace, the concept of "Soft, Warm, and Yielding."

In the wake of Susan's break with Mike, she and Dan drew closer. They did not date; after one platonic weekend trip together—which scandalized the elders of the church—Dan did not ask Susan out again. He was simply there, always "quiet, gentle, a sweetheart of a guy." Soon, Dan proposed.

> *Susan:* Three or four months after the trip Dan said, "I think we should get married." And I laughed and said, "What a ridiculous notion." But Dan said best friends make the best marriages, and he said we should go to the marriage counseling the church required for all couples before they got married.
>
> I was oblivious; it was like a lamb to the slaughter. The church psychologist told us he was in favor of Japanese culture with its arranged marriages. He said sex is automatic, and it will come afterwards; God puts the emotions in place. I said, "Wow, if that's the way it is, then Dan and I fit the paradigm." And Dan said that the reason he never touched me was that he respected me so much, he couldn't touch me at all, because if he started touching me he wouldn't be able to stop. I would tell him, "But my girlfriends are engaged and their boyfriends send them roses," and Dan would say, "I'm not going to be that way." For the counselor, roses didn't matter. What mattered was common goals and values.
>
> So I became willingly Mrs. Dan Jones. My earlier relationship had been very passionate and romantic and engaged, and I was on the rebound. And I married Dan.

For Susan the marriage would prove to be extraordinarily difficult.

■ MIND BLINDNESS

It is an axiom of couples counseling that spouses cannot read each other's minds. Wives are usually the targets of this homily: it is husbands (let's be honest) who seem so often to fall down in the empathy department. Women want their men to intuit what they need, to *know* what they are feeling and wishing without having to ask, or be told. In this, according to the tenets of marriage counseling, they are being completely unreasonable.

But when we look at love and marriage from the perspective of autism, we begin to see things differently. In fact, it is not unreasonable to expect one's mate to read one's mind, and on a daily basis, too: mind reading (the British call this ability mentalizing) is a fundamental talent wired in to all normal brains. We must read others' minds continually in order to function as social beings at all: in order to know when others are receptive and when they are not, when people like us and when they do not, who is a friend and who is a foe. We read minds just to carry on a conversation: one extremely high-functioning autistic man, a man so mildly affected that he is (accurately) self-diagnosed for the syndrome, reports that to this day he cannot tell when it is his turn to talk. Intelligent enough to have majored in mathematics at a major university, he does not know when the other person is ready to yield the floor. He is "mind blind"; he cannot read minds.

Liars and cheats must also mentalize: it is impossible to deceive another without some concept of how the intended target is likely to react. And indeed, autistic children do not lie. In one of the more fascinating recent investigations into the nature of autistic impairment, autistic children were set the task of trying to keep a piece of candy from falling into the hands of a wicked puppet. They were given two ways to do this: they could either lie to the puppet by pointing to an empty box (all the while knowing that the candy was safely stashed away in a second box) or they could simply sabotage the candy box by locking it up so that the puppet could not get inside. The children turned out to be quite good at sabotage, but terrible at lying. The experimenters concluded that while the children were entirely capable of manipulating the puppet's *behavior*, they were not able to manipulate his *beliefs* by deceiving him.

The idea that other people are independent agents harboring independent thoughts about the nature of the universe eludes them. If something is true (the box is empty) and the autistic child knows it to be true, he cannot imagine another person thinking otherwise. Hence he cannot lead that person astray, because he does not comprehend that it is possible for that person *to be* led astray, to see the world and its boxes differently from the way they are. Thus for butcher and baker, for liar and thief, for lover and beloved, the capacity to see inside another's soul is essential. In the words of Francesca Happé: "The ability to 'mind-read' may be of such evolutionary importance that it is performed by a special, innately determined part of the brain." Research into the biology of autism may one day tell us where this anatomy lies.

Investigations into the mind blindness of autism are known as "theory of mind" research, and are essentially an updated and subtle working out of the commonplace observation that autistic people lack empathy. The Sally-Anne experiments, already classics in the annals of research into the psychology of autism, were the starting point for theory-of-mind researchers. In the Sally-Anne task, the autistic child is shown a situation in which two dolls, Sally and Anne, are together in a room. Sally has a basket, Anne a box. Sally puts her marble in her basket and leaves. While she is gone, Anne moves the marble from the basket to the box.

The crux of the autistic child's problem occurs when Sally returns. The child is asked: Where will Sally look for the marble? The correct answer, of course, is the basket: Sally has left the marble in her basket, and does not know that the marble has been moved while she was gone. All normal children understand that Sally will look in the wrong place by the time they are four years old: they understand that other people can hold false beliefs, beliefs that are different from reality, and different from their own beliefs. Very young nonautistic children can, in short, "think about thoughts."

But autistic children, it seems, cannot do this: an autistic child with a mental age of four years will normally tell the experimenter that Sally will look in the box! He has seen Anne move the marble to the box; the box is where the marble actually is; hence, he concludes, Sally will look in the box. He is incapable of imagining what is going on in Sally's mind. Significantly, this inability is not due to a simple and pervasive "retardation" (though many children with autism are also mentally retarded): Simon Baron-Cohen, the author of this study, found that 80 percent of a sample of children with Down's syndrome, children who as a group were somewhat lower in mental age than his autistic children, could answer this question correctly as well. The Down's child, the "normal" retarded child, can work out what another person is thinking. The autistic child cannot.

While the theory-of-mind idea gives off a great deal of heat in autism circles these days, there are of course dissenters. Some believe that the problem lies not fundamentally in the ability to mentalize, but in the brain's executive function: the capacity to engage, and to remain engaged, with a problem or an issue until it is resolved. The capacity, in short, and the drive, to make things happen. This is a concept borrowed from the annals of frontal-lobe research. People with frontal-lobe injuries lose executive function; they become apathetic and still, and their families complain that they lack motivation. They cease to act as chief executives of their own lives (a deficit also found, as we have seen, in rage disorders and in ADD). Because autistic people do indeed show deficits in executive function, some theorists feel that this may be the central deficit. Further research will look more closely at the balance between and among the many and varied psychological deficits we see in autism. But however our conception of the disorder changes over the years to come, however the emphasis shifts, the social deficits of autism will always be seen as central, and crippling.

■□ LOVE AND MARRIAGE

A marriage without mentalizing is going to be, from the nonautistic spouse's perspective, barely a marriage at all. And so it has been for Susan. In her twenty-three years with Dan she has been living in a state of disconnect. Susan often feels profoundly alone, and unprotected. Certainly, such feelings overcome her whenever she confronts bad news:

> *Susan:* It's the inappropriate responses when there's emotional news or bad stuff going on. Yesterday I found out that I didn't get the job I had applied for, and I was really upset and crying; I was so upset that I had to cancel my entire day and come home. And Dan said in a little-boy voice, "Oh, better luck next time," and then moved right on to the next topic. Once, when I'd had a devastating blow, Dan just said, "Oh. Want to go swimming?"

The trouble is, Dan is oblivious. He is not narcissistic in the classic sense of the term; he is not selfish. Instead, Dan suffers a primary disability in social comprehension. He loves his wife; he is hers for life. He is a good provider, and he is a steady soul. But he cannot read her mind in even the most basic ways. He cannot read her face, her gestures, her tone of voice. He is blind to his lifelong mate; he cannot see her.

The "discovery" of Dan's autism, just eighteen months ago, has come as a blow to both. The revelation came as the very unexpected end to a tumultuous course of events that began with Susan:

> I had a breakdown that I perceived as job burnout and stress. I'd been trying to get all my needs met through achievement, and I had reached a point where I was having anxiety and panic attacks. I was agoraphobic; Dan would have to hold my arm to walk me into grocery stores. I was suicidal. I had to stop working, and it was terrifying because I felt that, if I lost that, it would be over.

In therapy I talked about work; very definitely I presented a united front that home was OK, and so that issue never got dealt with. Dan was always in sessions with me, and he was a quiet support. I was so afraid that Dan would leave me or divorce me.

But the united front could not hold. In fact, Susan was extremely troubled by her marriage, and by the autistic behaviors she was witnessing in her husband:

Dan would run in circles, jump, and flap; for years I had a whole list of behaviors I was so frustrated about, particularly when we traveled. He might also masturbate in front of me, and when we would have intercourse, he would suddenly call out strange phrases. I would say "Dan!" and he would say, "I was thinking about a computer problem." He was pushing me away from these behaviors; he was masking them.

I couldn't go to my family; it was a no-talk family. And I didn't tell my friends. I had felt so guilty and shameful about bringing any behaviors forward.

But inevitably, as time wore on, issues concerning the marriage arose. As the therapy began to circle Dan and his problems, Dan withdrew. He stopped going to sessions, and told Susan that whatever was going on with her was her problem and hers alone.

By this point Dan was a man locked in an unacknowledged struggle with the truth. He did not want there to be something major "wrong" with him; he did not believe that there was. But in fact he had heard the word autism at a critical moment in his life:

In college my mom mentioned autism to me in a casual conversation. I was always wondering why I was two years older than everyone else going into college, and I had been doing real good in high school, and now I was away in college and wasn't doing too good either socially or academically and I was having some self-doubts. And it was one of those mom-son conversations. And I said, "Do you think there's something about me?" And she said I was held back a couple of years in grade school and that my second-grade teacher helped me out a lot. And the phrase "autistic behavior" came up with the teacher. I got the feeling from my mom's conversation that she didn't understand it. She said that some people thought she had abused me, and she said, "We knew that wasn't true, so we knew it couldn't be autism."

This was in the days of the refrigerator mother theory of autism, when cold or abusive mothers were blamed for their children's handicap. The autistic child, it was then thought, had been pushed into a state of catastrophic withdrawal from the world by a mother who did not love him. While this theory destroyed many an educated, middle-class mother, Dan's working-class parents simply rejected it out of hand.

My dad wasn't a smart man, and he had a very bad mistrust of doctors and professional people and all that kind of thing; he thought they'd invent these terms like "autism" for ego's sake and he had no confidence in that at all.

So the family closed ranks. They refused the label, and they dealt with their son's idiosyncrasies as best they could. The story of Dan's military father trying to make a dent in his son's autism is touching:

If my dad had been a social climber, I would have been discarded. But he didn't care about any of that, and he wanted to keep things in the family, and solve things in the family. He was very conditioning- and training-oriented, from his years in the military: if you've got a problem with an individual, you train them and condition them, and train them and condition them again. One of the things I used to do was I would run for hours around the perimeter of the backyard. I would just go out there and run. So rather than stop me from doing that, my dad one day just decided "OK, I'm going to run with you." And he said, "I want at least five minutes of your time every day, and we'll run the way I want to run, and then you can run the way you want to run," which was full-bore. And what he was teaching me was cadence running, and simple marching songs where you'd change speed by changing the song. He thought he could shape the running into something constructive.

As her husband circled the yard with their son, Dan's mother set about making their house the social center of the neighborhood, the one place all the other children came to play. If her son had trouble going out and meeting other children, she would bring the children to him. And she did.

And so they found their way through his childhood without a diagnosis, a strategy that, in the psychoanalytic climate of the 1950s, was probably just as well. Unfortunately, it left Dan with few resources outside his family for confronting what was different about him. Thus in college, knowing and yet not knowing that he was unlike his peers, he found himself drawn to psychology courses. For one of these he worked at Camarillo State Hospital, where he encountered severely autistic children living in an institutional setting. The image of these children sparked nothing in him, he says, no hint of recognition. Dan had by now heard the word autism applied to him and had rejected it as firmly as his parents before him. So when the troubles in his marriage began, he honestly did not see them as having anything to do with his social difference.

Unaware of her husband's history, Susan drew her own conclusions. Having uncovered repressed memories of incest and abuse during the course of her therapy, Susan now began to think that something similar must have happened to Dan. Clearly, she thought, there was a secret troubling their marriage. Finally, she confronted him:

> Six to eight months into my therapy I finally came home and said to Dan: I need to put it on the line with you. There's something wrong here and I need an explanation.

She was expecting, at long last, a breakthrough; she was expecting her husband to confess to his own parallel history of abuse.

That was not what she got. Cornered, Dan responded very much as his mother had many years earlier when asked about her son's problems in college: he mentioned that autism might be a possibility; mentioned it, and dismissed it. He did not believe that he could belong to the same category as the severely impaired children at the state hospital; it did not seem possible.

But this time the subject would not go away. Within a few months something entirely serendipitous occurred: a colleague at work gave

Dan a copy of the *Scientific American* containing Uta Frith's article on autism. Frith is the British researcher who first translated Hans Asperger's classic paper on autism from German into English in 1991, thus at long last opening up inquiry into the high-functioning form of autism we now know as Asperger's syndrome. Asperger's syndrome is essentially autism with language; children diagnosed with this syndrome show no clinically significant delay in language and are fully fluent. Their problems are primarily social (though they may have mild learning difficulties as well). The history of autism is interesting in this respect, because the disorder was simultaneously identified in America by Leo Kanner (who published his paper in 1943) and in Germany by Hans Asperger (who published his work in 1944).

Remarkably, both men called the disorder autism. But there was a difference between the two groups of children whom they described in their papers. Kanner's children were classically autistic and severely impaired; Asperger's young patients were much higher functioning. Thus Hans Asperger's work raised the possibility that a person could be only mildly autistic. But because his work was not seen outside of Germany, the Kanner description of severe autism came to dominate. Once Asperger's original paper became widely available, the paradigm began to shift. (Today opinion varies as to whether Asperger's is simply another term for high-functioning autism, or a separate disorder altogether, albeit with highly similar symptoms. Consistent with current practice, we have used the terms interchangeably in this chapter.)

Dan's colleague had no idea what was going on in Dan's life; he had given him the magazine because it contained an article on computers. (Dan is a highly successful senior systems analyst.) Dan read Frith's work, and this time he saw himself; he could no longer avoid the truth. He took the magazine to an employee counselor at work, and asked her whether, in her professional opinion, he might be autistic. Needless to say, Dan's quandary was radically far afield from the kinds of problems she was accustomed to employees bringing to her, and she told him so flatly. But she did do one helpful thing: she referred him to the psychologist he and Susan see today.

To his eternal credit, this therapist, who had himself worked with autistic children only briefly at the same state hospital where Dan had briefly volunteered, and who had never heard of the concept of mild autism, did not flinch when Dan came in with his question. Psychodynamically trained, he recognized right away the challenge Dan presented:

> I come from a classically trained world: Freud, Jung, and Klein. In that world a person with autism is viewed as someone who misses something critical very early in life, sometime from the moment of birth to one month, so that the child is not invited into the world. That's why Bettelheim went for the bad-mother theory of autism; it was the enraged infant who went inside himself and never came out again.
>
> Working with an autistic patient from that model, the idea would be to build a safe place where emotions are OK. The biomedical model introduced the idea that autism is not caused by psychological trauma, but is a result of physiological factors. Therefore, it's imperative that you get an idea of what the person is capable of before you start treatment, and with Dan I didn't have a clear idea whether psychosocial or biochemical elements were involved and it would have been horrendous to put him through fifteen years of psychodynamic therapy. So I was confused about this issue when I met Dan, and I remain so today.

Every week Dan and his therapist confront the puzzle of what Dan can change and what he cannot; what "behaviors" are autistic behaviors and what are just classic "guy things" like not being tuned into a wife's feelings. For years, whenever Susan did venture to complain about her husband, her family would invariably respond that Dan was simply acting "like a man," and in fact, when one hears Susan's catalogue of issues, they do, on the surface, sound very much like the complaints of many wives. In fact, her problems with Dan are so familiar that Susan's story inevitably raises the possibility—at least to anyone sitting with the two of them, listening—that perhaps it is a case not only of men being more likely to be autistic than women, but that normal men may be somewhat more "autistic" than normal women. That normal women may indeed possess greater social intelligence, on the whole, than normal men.

Whatever the reality may be concerning innate levels of social intelligence between the sexes, the truth is that Dan's social difficulties do
move far beyond the realm of normal "guy" behaviors. He is, in many
ways, not just "insensitive" but nearly blind to the feelings and needs
of others. Susan tells the story of the time they had pulled into the
parking lot of Savon Drugs to make a purchase. Dan waited in the car,
while Susan went inside. When Susan emerged from the store, she saw
a man staggering between the cars, clearly very ill. She got in the car
and pointed the man out to Dan, but Dan did not register the situation; he had the keys in the ignition and was starting the car. He
wanted to go.

At that moment the man collapsed in front of their car and Susan
jumped out to see what she could do, leaving Dan profoundly frustrated—autistically frustrated—by the fact that their designated
course of action had been interrupted. Once an autistic person is on
track to do something, he needs to stay on track. Dan was shouting,
"What! What!" angrily at Susan as she ran back inside the store to get
help.

> *Susan:* When I finally got back in the car, Dan asked me, "Why did
> you jump out of the car?" And I said, "Look at all those peo-
> ple standing around that man—don't you see what's going
> on?" And Dan said, "No." So I said, "You would have left
> that guy on the ground and driven off?" And Dan said, "Yes."

Dan saw, but he did not *see:*

> *Dan:* I did see the man on the ground, and I thought it looked like
> he was having a seizure. I just watched and then people started
> coming around looking at him. And his friend came. It didn't
> register as anything out of the ordinary; it was like anybody
> walking down the sidewalk. There was no emotional coloring
> to the event.

For Susan, episodes like these are frightening—terrifying, in fact—
because she can all too easily imagine being hurt herself, with Dan un-

able to respond. Suppose, she asks herself, one day it is she who is lying there before him, collapsed on the pavement. Will Dan start the car and drive away? Will he know to find help? Will he know *in time?* Already she has confronted one such situation, after a car accident that left her with a dislocated shoulder:

> They sent me home that night—they weren't going to set the shoulder for two weeks, when the swelling went down—and I was in shock. And Dan did not appear to have any perception that I had been severely injured. My girlfriend had to stay the night with me at home.
>
> Then the next morning Dan is angry and agitated because he has to take off work and make arrangements with highway patrol and insurance. I physically cannot move, and Dan keeps handing me the telephone. "You do it," he keeps saying, "you take care of it, Susan, because I don't know how to talk to the insurance agent." In the following two weeks my girlfriend, who was a therapist, canceled all her patients and came and stayed. I couldn't cut my meat because of my injury; the food would fly off the plate. And Dan would just keep eating; he didn't perceive what was going on.

While frightening to his wife, for Dan these situations are painful harbingers of things to come. He is profoundly embarrassed by his social lapses, none of which he perceives until they are pointed out to him by his wife, and the diagnosis of autism has hit him hard. It is, he says, devastating:

> I don't know what's in the cards; it may be that we'll be in therapy for the rest of our existence. I know I'm beyond having to be in an institution, I'm way beyond all that, but this is the first step in the direction of having to have daily assistance to live life. It gives me a feeling of awkwardness, a feeling that something very significant is wrong. And I do not wish to be a victim; I do not wish to be labeled as this.

Autism cannot be cured; that is the hard truth. Dan knows this. Still, there is hope. Dan's case is certainly mild; his therapist believes he can make significant changes, that his emotional life can grow. It is entirely possible. Not long after Dan's blank response to the stricken man in the parking lot, the meaning of the scene came to him:

> Two days later it popped into my brain, and I asked Susan, "What happened to that guy on the ground?" And at that point I knew that the man was in trouble.

Suddenly, the scene flooded with color, the emotional tinting Dan so often misses. He *got it*. Perhaps some day not too long from now, he will begin to make contact with his wife's inner life as well. In any case, all of the shadow syndromes bring their blessings, mixed though they may be, and the autistic person, loath to change and not much of a mind reader, is as loyal, steadfast, and fundamentally honest as he is socially unaware. As Susan says,

> Children love Dan. They instinctively like him. He's childlike, simple; Dan is uncomplicated. What you see is what you get. That was one of the things that attracted me to Dan, and that is still the case today. Dan is a man of integrity.

Perhaps Dan can refashion himself into a likeness of the husband Susan wants and needs, perhaps not. But given his unchanging devotion to Susan, he will certainly try.

■ THE CEREBELLAR CONNECTION REVISITED: HAM NASH

Ham Nash came to John as a sixty-year-old man who had been depressed for forty years. Because of his difficulty paying attention, he had been given the diagnosis of attention deficit disorder two years before, and since that time had devoted himself to reading everything he could find about the syndrome and developing an awareness of how ADD had shaped his daily life. Nevertheless, the diagnosis and his subsequent self-education had not helped as much as he had hoped. He was still depressed, still unfocused, still arguing with his wife of five years over what level of social life the two would have together. She was a wealthy citizen of a small town populated by affluent retirees with time on their hands (Ham had moved to the community after their marriage), and she wanted to spend time with what Ham called the country club set. But Ham had no interest in the many cocktail parties and charity events to which they were invited. He disliked small talk intensely and, without alcohol (which he had given up a few years before), he could not do it.

Ham's therapists, and they had been many, had universally seen him as a thoroughgoing narcissist. He would sit in their offices with his wife, monologuing about himself, and they would invariably conclude: this man needs to think about his wife's feelings. And yet, no matter how often he was admonished to take his wife's feelings into account, Ham continued to talk about Ham. *His* feelings, *his* pain, *his* chronic lack of what he called cognitive clarity. That was Ham.

The possibility that something more than a case of everyday narcissism might be present in Ham first struck John with the issue of Ham's profound aversion to small talk. Ham was not shy in the least; he was a friendly fellow with a big smile on his face, a man who drove around the small town in a truck with a canoe on top, dressed in vibrant colors and, if the spirit moved him, a bolo tie. (Which he'd once worn with a tux to a formal affair. As to this fashion choice, he told John, "I'm not trying to stir up attention, that's just the way I want to be." The string tie had felt right, and so he'd put it on. The fact that no one else at the affair would be wearing a bolo tie simply did not affect his vision of himself one way or another.) A friendly person who cannot engage in small talk: this is an anomaly, and it raised a question for John.

The moment of revelation arrived when Ham himself brought up the subject of balance. He told John that he had always had problems with balance—with the physical ability to balance his body—in spite of the fact that he had been a good athlete all of his life. But he had never been able to balance on his left foot, and a few years earlier he had been sufficiently troubled by his difficulties with balance that he had experimented with Dramamine as a treatment. The results had been encouraging: the Dramamine had stopped the ringing in his ears, which he had heard all of his life, and, interestingly, had dramatically improved his ability to read a line of print:

> I could follow one line to the end and drop down to the next line without my eyes wandering all over the page.

His comprehension had not improved, but the physical act of reading, under the influence of the Dramamine, now flowed smoothly for him.

The fact that these issues were coming up so early in therapy suggested to John that he was dealing with more than a mood disorder; more, in fact, than a straightforward case of ADD. Here was a man with cerebellar issues so intense that he himself was aware of them and had been actively trying to treat them.

Now John began to wonder whether Ham and his wife might be struggling with autistic issues. The fact that Dramamine could affect Ham's reading probably meant that it had worked by affecting his vestibular system, which is the end organ of the cerebellum. The vestibular system tells us where our limbs are located in space; it is what allows us to stand up straight with our eyes closed. Dizziness, vertigo, the sensation that the world is spinning: all of these conditions result from problems in the vestibular system. This system is very likely significant for large numbers of the handicapped population; at the large state institutions housing the mentally challenged, it is always the merry-go-rounds that are the most popular playground equipment. Dan, too, reports that he feels better, and calmer, after a wild ride on a roller coaster, the wilder the better. As Susan says:

> The more shake-up he gets—he loves it. I bet we'd have the best sex ever if we could go to bed right after Dan got off a roller coaster. He always kisses me really warmly after we come down off the ride.

The possibility that Ham's vestibular system was an issue set John upon a novel course: he would prescribe the balance medication Antivert for Ham, and see what happened. The results, from his patient's point of view, were stunning. With the Antivert, a drug intended to address problems in balance (in people with middle-ear infections, for instance, or in elderly people who have developed chronic problems with balance), suddenly, almost overnight, Ham's depression of forty years simply vanished:

> I've even tried at times to get depressed since I started the Antivert. I'll think what is the worst thing that has happened to me. But it doesn't seem to do anything, doesn't affect my mood.

Having witnessed this unorthodox miracle, John now began to see Ham's life through the lens of autism. Sure enough, Ham reported many of the issues a very high-functioning (*very* high) autistic adult would report. He had no friends at all: as Ham himself put it, "I don't have one friend in this world; I don't get to know people." And while he had had three wives (and three children), none of these people came across as much more than a name, rank, and serial number in his brief mentions of them. While he loves his wife Jane very much, she does not seem to *register*. It is not that Ham does not care what her thoughts or feelings are; it is more that Ham, like autistic people in general, truly does not know what those thoughts and feelings might be. He does not know because he does not seem to possess a means of finding out; he does not, in short, possess a theory of mind—certainly not a theory of mind as developed as it should be in a man his age. To Ham the interiority of others is entirely inaccessible.

His social deficits are the most obvious autistic quality in Ham, but as John pressed further, he discovered that Ham also possessed a host of other autistic symptomatology as well. For one thing, he was extremely sensitive to noise; the minor din produced by so mild a civil setting as a society wedding could plunge him into agony. Often, he would sit among the guests on their white folding chairs, plugging his ears with his fingers. For another, and this was quite a discovery, Ham secretly indulged in a number of autistic stereotypies: rocking and bending his fingers back, humming to himself, even hand-flapping from time to time. He did this, he said, to relieve tension:

It is soothing. Say, if there's a loud noise, I can rock back and forth, maybe just a few inches, it's just the motion. And it helps in moments of stress. There are times, when the stimuli is more than what the rocking can help, where I hum. As I rock forward, I can go mmm-m-mmm-m-mmm-m-mmm.

With the hand-flapping and rocking, I remember as a kid banging my back and head against the couch over and over again. It always felt so good. And my hand and finger motion; this was the first time I ever told anybody about it. In Dr. Ratey's office I made a motion he said autistic people do where they take their hands and push outward like they're trying to hold the walls up. And I said, "What's so unique about that?" When I'm overstimulated and alone, I'll have my fingers extending out and clenching back and forth, then I move the hands all around; I sometimes will do little dances to myself. It's a release from frustration. Some people have temper tantrums; I, if I'm alone, will do these odd little dances and gestures with my hands and arms, and it's been relieving.

When Ham demonstrated these classically autistic behaviors in John's office, his wife exclaimed: "You don't do that!" And Ham replied, "Not when you're around."

Autistic aloneness, autistic stereotypies: Ham is more than a touch autistic. But perhaps most troubling to him are his autisticlike difficulties with language. Many classically autistic people are mute; those who speak often show a severely stunted grasp of their native language. Ham struggles with an invisible handicap: he *sounds* fluent, he does not sound autistic. But language is not a friend:

People say, "You're so articulate." Well, you put on your mask when you're feeling lousy, and it's usually that of a clown. And if you diffuse what people were asking you with some jokes, they forget what they asked. You can't understand the words coming in, and you get very frustrated because you know that life is there, and is better than what you're living. You know that you can answer a question in a classroom, but you don't dare raise your hand because it's gone. The answer is living in me, but I raise my hand and have to put it in words and I'm embarrassed because I can't. You don't fit in with the articulate people. I've kept people laughing for years so they don't know how I hurt.

Visual thinking is easier for Ham (yet another indication that his problems are related to those of autism), though his inner life is not as profoundly wordless as Temple Grandin's. In her book *Thinking in Pictures,* Grandin writes that she does not think in words at all, only in images, and this is not precisely true of Ham. Instead, Ham's thought processes seem to fall somewhere between the verbal inner stream of normal people and the all-out imagery of Temple and many other autistics. Ham relies heavily upon visual analogies, or pictures put into words:

> I speak in analogies when I can't verbalize; I make an analogy when the feeling is there but I can't get it out. The words don't come, but the pictures do.

Ham's conversation is strewn with visual analogies. He tells people that his brain is, variously, like a bird's nest, or a dumpster, or a ball of cotton; his best day on medication was like a blind man waking up and suddenly seeing his face in the mirror; and so on. He is thoroughly visual when it comes to learning new material. He tells the story of learning how to execute a ski turn (Ham and his wife are both experienced ski instructors):

> For three years there was a concept in turn initiation, where you finish one ski turn and start into another, that I didn't get. I always listened, but it didn't register, and for one to say "I don't get that, show me"—that becomes an inconvenience to others.
>
> So one day we were all gathered around a slight incline, everybody was leaning on their ski poles and listening to the instructor explain something. And unconsciously he just stood up a little bit taller, and what I noticed was that as soon as he did that it went right to his boots; his skis went from being on edge to flattening out on the snow, and he started to slide forward and he put out his poles to stop himself. I don't think he moved six inches, but for the first time in three years, I got what the turn consisted of. I got it in my personal skiing and I got it in my teaching. I could never learn it verbally.
>
> Then I made an analogy out of it. If you take a one-foot ruler and lay it on edge on a plush carpet so that whole length of ruler is in the

carpet, then you can't turn that ruler left or right because it's in the carpet. But if you take the ruler and lay it flat, then you can turn it because it's flat on top of the carpet.

For Ham the visual *can* sometimes translate effectively into the verbal, but thought and learning always begin in imagery or feeling.

The question in all of this for anyone who sees himself, or a loved one, in the lives of Dan, Joe, and Ham is, of course, what can be done about an autism shadow syndrome. For many years the conventional wisdom, in dealing with classic autism, was that there was no medication for autism per se. A clinician could medicate individual symptoms: hyperactivity, mood problems, tantrums. But for autism itself, as a pervasive syndrome, there was nothing.

Generally speaking, this feeling remains true today, though an opinion is forming that of all the various medications available to the practitioner, the SSRIs (Prozac, Paxil, Zoloft, and Luvox) plus Anafranil (a tricyclic antidepressant that is highly effective for obsessive-compulsive disorder) are the drugs of choice for autistic patients. Prozac does not erase autism the way it can erase depression, but it is often a help. A mildly autistic person taking an SSRI may be far less obsessive, anxious, and depressed, less "noisy." (We should add that since its recent introduction into this country the atypical neuroleptic Risperidone has become popular in the treatment of severe cases of autism as well, particularly for problems with sleep and aggression. Risperidone is an extremely potent drug that would not be used for mild or high-functioning autism.)

Unfortunately, thus far no one has developed a "smart pill," the pill for which so many are waiting, the pill that will address the cognitive and perceptual deficits of autism, mild or severe. (There are at present pharmaceutical companies making real progress in developing a drug that will directly treat and improve memory, certainly a smart pill function. But none of these medications has reached the market yet.) It is here, in the hope for such a medication, such a method of treatment, that Ham's story offers both heartbreak and hope:

January 3, 1994, was the only time in my recollection that I had a full day of cognitive clarity. I had started taking Norpramin (an antidepressant) and at five after twelve in the morning I can remember sitting bolt upright in bed. It was like somebody with a terrible cold and they woke up and everything was clear; my senses were just like the Fourth of July. When you go to a Fourth of July celebration, and everything is going off, it's green and white and there are showers and rockets—the Fourth of July is *clear*.

And suddenly, I could talk to someone without thinking of my words beforehand and I could receive conversation. All my life I've had to guess at some of what people are saying; then I give myself a minisummary of ten sentences about what they've just said to try to get it down. But that day I didn't have to look at the words as they came in. And I can remember making I don't know how many phone calls that day to people just to hear incoming.

I remember going to bed at nine, and I just lay there saying "I'm not going to sleep." Scenarios were going on in my head, and all kinds of things were coming back that maybe I had learned but I couldn't process at the time. It was like these people with the photographic memories and everything was clear as a bell.

And everything went in thirty seconds; I could feel it all go at seven minutes before eleven. For twenty-two hours and forty-three minutes, or fifty-two minutes, everything was clear. And then I could feel the cloud come in, I could feel the whole thing ending.

It was a devastating experience: a dramatic treatment effect, in the dry vernacular of the profession, that was to last only twenty-three hours. After that day the Norpramin no longer worked, and nothing, including the Antivert, has worked since. Ham mourns the loss. Like the comatose patients in Oliver Sacks's *Awakenings,* Ham awoke to the world, and then lost it again.

But the very fact of Ham's twenty-three hours offers hope: his experience shows that it is at least possible to treat so profoundly intellectual a mental faculty as language with a medication. One day, perhaps sooner than we imagine, the chemists of the brain may find an answer.

■□ SHY GORILLAS

Autism has long been thought to be a rare disorder; today opinion is increasingly coming to hold that it is in fact not at all rare. What is relatively rare, mercifully, is the classic, severe form of autism that consigns its victims to lives of dependence in institutions and group homes. But the milder forms of autism may be with us in significant numbers. Certainly, as one autistic reader of an early draft of this chapter pointed out, Silicon Valley is filled with potential candidates for a high-end diagnosis.

But apart from the microserf, there also exists a formal psychiatric category that may in fact represent a subset of autism: the so-called schizoid personality. To the clinician, what is actually autism may *look* like, and be diagnosed as, schizoid personality disorder. Just as for many years autistic children were diagnosed as suffering from "childhood schizophrenia," today high-functioning autistic adults may be mistakenly receiving a diagnosis of schizoid personality.

Psychiatrists think of the schizoid personality as a person who is halfway down the path to schizophrenia. He or she is socially isolated, displays poor empathy and emotional detachment, employs "unusual styles of communication," and is paranoid and highly obsessive in his interests. As Francesca Happé points out: of this list, only paranoia stands out as being not particularly autistic. Otherwise this collection of symptoms fits the mildly autistic person like a glove.

What makes paranoia leap out from the list is the fact that the classically autistic person is typically not paranoid. True innocents themselves, they are blind to other people's darker motives. (One mother of an intelligent autistic son living in Los Angeles lamented that every time he waited at a bus stop on Hollywood Boulevard he ended up "giving away" his backpack to a stranger!) They are happily—or unhappily, as the case may be—oblivious.

So how is it that the schizoid personality might belong to the autistic spectrum? British theorists of autism including Happé have worked out a brilliant and economical explanation of how a subtype of autistic beings with paranoia could come to be: their paranoia, Happé writes, is a theory of mind gone wrong.

In short, there is more than one way to be socially apraxic (apraxia being the formal term for the loss of the ability to carry out purposeful movements that can occur after damage to the brain): one can have *no* notion of other people and their ways, or one can have actively *wrong* notions of other people and their ways. As Happé points out, a significant number of autistic people do pass theory-of-mind tests and yet still show significant social deficits. It is likely that they arrive at the right answer on the Sally-Anne task through different means than normal people do. In order to work out social situations they must recruit higher centers of the brain to think them through; they do not possess the automatic social-processing capacity of the nonautistic person. Like the cerebellar patient who must think before he puts his foot down, the high-functioning autistic person who possesses a theory of mind must think, and think hard, before he speaks or gestures.

Happé suggests that the effort-filled nature of social life for such people may be due to the severe delay any autistic or autisticlike person will experience in acquiring a theory of mind in the first place. By the time he has developed an ability to read minds, valuable childhood time has been lost. And indeed, Simon Baron-Cohen found that of the four autistic children who passed a false-belief task that normal four-year-olds universally pass, three were older than fifteen years of age, and the fourth was nearly ten. That is a great deal of childhood to pass by without even a rudimentary understanding of other people's thoughts and feelings. (While these particular children were not tested at age four to see whether they could have passed the test then as well, the fact that no autistic child has ever been found who could pass the false-belief task at either a chronological *or* a mental age of four implies that these children could not have done so either.) Just as a child past age ten or so can never learn to speak a foreign language without an accent, it may be the case that an autistic child who does not acquire a theory of mind until age ten will also, always, speak the language of social life with a difference.

By the same reasoning, it makes sense that at the very high-functioning end of the autistic spectrum you would begin to see people who *do* possess a highly elaborated theory of mind—but who have got the theory all wrong. Paranoid people, in other words. There is a school of thought that schizophrenia may in fact be, at the psychological level, a disorder of mind-reading: hallucinations and delusions often represent magnificently wrong "readings" of other people's intent and behavior. The very high-end autistic, rather than make no reading at all of the people around him, may instead be tortured by readings that are altogether wrong.

John first saw the connection between the schizoid personality and the very high-functioning autistic when he began to identify a population of patients whom he came to think of as shy gorillas. These were brilliant people, all of them, with IQs in the 160 range. The majority were women. They were intensely, fiercely, profoundly shy, and they were invariably quite distrustful to some degree. So much so that not one of them has been interviewed for this chapter; they are too shy, and too suspicious, to give interviews, and John did not feel comfortable even broaching the subject with them. (In this they are quite the opposite of the ADD population, who will happily talk for hours about the most intimate details of their lives to any friendly stranger with a word processor. For the interviewer, at least, ADD is a great deal of fun.)

It was the image of Dian Fossey quietly observing her gorillas that caused John to think of these patients as shy gorillas. With these patients, John felt like an observer; he could not make the direct contact with them that he could with other patients. Like John's shy gorillas, Fossey's gorillas had their own environment, away from other creatures; they needed to stay in the upland, off and away. They were social only with each other, and only out of the way, although they desired sociability and would die without it. So, too, with the shy gorillas of the human population, who want and need people, but whose shyness is always a barrier. For a therapist, or for a friend or lover, making contact with a shy gorilla is never easy. They grow frightened and retreat internally; they do not belong in the city. They belong in the simple spaces and in the country, and they know it. The ones who are successful in life find a way to stay in their simple gardens of life.

Often, John's shy gorillas had in the past been diagnosed as schizoid personalities in the past. They were socially isolated: one fifty-eight-year-old man, a brilliant scientist for NASA, had never placed a social telephone call to a soul in his entire life. He made his first during his therapy with John. None were married; all were extremely successful in their chosen fields. Some had experienced psychotic breakdowns and been hospitalized.

All gave evidence of telltale cerebellar issues: one had never been able to clap in time to music, another had never been able to dance with a partner, and so on. (We foresee a day in the not-too-distant future when psychiatrists will routinely ask socially disabled patients questions concerning physical coordination and rhythm.) This is not to say that they lacked rhythm on their own terms; one was a musical genius. What they lacked was social rhythm; they could not move in time to the rhythms of other people. They marched to different drummers.

They were also acutely oversensitive to mundane stimuli, as are most if not all classically autistic individuals. Many refused to wear their glasses because they found 20-20 visual reality too intense: too sharp, too cutting, too much information all at once. (Buckminster Fuller, another shy genius who did not wear his glasses, may well have been a shy gorilla.)

As to the realm of the imagination—the lack of which is one of the most striking deficits in autistic children, who do not engage in pretend play—most of John's shy gorillas fancied science fiction. This is classic among the high-functioning autistic population; science fiction is the autistic genre, it seems. The *Star Trek* series is revered by many high-functioning types; Temple Grandin reports that she never misses an episode. Interestingly, one of the *Star Trek* series has cast an actress with Asperger's syndrome in the recurring role of (what else?) an alien. (Off the record, a film producer once remarked, speaking of a famous actress who was diagnosed mildly autistic as a child: "She can only play aliens.") All of which offers some insight into the reasons why the very high-functioning person might gravitate to science fiction: often he feels like an alien himself. It is not for nothing that Temple Grandin, describing how she feels when trying to parse out the social behavior of her fellows, calls herself an "anthropologist on Mars," giving Oliver Sacks a memorable title for the book in which he profiles her life.

Where the shy gorillas deviate from their high-functioning autistic cousins is in their profound and crippling shyness. They fear people. In contrast, while the "normal" high-functioning autistic person might *appear* shy, often this is due simply to his awareness that he does not know how to approach people. Dan is sociable in the extreme; he loves being around people, and relies upon his wife to bring friends into their lives, and keep them happy. This is probably the hardest part of his autism for Dan to bear: the not knowing, the not being able to *imagine,* who will like him or why, or for how long. Susan tells the poignant story of Dan panicking one week when she was forced to cancel their Bible study class, a group of friends with whom they had been meeting regularly for three years. "They won't like us anymore," he said, "they'll stop coming." He did not possess the essential concept that three years of fellowship do not vanish with one canceled meeting. When we spoke, Dan showed me a postcard print of his favorite painting: two cowboys slouched on horses beneath a sunny blue sky, leaning close in to each other and talking. This is the happiest scene he can imagine, the image of two people communing under the sun.

It is doubtful that a shy gorilla would produce such a picture as a vision of what he seeks in life. Shy gorillas are simply too shy. In this they may be doomed by their very ability to compensate for their inborn deficits. Shy gorillas do possess the best-developed theory of mind of anyone on the autistic spectrum. They know very well that other people have feelings, and they are more likely than the Temples and the Dans to surmise rightly what those feelings are. Unfortunately, too often they are wrong—but unlike Temple or Dan, shy gorillas assume that they are right. They are so confident of their perceptions that they think of themselves as empaths. Certainly they never question their darkest views of the people they know.

Thus, where his more autistic brother may be blissfully unaware of the nefarious doings of other people, the shy gorilla with the genius IQ has figured it out, or thinks he has, and is terrified by the vision of evil his rudimentary ability to read minds and hearts has brought him.

His basic neurology nature makes matters worse. All autistics live in a challenging state of hyperarousal; many live in prepanic states day in and day out. But whereas for the "normal" autistic these feelings of inchoate anxiety will attach to painful stimuli like loud sounds, for the shy gorilla the panic has attached itself to *people*. For the shy gorilla, people are the too-intense stimuli, the overwhelming source of noise that must be avoided at all cost. The shy gorilla is too close to "getting it" about other people to be comfortable living among them; for him and his kin hell is other people. One of John's shy gorillas once told him, during a session, that he didn't like doors. John had been interviewing him, taking him through a list of more conventional stimuli the mildly autistic person will avoid, such as sudden loud noises and the like (all of which, the patient agreed, he found extremely unpleasant), when the man brought it up: "I don't like doorways, either," he said. He did not like doorways because someone could walk through them! Another *person* could walk through them.

It is important to understand that, for the "schizoid personality," this is not a case of simple curmudgeonry. The problem with doorways, for a shy gorilla, is not just shyness, but also the pronounced startle response in autistic and autisticlike individuals. The startle response is innate: in infants it is called the Moro reflex, and the presence or absence of a startle forms part of the Apgar score. In order to pass this part of the test, the newborn, when his head is suddenly dropped down or when someone claps beside his ear, must move all four limbs, cross his arms, bring his legs up to his body, and all but shake like a leaf. If he does these things, it means he has a healthy brain-to-body connection, a brain that is responding naturally and normally. This is a "central check" (central referring to the central nervous system) to make sure that the brain is responding to the baby's change in position. If you don't see the startle, the baby may be unresponsive or hypotonic; he may suffer a rare muscle disease that prevents him from mustering the full physical response of a healthy infant. In any case, a lack of startle in a newborn is a sign of trouble ahead.

As we mature, the startle dwindles, though it never completely disappears; when we startle as adults, our shoulders go up a bit, we suck in our breath and tense our muscles—which is exactly what happens in the beginning of a panic episode, interestingly enough. The adult startle is, normally, quite subtle in comparison to the newborn's.

The problem for the person with any degree of autism is that his startle sequence is different. He will startle, and then, horribly, go right on startling; he does not recover himself as the rest of us do. The startle continues to build upon itself, driving the body into a state of chronic hyperarousal and prepanic.

The importance of the startle to autism cannot be underestimated. John learned this for himself when, at the beginning of his career, he took part in a study of babies born to schizophrenic mothers. He and his colleagues were looking to see whether they could find differences between the babies who went on to develop schizophrenia and the babies who did not.

One of the babies displayed an unbelievably fierce startle; he *never* accommodated to a stimuli. If you rang a bell once, he, like all babies, startled; if you rang it a second time, he startled again; if you rang it a third, fourth, fifth, and sixth time, he continued to startle just as violently as if he were hearing the bell for the first time. By then the other babies had grown accustomed to the sound, loud and intrusive as it was, and could weather it with no more than a blink. John and his colleagues had found what is called an outlier; the baby was off the statistical curve. He was like no other baby.

Three years later the baby was diagnosed with autism.

Autistic people must cope with a severe and unrelenting startle. The shy gorilla who feared doorways would startle at the sudden sight of a person standing in its frame; then, when he did not recover from his startle, he would panic. The startle would go on and on, he would begin to feel out of control, and his incipient panic would build into an adrenaline storm: his muscles tense, his heart racing, his body pouring flop sweat.

This patient's experience of doors is part and parcel of the autistic person's difficulty with change, which a doorway intrinsically represents. For this patient, having someone come into the doorway breaks into his inner space, interrupts his expectation of what is happening now and what is going to happen in the next moment; to him a person coming through a doorway is like a sudden handclap. It is the Big Bang. It is an abrupt *transition* from an empty room to a full room, from one state of being to another. The change produces a violent startle that builds to panic.

■ SHY GORILLAS AND THE "CENTRAL COHERENCE" THEORY

Shy gorillas are brilliant individuals; their IQs are extraordinarily high. They often achieve success far beyond what their parents and teachers might have predicted for them given their isolation and fearfulness. Where poor social skills will severely handicap an ordinary mortal, even the paranoid delusions of the shy gorilla do not, necessarily, block their paths. Instead, they make their way in tightly drawn professional worlds where colleagues recognize their brilliance and accept their idiosyncracies.

Their fellows do this because the shy gorilla possesses one critical advantage over the rest of us: he is *obsessed* with his chosen interest. In this, as in so much else, the shy gorilla is, ultimately, more autistic than not: all of these people (mathematics professors, NASA engineers, microserfs . . .), in their way, demonstrate the limited interests of their classically autistic brothers and sisters. And because they never let go of an idea, they see its ramifications throughout different domains; they make brilliant and unforeseen connections. It is what makes them geniuses in their fields, as opposed to merely Renaissance men and women with high IQs.

It is here, in the autistic person's ability to seize and pursue one subject for a lifetime, that we see the connection between the terrible deficits of autism, and its terrible brilliance, its "islets of ability," in the terminology of the professionals, its savantry. Even the most handicapped autistic child will obsess over some "interest," however pointless: train timetables, or makes of automobiles, or pieces of lint shimmering in the carpet. An autistic child may spend hours and hours of his day picking tiny pieces of lint from the floor. If his parents try to distract him, he resists with all his might, and soon returns to his obsessive quest. Very likely, he is *good* at perceiving tiny pieces of lint; the severely handicapped autistic child may be brilliant in the minute quests that grip him. Autistic, and autisticlike, interests all share one overriding quality: they are extremely narrow in nature. The autistic person thinks about, or does, the same small, circumscribed, thing over and over again, day in and day out. It must be the same, and it must be narrowly defined. Lint from the carpet. Or higher mathematics.

Recently, British theorists have developed a theory to explain why this should be so: the autistic person, they believe, suffers from a deficit in the ability to bring unity to the perceived world. Instead of seeing the world as a world, or the room as a room, or the carpet as a carpet, he sees the world in pieces. The normal person automatically, unconsciously, assembles his perceptual world into wholes. We see a face, not a nose, mouth, and two eyes. We read a story, not a collection of sentences. We experience a *gestalt*. We cannot do otherwise.

Dan describes himself as having enormous difficulty with "pattern recognition." He needs "autistic sameness," he needs objects and people to be in their proper places. If they are not, often he literally cannot see them. Susan tells the story of the time she moved his hairbrush from the right side of his sink in the bathroom, where he had kept it for twenty years, to the left:

> Suddenly, I heard this explosion from the bathroom; Dan was shouting and swearing because his brush was gone. So I called in, "It's on the left side of the sink," but he still couldn't find it. So then I went into the bathroom and pointed to the brush and said, "There it is," and he *still* couldn't see it. I couldn't believe it. Finally, I had to take his hand and put it on the brush. And he just said, "Oh."

Susan's story brings to mind the old schoolyard joke about Helen Keller: How do you give Helen Keller a nervous breakdown? Move the furniture. Dan, whose eyesight is fine but whose brain is not, needs the furniture, and the hairbrushes and the daily routines and the routes taken to church on Sunday to *remain the same.* Otherwise he is lost.

All of us have had the experience of not seeing something sitting directly before our eyes. It is entirely possible that sometimes, when this happens, we, too, are suffering a temporary lapse in cerebellar function. (And it is possible that those of us with less able cerebellar function have this experience more often. It is certainly an interesting possibility.) But almost none of us would find ourselves unable to perceive an object as large as a hairbrush when someone is pointing directly to it. This is the realm of autism.

We can see the hairbrush when someone points it out because our brains form coherent wholes from sensory input. That Dan's brain does not automatically see a hairbrush as a hairbrush, rather than a mosaic of bristles and plastic, may explain how it is that Dan can pick dead roses for his wife without knowing it: the flowers' two qualities of *being roses* and *being dead* do not cohere in his perceptual apparatus. He is missing an entire element of the flowers; he is missing the fact that they are no longer alive. The same process happens, or does not happen, at the social level: the baby sees the toy train but misses his mother's smile at the train. The British neuropsychological work on central coherence (the theory was first proposed by Uta Frith) is exciting because it rather precisely fits the neurological work of Eric Courchesne; the theory of central coherence works well as an explanation, at the psychological level, of phenomena Courchesne is finding to exist at the biological level. The slowness of the autistic person's shifts in attention, both Courchesne and British theorists like Uta Frith, Simon Baron-Cohen, and Francesca Happé might agree, results in the autistic person experiencing life as a series of freeze-frames. The data he takes in does not coalesce into a unified whole in memory.

Thus the autistic person, from the time of infancy, apprehends the world in parts, but the perhaps unexpected outcome of this early loss is that he becomes very *good* at perceiving the world in parts. This is a strength of autism, perhaps the key strength and the source of the autistic genius we see in the so-called idiot savants: an autistic person, while far worse than the normal person at grasping a whole, is often far better at perceiving the parts. In embedded figures tests, tests in which a child is asked to find a hidden figure in a picture, autistic children far outperform normal children; often they outperform the experimenters as well.

In practice, the autistic deficit in central coherence reveals itself in various ways. Happé cites several fascinating examples. In one an autistic boy was shown a toy bed and asked to name the parts. He identified everything correctly: bed, mattress, quilt. But when he came to the pillow, he said, "Ravioli"—and indeed, the toy pillow did in fact look exactly like a piece of ravioli. But a normal child would never have made this mistake; the normal child would have been guided by the context, by the *whole,* in making his answer. This is a bed, this is a pillow. Not: This is a bed, this is ravioli! But to this intelligent autistic child, the context made no difference. He viewed each part of the bed in isolation, not in relation to the other parts. The pillow did not relate to the mattress and the quilt; it was a thing unto itself, and it looked like ravioli. So ravioli it was.

Fascinatingly, autistic artists also show this penchant. It is well known that a small subgroup of autistic people can produce extraordinarily accurate and detailed drawings of buildings they have seen only once. The way in which many of them set about making these drawings is to begin with an isolated detail, such as a branch on a tree, or a doorway, and then progressively add on the surrounding details, one by one. This is not at all the way in which a professional artist who is not autistic goes about his work; the normal artist begins by roughing out a general outline of a scene, and only *then* filling in the detail.

A deficit in central coherence may explain, too, why autistic people so violently prefer and even require sameness in the universe: sameness is different for them than it is for us. For the nonautistic person, going inside the house by the front door and going inside the house by the back door *are the same thing*. Although the details differ, our brain's automatic globalizing capacity simply pulls the basic meaning from the two different acts, *going inside the house,* and renders them equivalent.

But for the autistic person, for whom God is in the details, the two acts are profoundly different, and can only be made to coincide with the most profound effort of reason and will. Trying to describe what it is like to live with an autistic mate, Susan has often told the story of Dan's coming-home ritual. He pulls into the driveway, gets out of the car, goes to the mailbox and collects the mail, then walks inside. Always this sequence; always the same.

He cannot correct his course if Susan picks up the mail first. Going to the mailbox and finding no mail completely throws him off, pushing him into a state of agitation, anxiety, and lower functioning. The change in routine is so distressing to him that their therapist has told Susan to stop getting the mail altogether. Dan needs to do it.

It is extremely difficult for a nonautistic person to understand this, to empathize with what it must feel like to be able to have your entire evening derailed by the fact that your spouse has picked up the mail. In talking about it, Susan offers an analogy to driving: she and Dan have attended the same church for years, and they always take exactly the same route to get there. If they deviate by so much as one street Dan is lost—lost, upset, and agitated. Having his wife pick up the mail is, for Dan, the perceptual equivalent of taking a different route to church. When you are a person who sees only details and not the whole, going inside the house when you haven't picked up the mail is a wholly different experience from going inside the house when you have. It is the details that count, that create the event, not the whole: not the central fact of having gone inside the house.

It is here, finally, that the value in autism lies. Temple Grandin has written that if we were to eradicate disorders like autism from the species we would give up vital, and vibrant, parts of the human gene pool. Certainly, if we lost the unusual ability to see parts *over* wholes we would lose some of our geniuses; perhaps many of our geniuses. Being able to see something out of context is the starting point of invention; it is the ability to see a thing anew, to apprehend it separately from its usual context, unique and uncontaminated by longstanding cliché of science or belief. It is to begin the process of creation.

The shy gorillas focus exclusively upon their narrow fields of interest; they cannot do otherwise. And they succeed brilliantly. Some are geniuses, some are near-geniuses. The rigidity of autism, the narrowness of interest, the need for sameness: these same qualities can produce a miserably unhappy and mentally retarded child, or an isolated genius whose work will alter the world as we know it. The strange and bewildering disorder we know as autism can move a person either way.

7

THE HIDDEN EPIDEMIC:

Attention Surplus Disorders: Shadow Forms of OCD, Addiction, and Anxiety

WHILE MANY OF THE shadow syndromes in these chapters suffer from attention deficits in one shape or another, it is also entirely possible to pay far too much attention to a subject: it is possible to become locked into a thought or a behavior and be unable to escape. This is precisely what occurs in the classic form of obsessive-compulsive disorder. The afflicted person becomes obsessed with the idea that, say, his hands are dirty; then, gripped by his obsession, he is compelled to wash his hands, over and over and over again, hand-washings numbering into the hundreds, until the skin is cracked and bleeding, the pores leaking white from soap, in order to make them clean. He cannot escape this loop; he is locked in. Addictions show the same "attentional surplus": the addict spends his hours craving, and consuming, and then craving and consuming again and then again, the drug (or activity—like compulsive gambling or shopping) that holds him in its grip. The content of his mental life is filled with images of his drug, and longings for it; he may have little room left to think of anything else. And finally, anxiety disorders, as well, are frequently, though not always, obsessive: the anxious person may spend hours of his day ruminating about whatever worry currently lays claim to his soul. The underlying, *felt* experience among these disorders, which are admittedly quite different in their surface, behavioral manifestations, is very similar: whether one suffers from obsessive-compulsive disorder, from addictions, or from an anxiety disorder, one's attention is seized and bound in a death grip. The person who suffers any of these disorders can feel that there is no way out.

Of all the mental disorders listed in the DSM, the anxiety disorders are most common by far. Taken alone, the individual symptoms of these disorders are universal: one study found that as many as 70 percent of the population may have at least one classic symptom (you need several symptoms in order to meet the criteria for a diagnosis). Scott K. Veggeberg, author of the *Scientific American* focus book *Medication of the Mind,* offers this useful formulation in his brief survey of the major mental illnesses:

> [Schizophrenia, major depression, and bipolar disorder] are devastating illnesses, but what psychiatrists actually see most are the ones that involve fear of some sort. These anxiety states go by names like posttraumatic stress disorder, panic attacks, and obsessive-compulsive disorder; all of them involve some form of fear and dread that is out of proportion with reality.

To evolutionary biologists, this state of affairs is entirely reasonable given the central importance of fear to the survival of the organism. In their work on Darwinian medicine, *Why We Get Sick,* Randolph M. Nesse and George C. Williams describe a study demonstrating this truth, a study that transcends the flat-footed nature of so much experimental research to achieve the level of parable. It is the parable of the timid guppy. In the experiment, guppies are divided into three groups: bold guppies, timid guppies, and ordinary guppies. When "confronted by a smallmouth bass," Nesse and Williams write, the bold guppies respond by "eyeing the intruder." The timid guppies hide from the smallmouth bass; the ordinary guppies neither hide themselves nor confront their much larger fellow creature, but simply swim away. Nesse and Williams conclude with a Darwinian moral to the tale:

> Each group of guppies was then left in a tank with a bass. After sixty hours, 40 percent of the timid guppies and 15 percent of the ordinary guppies were still there, but none of the bold guppies had survived.

Clearly, for guppies, an anxiety disorder (if a guppy can be said to have an anxiety disorder) is a good thing.

In the human realm, and doubtless in much of animal life as well, adequate levels of anxiety are equally essential to social survival. Certainly, it is possible to possess levels of anxiety that are too low. The child without fear can grow up to become the adult without guilt: in clinical terms, the psychopath. (It is thought that such children may have a flaw in the frontal lobe that causes them to be fearless; in threatening circumstances they simply do not register the same degree of apprehension other children do.) This equation works in reverse: as the preeminent British child psychiatrist Michael Rutter has shown, young children with anxiety disorders almost never grow up to become teenagers with conduct disorders. Anxiety, it seems, is the raw material of guilt. At the very least, anxiety is a standard companion to good behavior.

In short, anxiety is as indispensable to survival of the person as pain is to survival of the body. Just as the child who cannot feel pain (a common feature of autism) does not learn to draw his hand away from the fire, the child who cannot feel anxiety does not learn to bow before the disapproval of his fellows. Both are burned.

While the global link among generalized anxiety disorder, addiction, and obsessive-compulsive disorder has long been recognized, in practice the three have been treated as separate and distinct. Psychiatric specialties reflected this reality: one group of psychiatrists specializes in obsessive-compulsive disorder; another group altogether specializes in addiction. Practitioners do not, as a rule, view obsessive-compulsive disorder and addiction, not to mention anxiety, as varying presentations of the same underlying dynamic. In particular, specialists in obsessive-compulsive disorder have tended to define their field rather narrowly. Patients who act out wildly irrational compulsions—washing their hands countless times a day, checking the stove to see whether they've left it on, checking and rechecking the road to see whether they have run over someone—this has been traditionally the province of obsessive-compulsive disorder and those who treat it.

The prominent psychiatrist and researcher Eric Hollander, long an authority on obsessive-compulsive disorder and currently clinical director of the Seaver Autism Research Center at the Mount Sinai School of Medicine in New York, was one of the first practitioners to realize that the definition of obsessive-compulsive disorder needed to be broadened—and that the addictive disorders may in fact belong to an obsessive-compulsive *spectrum:*

> My interest in obsessive-compulsive spectrum disorders (OCSDs) grew out of seeing patients who complained of repetitive thoughts and strange behaviors that did not fit within the standard diagnostic criteria for OCD. I became fascinated with patients who were preoccupied with the way they looked and had had repeated cosmetic surgery because they were obsessed with their appearance, now known as body dysmorphic disorder (BDD); with people who had a compulsion to gamble over and over again; with compulsive hair-pullers; with autistic individuals and others with . . . Asperger's syndrome that includes a prominent compulsive component and stereotyped behaviors; and with patients who have neurologic disorders that involve motor compulsions focused around symmetry and completeness, including Tourette's syndrome.

Thinking about these patients, Hollander realized that while they did not fit the traditional diagnostic criteria for obsessive-compulsive disorder, they nevertheless "shared a common theme or core clinical symptoms that overlapped with OCD." Their problem behaviors possessed a compulsive quality; the thoughts that produced these behaviors were nothing if not obsessive.

The development of the SSRIs during the same period that Hollander and others were making this connection ensured that this insight would not be lost. Because the SSRIs are somewhat-to-fairly effective in treating obsessive-compulsive disorder (though not nearly as effective as they are in cases of "pure" depression or anxiety), Hollander now tried his atypical hair-pullers and plastic-surgery addicts on trials of Prozac and its cousins. When his patients responded, he had clinical evidence that the logical connection he had made among these disparate disorders was in fact correct. The idea that obsessive-compulsive disorder was not an entity but a spectrum, a spectrum linked both biologically and behaviorally to addiction, is fast gaining ground, and in March 1996 the journal *Primary Psychiatry* devoted an entire issue to the topic "Betting Against the OCD Spectrum." The subtitle: "New Dimensions in Treating Autism, Pathologic Gambling, and Compulsive Buying."

■ OBSESSIVE-COMPULSIVE DISORDER IN ITS CLASSIC FORM

Unlike manic-depressive illness, obsessive-compulsive disorder has until very recently been recognized only in its classic and severe form, which was thought to be rare, affecting as few as 0.2 percent of the population. For reasons having to do with the essential nature of the disorder, this estimate has proved to be startlingly low, and it is now known that obsessive-compulsive disorder—and here we are speaking of obsessive-compulsive disorder in its classic form—affects as much as 3.6 percent of the general public. In his excellent self-help guide to conquering obsessive-compulsive disorder, *Brain Lock,* Jeffrey M. Schwartz puts the disorder's frequency into perspective:

> Once thought of as a curious and rare disease, in fact, [OCD] affects one person in forty . . . or more than five million Americans. A disorder that typically has its onset in adolescence or early adulthood, OCD is more common than asthma or diabetes.

Obsessive-compulsive disorder can be, and often is, severely disabling: people who suffer from OCD can lose all ability to pursue a career, or even to hold a low-level, undemanding job, or to form and sustain important relationships. The reason a disorder so common, and so handicapping, could go unnoticed for as long as it did has to do with the nature of obsessive-compulsive disorder, as we will see. Suffice it to say here that, almost universally, people with obsessive-compulsive disorder never escape the feeling that their obsessions and compulsions are irrational, wrong, "crazy." Often, sufferers are ashamed of their behaviors. As a result, they hide their symptoms from their doctors, complaining of depression or anxiety instead. When we include the many variants of severe obsessive-compulsive disorder *and* its shadow forms in prevalence estimates, the numbers rise so high that Hollander has justifiably referred to the obsessive-compulsive spectrum disorders as a hidden epidemic. Shockingly, he reports that:

> A survey of members of the OCD Foundation found that they had to wait an average of seventeen years from symptom onset to receipt of an effective treatment.

Much of this lag is due to a simple failure on the part of treating psychiatrists to make the diagnosis in the first place.

As its name implies, obsessive-compulsive disorder has two facets: obsessions and compulsions. The obsession is an extremely disturbing, even catastrophic thought: I haven't turned off the stove, the house is burning down; I have run over someone on the road, I am a murderer; I will pick up this bread knife and stab my husband to death; I will harm my beautiful baby. They are terrible thoughts, and they cannot be turned off. The person with obsessive-compulsive disorder is besieged by horrific images—images he experiences as entirely alien. It is in this key element that obsessive-compulsive disorder differs profoundly from so many of the brain-based disorders people confront: unlike the depressed person, who truly believes that she will lose her job and her husband will leave, the obsessive-compulsive person does not believe what his brain is telling him. The woman who is obsessed with the idea of harming her child has no desire whatsoever actually to do this; instead, she is besieged with the idea that somehow she *will*. She is radically at odds with the thoughts that are surging through her brain.

OCD is not an easy disorder to grasp empathically. Nevertheless, all of us rely upon the same circuitry that has gone awry in obsessive-compulsive disorder, and this is the place to start. What happens in OCD—what *keeps* happening, over and over again with no end in sight—is exactly what happens when we feel we've made a mistake. Our brains are hardwired to detect mistakes; we could not function in the world if we did not possess this capacity. In order to understand what has gone wrong in obsessive-compulsive disorder, we can call upon the feelings we experience in a social situation where we have committed a significant social blunder. In a conversation with the boss, perhaps you make a faux pas; you leave her office feeling you have misspoken, or have sounded unintelligent or unmotivated or both, or have offended her sensibilities in some way . . . In short, you feel you have handled the exchange badly. You have made a mistake.

For most of us, this "mistake feeling"—and it is indeed, the biology of the brain shows, a *feeling*—is extremely uncomfortable. Here again, we have not developed a vocabulary to keep pace with the discoveries of neuropsychiatry: the classic language of emotion—love, hate, anger, joy, envy—does not capture the very powerful feelings evoked by conditions like obsessive-compulsive disorder. Just as we need a term to convey the stress feeling that plagues the mildly depressed, so, too, do we need a word to express the mistake feeling that can besiege the person with obsessive-compulsive disorder.

In any case, language or no, all of us know this feeling. The key to grasping obsessive-compulsive disorder is to understand that the brain is structured so as to make us feel *compelled* to correct our mistakes. In the case of having made a misstep with an employer, most of us would be gripped by the need to set things right: to write a memo repairing the damage, perhaps simply to have a friendly exchange with her so as to convey our intelligence, our cooperative spirit, our tactful nature and complete desirability as a colleague and a human being. And we will feel driven by the need to do this until we have finally done it.

For those of us whose brains are functioning properly, once we have written the memo, or engaged our employer in conciliatory conversation, the episode comes to an end. We have detected a mistake; we have suffered the mistake feeling; we have corrected the mistake. The alarm feeling ebbs away into calm. But in obsessive-compulsive disorder, horribly, this does not happen; the alarm continues to sound. Correcting the mistake has no effect whatsoever upon the mistake feeling; in fact, correcting the mistake only makes the mistake feeling stronger. For the person with obsessive-compulsive disorder, the obsession grows stronger each time the compulsion to correct the obsession is acted out. Every time the obsessive-compulsive woman checks to see that the stove is turned off, the need to check grows stronger yet (just as, in addiction, each drink makes the alcoholic need another). Obsessive-compulsive disorder is the ultimate vicious cycle. Schwartz offers a description of the disorder, given by one of his patients, that verges on the existential:

> Your brain can get into such bad things. You say, "Is the stove off? Is the stove off?" And then you get to the point of saying, "Well, what's *off*? When I turn the knob up to the off position, how do I know that's really the off position?"

For the person with obsessive-compulsive disorder, life's felt realities dissolve into a nightmare of trying again and again to right what is wrong, to turn off the mistake circuit, to satisfy one's churning brain that all is well.

■ THE PERSON WITH "TOUCHES" OF OBSESSIVE-COMPULSIVE DISORDER

As we have seen, obsessive-compulsive disorder differs from many other psychiatric disorders in one crucial way: its victims always maintain insight. Judith Rapoport, the world's leading researcher in child psychiatry, and chief of child psychiatry at the NIMH, first brought the world's attention to obsessive-compulsive disorder in her 1989 book, *The Boy Who Couldn't Stop Washing*. In it she writes:

> The certain sense that the obsessions are an intimate part of one's conscious intent, *and yet that they are senseless,* is so much the essence of the disorder, even for a six-year-old, that this state of mind is used to define it.

For the classic sufferer of obsessive-compulsive disorder, even in the grip of his worst obsessions, part of his brain continues to say: "This isn't real. I don't want to be doing this." The observer self, the part of the patient that watches the rest of himself having obsessive-compulsive disorder, never disappears. Following the philosopher Adam Smith, Schwartz terms this observer self the Impartial Spectator. (For the sake of accuracy, it is important to note that not all victims of obsessive-compulsive disorder maintain insight; as many as 10 percent can become psychotic, at which point they have lost the ability to make judgments about what is real and what is not, and are delusional.)

In contrast to obsessive-compulsive disorder without psychosis, a severe depression can swallow the Impartial Spectator whole. As we have seen, people can *become* their disorders; the disorder can grow to be indistinguishable from the self. But it is the very definition of obsessive-compulsive disorder that this does not happen. And it is this feature of the disorder, this preservation of insight, that poses an important obstacle in terms of defining what a mild form of the disorder might be: paradoxically, a person who suffers only very mild obsessive-compulsive disorder might in fact lose insight precisely because his obsessions and compulsions are so much less intrusive and painful that he does not recognize them as irrational, or as "not real." Once a person loses the separation between observer self and his disorder, by definition he no longer suffers from obsessive-compulsive disorder.

To understand how this might work, compare one person, a patient of Dr. Schwartz's, suffering severe obsessive-compulsive disorder, with another person who may be displaying only mild obsessive-compulsive symptoms. "Anna," a woman with severe OCD, suffered obsessive doubts about her boyfriend's past romances, and his faithfulness to her. The compulsion that arose from her doubts was a burning need to question him repetitively about what he had done in the past, what he had done that day, whom he had seen, even what he had eaten for lunch—all the way down to questions about whether he had put butter or margarine on his bread. She would have to ask him the same questions over and over again, needing to hear the same answer, precisely, without alteration, in response. If he deviated in any respect from a previous answer—and of course he deviated all the time since Anna possessed total recall for every word of his responses, while he did not—her world would collapse and she would have to begin the questioning all over again. She was literally grilling her lover, interrogating him with the ferocity of an enemy commander interrogating a prisoner of war. And yet throughout all of this relentless questioning, Anna never lost sight of the fact that she was, in her own eyes, acting "crazy." As Schwartz says, OCD patients do not lose the "small holy voice of reason."

Now compare Anna to Janet, a woman who certainly would not be diagnosed as suffering from obsessive-compulsive disorder according to classic DSM criteria, and who, in fact, has never sought help for any such problem. Like so many people who are part of Eric Hollander's hidden epidemic, Janet had seen therapists over the years, but always for problems with men, and with anxiety. Never did she, or her therapists, think along the lines of obsessive-compulsive disorder. And yet Janet, too, has obsessions concerning the bad behavior of the men in her life—obsessions which, in her case, are accompanied by the not so readily recognizable compulsion to record their behavior in her journal. Now in her late thirties, Janet has composed hundreds upon hundreds of pages of journal entries, filling fifteen journals in as many years, describing every transgression, every argument, every betrayal either major or minor, made by every man with whom she has ever been involved. She is *compelled* to write down what has happened. She keeps the fifteen journals in a large suitcase stored in the basement of the house she and her husband share.

What makes Janet's case interesting, in terms of mild forms of obsessive-compulsive disorder, is that her problems are so "transparent": they do not look like a disorder. Her writing behavior is not obviously "crazy," as Anna's relentless questioning is; Janet is a writer by profession, and writers write. What could be more natural? Moreover, many therapists encourage the use of journal-keeping as a beneficial approach to life and its problems; Janet has always felt good about her many journals. Journal-keeping, for Janet, is ego-syntonic, meaning that it reinforces her best feelings about herself; journal-keeping feels right and true to the essence of her being.

To most authorities on obsessive-compulsive disorder, the ego-syntonic nature of Janet's "symptoms" would rule out the diagnosis of obsessive-compulsive disorder, mild or otherwise, because in true OCD the obsessions and compulsions are distinctly ego-*dys*tonic. The person with obsessive-compulsive disorder feels ashamed and distraught over his thoughts and acts; he does not experience them as being intrinsic to himself. He feels them as intrusions.

And yet, in all likelihood Janet's journal-keeping does represent a very mild form of obsessive-compulsive disorder. There is evidence for this interpretation in the reaction of Janet herself to the subject matter of this chapter. She took to the material at once, and went that day to her bookstore to purchase a copy of Judith Rapoport's book. That she was drawn to the topic in the first place suggests that a part of her did *not* feel entirely comfortable with her thoughts and acts. And as she read the book, she thought of her journals. Although without having happened upon Dr. Rapoport's work she might never have identified her journals as an instance of compulsive behavior, as she read graphic descriptions of very severely afflicted patients, she saw her diaries in a new and far less favorable light:

> If you read those journals, you would never find a single good thing that anybody ever did for me in any of them. Even my husband, with whom I have only one major fight every six months—and for the last three months you couldn't write up a husband as wonderful as he is—you won't find a word of that, of his goodness, not a hint. But the next time he slips, you'll find eighty pages.

Each major argument with her husband spins Janet into a suspiciously OCD-like spiral of thought and behavior. After an argument she will find herself spending hours ruminating over her husband's conduct, and she will feel driven to write the entire episode down in her journal. She will *have* to do this; she will not be able to find any peace until she has done so. As she puts it,

> That is how I manage the anxiety, I get through it through writing it down.

But the truth is that for Janet, as for the sufferer of classic obsessive-compulsive disorder, acting on the compulsion to record an argument in her journal does not make the anxiety go away. Janet remains just as obsessed with the argument as before, perhaps more so. Acting on the compulsion makes the obsession worse: what Janet may need to do is to refuse to record the next argument, to force herself to do something else instead.

In all likelihood, Anna's and Janet's problems lie on a spectrum, regardless of the fact that Anna has never lost insight even under the worst assaults of obsessive doubt, while Janet, until reading Dr. Rapoport's book, had never fully *developed* insight. Perhaps more than any other shadow syndrome, the mild forms of obsessive-compulsive disorder teach us the lesson that mild is not always so mild. A mild disorder can defeat insight; a mild disorder can become the self, become the Impartial Spectator whose task it is to watch over a life. In the mild forms character wraps around biology, and the soul slips away in the mists of a disorder that is not recognized as a disorder. A disorder that feels like the self.

■□ SCANNERS

The mildly obsessive-compulsive souls among us are the *scanners*.

Lou Marks is a good example of a person who lives his life on the mild side of the OCD spectrum. Lou has not received a diagnosis of obsessive-compulsive disorder; nor is he likely to. And yet the problems that plague him possess an obsessive-compulsive quality. Lou is a scanner of the hypochondriacal sort: he continually scans his body for signs of trouble—this in spite of the fact, which is obvious to all, that he is in excellent condition for a man of fifty. Needless to say, his obsession drives his health: he spends one hour a day, every day, running on his treadmill with the pace set at the highest level; he was a star athlete as an adolescent; he was a swimmer for many years; he is an accomplished golfer today. The reality of Lou's physical existence is that he is in excellent health.

But Lou cannot feel this. Judith Rapoport has called obsessive-compulsive disorder the doubting disease, and for Lou this formulation is dead on: Lou is besieged by doubt. When something happens to his body, when *anything* happens, his brain seizes the symptom and worries it to the limit; he is like a terrier shaking a rat. And he cannot help himself; he cannot *stop* thinking about what his physical symptom may mean. Most recently, he has been tormented by worries over a kink in his shoulder:

> One year when I was away on vacation with my present wife, I noticed that whenever I took my shirt off after a game of golf there was a sharp pain in my left shoulder. Then over the next couple of years it seemed to get worse and worse, and when it got to the point that I felt it continuously, I started to worry about it. It started off as a minor pain that I was afraid would get worse, then became a true pain that I was scared wouldn't go away, and I found myself after playing golf, which was my love, a couple of hours later in quite a bit of pain.

For Lou this situation, which would have been distressing to anyone, quickly grew to devastating proportions. He thought about his shoulder constantly; he dwelled upon the possibility that he would be forced to give up golfing, an eventuality that loomed before him, a catastrophic life event. Deeply concerned, he began a lengthy round of draining visits to physicians:

> To make a long story short, after a negative MRI and about a year of anti-inflammatory medication, my shoulder did not improve, and I'm going nuts because I have pain and they don't know what it is,

and it's going to be there the rest of my life and it hinders my golf, which is important to me—it scares me, thinking of losing my ability to play—I would get fight-or-flight hot flashes just thinking about it.

Finally, I went to another doctor, who told me about a new type of MRI they had that would allow them to inject a new type of medium in the shoulder so it would show up better on the screen.

My wife, who is a physician, an ob-gyn, wanted to go with me, and I thought it would be nice to have her there, because the MRI is an awful test because I am terribly claustrophobic. Apparently, it is a control issue; when I am not in control of something, my movements or anything, I get crazy. I dwell on things and get terribly obsessive about problems. So my wife said the only time she had available was Thursday afternoon, and it turned out that it was going to take one month to get a Thursday appointment.

And this was my mistake. I spent a month obsessing about what it was going to be like to be inside this machine. I spoke to the technicians and saw the machine, which was very small—and I spent the month taking different medications to see which knocked me out the best—Ativan, Valium, Xanax; I took a heavy dosage on different days to see which would work. That month had a lot to do with bringing on my latest bout of depression and anxiety.

Lou's obsessive worries about his shoulder and the impending MRI clearly show the connection between obsession and anxiety: patients like Lou, and they are legion, confirm the official DSM placement of the obsessive-compulsive disorders among disorders of anxiety. But the link between classic OCD and Lou's shoulder saga is less clear. Most obviously, the question of whether Lou's obsessions are accompanied by behavioral compulsions comes immediately to mind. Is Lou simply a man who "thinks too much," or does he truly belong in an OCD spectrum?

This is the point at which mild forms of obsessive-compulsive disorder become shadowy, perhaps fading into simple anxiety disorders, because if Lou does have a behavioral compulsion—and we believe that he does—it is so normal in form that it does not draw attention to itself as aberrant or bizarre. In Lou's case, very likely the compulsive part of his brain's functioning is the compulsion to question his wife repeatedly about whatever condition he is preoccupied with at the moment. Laughing, Lou tells a story on himself:

> I always get cancer worries as well. Being married to a doctor—she has an incredible memory and knows so much about different kinds of medicine that it's scary. So she can say to me, "You don't get cancer there," and that will help me. At least, it started to help me once I began to believe her opinions; when we first got together, I would think: "What does she know about lung cancer? She deals with women's unmentionables."
>
> But once I began to believe her, it would help, and for the most part—not completely—I could stop worrying. Being the type of person that I am, I can't totally believe her.

This sounds very much like Anna's questioning, except far milder. In mild forms of obsessive-compulsive disorder very likely the brain biology that tells us when a mistake has been corrected, or when a worry has been satisfied, is simply less impaired. The person suffering from severe obsessive-compulsive disorder *cannot* turn off his something is wrong circuit, no matter how many times he checks the stove. But the person suffering from a mild form has a greater capacity to achieve the feeling normal people experience when they recheck the stove once or perhaps twice, see that it is turned off, and then are satisfied that yes indeed the stove is turned off, and will remain so until further notice. Lou has some capacity—not enough, certainly, but some—to *hear his wife,* some capacity to listen to reason. Judith Rapoport speaks movingly of obsessive-compulsive disorder victims sometimes being able to "borrow" the ability to *know* from friends and loved ones, and Lou depends heavily upon his capacity to borrow his physician-wife's knowing, where his physical symptoms are concerned. If she says he does not have cancer, then an important part of him believes her. He still worries; very likely he still continues to question her. But his case is mild.

And, as with Janet, the very mildness of his problems militates against his development of insight: Lou does not view his concerns as being entirely without base in reality. And yet, he is by no means at one with his obsessions; he is aware that he ruminates continually about his shoulder, or his elbow, or the possibility that he has cancer—and he does not want to be doing so. In this his problem is quite different from the disorder known as obsessive-compulsive personality disorder, or compulsive personality. A person with a diagnosis of obsessive-compulsive personality disorder (OCPD) is so perfectionistic and inflexible in every conceivable realm that, in the words of John M. Oldham (a member of the advisory committee that revised the definitions of the personality disorders for the DSM-III-R), and his coauthor Lois B. Morris:

> . . . they can no longer adapt to the demands of reality or meet their personal and professional goals, and to others they may seem exasperating, even impossible, to deal with.

These are the stingy and rule-obsessed hoarders who demand that everything be done their way—and who are just as withholding of their affections as they are of their time and money. But this population, whose problems are so pervasive they have overtaken the entire personality, are far less troubled by their situation than are sufferers of "simple" OCD. Schwartz writes:

> The . . . crucial difference between OCD and OCPD is that although people with OCPD are rigid and stubborn and let their ideas run their lives, *they have no real desire to change their ways.* Either they are not aware that their behavior annoys others or they simply don't care. The person with OCD washes and washes, even though it causes him great pain and gives him no pleasure. The person with OCPD *enjoys* washing and cleaning and thinks, "If everyone cleaned as much as I do, everything would be fine. The problem is that my family is a bunch of slobs."

Dr. Rapoport confirms this account:

> Obsessional personalities are cold, rigid, and righteous. And often very neat . . . Compulsive personalities don't usually come for treatment for their habits; their complaints are about everyone else.

Clearly, Lou does not suffer from a personality disorder. He is neither cold, rigid, nor righteous; his complaints concern himself, not his family. He is a loving husband to his second wife, a committed father to a son who is now experiencing severe forms of the problems that have plagued Lou throughout life, and a generous and beloved friend. On balance, Lou's story teaches us that in the mild forms of obsessive-compulsive disorder the observer self is alive and well, just as it is in the severe forms. Still, as we see with so many of the shadow syndromes, the very mildness of Lou's problems is a danger in itself. A person with severe obsessive-compulsive disorder cannot help but know something is wrong: Unless he is psychotic, a man who finds himself scrubbing imagined battery acid from city streets in the middle of the night, as one of Dr. Schwartz's patients did for many years, knows that he is doing something no one else in the world is doing. He knows he is behaving irrationally.

But a man like Lou who is worrying obsessively that his shoulder injury may prevent him from playing golf, and who is questioning his physician-wife obsessively about whether cancer can manifest itself as joint pain: this level of obsession and compulsion is not so obviously irrational. It is to Lou's credit that he has not allowed his character to become wrapped around his biology: he has chosen not to take his obsessions to heart. Instead, he fights them.

Luckily for Lou, in the case of his shoulder the advanced MRI did yield a clear diagnosis: reading the scan, his physician discovered a small tear in the shoulder located in a position where surgery would be neither helpful nor indicated. While Lou was distressed by this ("It was a blow to me because it was like saying there's nothing to do about it"), he has not continued to dwell on his injury and the potential loss of his hobby, or to pepper his wife with questions about it. As an interesting sidelight, the diagnosis itself affirms his obsessive-compulsive makeup:

The guy said he's only seen an injury like that in professional baseball pitchers and competitive swimmers. But I was a pitcher as a kid; I pitched constantly. I'm obsessive about everything, and I wouldn't just pitch one hour a day; I would stand in front of a wall and make five thousand pitches against that wall. I might do it all afternoon, eleven o'clock to four o'clock; I'd make up games for myself like a nine-inning game, Mickey Mantle is up at bat—I'd just keep going. I was obsessed with getting it right.

I swam, too, starting at the age of thirty-three or thirty-four, and again, it wasn't good enough for me to swim ten minutes every other day. I would do two miles every day. So that's obviously where this thing came from.

This is the intersection of shadow syndrome and normalcy: obsession can drive ambition—and when it does, obsession becomes a useful quality to possess. Lou is a highly successful entrepreneur who started his business when he was still in his teens; it is in large part his obsessiveness, coupled with ability and intelligence, that has made this possible. To friends and colleagues this quality simply looks like perfectionism and drive, and at one level it is. But the compulsive behaviors are there. The need to *continue* to pitch a ball against a wall for five hours in a row crosses the line into compulsion: Lou had to continue pitching the ball, because he could not overcome the something-is-wrong feeling that plagues people with obsessive-compulsive disorder ("something is wrong with my pitch"). He could not practice his pitch for an hour and then achieve the critically important "it's alright now" feeling normal folk take for granted. Here again, we lack the vocabulary to express the inner experience of the obsessive-compulsive person. For all of us the everything-is-alright-now feeling is the soothing answer to the something-is-wrong feeling. We have a *feeling* that the stove has been left on, we check the stove, then we have a *feeling* that the stove has been turned off and all is well. We do not simply know these things, we feel them. Emotion is involved; biology shows that it is invariably involved. The same sequence operates in the social realm. We experience a feeling that we have committed a faux pas with our employer; then, after we have repaired whatever breach may have occurred, we experience a feeling that the situation has been corrected. It is this feeling that people with severe obsessive-compulsive disorder cannot capture—and it is the ability to achieve this feeling that contributes to their anguish, to the torture that is their entire existence. They are *compelled* to wash, for many hours on end, until their hands are cracked and bleeding, not because they enjoy washing, but because their brains continue to broadcast the choked and panic-stricken bulletin that something is wrong! They cannot wash their hands and *feel right.* So, too, with Lou, at a far less devastating level. Even so, Lou's obsessive-compulsive tendencies were serious enough to result in physical injury. He could not stop pitching the ball, or swimming lengths of the pool, when he should have. He could not feel that it was alright to stop—although in adult life he *has* been able to respond rationally to the MRI results. He has cut back sensibly on his golf, just as a person with no traces of obsessive-compulsive disorder would do, and eventually his shoulder pain has diminished. In short, his obsessive-compulsive qualities are mild enough to allow him to take the sensible step of slowing a semicompulsive behavior that needed to be slowed for a time.

■□ SOCIAL SCANNERS: CIVILIZATION AND ITS DISCONTENTS

Janet's compulsive journal-keeping raises an interesting possibility concerning the nature of a mild form of obsessive-compulsive disorder: is it possible that mild obsessive-compulsives are not just mildly obsessed with cleanliness and contamination, but have actually moved on to different concerns altogether?

We think this is likely. The classic fears of DSM obsessive-compulsive disorder, Dr. Rapoport argues, involve certain universal, and primitive, themes we share with our animal ancestors. As she writes:

> I see OCD patients as victims of evolutionarily meaningful but personally horrific "orders from the brain."

The urge to wash is hardwired into our brains, she believes, and somehow the disorder we know as obsessive-compulsive disorder throws the circuit that controls this innate impulse into a permanent ON position. In support of this argument she offers fascinating data concerning the development of snake phobias in laboratory-raised monkeys. Monkeys in the wild, she writes, universally fear snakes. But a monkey raised in captivity, as one might expect, demonstrates no fear of snakes, and will even reach out to play with one if a lab worker drops a snake inside his cage.

However, teaching a monkey to fear a snake is easy: all a monkey needs to be convinced of the malevolence of snakes once and for all is *one* exposure to the sight of a field-reared monkey being afraid of a snake. For laboratory-reared monkeys, simply watching a brief video-tape of a live monkey recoiling from a live snake will suffice. One vicarious experience of fear, and the monkey's consciousness is altered forever: snake-fear is firmly established, and lives on in the heart of the captive monkey for life.

That the inclination to fear snakes is hardwired into the monkey brain, Rapoport continues, becomes evident when researchers attempt to duplicate this experiment using an evolutionarily benign stimulus such as a flower. As it turns out, it is impossible to teach a monkey to fear a flower using the same means. A videotape showing a shot of a flower followed by a shot of a monkey looking terrified has no effect whatsoever upon its monkey viewer. Rapoport concludes that certain fears, or the potential for certain fears, are present in the animal brain at birth. And the same is true of people:

> Phobias emerge in humans after only a single unpleasant experience and they are very hard to cure. Remarkably, the most common phobias concern mankind's most ancient dangers: closed spaces, heights, snakes, and spiders. People are rarely phobic about the really dangerous objects in modern life: automobiles, guns and knives. This ability to easily "learn" a selected pattern of fears is also present, then, in ourselves.

The link to obsessive-compulsive disorder is clear: the obsessions of OCD may be, Rapoport believes, like the snake phobias of monkeys (and humans), built into the basic makeup of the brain:

> Grooming behaviors are particularly interesting to me because washing and rituals of dress are by far the most common of all the obses-

sive compulsive patterns. Almost all of our youngest patients who start out counting and checking spend some months or years as washers before their teenage years are over. And once the washing ritual appears, it seldom leaves.

If classic obsessive-compulsive disorder is largely concerned with evolutionarily primitive dangers to the organism, we have come to believe that the milder forms may in fact be concerned with "higher order" dangers: with threats to the *self,* not the body (or with the self as well as the body). And threats to the self are largely social in nature. As James Gilligan writes in his book *Violence, Our Deadly Epidemic and Its Causes,* the self depends upon the goodwill of other people in order to survive:

> The psyche is as dependent on being nurtured by . . . relationships and community . . . as the body is on being nourished by food.

Thus the higher-order threat to the self that preoccupies the mildly obsessive-compulsive person is the possibility of being scorned and rejected by his fellows. The mildly obsessive-compulsive person is not predominantly a hand-washer or a stove-checker (though, as we will see, he may show traces of these behaviors as well); instead, he is a social scanner, a person who scans the social environment obsessively for signs of danger. Social scanners do not receive a diagnosis of obsessive-compulsive disorder because they do not report obsessions with contamination or coffeemakers; nor do they engage in obvious rituals. Instead, like Janet, they ruminate and react to social dangers or to social mistakes. Theirs is the territory of the faux pas.

The situation comedy *Seinfeld* is virtually a textbook study of mild obsessive-compulsive disorder: the entire show is structured around the preoccupations and follies of the socially obsessed. The characters— Jerry, George, Elaine, and Kramer—spend countless hours debating the minutiae of social life: whether a woman can be attracted to a man who is bald, how to break up with a lover without coming right out and saying it, how to command the respect of pretentious salesmen in expensive men's stores. Always, the humor in *Seinfeld* stems from the social dangers that inhere in trivial situations. While the producers of *Seinfeld* have been widely quoted as saying that the show is about "nothing," in fact it is about a very particular kind of nothing: it is about the "nothing" situations that threaten embarrassment and social rejection to the person going through them. In other words, *Seinfeld* is not simply a program based upon the form of humor commonly called recognition humor, the pointing out of small realities we normally miss. (A classic instance of recognition humor is George Carlin's old line about rotary telephones: "When you dial a number," he asks the audience in one of his routines from the 1970s, "do you let your finger ride back?") While Jerry's opening monologues often rely upon recognition humor, the story line is invariably based upon the small realities of life that threaten excruciating embarrassment and humiliation to anyone caught in their grip.

This is the realm of shadow OCD; in emotional terms it is the realm of *shame.* This is the fate social scanners dread: the experience of being humiliated and shamed, of losing face. Shame means the loss of respect, both in the eyes of others, and in the eyes of oneself. In real life, of course, this is a very serious danger. Psychiatrists like Gilligan have shown that shame threatens the self in precisely the same way contamination and illness threaten the body: profound shame is to self-respect what death is to life. When shame is too overwhelming—as it is in severe cases of child neglect and abuse—the soul dies.

Of course *Seinfeld* is not remotely about soul-destroying levels of social rejection and loss—and that is precisely what makes it an example of shadow OCD: the fact that none of the social dangers the characters face are "real." In classic obsessive-compulsive disorder the sufferer's emotions and preoccupations are out of all proportion to any actual threat (no one is going to die if he fails to wash his hands one more time); in *Seinfeld* the characters' *social* preoccupations are out of all proportion to the actual social traps and pitfalls that loom before them. Thus an entire episode can be built around nothing in the sense of a problem that shouldn't, and wouldn't, *be* a problem to a rational person. For example, *Seinfeld* fans fondly recall the incident of the marble bread. Invited to dinner at the tasteful home of George's future in-laws, George's own loud and obnoxious parents come bearing the gift of a prized loaf of marble bread—which the future in-laws naturally neglect to serve with dinner. This perceived slight so infuriates George *père* that he swipes the loaf on the way out, leaving his (to George) life-threatening faux pas to be discovered by their host.

The entire setup, of course, is fraught with wildly exaggerated threats to social survival, but the really flagrant shadow OCD sets in now, with the story's resolution. George becomes obsessed by the absolute conviction that his fiancée's parents *must not discover what his father has done,* and, in a state of near-panic, he draws Jerry and Kramer into a scheme to secretly return the bread to the in-laws' apartment—a scheme that is nothing if not compulsive. George's obsession so utterly drives the story that by the episode's end Jerry has mugged an old woman and Kramer has subjected the in-laws to a ride through Central Park in a hansom cab pulled by a massively farting horse, all in the service of covering up Mr. Costanza's social crime. One of the funniest things about *Seinfeld* is that the characters' worst paranoid visions of the social horrors that will befall them if they don't *act now* invariably turn out to be mild in comparison to what actually *does* befall them when they do act. The insult of taking back one's gift bread from a dinner party inevitably turns into the insult of sending a horse to fart in the host's face. This is the world of *Seinfeld.* An OCD world, only funny.

In every *Seinfeld* episode, the feared result of whatever horrible thing is about to happen is the experience of being humiliated in the eyes of an important or desirable person (wealthy in-laws, fashion-model dates, jazz-musician boyfriends who do not perform oral sex, and so on): the feared result is the primal emotion of shame—or, in the lighter vein of situation comedy, at the very least, severe and even terminal embarrassment.

When we view *Seinfeld* through the lens of shadow OCD and the psychology of shame, the oddness of the story lines makes perfect sense. Perhaps most obviously, shame is closely tied to the genitals, to the idea of the genitals being exposed. This is the story of Adam and Eve: after eating the apple they see that they are naked, and they are ashamed. Of course *Seinfeld* is well-known for building entire episodes around dilemmas that are simply grandiose playings-out of bathroom humor, which always involves exposure of activities normally kept private. But beyond this some of the funniest episodes are explicitly about the experience of being naked before the world. Invariably, these story lines seem to involve Elaine. There is the Christmas episode in which Kramer takes a photograph of Elaine for her Christmas card; after she has sent the card to everyone she knows, she discovers that in the picture her nipple is showing. Mass fear and loathing ensues. In another episode, when Elaine is blasted by water from a storekeeper's hose, she does not realize that everyone can now see her breasts through her soaking-wet blouse. Later in the same episode she loses the top button of her blouse and, yet again, does not realize that her brassiere is now exposed for all the world to see.

Obviously, exposure humor is a main event on *Seinfeld:* exposure in every possible sense. Where the nipple episode is built around the theme of other people being able to see some body part they should not, there are dozens of episodes structured around the theme of other people being able to see *behaviors* they should not: nose-picking, men peeing in showers, the list goes on. The characters of *Seinfeld* are being chronically caught in the act.

Then, too, the very triviality of the events that torment the characters—the nothingness of these occurrences—is another link between *Seinfeld* and the psychology of shame, between *Seinfeld* and shadow OCD. As Gilligan writes:

> If we want to understand the nature of the incident that typically provokes the most intense shame . . . it is precisely the triviality of the incident that makes the incident so shameful . . . as the shame-sensitive person knows better than anyone else, only an unimportant and slight person would be vulnerable to, and upset over, an unimportant slight.

This is *Seinfeld* to the nth degree: the characters live their lives in a constant state of horror over the most minor embarrassments, such as, to return to the beleaguered Elaine, wearing an unflattering dress in public that looked great in the store. This experience, universal to all women who try on garments in the presence of enthusiastic salesclerks, creates *hours* of agitated scheming and plotting on the part of Elaine and her friends to right the appalling wrong Elaine has suffered.

The utterly deficient love lives of the characters—none of whom is presented as remotely capable of forming a genuine romantic attachment to another human being—is part and parcel of the psychology of shame as well: people who wrestle with shame typically lead emotionally blunted lives. It is a truism that in order to love others we must first love ourselves, and shame is the opposite of self-love. Thus when Jerry meets a woman exactly like himself, and subsequently proposes marriage to her, he quickly becomes horrified by this rash action, shouting at his neighbor Kramer, "I can't be with someone just like myself! I hate myself!"

This is the realm of shadow OCD: the person with higher-order obsessive-compulsive disorder is constantly fending off threats not to physical survival but to sheer psychic survival in the form of self-respect. The mildly obsessive-compulsive individual is preoccupied with threatened feelings of shame and humiliation. And, like his classic counterpart, he suffers the resulting problems in intimacy, living his life at a distance from the people around him.

Mild OCD is in fact a true shadow in the sense that often the original, classic form remains visible in outline: social scanners are often cleanliness obsessives as well. This is true of *Seinfeld;* not only are many of the characters' preoccupations overtly tinged with issues of cleanliness and order, but the central character of Jerry himself is presented as an obsessively neat person too squeamish even to eat meat.

By the same token, people with classic obsessive-compulsive disorder are highly prone to developing higher-order social obsessions in addition to their washing and checking compulsions; the obsessive handwasher may be an obsessive social scanner as well. In other words, the distinction between mild social scanning and severe contamination scanning is a matter of emphasis and degree. Classic obsessive-compulsive disorder can in fact include a pronounced social, and psychic, element, as it does in those sufferers who obsess that they have

killed someone (or that they will kill someone), or who find themselves
driven obsessively to think blasphemous thoughts about God. Still,
even in these forms of the disorder, which occur less commonly than
washing and contamination obsessions, a distinct threat to physical
survival is involved. Aggressive behavior is dangerous to all animals
who display it (remember the bold guppies), and all animals possess
wired-in responses of submission to any animal strong enough to kill
them. It is entirely possible that when OCD takes the form of causing
a person to be terrified of his own aggressive thoughts, this fear, too, is
hardwired into our primitive brains. And, of course, when it comes to
the religious forms of classic OCD, blaspheming the creator of the universe is obviously risky business. In any event, there is no stark dividing
line between classic obsessive-compulsive disorder, with its emphasis
upon physical dangers to the body, and shadow OCD with its list toward social dangers to the self. Still, the distinction is useful when it
comes to understanding—and particularly when it comes to recognizing—shadow forms. Compulsive journal-writing can be OCD just as
surely as compulsive hand-washing. But without a name for compulsive journal-writing, we miss the possibility that such an activity may be
doing more harm than good.

■□ ANXIETY DISORDERS AND SHADOW OCD

The concept of shadow OCD casts a new light upon garden-variety
anxiety disorders—which, for many, are simply mild OCD-without-
the-C (much like ADHD-without-the-H for dreamy children with
attention deficits). Anxious people struggle with obsessive and exaggerated fears of situations that may involve threats to the body or threats
to the self: threats to a sound and happy life in every sense of the term.

Many of Lou's problems locate him here, among the anxiety disorders proper. For all of his adult life, dating back to his years in high
school, Lou has suffered a phobia about soiling himself. There is some
realistic basis to this fear in that Lou has a nervous stomach; he can develop cramping and diarrhea in response to stressful situations. But

Lou's anxious brain chemistry is such that he has magnified the reality of his situation into a crippling phobia that has circumscribed every corner of his adult life. He is terrified to go places that do not have public restrooms. Baseball games with his children, grocery stores: just the thought of being in one of these situations is extremely aversive.

He dates his fear to a lone traumatic event that occurred when he was in the eighth grade:

> I was taking a shop class that ran for two periods in a row. And one day, somewhere in the middle of the first period, I began to feel stomachaches like I had to go to the bathroom. I was afraid to ask the teacher to let me leave; I was hoping he would give us a break at the middle of the class, when the first hour was over.
>
> But he didn't. I had to go up to him in front of the class and ask him to let me go, and he wouldn't. Everyone was watching, and kind of laughing, and I had to go. Finally, he said, "You go ahead, but don't come back. Go to the principal's office." I was so humiliated I dropped out of school. And I was only thirteen years old.

This story reveals the disabling nature of anxiety disorders: for Lou, an innately anxious boy, just *one* distressing scene with his shop teacher was enough to devastate him for life. Where a naturally sanguine thirteen-year-old would easily have shrugged off this episode, Lou responded with full-blown trauma; after that day, he was never the same again.

Things went from bad to worse, as they can when anxious children try to negotiate the school system. When his parents finally convinced him to reenroll, Lou had to have a note from the principal stating that he was to be allowed to leave class at any time, no questions asked—a humiliating state of affairs for a boy who was accustomed to being the class star. Lou's experience reveals the social handicaps that can result from even subtle differences in the brain, because his abilities and character were so completely at odds with his anxious biology:

> All my life I was an all-star, I was the smartest, I was the best athlete, I was the best built, I was the class president. I was looked at as the perfect one; I had it all.

Yet this extremely high-achieving boy was so traumatized by one incident with his shop teacher that he essentially never recovered:

> After that, in high school, starting a new school, I was just too scared. So my parents finally had to take me out for half the year. I did finally go back, but it was never the same. I was reasonably bright, so I got through OK, but then I went to college, and I couldn't hack that. I was not any dummy; that wasn't the problem. Even then I was running a very successful business. So I made it through a local school that sort of stunk, but then I got through a pretty good law school. There was a resolution in my life when I got accepted into law school, but I was scared of the law all the time—because what would I do in the courtroom if I had to go to the bathroom?

Today, Lou is fifty years old, and his fear of soiling himself in public has held him in thrall for thirty-seven years:

> I'm a person who loves life. This hang-up I had about being near bathrooms has held me back. Finally, I bought a motor home, so that wherever I was the bathroom was there with me; I have a vehicle that has a bathroom in it.
> My mother was agoraphobic; she would very rarely if ever leave the house. She didn't go out with my dad, and my father said many times, "I had to learn to live with that part of your mother's personality." But her children were very important to her, and she always took us to dentist appointments, always came to school functions; these things would make her come out. Left on her own, she would never have done it. And I feel the same way about my own kids. Some of the places I've taken my kids I would never have gone myself because of the bathroom hang-up. Just going to a baseball game where there's an open field, nowhere to escape: I would only do it for my kids. The girlfriends that I had through the years, before I met my second wife, would say, "You would do anything for your children, but not for me," and they didn't realize it had to do with this phobia that I have.

In Lou we see the intersection of the various stopping points along the anxiety spectrum: obsessive-compulsive disorder, phobia, generalized anxiety. We see, too, how a psychiatric issue that would normally be diagnosed as a phobia—Lou's fear of being in a place with no bathroom—contains strains of primitive, and classic, obsessive-compulsive cleanliness concerns; at the heart of his fear of soiling himself lies a dread of contamination. And finally, the social nature of Lou's phobia is clear as well: he is afraid of soiling himself *in public,* with a classroom of snickering thirteen-year-olds looking on. A bad case of the "runs" somewhere in the middle of a deserted forest holds no particular terror.

That his phobia is related to obsessive-compulsive disorder is further supported by the fact that his sister very likely suffers from the disorder, which is highly genetic, in its true form:

> My sister has it terribly. Both she and my mother were terrible neat freaks, and I am one myself, but not that bad. My sister is so bad that her silverware has to be in certain piles, and if she closes the drawer and hears a clink, she has to open it up and redo the pile exactly the way it was. And she continuously counts her money. If she leaves her house to go somewhere, if there are five lights she stops at, then at each light she will open her pocketbook and count her money. She will lock the door to the office, and a mile away she'll turn around and come back to check. She said to me, "How do you know when it's so bad you need help?" And I said, "When it's so bad it affects your life." And she said, "That's how bad it is."

Thus in the anxiety disorders, and in the shadow forms of obsessive-compulsive disorder, the sufferer has "graduated" from the fears of our Neanderthal ancestors to the anxieties of modern man, albeit with remnants of our ancient washing and checking needs still visible to the naked eye. Mild obsessive-compulsive disorder brings us in direct contact with civilization and its discontents; mild obsessive-compulsive disorder produces the person who is obsessed with injuries that prevent him from playing golf, or with offending the boss, or, in the worst of all possible worlds, with both. Mild forms of obsessive-compulsive disorder and anxiety are the maladies of contemporary life.

■□ "BRAIN LOCK"

The biology of obsessive-compulsive disorder has come to be fairly well understood. Jeffrey Schwartz has coined the term "brain lock" to describe it, and by brain lock he means precisely that: three sections of the brain locked together in metabolic functioning, each structure rising in activity as the other two rise, and falling as the other two fall. In the normal brain the three can and do operate freely and independently of each other, a state of affairs that is true even in depression, which may show many features of obsessive-compulsive disorder up to and including transient obsessive-compulsive behaviors and rituals. However, in depression the three structures do not become locked together in the distinctive pattern researchers have identified in OCD.

Although obsessive-compulsive disorder always involves three main regions of the brain's circuitry, the primary causal factor seems to reside in one area alone: the caudate nucleus. *Any* damage to the caudate, whether from "bad genes" or from brain damage following head injury, or even, as we will see, from an autoimmune attack upon the region, can result in obsessive-compulsive disorder. Damage to the other two areas involved in OCD, the cingulate gyrus and the orbital cortex, will cause problems, but will not result in obsessive-compulsive disorder per se.

The caudate nucleus, in Schwartz's analogy, is essentially the automatic transmission of the brain's thought processes: it is the part of the brain that allows thought to flow smoothly, easily, "naturally." How exactly this happens is not clear, but an analogy to Huntington's disease may be helpful in terms of visualizing what happens in the obsessive-compulsive brain. Huntington's disease involves the caudate's "twin," the putamen, which does for movement what the caudate does for thought: the putamen allows us to move our bodies automatically, effectively, without thought or concern. The putamen and the caudate nucleus sit side by side in the brain, making up the striatum.

In Huntington's disease the putamen has been destroyed, just as in obsessive-compulsive disorder the caudate nucleus has sustained damage of some kind. (The two disorders differ in that in Huntington's disease actual cell death has occurred. In Huntington's disease the putamen has been destroyed, whereas in obsessive-compulsive disorder the neurons of the caudate appear to be alive, but not functioning properly. Nevertheless, the analogy holds. For all practical purposes, a malfunctioning neuron may be of little more use than a dead neuron.) In any event, once the putamen begins to die off, the Huntington's sufferer can no longer *automatically* perform the simple, everyday movements we take for granted. The Huntington's patient can still sign his name, for instance, but he has to think to do it. Just to write his name on a sheet of paper requires that he summon all of his concentration and will to the task. In brain terms, he has had to enlist the cortex to guide an action normally controlled by the putamen; he has moved to an evolutionary higher region of the brain, taking away from the normal automaticity of life. When the cortex must do what the putamen should, the action becomes effortful, awkward, difficult.

What is going on in the brain is that the Huntington's victim has had to shift control of name-signing from his now diseased putamen to his cerebral cortex, to the thinking part of his brain. To sign his name, he must literally—not just metaphorically, but literally—think about signing his name. In a sense, the Huntington's patient has been put in the position of always having to do things for the first time. For all of us, at the outset, trying to acquire any new physical skill is highly effortful; it takes thought and concentration, for instance, to try to learn how to serve a tennis ball over the net. But as we achieve mastery of that skill, the skill becomes automatic; it becomes, as we say, "second nature." What has happened, of course—and brain-mapping expert John Mazziotta of UCLA has demonstrated this process in the brains of subjects learning a particular series of novel thumb-finger movements—is that the control center for learning to serve the tennis ball has shifted from the cortex to the putamen. Serving the ball has become automatic because the putamen has taken over that function. To grasp what Huntington's disease feels like from the inside, imagine this process happening in reverse. The physical movements we all perform automatically every day, now revert *back* to the cortex: all become actions one must think about in order to perform. Signing one's name on a check becomes exactly like serving a tennis ball for the first time.

The putamen allows actions to become automatic by serving as the filter to all incoming sensory information, allowing some stimuli through, rejecting other pieces as irrelevant. Thus the tennis player takes in only what he needs to take in; he is not responding to an infinite number of different stimuli as he tosses the ball into the air and swings. The phenomenon of automaticity depends upon a critical *gating* action in the brain.

This same gating action is lost in obsessive-compulsive disorder at the level of *thought:* the person suffering from OCD loses the capacity automatically to filter the flow of thought. In Schwartz's words:

> In all likelihood, what happens in OCD is that evolutionarily old circuits of the cortex, like those for washing and checking, break through the gate, probably because of a problem in the caudate nucleus. . . . The thought comes in the gate, the gate gets stuck open, and the thought keeps coming in over and over again. People then persevere in washing their hands or checking the stove, even though it makes no sense to do so. These actions may bring them momentary relief, but then—boom—because the gate is stuck open, the urge to wash or check breaks through again and again.

In the normal brain, we wash our hands once, and afterward the caudate nucleus filters out any further "grooming" thoughts; they don't rise to consciousness. They are gone, and we move on. But in obsessive-compulsive disorder the thoughts never cease; the gating mechanism of the caudate cannot suppress them.

In a certain sense, the breakdown of the brain's filtering mechanism in obsessive-compulsive disorder is the mirror image of what happens to the brain in attention deficit disorder: essentially, whereas the person with obsessive-compulsive disorder cannot filter out *internal* stimuli (the impulse to wash or check), the person with attention deficit disorder cannot filter out *external* stimuli. Both patients are besieged, but one, the person with obsessive-compulsive disorder, is besieged by stimuli generated from within his own biology. All of which leads to a second observation, which is that often, when the brain is not functioning well, we see *too much* activity, not too little. When brain systems go off-line frequently—not invariably, but frequently—the result is chaos, not silence. The sluggish brain mechanisms of attention deficit disorder tend to result in *hyper*activity, not *hypo-* (though certainly brain disorders can and do produce hypoactivity in some cases); likewise, the malfunctioning caudate results in a hyperactivity of thought and compulsion.

Two other areas of the brain are involved in the brain lock of obsessive-compulsive disorder: the orbital cortex, and the cingulate gyrus. The orbital cortex, part of the cerebral cortex, houses the brain's error-detection circuit. Schwartz cites a wonderful study by E. T. Rolls of Oxford University demonstrating what happens in the brain of a monkey when a mistake has occurred. Rolls taught his monkeys to expect juice, a universal monkey treat, anytime they saw a blue signal on a screen. Then he taught them that a medicinal syringe offered to them would be filled with salt water, a substance monkeys dislike intensely. Cells in the orbital cortex fired under both circumstances. It is the orbital cortex that tells a monkey: Here is something good; here is something not good.

But when Rolls reversed conditions, suddenly delivering salt water to his monkeys when the blue signal appeared, an entirely different set of cells in the orbital cortex fired, with far greater intensity. Both sets of cells, taken together, form the brain's mistake circuit: some fire for right answers, others fire for wrong answers. They do not fire simply to signal sensory recognition: under normal circumstances they do not fire when a monkey eats something either sweet or salty. Another part of the brain handles that task. The cells of the orbital cortex fire in response to "sweet" and "salty" only when there is a *question* about sweet or salty. Can Rolls's salt-and-juice findings in monkeys be related to the biology of obsessive-compulsive disorder? Schwartz believes so:

> We know that the error-detection system in the orbital-cortex system is strongly connected to the caudate nucleus, which modulates it and can turn it off . . . . There is now excellent evidence from a variety of scientific studies that damage to the basal ganglia (of which the caudate nucleus is a part) can cause OCD, with its terrible feeling that "something is wrong," feelings that don't go away.

In the normal monkey, in other words, the "mistake neurons" cease firing once the monkey has assimilated the startling information: This is salt water, not juice! But for the obsessive-compulsive brain this process of assimilating the mistake does not happen: the obsessive thought is *always* followed by a psychic exclamation point, each time it recurs. In the obsessive-compulsive brain mistake information never grows old; it remains as fresh, new, and jarring as it was in the very moment that it first dawned. The OCD sufferer is shocked anew, over and over again, by the error message: "I have forgotten to turn off the stove!"

The final cog in the relentlessly turning wheel that is the obsessive-compulsive brain is the cingulate gyrus, part of the limbic (or emotional) system of the brain. The cingulate gyrus is responsible for the severe psychic pain of obsessive-compulsive disorder. And obsessive-compulsive disorder is profoundly painful, so painful that sufferers speak of being tortured by their own thoughts. If obsessive-compulsive disorder were simply a matter of having a neutral thought replaying itself in one's head, like a song that has gotten "stuck," it would not be a disabling condition. Instead, in OCD the thought brings with it severe pain in the form of *terror,* courtesy of the cingulate gyrus. The error message from the orbital cortex shoots down to the cingulate gyrus, producing a state of fear, panic, and alarm that is precisely what we would feel if in fact the world *were* caving in around our ears. This is the essential element linking all of the anxiety disorders: in response to what should be a neutral or at most mildly worrisome stimulus, the sufferer feels the exact same fear that he would experience in response to a catastrophic threat to his or his family's safety and well-being. To grasp the anxiety disorders intuitively, we must remember the most frightening moments of our lives, and then imagine the emotions of those moments being triggered, again and again, by meaningless events. The OCD sufferer, in short, does not simply say to himself, "I've left the stove on," and then return calmly to the stove to check. The OCD sufferer lives in a state of panic, or near-panic, that *he has left the stove on and the house is burning down.* Obsessive-compulsive disorder in its full-blown form torments its sufferers, who are driven, against their better judgment and against their will, to check, and check, and check, and then to check again—and to do all this even though they absolutely do not want to be checking. They cannot stop themselves (they *feel* as if they cannot stop themselves); they are gripped by terror and they *must act.*

■☐ CHILDREN AND THE PANDAS

Obsessive-compulsive disorder appears to be highly genetic. It can be glimpsed descending through family trees, passing from long-deceased great-grandparents, great-aunts, or great-uncles to their children, then on to their children's children, and so on down the line. The genetic nature of obsessive-compulsive disorder can also be seen in its apparent lack of psychodynamic roots: it is not at all clear that one can be traumatized into an obsessive-compulsive disorder by bad parenting, just as we now know that a child cannot be traumatized into autism by bad parenting, or by being abandoned to the care of a Romanian orphanage. Very likely, a restrictive and punitive parent cannot make a child obsessive-compulsive.

Research in psychopharmacology has produced further confirmation of the highly biological nature of the condition: only 10 percent of patients with obsessive-compulsive disorder respond to placebos—a lower figure, even, than that for schizophrenics. (Some authorities have put the placebo response rate for OCD closer to zero.) The normal placebo response rate among depressives is 30 percent. Interestingly, the 10 percent for OCD has crept up as patients have become aware that psychiatrists now possess medications (the SSRIs) that work.

Of course, "biological" does not invariably mean "inherited," a fact we take for granted in the realm of physical health. When we think about the problems of the body, we do not assume that we have caught cold because of bad genes. However, when it comes to psychiatric health, we tend to equate the biological causes of mental disorders almost entirely with genes and the mechanisms of heredity. For most, the existence of an entire field called environmental psychiatry, the study of the ways in which the physical environment affects mood and thought, remains a fairly well-kept secret, apart from annual Lifestyle features on winter depression. This is as far as most of the reading public, as well as many therapists, travel when it comes to thinking about the biological—yet nongenetic—causes of everyday mental disorders.

Thus it came as a shock to the professional world—a shock of paradigm-shifting magnitude—when NIH researchers first announced the discovery of a group of children, affectionately dubbed the PANDAS (for "pediatric autoimmune neuropsychiatric disorders associated with streptococcal infections") who had developed obsessive-compulsive disorder as a *direct result of having become infected with strep throat.* In many cases these children were completely normal before the infection; in others the children already had well-controlled cases of OCD that sharply deteriorated immediately after the child had fallen ill. In the most dramatic cases a psychiatrically normal child might develop a case of strep throat on a Saturday, and present as a full-fledged obsessive-compulsive by Monday, as researchers Albert J. Allen and his colleagues report in their case study of "T. J.":

> T. J. was a 10-year-old who had no history of psychiatric or neurological problems. The weekend after several family members had the "flu," he had sudden onset of severe obsessions about viruses and chemicals and he began compulsive hand-washing. After a month of continuous illness, psychiatric treatment was sought and he started sertraline [Zoloft] therapy, with only partial symptom relief of his OCD after 2 months . . . At that time his forearms and hands were chapped and red [from repeated washing], and contamination fears prevented him from fully opening his mouth so that he was unable to eat in the hospital or have a throat culture.

Cases like T. J.'s stunned practicing psychiatrists, virtually all of whom had been schooled in the classic Freudian view that obsessive-compulsive disorder stemmed from a disturbance in toilet training. Even for the biologically inclined, Freud's psychoanalysis of OCD had remained a defining vision well after the discovery that the neurotransmitter serotonin was involved in the disorder—largely because, after all, serotonin is involved in practically every disorder of mood and functioning, or so it can sometimes appear. In short, the introduction of serotonin findings, and of the SSRIs as treating medications (which were not all that effective in any event) into the field of OCD, left the disorder's etiology too diffuse to change clinical thinking radically. After the introduction of SSRIs, obsessive-compulsive disorder came to seem a vaguely biological problem in social learning that could be treated by the relearning produced by cognitive-behavioral therapy techniques.

Thus the news that a completely symptom-free, altogether normal little boy like T. J. could develop a flagrant case of the disorder *overnight* was profoundly shocking: acute onset cases like these wrenched obsessive-compulsive disorder radically out of a psychodynamic, interpretive framework—even the updated, biologically aware versions. Essentially, these children were *catching* OCD (or catching tics—many ended up with diagnoses of Tourette's syndrome as well) the way a person catches cold. There was nothing social about it.

Research subsequently showed that this was almost exactly what had occurred: in a sense, the children's *brains* had caught cold. MRI scans revealed that in these children the caudate nucleus, the very area affected in obsessive-compulsive disorder, had swollen to a size as much as 24 percent greater than normal; what is more, the degree of swelling directly correlated with the degree of severity of obsessive-compulsive symptoms. Researchers surmised that the immune response to the strep infection had somehow become an *auto*immune response to the cells of the children's own brains; they speculated that the caudate neurons and the strep cells must possess a look-alike protein on their surfaces, causing both to attract the strep antibody that then killed them. The antibody created to attack the strep bacteria was attacking the brain as well.

The logical approach to an autoimmune response is to suppress the harmful antibodies, and that is exactly the tack researchers have taken. Some of the PANDAS were given intravenous doses of immunosuppressant medications; others underwent plasma exchanges in which doctors removed the children's blood plasma, treated it, and then restored it to the body, free of antibodies to strep. Thus far, these approaches have been successful:

Because of the abrupt onset of his symptoms and their severity, T. J. was treated with six plasma exchanges over a period of 2 weeks . . . His symptoms declined noticeably . . . after the fourth exchange he could eat at the hospital and permitted a throat culture. His symptoms were so improved 1 month after plasmapheresis that his sertraline dosage was being tapered, with only subclinical obsessions and compulsions remaining. He was reported to be doing well several months later.

It is entirely possible that some of the very mildly OCD population may be unrecognized PANDAS themselves. At the very least, one lesson to take away from the PANDAS is the potential seriousness of any infection with group A streptococcus. (Even more troublesome is the fact that at least some of these children, T. J. included, appear to have developed obsessive-compulsive disorder after infection not with bacteria which are treatable by antibiotics, but with viruses, which are not.) In the future, keeping an eye open to any rapid-onset psychiatric symptoms *as well as* to bodily symptoms may become standard practice in times of physical illness.

■□ OCD AND ADDICTION: THE GENETIC CONNECTION

At the same time that practicing physicians like Eric Hollander were discovering the efficacy of SSRIs in disorders previously not seen as part of an OCD spectrum, geneticists were traveling a parallel path in their efforts to find a gene implicated in alcoholism. Their work had led them to the D2R2 receptor gene, a gene that codes for the dopamine-2 receptor, and lies on chromosome 11. Dopamine is, like its better-known cousin serotonin, a neurotransmitter in the brain. At present, we know of four different dopamine receptors. The D2R2 gene possesses a common allele that appears in 20 to 25 percent of the population, an allele being a variation of a gene—often a variation created by a "genetic repeat" within the gene in which a segment of the gene is duplicated over and over again. Some geneticists call this phenomenon a genetic stutter. In 1970 researchers Kenneth Blum and Ernest Noble published a paper showing that the D2R2 allele occurred *70 percent of the time* in severe alcoholics suffering from cirrhosis of the liver.

The media response was immediate: to many if not most reporters, the gene for alcoholism had been found. While Blum and Noble underscored the point that the gene was merely associated with alcoholism, rather than causal, this was not the message that reached the reading public. Unfortunately, the media portrayal of Blum and Noble's work influenced not only the public's reaction but the scientific reaction as well. Blum and Noble became a target, and a succession of studies quickly appeared, all of which seemed to disprove the link. The two researchers were embattled on all sides, with a consensus soon forming that their results could not be, and would not be, duplicated. Blum and Noble, their peers believed, had simply selected an idiosyncratic population, producing a chance association between an allele and a behavior that did not actually exist.

Blum and Noble's response was interesting in light of the distinction we have made throughout this book between hard and soft versions of mental disorders. They argued that in fact they had chosen *precisely* the correct population to assess: by choosing only alcoholics who had developed cirrhosis of the liver, they said, they had selected out for the most severe cases. These alcoholics were *most* likely, in other words, to reveal the genetic contribution to their addiction. To find a genetic association with a given behavior, they held, we must look at that behavior in its "purest" form.

Subsequent research has proved them right. Since their study first appeared, fourteen major, independent studies have been published confirming the fact that a very high percentage of cirrhotic alcoholics will indeed bear the D2R2 allele. The most recent of these studies was done by a researcher in Pittsburgh who set out to show precisely the opposite: she believed, going in, that the D2R2 allele was not associated with alcoholism. Yet she, too, found that cirrhotic alcoholics carried the allele.

Now other addiction researchers, looking at other addictions, began to search for the D2R2 allele. They soon found it. Fifty-one percent of cocaine addicts had the allele; when researchers looked at cocaine addicts who had other forms of substance abuse as well, the rate went up to 80 percent. In patients with severe obesity, also considered a form of addiction, the allele was present 50 percent of the time; this figure rose to 87 percent in patients with substance abuse as well as severe obesity. Pathological gamblers carried the allele 51 percent of the time; with pathological gamblers who also had substance abuse—and whose fathers had substance abuse as well—the figure rose above 80 percent. Consistently, researchers found what Blum and Noble had found: the worse the condition of the patient, the more likely the allele was to be present. The D2R2 allele is associated with severe forms of addictive behavior.

It was researcher David Comings who would make the genetic leap from addiction to the obsessive-compulsive disorders. Comings, of the City of Hope Medical Center, was a gene hunter; he had created one of the first academic journals devoted to genetics. He was studying Tourette's syndrome, because at that time researchers believed that the gene or genes for Tourette's were autosomal dominant, meaning that only one parent had to carry the gene, and if the child received the gene, the child invariably developed the syndrome. This proved to be too simple an account, and eventually Comings came to believe that in fact Tourette syndrome is probably caused by the inheritance of a number of genes from each parent—a pattern called polygenetic inheritance. When Comings realized that no one was treating people with Tourette's, he opened what is now one of the leading centers in the country for treating Tourette's syndrome in children and adults.

Comings's research had nothing to do with alcoholism. But in his Tourette's subjects, Comings discovered the D2R2 allele. This makes sense, since Tourette's patients show a wide range of impulsive, compulsive, and addictive behaviors along with their tics. But the link had not been suspected before, and Comings' discovery marked a major step forward in the biological understanding of addiction. At the genetic level, the connection between disorders of "compulsion" and disorders of "addiction" had been made.

■□ THE SYNDROME OF REWARD DEFICIENCY

Although the discovery of the D2R2 allele in Tourette's syndrome, obsessive-compulsive disorder, and in the addictive disorders established a genetic link among the disorders, researchers still lacked a theoretical understanding of how the allele resulted in these rather diverse states. Until recently, the connection between Tourette's and obsessive-compulsive disorder was the only part of the puzzle that was fairly well understood. It has always been known that Tourette's and OCD are closely connected, if only because the comorbidity rate between the two is so high: fully one-half to three-fourths of Tourette's sufferers qualify for a diagnosis of obsessive-compulsive disorder as well, and people with OCD frequently have motor tics. The difference between the two syndromes appears to hinge upon the question of whether the damage has occurred to the caudate nucleus, which controls automaticity in thought, or to the putamen, which is responsible for automaticity in actions. Thus a compulsive behavior can be seen as a "tic" of the mind, while a motor tic can rightly be understood as a "compulsive behavior" of the motor system. (Such commonplace compulsive behaviors as fingernail- and cuticle-biting are now thought to be mild tics.) As Dr. Schwartz puts it:

> In essence [Tourette's victims] get a strong intrusive urge to move and then perform tics to relieve themselves of the discomfort. Or they may get vocal tics, starting with an urge to do repetitive throat clearing, an urge that may later develop into yips, yelps, barks, or other animal sounds. . . . Many people with OCD also have motor tics, and a lot of people with Tourette's syndrome get compulsive symptoms.

In an effort to explain how one allele, the D2R2 allele, could underlie several different disorders, geneticists Blum and Comings have developed a novel and intellectually dazzling account of the brain difference the allele creates in its bearer: many D2R2 individuals, they believe, regardless of the form their problems take, struggle with an underlying deficit Blum and Comings term reward deficiency syndrome.

In the simplest terms, reward deficiency syndrome is precisely what the words imply: it is a flaw or a deficit in the brain's capacity to feel rewarded by the things that reward other people: love, sex, food, drink, the laughter of children. The reward-deficient person, while he can enjoy the bounty of life to some extent, cannot enjoy life *enough*. At heart, a deficiency of the D-2 receptor impairs a person's capacity simply to feel content. Blum and Comings explain:

> Consider how people respond positively to safety, warmth and a full stomach. If these needs are threatened or are not being met, we experience discomfort and anxiety.

This is the normal, and essential, function of anxiety in the healthy brain. Anxiety rightly signals to us that we need more of something: more food, more safety, more warmth. But in the person whose anxiety system has been impaired by a faulty gene, anxiety runs amok. We may be surrounded by food and warmth and safety, yet find ourselves suffused with foreboding and concern. With only one small, and entirely common, difference in our genetic makeup, we lose the capacity to feel adequately rewarded by the elements of life that reward our fellows. Good things and good people may embrace us, but we cannot *feel* them, or take them in:

> An inborn chemical imbalance that alters the intercellular signaling in the brain's reward process could supplant an individual's feeling of well being with anxiety, anger or a craving for a substance that can alleviate the negative emotions. . . . *This syndrome involves a form of sensory deprivation of the brain's pleasure mechanisms.* (our emphasis)

In essence, people suffering from this syndrome find it nearly impossible to feel "full" at any level, intellectually, emotionally, or physically. A large meal does not satisfy, hence the eating addictions; nor does the first glass of wine, or the second, or the third. A loving conversation with a spouse, an afternoon playing in the sun with the children: these golden moments can leave the reward-deficient person feeling strangely alone, alienated, "empty." A felt emptiness is the hallmark of this syndrome: the concept of reward deficiency syndrome speaks directly to that population of people who describe themselves as feeling hollow inside. These people may feel empty not because their childhoods were bad, or their work is not meaningful (two of the most commonly intuited culprits), although either or both may be true. Instead, for many the "real" problem, an important piece of the problem, is a defect in the basic brain mechanism that allows us to feel pleasure.

Reward deficiency is not depression, though it may certainly lead to depression in time. (There are those who view depression as the base level disorder, the one mental illness everyone in the DSM ends up with sooner or later. Schizophrenics, obsessive-compulsives, borderline personalities: most will eventually qualify for a diagnosis of depression, too. All roads lead to Rome.) As we have seen, depressed individuals often suffer from anhedonia, which is the inability to experience pleasure *at all.* But the reward-deficient person suffers a different problem with pleasure: he can experience pleasure, but he cannot experience pleasure *enough.* Moments of pleasure in his life do not turn off the signal in his brain that is telling him, "I need."

It is easy enough to see how reward deficiency syndrome would result in addiction: the alcoholic needs one more drink, and then one more still; the food addict needs one more slice of pizza; the sex addict needs one more sexual encounter. If the brain cannot feel satisfied, cannot construct the subjective state of being expressed by the English word "enough," a relentless pursuit of the object of desire will result. This pursuit takes on a life of its own, as the sufferer becomes *compelled* to drink, eat, gamble, or shop, as the behavior slips out of his control and evolves into full-blown addiction.

Thus the connection between a reward deficiency and an addiction is easy to grasp. But the link between a reward deficiency and a disorder of compulsion, like obsessive-compulsive disorder and Tourette's syndrome, is less intuitively obvious. To understand what has happened, we can think of the person with OCD essentially as being addicted to his *compulsion* (and the Tourette's victim addicted to his tic)—even though he gains no gratification in the performing of his compulsion.

The fundamental difference between the obsessive-compulsive and the addict is simply that the obsessive-compulsive does not enjoy the behavior he is driven to, where the addict does enjoy—though he does not enjoy it *enough*—each hit of cocaine, each drink. Both the addict and the obsessive-compulsive are trying to silence the voice in their brains that is saying, "I need to do this (check this, wash this, drink this, smoke this . . .) in order to be well!" Both are trying to still an anxiety circuit that has become stuck in the ON position. And both will fail miserably. Just as the glass of wine does not quench the alcoholic's thirst, the checked stove does not quell the obsessive-compulsive's need to check (or the tic extinguish the need to tic). The wine and the checking and the tic-ing just make matters worse.

■□ DOPAMINE LEVELS AND THE REWARD DEFICIENCY

The immediate biological effect of the D2R2 allele is fairly well understood: D2R2 results in lower-than-normal levels of dopamine activity in the brain. Exactly how it does this is complex. Briefly reviewing brain biology: brain cells (or neurons) communicate with each other via the release of neurotransmitters—such as dopamine, serotonin, norepinephrine, and the like—into the spaces between cells. These spaces are called the synapse; the cell "before" the synapse is called the presynaptic cell; the cell "after" the synapse is the postsynaptic cell. (Of course, all brain cells are both: any given cell is a presynaptic cell to the cells coming after it, and a postsynaptic cell to the cells coming before it.) When brain cells communicate, presynaptic cells release neurotransmitters into the synapse, and the neurotransmitter then docks at a receptor site on the postsynaptic cell.

What happens with the D2R2 allele is that the D2R2 brain has up to 30 percent fewer dopamine receptors in the postsynaptic receptor area. This means that there are simply not enough receptors on the *post*synaptic side to take up all of the dopamine being produced on the *pre*synaptic side. This out-of-balance state of affairs leads directly to a decline in dopamine activity because of the brain's "use it or lose it" principle: when a neurotransmitter is not being taken up and used, the brain simply ceases to produce so much of it. Production drops (in the language of the field, it is "down-regulated") to match the reduced number of dopamine receptors available, and the brain is left with, in the vivid imagery of working neuroscientists, "skinny neurons," presynaptically. In short, when dopamine (or any neurotransmitter) is not used, it is lost; nerve cells down-regulate production and the brain goes hungry.

With the loss in dopamine, three major brain functions are affected, all of them impaired across the entire addiction-to-ADD-to-OCD-to-Tourette's-to-GAD (generalized anxiety disorder) spectrum:

The attentional system. Dopamine is the major neurotransmitter for the attentional system. We see this clearly in attention deficit disorder, which we treat with dopaminergic medications. Ritalin, Cylert, amphetamines in general: all increase dopamine levels in the brain.

The reward/satiety system. Dopamine is one of the key elements in the reward/satiety center of the brain. A person who is in chronic lack of this neurotransmitter has a difficult time feeling a sense of reward, fullness, or satiety, at any level, emotionally or physically.

The stress/resiliency system. Dopamine, along with serotonin and the opioids, is one of the primary neurotransmitters that responds to stress. Whenever we are stressed, whenever we *feel* stressed, dopamine levels rise to help us equilibrate to that stress. At the level of biology and the brain, this is what resilience is: resilience is *having adequate levels of dopamine in the brain.* This is also where, looking back to attention deficit disorder, the concept of the "stress junkie" comes into play. People who are addicted to stress are using stressful situations to pump up their brain's production of dopamine: they are "stressing up" in much the same way, phenomenologically speaking, people with normal brain chemistry speak of "psyching up." Stress addicts are using stress to boost their dopamine to normal, or near-normal, levels.

With all of the biological and genetic similarities among these seemingly disparate conditions, of course, the question remains: why does one person become an addict while another person develops obsessive-compulsive disorder? We do not know. Other alleles, alleles perhaps specific to the various disorders on the anxiety spectrum, will doubtless be identified; environmental factors (biological and social) that steer a person in one direction and not in another will come to be understood.

Thus, the question of how much flexibility is possible in terms of *which* disorder (or disorders) the individual carrying the D2R2 allele will develop, we cannot answer. But that there is a strong element of, for want of a better term, chance involved *within* each of these disorders does seem to be the case. Whether a particular person with OCD, for example, will end up washing his hands or checking the stove (or both) appears, at present, to be to some degree a matter of personal history and environment. Similarly, the life history of many an addict shows us that the "addictive personality" concept, popular within the recovery movement, is essentially correct (although it is important to note that there is no such thing as an addictive personality disorder— there is no one unique personality disturbance universally associated with all cases of substance abuse). Clearly, the same person can become addicted to many and varied substances or pleasures, just as the obsessive-compulsive person can, and will, move from a counting obsession to a washing obsession in time. The *particular* symptoms of the OCD-addiction-anxiety spectrum disorders do not seem to be as rigidly determined by heredity as the basic fact of simply having one or more of these disorders in the first place seems to be. If we are born with the allele, we are going to land on the spectrum. But what form, precisely, our problems will take, whether we will be addicts or obsessives or neurotic worriers or people who bite their fingernails down to the quick: perhaps it is life that determines this.

■□ **THE SHOPPER**

At one time or another in her thirty years of life, Sandra has shown streaks of most of the syndromes on the anxiety spectrum. She has been obsessive; she has been compulsive; she has been addictive; she has been unfocused in the extreme. Although the face she presents to her women friends is that of a relaxed and loyal friend, internally she is never at ease—a reality she cannot keep hidden at home:

> If things don't go exactly as I think they should go, I get upset. And I've always been that way, even as a child. I had to know exactly what was going on, and if something interrupted that, I would get upset.

This is the classic rigidity of the obsessive child: for Sandra things had to be "just so" for her to *feel right;* things had to go the way they were supposed to go. By an accident of fate this proved not to be an insurmountable problem in her childhood, for she had been blessed with a twin sister, a fraternal twin, who took on the task of protecting Sandra and keeping her safe.

It was her twin who helped her through her first serious brush with obsessive-addictive behavior, when she developed an eating disorder in college. A gymnast since the age of nine, Sandra chose to major in physical education at the two-year college where she and her sister had enrolled. The need to be thin, and still thinner, soon engulfed her:

> I was always striving to be small and skinny—it was that mentality that to be smaller is better. But I still had that impulse to eat, so I would eat when no one would see me eating, and then I would get rid of it. It looked normal to everyone else; I'd eat my three meals. But I would always be hungry after them because I kept the portions small. I would be training eight to ten hours a day, and I was not getting enough calories. So then I would be starving, but I wouldn't want anyone to see me eating. People would say, "How do you do it? How do you stay so thin?" And I would have this facade that "I don't know, I just eat my three meals." I got attention for being thin. I was mysteriously thin.
>
> It was very hard for me to make myself throw up, so I said, Well, maybe I'll control my weight if I take weight-loss medications. So I started taking over-the-counter medications.
>
> Finally, when I was down to between ninety and ninety-five pounds—I'm five feet one—I confided in my sister. We were drinking one night, and I told her what was going on, and she said, "That's ridiculous, you're a good person, you can't do it anymore." My roommate was there, and they both helped me get over it.

While at least in Sandra's memory her dieting compulsion did not reach the level of an addiction, it was close enough: certainly, she was very uncomfortable with her vomiting, and yet she felt compelled, for a time, to do it.

If Sandra had simply pushed on with her studies, she probably would have fared well enough. But instead, she added a major environmental stressor to her life—and to her brain's biochemistry—when she became pregnant shortly after meeting Ron and dropped out of school to devote herself to marriage and motherhood. Although she had always loved children (she imagined having six of them), she did not fare well in the postpartum period, particularly after the birth of her second child:

> I went into counseling after I had my second baby, because I had what they thought was postpartum depression and I just couldn't cope with having a second child. I think I had it after the first baby, too, but I didn't recognize it. With the first one I attributed my feelings to how much breast-feeding I was doing, that the baby wanted to breast-feed all the time. So I didn't breast-feed the second time, and the feeling was still there. I knew pretty much immediately something was wrong, the first day I left the hospital. I could feel that emptiness inside, and that first week I was home, I called my doctor and they set me up with a counselor.

Under the pressure of new motherhood, Sandra progressed from reward deficiency to full-blown depression, and her feelings of stress were pervasive and severe. She was showing most of the symptoms of an attention deficit as well.

Sandra's difficulties with reward deficiency have not abated in the two years since her second son's birth. Although she now understands her problem, thus far she has not been able to make much headway against it:

> My depression lifted (I wasn't taking drugs at that point, just going to therapy), but it seemed that I hopped around from counselor to counselor. I've seen two therapists and two psychiatrists in the two years since my second child was born. I couldn't find the answers that

I was looking for, I couldn't understand why I couldn't cope with the kids, why I would feel that overwhelming sense of just wanting to run away. I have this overwhelming guilt about, Why can't I play with my kids, why don't I want to be around them? And I was looking for someone to help me develop those skills. I would find much more pleasure in going to the store and buying them things than in reading them a story.

So I kept seeking people out, therapists and doctors, and it's been more of a chore for me to go once a week than a benefit. I always found, with everyone I saw, they'd always say things like, "Oh, how do you feel about being adopted?" I've never had any thoughts on being adopted, or any resentment, and I was getting sick of talking about it. They'd hear I was adopted and jump on it and it was not ringing a bell with me. It wasn't helping.

However her own childhood may be affecting her as an adult, Sandra faces challenges beyond the historical facts of her early years. She must grapple with the facts of her biology as well, and she needs the help of her therapists in doing so. She is highly compulsive; she is *driven* to clean the house obsessively—or to diet obsessively, or to shop obsessively, or whatever it is. Recognizing this quality in herself, she struggles against it:

One good thing is, I stopped the compulsive cleaning. But now I've gone to the opposite extreme, and I can't clean at all. I feel too overwhelmed being in my house and cleaning it, so I'd rather get out of the house, and I'm always trying to get away. I can't find a controlled center.

Sandra's problems are worst at home, which is typical of patients with any degree of obsessive-compulsive biology; for the obsessive, the confines of hearth and home can be deadly. Obsessives need the distractions of work and the outside world to suppress their compulsive behaviors—a harsh reality that makes full-time motherhood challenging in the extreme to any woman with obsessive-compulsive tendencies.

Not surprisingly, Sandra soon developed a new addictive behavior

under the stress of stay-at-home mothering: she has become a compulsive shopper. This is an extremely common low-level (and occasionally not so low) addictive behavior in women that therapists often
miss:

> I justify myself in getting a lot of little things that add up. I'll say,
> Well, OK, I won't feel guilty because I'm not buying something for
> me—but then I'll buy something for the kids. So we'll go to the store
> and I'll spend twenty dollars on toys for them, for no reason. I'll buy
> a lot of cleaning products for the house. Never big purchases.
>
> The other day I wanted to buy clothes and sneakers for my kids,
> but I thought, They really don't need that now, and so I went and
> spent ninety dollars at the grocery store. If I'd just gone to the cloth-
> ing store, I would have spent forty-five dollars. I justified it that we
> need the food, and it was all healthy.

While this sounds harmless enough—and no doubt familiar to
many of us—Sandra's shopping clearly reveals an addictive quality. She
would far rather shop than interact with her children, and thoughts of
shopping consume a fair portion of her day:

> When I get a thought that I want something, or my kids need some-
> thing, I don't let it go until I get it. Three hours a day go into think-
> ing about what I want, or going to stores; I used to go to stores every
> day. Now I go at least four times a week. If I don't go into a depart-
> ment store, then I go grocery shopping and spend a lot of money
> there.
>
> Recently, there was this purse that my girlfriend had in her room,
> a really nice purse. I found out it was $165, and now I'm obsessed
> with getting that purse. And that thought won't let go until I get the
> purse. Two or three times a day the thought that I want that purse
> will come; it's driving me crazy because I know that $165 for a purse
> is ridiculous. But then the other side of me says, I deserve it. So then
> I will go out and buy thirty dollars' [worth] of makeup instead. I
> work for Estée Lauder and I spend the thirty dollars on makeup be-
> cause I can't get the purse, and buying the makeup makes me feel
> better. But I still think about the purse. And when I'm thinking
> about the purse, I get frustrated, so then I try to think about another

purse that would be cheaper. The other night I walked around the mall and looked at purses that were sixty dollars instead of a hundred and sixty. But I still wanted that purse.

Obviously, a shopping addiction differs from a washing compulsion in that constant shopping can be pleasurable, whereas constant hand-washing is not. Still, the distance between the two is not vast. Sandra's shopping brings her family pain; it causes her pain as well. Within only a few years' time she found she had run up a debt of $15,000; to pay it off she and her husband were forced to use his share of the proceeds from the sale of a family business. The two argue constantly because she yearns to escape house, husband, and children for the calm of her beloved department stores; he rightly views her decision to work for Estée Lauder as a rejection of life at home with her family. And yet still she shops. She cannot stop herself.

> I was selling Tupperware before, but I wasn't making any money because I kept buying Tupperware, and now working for Estée Lauder it's even worse because I'm there in the department store. Now I'm trying to convince my husband that I should open up a checking account so I can put the money in and know it has to be there to pay for the girls' nursery schools; I'll know I have to pay for that, and that the money is already spent.

It is only recently that Sandra has come to view the behaviors that trouble her as forms of addiction:

> I don't know if I was always like this, but I see it now as a problem and I've really been examining myself. I was a smoker when I met my husband, and he said, "Forget it, see you later," so I stopped. Now I've just started again. I don't know if that's an addiction. I would say I'm a social drinker; I could come home at night and have a beer or two every single night. But I have stopped doing that because I got nervous that that could go somewhere.
> I think shopping is immediate gratification because I feel I gave up a lot to marry my husband and I haven't let that go. I almost kick myself for saying, "I deserve it because I've given up gymnastics, I'm

home with the kids now, and they're driving me crazy." When in reality I know shopping is not making me happy.

Being compelled to do something that feels good but does not make her happy: this is the essence of Sandra's problem. Whatever her genetic makeup, Sandra can surely be said to suffer from a reward deficiency: she cannot feel *good.* She is not clinically depressed—although she might qualify for a diagnosis of chronic mild depression. She simply cannot feel centered, whole, *satisfied.* She speaks spontaneously of an emptiness inside, and all of her shopping and smoking and running away from home to the marble walkways of the beckoning mall is an effort to fill that hollow place inside.

And, as is probably the case with most who suffer this emptiness within, Sandra is highly obsessive as well as addictive:

> When I get a thought in my head, I don't let it go. I might run an argument I've had with my husband through my head over and over again; it doesn't stop. Lately things have been so bad here that I'll think, Oh, let's get a puppy, and I'll obsess about getting a puppy when I know I already have a dog and four cats. But I keep thinking about it, about how much I want to get a puppy.

The toll her obsessive brain takes on her family is immense. Obsession and motherhood are a destructive, even catastrophic, mix:

> My kids intrude on my obsession. I'll be thinking, thinking, thinking, and the kids get in my face, and I have to stop the thought process and I get angry.

Obsession invades the intimacy between spouses as readily as that between parents and children, and Sandra's marriage is precarious:

> My husband and I have a real hard communication problem right now. He really thinks that I don't do a good job with the kids because of my not wanting to be alone with them. And I am very demanding of him; I expect him to take over everything when he gets home, while I would prefer just to leave the house and go to the mall.

We argue every day. Each of us always wants to be the winner. It's sad because we were best friends and I know that friendship is still there, and we're just kind of split apart. We have to find something to get us back.

Obsession, addiction, reward deficiencies of every stripe: all lock Sandra inside herself, closing off her felt connection to life and love. Surrounded by family, she is alone.

■ USING MIND TO ALTER BRAIN

Although Sandra has not found the answers she seeks, she does possess a powerful weapon in the struggle against her own biology. And this is simply the fact that Sandra *knows what is wrong*. She is able to stand outside herself and observe; she is able to see herself as others see her. In this way at least, she is fully connected with the inner reality of the people she loves. She is not in denial, as the saying goes; nor is she a person who blames others for her woes.

In short, Sandra possesses insight in the clinical sense of the term; she does not experience her behaviors and preoccupations as purely and simply "me." Sandra has developed the necessary split in subjectivity that is essential to mental health: there is the Sandra who obsesses over purses and puppies, and there is the Sandra who *watches* the Sandra who obsesses over purses and puppies. This split allows her to make judgments about whether she wants to be the kind of person who ruminates for hours on end about a $165 purse, rather than simply and unquestioningly being that person. And the Sandra who watches has decided that she does not want to function this way. While she does not feel the same level of ego-dystonia we find in the classic sufferer of obsessive-compulsive disorder—she really, truly wants that $165 purse—nevertheless, an important part of her is saying, even as she cruises the mall scanning the merchandise: I do not want the purse. Or, perhaps more accurately: I do not want to want the purse.

How a person with a shadow form of obsessive-compulsive disorder uses this insight can be the key to his salvation. In a study that has made headlines throughout the professional world, Jeffrey Schwartz and his colleagues at UCLA have demonstrated through PET scans that obsessive-compulsive patients can actually change the chemistry of their brains entirely through behavioral means. While psychiatrists and geneticists alike have said for some time that "environment" (which by definition would include any purely behavioral treatments patients undergo) affects the brain's biology, the UCLA team has actually documented, via imaging technology, a tangible example of just such a change.

In the study, eighteen patients suffering from classic obsessive-compulsive disorder underwent baseline brain scans before treating themselves with cognitive-behavioral therapy. They took no medication at all. The therapy itself was a modification of classic behavioral therapy for the disorder, which usually emphasizes such techniques as "exposure" and "flooding" in which patients are essentially trained to steel themselves against the normally triggering stimulus of dirty towels, or unchecked stoves, or whatever it is that sparks their obsessions.

Seeking a form of behavior therapy that could be self-administered, Schwartz's innovation was to drop the desensitization techniques and substitute a distraction approach that requires the patient, when he is gripped by the overwhelming need to wash his hands or check the stove, to do something else instead—something "wholesome." Patients first exercise their insight, telling themselves that the obsession they are experiencing is not real, that it is entirely a figment of their OCD. Then, having done this, they resist performing the compulsion (for short periods at the outset, longer periods as they gain control) and instead force themselves to do something productive, and enjoyable, for at least fifteen minutes. Hobbies of any kind are particularly useful for this step, but some patients have found that doing something good for other people—volunteer work, or simply a nice gesture to a friend or loved one—was an excellent diversion. This strictly behavioral step is essential: the UCLA team has found that it is not sufficient for a patient simply to experience awareness that his obsessions stem from a brain disorder. Insight is not enough; action is required—the action of performing an alternative behavior, as well as the "action" of *refusing* to perform the compulsion.

The twelve patients who responded to this therapy (six patients did not) experienced striking reductions in their obsessive-compulsive symptoms. One patient, "Michael," had long been too preoccupied by his obsessions to read; after treatment he reported that he could now read more books in one month than he had previously been able to read in a year. Another patient, "Jack," a man who washed his hands from fifty to a hundred times a day, estimated that he had reduced his symptoms by 90 percent, and reported that he now was able to wash his hands only a "socially acceptable" number of times each day. And a third, "Karen," a hoarder whose home was so filled with yard-sale purchases that she and her husband could not light the pilot of their furnace for fear of starting a fire, or allow a repairman inside for fear of being reported to the Department of Health, was able to begin the long process of excavating her house out from under the jumble. Two years later she was 75 percent of the way to her goal and had opened her own small business. These are dramatic changes, all achieved with no medication at all.

The changes were reflected in the scans. In graphic before-and-after images of the brains of these twelve responders we can see clear changes in brain function. Moreover, the greater the difference in the scan, the greater the clinical response—the better the patient's self-report of his or her functioning. In all twelve, two biological changes occurred: activity in the caudate nucleus "cooled" considerably, and the tight correlation in activity among the caudate nucleus, the orbital cortex, and the cingulate gyrus decreased significantly as well. In other words, the brain lock of obsessive-compulsive disorder diminished, and the three brain areas began to operate more independently of each other, as they do in the normal brain.

This is revolutionary data, revolutionary in its physical demonstration of the power of thought and behavior to alter basic brain function; revolutionary, too, in its offer of hope to all who wrestle with recalcitrant biology—a category that, while it may not include all of the people all of the time, very likely does include all of the people *some* of the

time. The UCLA researchers have demonstrated that the mind can
bend a stubbornly malfunctioning brain to its will.

What does this mean for the mildly afflicted person like Sandra? What
does it mean for any of the people in this book?

In the first place, anyone who struggles with any form of brain difference must begin by monitoring his thought processes, and the actions sparked by his thoughts, throughout the day. To do this well he
must learn to see himself from a distance; he must cultivate the Impartial Spectator within. The goal is simply to chart one's thoughts objec-
tively, exactly as a classic behaviorist charts behaviors: how many
depressive thoughts one thinks in an hour, how many manic thoughts,
how many addictive thoughts, and so on.

Interestingly, the very act of consciously noting an unproductive
thought or stream of thoughts may in fact decrease those thoughts. As
long ago as 1970 behaviorists discovered this effect, as Gerald Patterson
describes in his now classic behaviorist text for parents, *Families: Appli-
cations of Social Learning to Family Life:*

> The simple act of counting the occurrences of some of your own be-
> haviors can change their rate of occurrence! For example, if you wish
> to increase time spent reading, you might begin to count the number
> of minutes spent reading each day. For some people, the act of ob-
> serving and recording produces increases in reading. On the other
> hand, if you were interested in reducing fingernail-biting or angry
> thoughts about your spouse, daily recordings of these behaviors
> could produce decreases in their occurrence.

For anyone grappling with a shadow syndrome, this is extremely useful advice, since shadow syndromes are, by definition, only mildly
problematic. Where the patient with the full-blown, classic obsessive-
compulsive disorder can hardly miss the fact that he is spending vast
amounts of time obsessing about the stove, the person with a shadow
form *can* miss the fact that he or she is spending many hours a day obsessing about the bad behavior of his spouse. People can, and do,

squander hours of their lives in thought streams that produce nothing of value at all. Making mental note of these thought streams, knowing exactly what content is going through our minds, for how long and how often, is in and of itself an important tool for improving one's life. (Interestingly, Patterson reports, too, that consciously noting the behaviors of *others*—namely, one's misbehaving children or even spouse—can have this effect. It is well known within the world of special education that even in a disorder as serious as autism the simple act of a parent recording his autistic child's negative behaviors on a chart will cause a decrease in those behaviors. How this happens, no one can say.)

However, insight alone is not sufficient to change brain function: simply knowing that we have a problem does not solve the problem, although it helps. As we have seen, the UCLA team found that, in addition to developing insight, their patients needed to adhere to the behavioral component of the program as well: they had to prevent themselves from performing their compulsions—and, more than this, they had to put a wholesome and enjoyable behavior in their place.

To what degree can we alter basic brain biology using strictly cognitive-behavioral techniques? At present, we do not know. At least gauging by their own testimony, the UCLA patients are some distance from being "cured": they do not become symptom-free. (We do not know how similar their PET scans are to those of normal people, because the experimental design called for each patient to act as his own control. That is, the eighteen patients' posttreatment brain scans were compared not to the scans of eighteen people without obsessive-compulsive disorder but to the patients' own before-treatment scans.) These patients are vastly improved, but most of them must work very hard in the day-to-day to maintain that improvement. Barbara, a patient who had been severely handicapped by the disorder, is quoted as saying that "her few remaining OCD rituals are 'just a minor nuisance, like having to floss my teeth every day.'" While this description of her treatment outcome sounds nigh unto miraculous, a few paragraphs later she produces a second formulation: "[My

OCD] is a presence in my life as real and insistent in its own way as a fussing infant."

For anyone who does not suffer from obsessive-compulsive disorder—and who has spent a significant amount of time in the company of a fussing infant—this statement poses its complexities. It seems fair to say that, in essence, patients like Barbara have managed to move themselves from the category of severe obsessive-compulsive disorder up to the far less handicapping category of moderate or even mild obsessive-compulsive disorder. Or, in the language of autism and special education, from low-functioning to high-functioning. This result is certainly a therapeutic triumph, given the alternative. However, when we look at lives like Sandra's, we again confront the stubborn reality that, at least when it comes to the realm of family and children, mild may not be all that mild. Sandra's problems are mild already, as are the problems of all of the people described in this book, none of whom suffer from severe disorders of the brain (though some, it is true, have suffered severe psychological disorders in the past). And yet for every person interviewed, mild brain issues have *at times* proved crippling. Even a mild brain flaw can be devastating, under the "right" circumstances.

Given this reality, we cannot make the logical assumption that if the severely obsessive-compulsive patient can alter his brain function to a satisfactory degree strictly through behavioral techniques, then the mildly obsessive-compulsive patient can certainly do so. What interventions any individual will require in order to be the person he needs and wants to be will always depend upon the level of challenge he faces. For those individuals who are trying to do something too "difficult" for their own particular biological makeup—something that, at a profound level, they are simply not cut out to do (and this is Sandra's situation)—behavioral therapy may never be enough.

■□ THE GOOD CITIZEN

Of all the shadow syndromes, mild obsessive-compulsive disorder is perhaps the one constellation of mood and thought society cannot do without. Oldham and Morris's discussion of the normal variant of obsessive-compulsive personality disorder is an ode to the virtues of the mildly obsessed, whom they term "Conscientious" in their book:

> Call them the backbone of America. Conscientious-style people are the men and women of strong moral principle and absolute certainty, and they won't rest until the job is done and done right. They are loyal to their families, their causes, and their superiors. Hard work is a hallmark of this personality style; Conscientious types *achieve.*

And while many of the shadow syndromes can be helpful at work but toxic at home, a streak of obsessive-compulsive dedication *can* be (though not always) beneficial in love as well as work:

> Conscientious people can make great husbands or wives and good and lasting friends. . . . They're loyal, faithful, responsible, and will take extremely good care of their mates—but they're unemotional and unromantic about it . . . intimacy is hard for a Conscientious person. . . . During times of stress, Conscientious people may bury all suggestion of emotion as they dive deep into their work, but they won't run away from you unless you push them.

And, of course, there is the powerful conscience of the anxious or obsessive person—a highly developed moral self that is essential to work *and* to love:

> Conscientious people measure themselves and their behavior along the strict yardstick of a strong, demanding inner authority. When you listen to a Conscientious person speak, count how many times he or she says, "I should . . ." or, "You should . . ." (Conscientious types do like to give advice). Because of this very developed conscience, Conscientious people often contribute greatly to our society. They demand perfection in their own moral behavior and often expect it from everyone else.

While Judith Rapoport has not yet made up her mind whether "good OCD"—as Oldham and Morris describe it—is simply the healthy side of "bad OCD," she, too, has given the subject thought. Pondering the question, she writes:

> We also wonder about people with a great many "good" habits, whom we often think of as "super normals." These are people who have every minute of every day scheduled. As students, they were on every team, in every club, volunteer or community group, and they also took exercise and music classes. . . . Super-organized, neat, and careful, such people answer "yes" to a high number of questions in our obsessional questionnaire. Yet they feel that their habits are useful and in no way interfere with their lives. If they have a complaint it is that they might not meet all their obligations every week of the year. Sometimes they feel frantic. But they are not complainers. They don't want anything to change—just to do it all.

In short, *some* obsession is a good thing. *Some* addiction can be a good thing, too, when the addiction is put to a positive end. Physicists are addictive personalities in this sense; Albert Einstein can be said to have been addicted to field theory. Einstein was always, at all times, no matter what else might be going on in his life, thinking about electromagnetic fields. He spent his days and nights worrying about electromagnetic fields, thinking and fretting and theorizing and obsessing about electromagnetic fields; the problem of electromagnetic fields was invariably in the back of his mind if not the absolute forefront.

This is the place where addiction and obsession meet and bloom into something good. The notion that one can become addicted to work and productivity is already present in our term "workaholism": it may be time to endow the term with a positive valence as well as the negative one it has carried until now. Certainly, great thinkers and scholars throughout history reveal an addiction to work their spouses might have called workaholic, if they had known the term. Philosophers, historians, writers of every stripe: these people could not do the work they do if they were not obsessed, if they were not addicted to doing what it is that they do. These people *do* have a "monkey on their back," but it is a cherished creature they have no wish to live without.

Thus the goal for the Lous and the Sandras of this world is not to defeat their obsessive and addictive natures but to turn those natures toward the light. The mildly obsessive, the mildly anxious, the mildly compulsive, the mildly addicted—all have their contributions to make. When obsessive qualities are yoked to the service of projects larger than losing weight, or scrutinizing one's body for signs of cancer, or restoring a loaf of marble bread to a rich man's apartment—this is when good lives, and good societies, are built.

8

CARE AND FEEDING
OF THE BRAIN

"Orandum est ut sit mens sana in corpore sano."
"One can only ask for a sound mind in a sound body."
Juvenal, *Satires*, X.L. 356

SHADOW SYNDROMES BRING US face to face with the biology of
everyday life. So much of what we take to be bad character or unattractive personality is not, or not exactly, flawed personality (though in
time, as we have seen, a shadow syndrome may become personality): it
is flawed biology instead. The everyday emotional problems we confront, in ourselves and in others—hot tempers, mean spiritedness, lazi-
ness, pessimism, chronic worry, overeating or overdrinking—all find
their roots in the biology we bring into the world, and in the biology
our environments call forth from us as we live our lives.

But the fact that difficult behavior may have its source in "difficult"
biology does not excuse the behavior. Quite the opposite, in fact. That
behavior may be influenced by biology adds further responsibility to
our lot: the responsibility to tend to our biological lives *as well as* to our
social and emotional lives. If a biological difference in the brain moves
us to act in ways that are destructive or hurtful—in ways that are, in the
secular terminology of our time, dysfunctional—then it becomes our

job to address that difference. Our job is to care for our brains as well as our souls.

The first step is understanding. As the discoveries of neuropsychiatry become clear, people can begin to "know" themselves in a way that is historically unprecedented: we can begin to know our biological selves as well as our psychological selves. A woman who has always thought of herself as "codependent" might now come to see herself as "environmentally dependent," a difference that may be profound, and life-altering. A man with a "bad temper" may see himself as a person with too-low levels of serotonin—again, a difference in perception that may direct him toward new solutions to this problem. In both cases blame shifts: The woman who reaches the conclusion that she is biologically compelled to overinvolvement with other people's problems may cease to blame her alcoholic mother for this trait; she may cease to blame *herself.* The man who berates his children and whips the dog begins to see that it is not the children's fault, or the dog's fault, that his life is so miserable; the problem lies within himself. His anger is the product of his own chemistry.

■ COMPLEXITIES AND TIPPING POINTS

Altering that chemistry is not as daunting an undertaking as it may seem. The brain scans of obsessive-compulsive patients at UCLA tell us that the brain remains plastic throughout life: these were people, some of them in middle age, all of them suffering from a severe disorder, who used cognitive-behavioral therapy to change brain function in a matter of weeks. If the UCLA patients could alter the working of their brains, those of us struggling with far milder issues can certainly hope to do the same. The biology of the brain is complex, reactive, and always subject to growth and change.

The first principle to absorb as we set about attempting to influence the course of our own biology is that the brain is infinitely complex. It is a widely accepted view among neuroscientists that the brain is the most complex system in the known universe. A quart-sized mass of tissue, the brain contains roughly 100 billion neurons, *each and every one* of those 100 billion neurons possessing an average of 10,000 links to other neurons. For all practical purposes, the brain is infinite.

Which means that when it comes to altering brain function, there is no simple, one-stop cure—or not for most of us, at any rate. For instance, while we have spoken frequently of "low" serotonin levels in this book, in fact the concept of a low serotonin level is extraordinarily complex. There are thirteen different kinds of serotonin receptors in animals—and counting—and it is still unknown how many serotonin receptors humans possess. Each and every one of these receptors exists within *each* synapse—and when a "serotonin-raising" medication like Prozac hits the synapse, each different serotonin receptor is affected in a different way. Some receptors alter electrical transmission in response to the drug, other receptors alter chemical transmission, and so on.

But the real story of serotonin levels isn't told even by the individual synapses being affected, because each and every synapse is always affected in turn by the neurons lying "downstream." "Downstream" neurons are the neurons lying *past* the neuron being treated by the Prozac—the neurons being "fed into" by the neuron responding to the drug. The downstream neuron may feed back into the upstream neuron and actually *decrease* serotonin release—or the downstream neuron's feedback may *increase* serotonin release further—we simply do not know, at least not yet. God did not make us simple.

Then you have to take the cascade of enzymes that make up the serotonin molecule into account; these enzymes may be influenced by the feedback loop as well, and the enzymes are in turn affected by even smaller hormones like peptides and the chemistry that guides them. . . . And we have yet even to *mention* genes and cell functioning!

In any event, psychiatrists are forced to speak of "high" and "low" levels of serotonin in order to hold any kind of dialogue at all with any reader who is not a seasoned neuroscientist. Nevertheless, the fact remains that, at this point, the workings of the serotonin system are still unknown. The scientists at Eli Lilly, manufacturer of Prozac, simply do not know what Prozac does to the brain downstream. They know what it does in the synapse; they do not know what cascade of feedback loops and genetic mechanisms this synaptic change sets off.

John once organized a conference on serotonin and aggression for the APA. He invited one of the most prominent researchers in serotonin studies in animals. After one presentation on the atypical tranquilizer BuSpar, a simple drug which we know acts upon just one of the serotonin receptors, the researcher stood and objected to the paper as being far too simple. Rather than BuSpar raising serotonin levels, as most believe, he remarked that the downstream neurons may actually act to shut down the flow of serotonin, as he had found studying isolated neurons in the laboratory. He was an old man by then, and he had spent a lifetime at the bench trying to sort out the puzzle. And still he did not know.

Thus for anyone trying to improve brain function, it is essential to recognize the fact that whenever we treat the brain with a medication like Prozac—or with a change in diet, exercise, marital partner, or anything else that affects the brain—we invariably produce a cascade effect: one small change in one receptor leads to another small change in another receptor which leads to more changes in the neurons lying beyond, and so on down the line. Because each brain in the universe of human brains is completely distinct and unique—including the brains of identical twins—any treatments of any kind produce effects unique to that individual. No doctor, no psychotherapist, can predict what effect this pill, or this "talking cure," will have upon this person's biology. The clinician can only rely upon statistical averages: how many patients with this cluster of issues typically respond to a particular treatment? After that, it is a matter of trying the treatment and seeing what happens. (This should not be taken as an unduly pessimistic observation: in fact, the majority of patients who choose to take medication do end up experiencing very real and significant improvement. At least half, and probably more, of all patients who consult a psychiatrist will find the help they need.)

To the uninitiated, this image of cascading brain-changes can be a bit horrifying on first view—particularly since by far the best-understood cascade effects at this points are the bad ones. Traumatic head injuries produce cascading damage to the brain: a "bruise" to the brain in one location produces toxic chemicals that spread rapidly to other parts of the brain, killing off neurons far removed from the original site of injury. Inside the brain, a car crash today keeps right on happening tomorrow and the day after; it is a terrifying process to contemplate. Because within the brain everything is connected to everything else, trouble in one "spot" eventually means trouble in another—which is why we are now starting to see, at the genetic level, connections being made between mood issues like anxiety, and cognitive issues like attention, as we saw with the D2R2 allele. Below-the-norm levels of just *one* receptor can produce wildly varying unpredictable effects.

The startling complexity of the brain can also be discouraging when we contemplate the possibility of improving our mental lives. If the brain is so complicated, and if everything we do affects everything else—and worse yet, does so in unpredictable ways—where does the person slogging through her day under a cloud of mild depression go from here? Trying to achieve "mental fitness" is not like trying to achieve physical fitness, where studies have demonstrated that thirty minutes of exercise three times a week and five fruits and vegetables a day will pretty much do it. The government has yet to produce a pamphlet containing the basic rules of biological brain fitness; given the brain's complexity, whether or not it will ever be possible to produce such a pamphlet remains an open question. "Predicting" the brain—predicting the effects of positive behaviors on our brains—may be like predicting the weather: almost impossible.

We bring up the weather because we feel that for anyone contemplating making "brain changes," a brief lesson in complexity theory is essential. As we will see, the principles of complexity theory—and of its cousin, "tipping point" theory—are extremely useful when it comes to guiding and motivating brain-positive actions. Complexity theory originally grew out of efforts to predict the weather. What meteorologists found was that tomorrow's weather cannot be forecast with a high degree of reliability because weather is a complex system. An infinite number of variables coalesce to create a rainstorm over the Midwest.

What is more, weather systems are *nonlinear* in nature: When it comes to the weather, or to any complex system in nature or in society, two plus two may not equal four. Climatologists cannot simply add up the various factors that go into producing a storm—temperature, air pressure, ocean currents, and so on—and come up with a probability that says anything useful at all about what will or will not happen over the cornfields of Iowa tomorrow. Linear mathematics do not work. You cannot predict the weather the way you can predict the direction and velocity of a pool ball in billiards. The same principle holds true of the brain.

All of us are familiar with nonlinear phenomena in real life: the nonlinearity of life is what people are getting at when they make observations along the lines of "twins aren't double the work, they're quadruple"—a commonplace among parents of multiples. Husbands and wives invariably make the same observation concerning the jump from one child to two: The increase in work load and stress is far higher than simple addition would predict. The effect of the second child upon the family system is not a simple addition of one child to one child. It is *more*. Thus when it comes to families, we intuitively understand that one plus one may not equal two. Complexity theory grew out of this observation, and is an attempt to discover the rules and principles that govern complex systems. Complex systems like the weather, or like the family, or like the brain.

While most of the metaphors and principles of complexity theory are relevant to the brain, perhaps the most useful theorem for anyone trying to change his brain is meteorologist Edward Lorenz's now famous "butterfly effect": a butterfly flapping its wings in Tokyo, he observed, could set off a cascading chain of events that ended up as a hurricane over Texas. Or, as John L. Casti puts it in his book *Complexification*:

> . . . the purely deterministic laws governing weather formation are unstable in the worst possible way. As a result, they allow minuscule changes at one location to percolate through the system so as to bring about major effects somewhere else.

The negative implications of this principle for human behavior, and for the biology of the brain, are immediately apparent: this is the "one false move" notion ratified by higher mathematics. New lovers, for instance, understand intuitively that in the intricate calculus of the love affair just one small misstep can ruin a whole day. Tiny inputs—minuscule changes—at one location can and do bring about major effects someplace else.

Researchers have now demonstrated this phenomenon with transgenic mice—mice who have been bred to be missing one particular gene. These mice have given us fascinating evidence of what can happen to the brain when just one element is lost. For instance, one strain of transgenic mice is missing the brain enzyme CAMKA II. And in losing this one, lone enzyme the mice are devastated. They cannot learn to swim underwater; their spatial memory is poor; they are a bit parkinsonish. In the CAMKA II mice, a small change mushrooms into many and devastating consequences. (When researchers return this one enzyme to the brains of the mice the animals are restored to normalcy—an extremely heartening discovery to all who cope with severe brain disorders such as autism and schizophrenia and the like. This is the kind of data that parents of autistic or mentally retarded children hold on to: a profoundly handicapping brain condition, a condition that to the layperson *looks* like it would have to result from massive brain damage, can, because of the brain's complexity and interconnectivity, result from just one small defect.)

When it comes to applying these principles to creating a program of "mental fitness," the brain's interconnectivity immediately tells us why it can be important (though not always, as we will see) not to let even minor mental issues slide. Small problems may cascade into large ones; that is a First Principle. Probably the most vivid formulation of this reality, when it comes to making changes in our lives and brains, is the "tipping point" idea, developed in the 1970s by Thomas Schelling, a political economist from Harvard. Schelling is not a complexologist; he is a social scientist. But the two schools of thought are similar in that both Schelling's work and complexology use nonlinear dynamics to explain complex phenomena. The tipping point in any social situation (and very likely the brain as well) is the straw that breaks the camel's back; it is the tiny additional factor that can touch off a shocking explosion of change. In his 1996 *New Yorker* article on tipping point theory Malcolm Gladwell uses the work of sociologist Jonathan Crane to illustrate the point. Crane set out to correlate the rate of teen pregnancies in any given neighborhood with the number of "high status" workers living in that neighborhood. By high status Crane meant grownups who could serve as role models for the young people around them: professionals, managers, teachers, business people. And what he found was entirely nonlinear. Given a high-status population of anywhere from 5 to 40 percent—a large range indeed—in a neighborhood, teen pregnancy rates held steady. Pregnancy rates were the same with just 5 percent high-status workers in the neighborhood as they were with 40 percent of the adults holding high-status jobs. But virtually the instant the proportion of high-status to low-status workers fell below the 5 percent "threshold," the teen pregnancy rate *doubled,* as did high school drop-out rates—which also held steady throughout the 5-to-40 percent range. Below 5 percent the neighborhood *tipped:* it crashed into chaos and disorder. As Gladwell writes:

> Crane's study essentially means that at the five-percent tipping point neighborhoods go from relatively functional to wildly dysfunctional virtually overnight. There is no steady decline: a little change has a huge effect. The neighborhoods below the tipping point look like they've been hit by the Ebola virus.

The brain can tip as well: a very mild depression, in a person who is already close to the edge, might destroy a marriage, a family, a job, a life. The effects of a shadow syndrome, however mild, depend upon where a person stands in the 5-to-40 comfort range.

But even when an individual starts out in life living well above the 5 percent tipping point, a shadow syndrome may ultimately wreak havoc. A very mild depression, lived through day in and day out, can percolate through a life system just as easily as a butterfly's wings can percolate through a weather system. Take a person whose life is in excellent shape apart from a chronic problem with mild depression: in time a persistent state of subtle hopelessness and despair can wear away at the good things with which this person is blessed—friendships, job, marriage—until he has sunk to the 5 percent borderline. Once the tipping point has been reached, just a slight deepening of the depression might cause that person to crash.

Trying to discern a butterfly effect at work in a life is not easy. The essential question is: How many times a day does mild depression (or mild ADD or mild OCD, etc.) shape the course of events? How often does a shadow syndrome produce an argument between husband and wife instead of a moment of shared joy? How often does it produce a solitary bout of suspicious brooding over a colleague's behavior, instead of an afternoon spent working together with that person to get something done? How often are interactions and thoughts nudged just two degrees toward the negative? And how do these many small moments multiply each other's effects in the overall scheme of things? Obviously, these are the questions it is important to ask well before we reach the tipping point: these are the questions that, if we were to address them honestly while we are still safely residing well within the 5-to-40 percent realm, might allow us to avoid a "tip."

The problem with "butterfly" questions (and with tipping questions as well) is that, of course, they are not easy to answer. Trying to discern a butterfly effect in one's own life requires extremely close and nuanced scrutiny of the smallest of social interactions—no easy task for anyone whose shadow syndrome in and of itself creates minor deficits in social awareness. Perhaps somewhat easier for most, the butterfly effect also tells us that we should take close note not just of our actions (and interactions) throughout the day, but of our thought stream as well. How much sheer *time* do we spend on our shadow syndromes? If we sat down and kept a running log, most of us would be surprised.

As we have neared the end of this book, we have found that many of the people we interviewed connect instantly with tipping points and butterfly effects when we bring these subjects up. Ellen, for instance, the overrun working mother of two who eventually decided to use

Prozac to treat her mild depression, had in fact tipped after the second baby. While her work was going well, and her marriage was certainly surviving, her mothering skills had pretty much gone into free fall. And, of course, when one part of a life goes into free fall, other parts can follow. As the saying goes, troubles come in threes—a piece of folk wisdom that precisely captures the nature of what it means for a life to tip down. When we contacted Ellen recently, and described tipping point theory to her, she got it at once:

> There's no question in my mind that the second kid was the tipping point for me. This summer we sent Laura to camp—she stayed overnight—and it was amazing. Tom and I could go out to dinner with Elaine every night and relax and have fun; we could hardly believe it. With just one child again, for the first time in three years, everything was unbelievably easy. We were having a party.

Would Ellen be taking Prozac if she had had just one child? Quite possibly not. Abstract concepts like tipping points and butterfly effects can help us visualize the point at which we need more help than proper exercise and diet can supply. And, when we do need a stronger treatment, tipping theory can help relieve the sense of failure we often experience when we make a first appointment with a therapist, or fill a first prescription. One of the messages of tipping and complexity is that seeing a therapist, or taking a pill, is not a sign of weakness. Seeing a therapist or taking a pill can mean many things, but often the necessity of these acts means simply that our reach has finally exceeded our grasp.

■□ THE GOOD NEWS

The revelations of complexity and tipping point theories are extraordinarily useful, but at first glance daunting. People's lives and brains can and do crash, and they can crash because of small problems. A shadow syndrome *can* be dangerous.

However, the good news is that both theories also establish the possibility that a system can tip up as well as down. In other words, complex systems do not list in just one direction: life is not inevitably a downhill proposition. The main subject of Gladwell's article, in fact, is the sudden "crash" in murder rates—or skyrocketing *rise* in safety—in New York City after the fall of 1994, following a series of small changes instituted by then Police Commissioner William J. Bratton. Under his command police officers made small changes in high-crime neighborhoods: breaking up groups of young men lounging around on street corners, stopping drunk drivers, shutting down drug bazaars. These were small, or smallish, changes: the police weren't out on the beat every day arresting serial killers. And yet these small changes in nonviolent crime led to a large change in violent crime, with the murder rate in New York City dropping to the level of the early 1970s, half of what it was in 1990. Gladwell writes:

> . . . it is the nature of nonlinear phenomena that sometimes the most modest of changes can bring about enormous effects.

When it comes to the brain, this is tremendously good news: depending again upon where you are vis-à-vis your tipping point *up,* just so small a change as a new exercise program or a satisfying hobby might make all the difference in the world. Complexity theory has its own name, and description, of this phenomenon: complexologists speak of levers within the system—points at which small changes can yield large and entirely positive results. They speak, too, of "self-organizing" systems: those moments where, out of chaos, a complex and ordered form spontaneously emerges, like the snowflake out of random rain and chill.

For most of us, the notion that a complex system may tip up as well as down, that what goes down may also go up, is counterintuitive. Collectively, as a culture, we have taken the second law of thermodynamics to heart: entropy rules. We have taken our college textbook knowledge of physics to mean that all of life drifts inevitably toward disorder and decline. Things fall apart.

Thus the notion that things might naturally come together—might naturally, inevitably and suddenly cohere: this is something rather new under the sun. It is such a novel concept that some complexologists believe a fifth fundamental force (in addition to gravity, electromagnetism, and the strong and weak forces that govern the atom) will be discovered to exist in nature.

When it comes to social reality, we *do* possess some intuitive understanding of this possibility, of an anti-entropy force at work in life and love. We speak of "things falling into place" or of being "on a roll"; athletes strive to move into the "zone" or to hit on a "winning streak." All of these experiences are, in a sense, self-organizing systems. Peter Kramer's patients who, taking antidepressant medication, suddenly and miraculously became better than well, were experiencing exactly this: their previously chaotic existence had suddenly coalesced into perfect, crystalline form. (In tipping terminology, they had tipped up.) In any event, they weren't just better, they were better than better.

These are the images to carry with us when we think of changing our lives. We are looking to tip up; we are hoping to reach that magic moment when life and love "self-organize" into something splendid. That is the hope.

■ THE CARE AND FEEDING OF THE BRAIN

When it comes to making small changes in our lives and brains, the motto to embrace is: everything matters. Exercise, food, sleep, whom we marry, the work we do—all of it counts; all of it affects our brains. The advancing field of neuroscience tells us that our mothers were right: eat your vegetables, say your prayers, and do your homework before you turn on the TV. Or, as Ben Franklin put it, early to bed and early to rise. The folk wisdom of our ancestors was intuitively correct. Paying attention to the detail of daily life, and making good choices, is the way to mental fitness.

Perhaps the most important modest change any of us can make will be to establish an exercise program, and stick to it. A growing body of evidence links aerobic exercise to sharpened memory, faster response times, elevation of mood, increased self-esteem. Most of these studies have been conducted on elderly populations, but the results are so encouraging that many clinicians are convinced that even young children may benefit from a program of daily exercise. Researchers have found significant improvements even in the behavior of severely autistic adolescents following intensive aerobic conditioning (although in this case the youngest subjects did not respond). If aerobic exercise can cause change in the behavior of brain-damaged autistics, this discovery alone is reason enough for the rest of us to take it up.

On balance, the research shows that the majority of positive neurological alterations to the brain occur as the result of long-term, regular exercise. Nevertheless, some changes do occur from the first day a program is begun: neural levels of dopamine, serotonin, and norepinephrine rise after a single workout. Mild depression and anxiety in particular can be very responsive to the effects of exercise. Exercise increases alpha-wave emissions in the right (or "depressive") hemisphere; this is beneficial because an *increase* in alpha waves appears to correlate with an overall *decrease* in activity in that area (since alpha waves are slower than the beta waves produced when we concentrate). In short, exercise appears to slow the right side of the brain to some degree, and to stimulate the left side. That is a good thing, because the left-dominant brain is generally a tougher, more adaptable, more stress-tolerant brain. Which is what most of us desire.

Exercise treats anxiety via a slightly different mechanism. Anxiety increases under two conditions: when neural feedback indicates either that the brain is losing control over its environment, or that it is operating under some degree of uncertainty. Because exercise is a self-driven activity, both of these messages cease. The normally anxious person who is engaged in a vigorous game of squash is continually receiving the message that his brain is in control of his body, and that movement and flow are happening as they should. Both messages relieve anxiety. They do so at a physiological level; the actual score of the game— whether the person is winning or losing—has nothing to do with it. A person jogging alone will experience exactly the same effect. Anxiety is allayed by the brain's perception that the brain and body are fully connected and firing in sync. Thus, some drop in anxiety is a virtual certainty after a vigorous workout.

Ongoing exercise has also been shown to increase levels of neurotrophins—or nerve growth factors—in the brain. We will be hearing more about nerve growth factors in the coming years; neuroscientists are experimenting with these chemicals as treatments for brain deficits of every conceivable kind, ranging from genetic defects like autism or Down's syndrome all the way through Alzheimer's disease and traumatic head injury. In the brain, nerve growth factors do exactly what the name implies: they trigger and guide the growth of new neural connections between cells. This may explain the fact that older people who exercise consistently appear to be less susceptible to the mental effects of aging than those who do not exercise. Exercise increases neurotrophin levels, allowing memory and attention span to remain intact well into advanced years.

Some of the most interesting work on the neurophysiology of exercise and its effects upon nerve growth factors is that of William Greenough, professor of psychology at the University of Illinois. Greenough studied rats who had been raised in environments that differed in amount and kind of exercise obtained each day. One group of rats led sedentary lives, a second played aimlessly on pieces of wood and plastic in their cages, a third ran on an automated running wheel several hours a day, and a fourth group were made to navigate an intricate construction of wires and metal bridges in order to move from one part of their cage to another.

Greenough found that all of the rats who exercised in any way developed a greater concentration of blood vessels in their brains, indicating that a better supply of nutrients was reaching their neurons. Predictably, these blood vessel-enriched rats far outlived their sedentary brothers. Interestingly, the rats who had improved dexterity and coordination (the wires-and-bridges group) showed significantly more neural connections upon postmortem examination than did any other group. Their increase in degree of neural connectivity is almost certainly linked to the rise in neurotrophins that accompanies complex exercise—and offers a strong argument for taking up a sport beyond the treadmill. Tennis lessons at fifty may be the right way to go. Tennis, or dance: anything that requires working on coordination as well as speed and stamina.

Whether or not exercise improves strictly cognitive abilities (reasoning and comprehension) is not clear at this point. Some studies have found rises in IQ after a year of exercise, but we do not yet know whether the improvement can be attributed to an increase in intelligence per se, or to an improvement in the substrates of cognitive performance, such as reaction times, attention span, and memory. In any event, since reaction time and attention are in fact an issue in many of the shadow syndromes, if these are the only areas affected that is reason enough to take up a sport and stay with it. An increase in any or all of these factors can produce a corresponding bump up in IQ scores. While drugs, foods, and other treatments often vary wildly in the degree to which they improve our "hidden handicaps," exercise is the one intervention that seems to help across the board. Exercise toughens the brain as well as the body, making the brain more fit to cope with the stresses of life.

■ SMART MACHINES

As to what sort of exercise to choose: at present our knowledge on this front, too, is somewhat limited. Aerobic exercise is clearly good; aerobic exercise that requires improvements in coordination and dexterity is probably better. In the future we will know more: psychiatrists already speak of "brain training"—of precision exercise routines, and computerized exercise machines, that will directly address a person's individual brain deficits and needs.

Eventually we will see the personal gymnasium of the future, a high-tech workout machine designed to exercise the brain as well as the body—designed to exercise the brain in tandem with the body. These will be smart machines, equipped with computers that can learn from its user's response to each day's workout. The machine will take measures such as pulse, respiration, the composition of the user's sweat (recording pH, glucose, alcohol, and hormone levels), galvanized skin response (a measure of sweat gland activity); perhaps at some point such exercise equipment will be able to take inexpensive EEG readings. The smart machines of the future will be interactive; they will be equipped with software that can learn from the user each morning, and adjust the day's exercise progam accordingly. The computer might ask its owner how yesterday's business meeting went, and in what ways yesterday's workout kept him or her feeling sharp and self-assured throughout the day. Or it might ask how patient and focused he or she managed to be with the children—the questions asked will be determined by the kind of life its owner is trying to lead. How did you sleep last night? What have you eaten today? How worrried are you about this afternoon? All of this data will go into refining the body-and-brain-training regimen the machine has evolved.

Smart machines will use active testing as well, challenging the owner's memory, attention, alertness, perceptual acuity, and reaction times with a a series of puzzles and video games. All of it geared to the day ahead: The personal gymnasium will design a total-body workout tailored to the user, and to the user alone. Light, rhythms, harmonies, aromas, negative-ion-rich air—any or all might be incorporated into the physical workout in order to fine tune the owner's brain for the day ahead. If the user were feeling slightly depressed, the machine would deploy various means to up-regulate the left hemisphere while down-regulating the right; if the user were scheduled to make a creative business presentation that day, the machine might work to boost right-brain function instead.

The smart machines of the future will go a long way toward enabling us to bring our brains up to speed without medication or extended psychotherapy—a gift to anyone who prefers to take more conservative routes to well-being. Such machines are of course only a theoretical possibility at present. But we will begin to see them sooner than we might think.

Owners of these machines will set parameters according to their own neurology. The biology of the brain is such that it will probably never become feasible to formulate a set of precision norms for all to follow. Normalcy is always a range, and a wide one at that. This is why the UCLA studies of obsessive-compulsive disorder employed a before-and-after design instead of matched controls (a standard form of experimental design in which two groups of subjects are used, the only difference between them being the variable—in this case OCD—under study). In the UCLA study, patients' scans were compared not to a group of normal scans, but to the patients' own scans before the treatment.

The fact is, there probably is no such thing as a normal, one-to-one correlation between specific brain functions and specific behaviors. Brain scans have shown that different people may use different parts of the brain to perform the same functions. Not surprisingly, Alan J. Zametkin's now-famous scans of the brains of adults with attention deficit disorder overlapped significantly with the brains of adults who showed no sign of attention deficit disorder: the brain is profoundly diverse. The exact same scan on one person might signal attention deficit disorder, and on another person correlate with entirely normal attention and impulse.

Thus, those who worry that advancing knowledge of the brain will lead to a day when we have drugs or gene therapies or Big Brother exercise machines capable of forcing everyone into the same strict mold of normalcy can relax. This is not the way brains were designed to work, can work, or ever will work. Which means that anyone using a smart machine for exercise will, like the patients in the UCLA study, simply compete against himself: he will set norms specific to his own brain and body.

It is entirely possible, of course, that neuroscience may one day establish general ranges of brain function, much as we now possess optimal ranges for blood pressure, cholesterol levels, and the like. Researchers into the psychology of "well-being" have already begun the process of establishing one such parameter: college students, they have found, tend to average seven "good days" for every ten. *Three bad days in ten:* this figure is, at least for college students, a normal level of "depression," or "anxiety," or relationship problems, or whatever it is that produces a bad day for any particular person.

It is easy to see where figures like these might be helpful: once you have the 70 percent figure in mind, a college student who finds himself having seven bad days out of ten becomes a person who does not have to spend a great deal of time wondering whether he is like "everyone else." He is not. Simple behavioral averages like these, along with their biological analogues, may come into being one day, and will no doubt be useful when they do. But the idea of absolute behavioral and biological norms: this will not, and in fact cannot, happen.

■□ TAI CHI AND THE ART OF BEING WELL

In the meantime, miracles can be worked, sometimes, with the forms of exercise we possess today. In particular, several of John's patients have thrived as a result of taking up the martial arts: karate, aikido, tai chi, and tae kwan do. Like the smart gym of the future, these forms of exercise integrate the physical with the mental: the martial arts involve both strenuous exercise *and* focused awareness. It is this dual focus that gives the martial arts a unique power to improve a variety of brain functions.

Unlike most Western sports, the martial arts specifically train the mind as well as the body: novices are taught to pay attention—conscious, focused attention—to their balance, timing, endurance, ability to act sequentially, the speed and strength of each muscle, and the way they move through space. Like many forms of meditation (which is also an excellent tool for treating and managing the shadow syndromes), the martial arts train the body and brain to achieve a state of relaxed readiness, a condition in which the trainee is able to react effectively to any challenge without having to anticipate it. Training is a process of constantly learning new moves. Learning a martial art is a bit like learning to draw in a mirror; it is not likely to be a natural or inborn talent, the way tossing or kicking a ball seems to be. (The ability, and desire, to catch and kick balls are basic developmental steps, at least in Western development psychology.) Thus anyone who takes up a martial art begins as an absolute novice.

Two of John's patients have made tremendous progress in their lives through their commitment to the practice of a martial art. One patient, Rick, had been a varsity athlete in high school who managed to make it all the way to college before his learning disabilities caught up with him. Struggling with college-level course work, he found himself virtually unable to concentrate. Always the highly distractible, impulsive, stimulus-seeking type, he began to drink and party his way through college, drifting from subject to subject, making low B's and C's in all of his classes. He had no idea what he wanted to do with his life, although he possessed good visual spatial skills, and might have pursued his interest in architecture if he had felt any confidence in himself at all. Rick's father was an accomplished neuroscientist, his mother a government official, and both of his high-achieving parents were heartbroken over their son's lack of direction and motivation.

It was his parents who steered Rick to John the summer before his senior year. John asked him to read literature on learning disabilities and attention, and put him on a mild course of Ritalin. Then, he advised him to sign up for a class in karate.

It was the karate that made the difference. Rick now studies tae kwan do, a Korean martial art similar to karate, five days a week. He has found an activity that he truly enjoys, one that keeps him interested and striving to improve himself. He thrives upon the discipline tae kwan do requires of him, and he loves the fact that it is so difficult—yet eventually possible—to master each new move. Tae kwan do has trained Rick to wrestle with frustration and hardship rather than shying away from challenges and procrastinating.

That fall his grades rose into the A-minus range, in part because he now possessed the confidence to take difficult courses that would keep him intrigued and motivated—courses that seized his attention and held it. Today he has virtually stopped drinking; he is committed to school, and eager to graduate when his senior year ends and move on to the work world. He has found his mission in life: he plans to become involved in a local organization dedicated to protecting the environment.

Rick's diagnosis, as well as his newfound love of self-discipline, has motivated him to write a few paragraphs every day as a way to overcome his learning disabilities. He consciously applies the techniques of tae kwan do—careful self-observation and practice—to seek out and attack his own intellectual weaknesses. And his shame over his former mediocrity, as well as his once constant fear of failure, has vanished completely. The self-awareness and discipline of tae kwan do have given Rick a mental toughness. Now, confident in his ability to change his habits and tendencies when he needs to, he no longer puts off and denies issues that in the past would have been too painful to confront. More often than not, Rick feels in control of shaping his actions to achieve his dreams.

An even more startling case of improvement through the discipline of the martial arts is the story of Anthony, himself a psychiatrist and the father of two. Ironically, it was only during his own psychoanalysis that Anthony realized that he himself suffered an autisticlike social deficit that left him incapable of relating well to other people. As a child he had not talked until the age of three; thereafter he had found the practice of speaking to other people so difficult and painful that his grade-school teachers thought him retarded. (Today, in the not uncommon savantry of the high-functioning autistic spectrum, he is a philosopher, a lecturer, and an M.D.)

Probably suffering from mild cerebellar deficits, Anthony could not play sports well; he was exceedingly uncoordinated, and never able to feel good about his body. Although he had taken karate classes off and on for nearly sixteen years, he had slacked off of late, and he was stewing moodily in his various addictions: smoking, food binges, purchasing scratch tickets for the lottery, and a host of other compulsions.

John recommended that Anthony return to his karate lessons, and that, more important, he do so wholeheartedly. Anthony quickly rediscovered how much he loved and needed these classes. Almost at once he noticed not only a decrease in his moodiness, but also an improved ability to focus his attention, with the result that he was able to give more real time—focused, loving time—to his wife and children.

Anthony now became fascinated with the intricacy of karate, and began to be aware of himself and his body's well-being. He was able to stop smoking, and he found it easier to contain his bingeing and ticket buying. His sense of rhythm and timing improved. He found that the focus and determination fostered in the dojo accompanied him home at night, making it easier to do the things he normally would dread and put off until the last moment. The slew of telephone messages that awaited him every morning, the bane of any therapist's existence, no longer troubled him. Rather than dragging himself through the pile, as he had done for many years, now he was able to sit down at his desk, size up what was required of him, and set himself to it.

To his delight, Anthony found that the Japanese karate he practiced also improved his ability to relate to others. The particular form of Japanese karate Anthony was studying devoted half of each class to "partner training." During this thirty-minute period Anthony was required to observe and move in concert with another human being—a perfect exercise for a person who had never truly mastered the smooth, automatic social interactions most people take for granted.

Both Rick and Anthony have tipped up, and they have done so by making only modest changes in their lives. A fullhearted commitment to a hobby—in Anthony's case a hobby he had already dabbled in for years—has percolated through the systems of their lives and pushed both up above the 5 percent line. For Rick and Anthony, things have fallen into place.

The experiences of Rick and Anthony tell us that very likely any form of general training for the brain and body can cause specific brain functions to work better. The physiological reasons for this phenomenon are still poorly understood, but it is clear that any activity that provides constant challenge, and requires sustained self-discipline, has the potential to benefit many and various areas of our intellectual, social, and emotional lives.

We can influence brain function through many other "natural" means, of course. Food, light, and sleep—all can alter brain chemistry for the better. In terms of light and sleep the data are fairly clear: light is good (unless you are manic); sleep is good (unless you are depressed, when it may be bad). Michael Norden's *Beyond Prozac* provides an excellent summary of the uses of light and sleep. And Herbert Benson's now classic *Relaxation Response* probably remains one of the most useful guides to the capacity of meditation to soothe the noisy brain.

Food is a more complicated issue, with experimental results, at this point, often contradictory or unclear. Thus pure carbohydrates unaccompanied by fat may soothe anxiety, but decrease alertness at the same time. Certainly we know that almost everything we eat can affect the way the brain works, not only directly, through psychoactive substances such as coffee, wine, and chocolate, but indirectly through foods that alter the ratio of one hormone to another, or one protein to another. The brain is connected to the body not only through the nervous system, but also through the evolutionarily more ancient system of chemical regulation, which means that whatever enters our bloodstream, from wheat germ to pork crackling, may affect the brain in a matter of seconds.

Beyond the common-sense tactic of striving to develop good habits in exercise and diet, we should hold ourselves open to the mysteries of the body and its brain. Solutions can come from places we would never think to look, and if we aren't paying attention we may miss an answer that is staring us in the face.

John once had a patient on the locked unit of the hospital, the ward where people with developmental disabilities and extremes of agitation, self-abuse, or aggression were kept for around-the-clock observation. This woman had been there for many, many years, and had a combination of cerebral palsy, autism, panic disorder, and aggression. As time went by she had become progressively more confrontational with the staff, and was one of the two women on the unit who consistently managed to cause a brouhaha of one sort or another on almost a daily basis.

She had been tried on every program available in the state system, including special diets, vitamins, behavior training, cognitive therapy (adapted to her level of mental functioning), not to mention traditional psychotherapy also adapted to her special needs. Although her initial guardian had been opposed in principle to the use of medication, eventually drugs were tried as well, and she had received every combination of medications imaginable. It was all to no avail.

But there was one curious thing: over time the nursing staff had noticed that whenever this patient came down with a cold, and was treated with Dimetapp for her cough and runny nose, her behavior improved. She stopped confronting and assaulting other patients, and generally stopped making trouble. This observation had been made by the staff for some years, but they passed it off as just another example of the old saying that patients get better when they get sick. (This is a common observation made by the parents of developmentally disabled children. Often these children function better—better attention spans, even better language—when they are ill.)

At one point, during a particularly long and pronounced patch of escalating misbehavior, the patient developed a cold, and was put on Dimetapp. This time her behavioral problems disappeared so abruptly and completely that it caught the staff's attention. Everyone was awed, although skeptical—and then all were further amazed when, after the patient's cold subsided and the Dimetapp had been discontinued, her challenging behaviors returned in force.

That was enough for the nurses. They insisted that the doctors reinstitute the Dimetapp, and the doctors complied. Remarkably, the patient's behavioral symptoms vanished once again. Near-believers now, her doctors took away the Dimetapp and *voilà*: the symptoms were back. Everyone was convinced.

But from the point of view of traditional pharmacology, this was beyond the pale. There simply weren't any known psychoactive properties to either of the active ingredients in Dimetapp, an antihistamine and a decongestant. The staff tried the patient on each of the compounds separately, and neither had any effect. The Dimetapp, however, worked like magic, and for six months the unit was as peaceful as could be.

Sadly, her behavior eventually began to deteriorate in spite of the Dimetapp and, because it was a nontraditional treatment and thus difficult to justify medically, she was taken off it. Her behavior problems returned for good. Whatever it was in her brain that had responded to the drug had now changed. This is one of the frustrating facts of clinical life; the brain can defeat a medication that has worked in the past. (Although this can happen on occasion with any psychotropic medication, psychiatrists have actually coined a term for it with Prozac: it is called "Prozac poop-out.")

The moral here is that when it comes to the brain we are still feeling our way, and we must respect what we do not know as much as what we do know. In terms of daily living this means simply staying connected to ourselves, and to our brains. If we notice a Dimetapp effect in our own life, whether it happens with food or exercise or sleep or light or negative ions or simply the scent of autumn in the air, we should take it seriously.

Apart from food and exercise and the random Dimetapp cure, the single most critical improvement anyone can make in brain function, and in character, is to find his mission in life. Passion heals; a wholehearted commitment to a calling, or a career, or an avocation focuses the mind and the soul. And neuropsychiatry tells us that idleness is indeed the devil's playground. It is well known that idleness increases psychiatric and physical symptoms of all kinds; this is true even of schizophrenics. Psychotic patients often report that, while they are working, they do not hear voices. The effect is so pronounced that some authorities speak of work as a wonder drug.

Almost any form of work, even including work we do not particularly enjoy, can quiet the noisy brain. But work we love is more powerful still. As always, there is a biological reason for this: for most of us, work stimulates the cheer-seeking left side of the brain, taking us out of the stewing morass that is the right. An impassioned commitment to an activity, to any activity at all, pushes brain function in the direction of health, sanity, and well-being. Work soothes the soul.

■ □ THE CARE AND FEEDING OF THE SOUL

Which brings us to the question of whether it makes sense to speak of a soul at the conclusion of a book that has had much to say about the biology of personality. If brain function makes us irritable or depressed or alert or manic or socially ill at ease—how is it that we can speak of a soul that is somehow separate from brain?

Some would say that we cannot. Francis Crick and his partner Christof Koch are perhaps the foremost proponents of the *materialist* position, which holds that the mind is simply what the brain does: consciousness is an effect of biology. There is no soul separate from brain, no mind that is not also body. As some put it, instead of mind-and-body, we should say "mind-body."

But many neuroscientists in fact do not believe that the mind can be entirely reduced to its biology. This group sees consciousness as an *emergent property:* consciousness, they argue, emerges from biology, but once it has emerged consciousness takes on, literally and figuratively, a "life of its own." This is the Hal-the-computer view of mind and self: the perception that, at a certain point of biological complexity, the mind appears and begins to think—and to act—for itself. (Some members of the emergent property camp believe that a computer could one day produce a mind, as well. Certainly this possibility is not incompatible with the emergent property hypothesis. One researcher calls the brain a "computer made of meat.")

Finally, beyond this large middle category is a small but committed band of outright dualists, neuroscientists who believe that mind and body are separate and distinct. Their leader is the Nobel Prize–winner John C. Eccles, whose position on the subject is frankly religious: as he tells science writer John Horgan, in his book *The End of Science,* "the very nature of the mind is the same as the nature of life. It's a divine creation."

It is the position of Eccles, and of his admirer Jeffrey Schwartz, that in fact we do possess free will: a soul that is not reducible to gray matter. The UCLA scans showing that patients were able to alter brain function entirely through cognitive-behavioral means, Schwartz argues, prove the point.

Most of the time, biological brain function is running the show: the person suffering from obsessive-compulsive disorder is literally besieged by thoughts, feelings, and impulses coming to him directly from his brain. But we can find this patient's free will in the split second between the obsessions and the compulsions:

> What I do not think is reducible to brain function are the moments of decision in which you make considered opinions about the next thing you're going to do about the information your brain is sending.

This is the domain of the soul: the moment of decision, the moment in which the *self* decides whether to act upon the impulse the brain has sent. It is the self or soul that possesses the power to decide whether to act on the obsession: to take the drink, eat the chocolate ice cream, shout at the children. Not the brain.

The self's decision then feeds back into the biology. When we make a decision *not* to act on the impulse our biology has sent, we weaken the circuitry sending the message ever so slightly, while strengthening the vital circuitry of resistance. This is the biological mechanism through which cognitive-behavioral therapy alters the brain.

This view is explicitly moral; to the mind/brain dualist, human beings bear an irrevocable moral responsibility *not* to act blindly on the negative or destructive impulses our gray matter sends out to us. But even a dualist recognizes that often responsible behavior is not easy. The neuropsychiatric soul is a soul under siege, a soul bombarded every second of every day by a cascading stream of messages from the always churning brain. On this much, at least, everyone agrees.

One of the people interviewed for this book—Diane, a woman with shadow OCD—spends her days so awash in low-level repetitive thoughts that she no longer remembers a time when she did not have a song cycle running through her head. For years, every night when she pulled up the covers, Diane would abruptly hear the words, "Open a new window, Open a new door!" from her childhood Girl Scout troop playing in her mind. This was still going on when we spoke again some months after our interview, although Diane told us that just a couple of nights before she had collapsed into bed at 8:00 P.M. and, when she thought to herself, I'm going to bed too early, I'll sleep from 8 to 4, suddenly the lyrics from the song *9 to 5* had burst into her brain. Then she couldn't make them stop.

When we told Diane the idea that the soul might exist in the moments between the thoughts (or in Diane's case, the songs) that stream into our heads unbidden, she burst out laughing. "Well, I must have a very tiny soul," Diane said.

Neuroscience is probably never going to resolve the question of the human soul. But neuroscience does tell us that, when it comes to a life well-lived, we must take the existence of a soul on faith. Pure materialism, the assumption that we possess no free will at all—that our biology makes us do the things we do—is a working proposition only for those of us fortunate enough to be born with high serotonin levels and a long attention span. For the rest of us, leaving our lives to the biology of our brains will not do. Over the long haul of life the shadow syndromes, even with the blessings they can and do bestow, are simply too troubling.

It is our hope that this book will give people some of the understanding they need in order to embrace the good that comes of differences in the brain, while honestly confronting the bad. We want to state unequivocally that a person who comes away from these pages saying to himself and his loved ones "I can't help it, this is the way I am" is a person who has misread our intent.

On the other hand, we hope, too, that readers will gain not just greater understanding, but greater acceptance of the fact of biology's force and influence in our lives. We must strike a balance between acceptance and resistance. In psychoanalytic terms we are speaking of the difference between shame and guilt—and of the two, it is shame, and not necessarily guilt, that we hope to relieve by offering the information we have here.

Shame is wounding. People feel shame over qualities they perceive to be intrinsic to themselves, qualities they feel helpless to change. We might feel ashamed that we are not successful, or thin, or brilliantly intelligent or creative. Certainly many of us may feel ashamed of any shadow syndrome with which we struggle; the stigma attached to the mental illnesses has long been powerful indeed. People are ashamed of psychiatric problems; just the phrase—*psychiatric problem*—bears profoundly negative connotations. It is this feeling of shame we hope to lift.

What is more, while shame is generally hurtful to adults, for the child who suffers from a shadow syndrome the experience of being shamed—of being ridiculed and scorned by parents, teachers, or peers—can be devastating. This is especially true when a child's particular shadow syndrome means that he has poorer self-observation skills than other children his age. A child with built-in social deficits will take such ridicule wholly to heart, making it his own. He is defenseless in the face of criticism, because of his diminished capacity simply to *perceive* that what others think of him may actually be wrong. In his own eyes he becomes the failed and shameful child others think him to be.

Guilt is different. We feel guilt over actions, or over failures to act, as Andrew B. Morrison writes in *The Culture of Shame:*

> [Guilt focuses on] . . . a *deed* that causes pain to another. As guilt generates confession and the goal of forgiveness, shame generates concealment and hiding . . .

Guilt is the emotion of responsibility; it is the emotion we feel when we hold ourselves accountable for our acts. And guilt, when it is not so strong as to be paralyzing, can be an excellent social motivator indeed. Often the shadow syndromes are not intrinsically painful enough to demand our attention; that is why we call them mild. As a result, if we are going to escape their grip we will have to establish to internalized standards of behavior and life success to guide our choices. And as we all know, the superego maintains and enforces internalized standards through the emotion of guilt. Thus for many of the people interviewed throughout this book it was feelings of guilt—and not overwhelming feelings of unhappiness—that moved them at last to address their problems. Thus we are not, with this book, seeking to extend the therapeutic culture; we are not looking to lead the way to a new day in which people will devote themselves full-time to analyzing not only their bad childhoods, but their "bad" biology as well.

Instead, we hope that with increasing knowledge of the brain and its biology, people can begin to accept the limitations—and the gifts—of their biology, while at the same time assuming responsibility for which actions they will and will not allow their biology to provoke.

For all of us knowledge is, or should be, power. Another woman interviewed in these pages, a friend who struggles with anxiety in her own life, and who has followed the development of the book over the past two years, put it this way:

> This information is not depressing, it's empowering. Now I can say to myself, This is just a pattern in my brain chemistry. Maybe I was born with it, maybe it's from a semi-traumatic childhood. But however it came to be it's here, it's been here to stay for a long time, and now I have the ability to get rid of it. These shadow syndromes are the albatross, they are the monkey on your back. They are the thing that defeats life, and makes the mass of men lead lives of quiet desperation. If I added up all the moments in every day where I have intrusive, morbid thoughts, or where I have obsession over some injustice someone has done to me, I bet I would come up with a good ten hours a week. And that is going to color the rest of your existence in a major way. Those ten waking hours are like someone stomping on your foot; even after they've gotten off your foot for the next hour your foot still hurts.
>
> I do not want to live that way.

We hope that, with the knowledge of the brain's biology offered here, people who struggle with shadow syndromes can move closer to that goal; closer to the goal of not living in ways they do not wish to live. We hope that as knowledge of the brain and its problems grows, the shame of having to live life as a flawed human being will fade, and the potential to free the soul, or the self or the will or whatever word we wish to use for this part of human experience, from the bonds of biology will grow strong.

We hope that in reading this book people will begin the journey out from the shadows and into the clear light of day.

ACKNOWLEDGMENTS

CATHERINE JOHNSON

My friend Teri Von Ende introduced me to John's work. Teri was my first special ed chum and my main source of the photocopied materials special needs parents live by. In the midst of one of her batches of papers and bibliographies was John's article "Paying Attention to Attention" for the CH.A.D.D. newsletter. Teri, thank you.

Working with John is like having a bolt of lightning in your office every day. John is inspired and inspiring, and writing a book with him has been a life-altering experience. John is the best.

The psychiatrists my husband and I have turned to over the years since Jimmy's diagnosis have also been important to me and to the book: Greer Sullivan of the Centers For Mental Healthcare Research in Little Rock (and previously of UCLA's Neuropsychiatric Institute), Ed Ritvo of UCLA, Allan Phillips, Arthur Sorosky, and Mark DeAntonio (also of NPI). Their insights into mild, everyday mood disorders spurred my own interest in the subject of neuropsychiatry; it was Dr. Sullivan who first explained the concept of a shadow syndrome to me.

My husband, Ed, my friends Cindy Cassutt, Donna Jackson, Deborah Gieringer, and Veda Semarne, and my sisters, Rosalyn Clement and Elizabeth Caslin, all helped shape the ideas in the book. They talked things through with me, and always listened thoughtfully and critically. Donna did a careful edit of several chapters as well—though this is the point where I want to say that if a reader should stumble over a bumpy sentence, this is no one's fault but John's and mine.

My agent, Geri Thoma, knew that John and I should write the book together; once we finished the proposal she did a terrific job selling it. Linda Healey at Pantheon is an amazing editorial tactician. I've learned something new about editing and publishing in every conversation we've had.

Next comes the without-whom-this-book-would-not-exist group: Martine Saidi (treasured nanny and baby-wrangler to the twins), Kim Firment (surrogate big sister to Jimmy), Tony Orsini (Kim's successor and natural-born child management talent), Marco Martinez (therapeutic companion extraordinaire), Patty Sorge (brilliant Lovaas therapist), and the entire Lovaas crew: Jacquie Wynn and Janet Yi, Mario Tamayo, Mike Lee, Miriam Bakcht, and all the rest—thank you for everything. And to Ivar Lovaas, who recruited and trained the talented and hardworking therapists who got us (and Jimmy) through the first two years of the babies' lives: you are in our pantheon. Thank you.

I also want to thank my parents, Robert and Patricia Johnson. Writing this book made me see that they were early proponents of taking biology into account in bringing up children. All of us were taught to use the God-given talents we had, and to strive to overcome our equally God-given flaws. Working with John, I had the happy experience of realizing that my parents knew what they were doing!

And to Ed: writing this book convinced me that my husband may be one of the few people in the known universe who doesn't have a shadow syndrome. Thank you for your calm, your good cheer, your steady love, and your willingness to fight the good fight for Jimmy on a daily basis, giving me a quiet place to write. Without you this book would certainly not exist.

And finally, to the people who gave John and me their stories and thoughts for strangers to read: you *are* the book. Thank you.

JOHN RATEY

My debts begin with my patients, who have been the constant source of inspiration and learning throughout the years. Many of them have been so gracious by sharing their stories with us in an attempt to shed light on the shadows of others. They are a daily reminder of the triumph of the human spirit.

Catherine has been a wonderful partner and companion via phone, fax, and e-mail. She came up with this wonderful idea four years ago and carried us through to the end, despite having twins and continuing her many mothering demands. She has been brilliant and has become a great friend and a respected colleague. Her challenging questions and tireless attempts to get it just right kept me and the book as close to accurate as we could come. But most of all I am thankful for her talent that has allowed her to make these miracles of science accessible to all and blend our remarkable knowledge into the fabric of everyday life.

I thank my good friend Ned Hallowell for making my life richer in so many ways. He blazed the trail for us through the *Distraction* books and beyond. His ideas and his passion for making the complex simple run through these pages and his friendship remains a sustaining force.

I have had the best supervisors in the world at the Massachusetts Mental Health Center. Mentors such as George Vaillant, Richard Shader, Alan Hobson, Les Havens, and Jules Bemporad are unique. Their tireless pursuit of the truth helped mold my thinking and provided the groundwork for my entry into neuropsychiatry.

To Shervert Frazier, Barbara Goren, Gillian Walker, Temple Grandin, Jeff Sutton, and Ben Lopez, my thanks for their readings of the manuscript and their helpful comments and enthusiasm. And a deep debt of gratitude to Linda Healey for guiding the editing and once again pushing the book to completion.

Catherine and I both warmly thank Andrew Littman, Maurizio Fava, Mark George, Jeffrey Schwartz, Susan Swedo, and David Comings for taking time away from their academic pursuits to describe their important findings and share their thoughts.

My thanks to the staff at Medfield throughout the many years of the writing of this book, especially to Andrea Miller, Jill Mullen, Robert Kirkpatrick, Gail Garber, and David Hoffman for their help with the researching and writing of the scientific material in the text.

I also thank my beloved family. I could not have had a more supportive wife than Nancy, who made time and room for me to do the work and withstood my ups and downs. My wonderful children, Jessica and Kathryn, put up with their madcap father, who once again had a very long and compelling project that challenged the flow of the household and our lives.

INDEX

ABOUT THE AUTHORS

John J. Ratey, M.D., is an assistant professor of psychiatry at Harvard Medical School and executive director of research at Medfield State Hospital in Massachusetts. He is the co-author of *Driven to Distraction* and *Answers to Distraction*. He lives in Wellesley with his wife and two daughters.

Catherine Johnson, Ph.D., is a trustee of the National Alliance for Autism Research, a contributing editor at *New Woman* magazine, and the author of *When to Say Goodbye to Your Therapist* and *Lucky in Love*. She lives in Los Angeles with her husband and three sons.